THINKING THROUGH THEORY

Thinking Through Theory

Vygotskian Perspectives on the Teaching of Writing

JAMES THOMAS ZEBROSKI

Boynton/Cook Publishers
HEINEMANN
Portsmouth, NH

Boynton/Cook Publishers, Inc.
A subsidiary of Reed Publishing (USA) Inc.
361 Hanover Street
Portsmouth, NH 03801-3912

Offices and agents throughout the world

Editor: Peter R. Stillman
Production: Renée M. Pinard
Cover design: T. Watson Bogaard

Chapter 1 originally appeared in slightly different form as "The Uses of Theory: A Vygotskian Approach to Composition." In *The Writing Instructor* 5 (2): 57–65. Winter 1986. Used with permission.

Chapter 11 originally appeared in slightly different form as "The Social Construction of Self in the Work of Lev Vygotsky." In *The Writing Istructor* 8 (4): 149–156. Summer 1989. Used with permission.

Library of Congress Cataloging-in-Publication Data

Zebroski, James Thomas.
  Thinking through theory : Vygotskian perspectives on the teaching of writing /
James Thomas Zebroski.
    p. cm.
  Includes bibliographical references.
  ISBN 0-86709-324-2
  1. English language—Rhetoric—Study and teaching—Theory, etc.
2. Vygotskiĭ, L. S. (Lev Semenovich), 1896–1934. I. Title.
PE1404.Z35 1994
808'.042'07—dc20   93–26406
                                                                          CIP

Printed in the United States of America on acid-free paper.
99 98 97 96 95 94   BB   1 2 3 4 5 6 7 8 9

*This book is dedicated to
Donald Bateman*

Contents

Acknowledgments

For over twelve years, I have written and spoken on Lev Vygotsky's theory of language and mind. I believed from the time I did my dissertation on his work that Vygotsky had much to contribute to our understanding of writing. That this book has at last become a reality owes much to those few who have strongly and consistently supported me in my quest.

First, my students, who for nearly twenty years have challenged and energized me. They have contributed to the development of my ideas about writing and teaching. I see them as coauthors with me of our writing classes. They have taught me much, not the least of which has been to be more patient, never one of my cardinal virtues.

I especially want to thank Stephen Lisauskas for being a great student and for allowing me to use his writing as an example that might help other teachers get a better sense of how they can use student portfolios.

I also want to recognize Fran Lambrecht and Elaine Starinchak who gave me good models for and good memories of my first teaching experiences. Those positive experiences have gotten me through the tough times. Fran and Elaine invited me into teaching at the moment when innovation in the English curriculum seemed a possibility. Their excitement about teaching English was infectious, their practice artful.

Donald R. Bateman is a good friend and mentor who introduced me to Vygotsky and Russian, and to intellectual work as an exciting and integrity-creating enterprise. Don, this book's for you.

Nancy Mack, your dialogues have made this possible. Thanks for your constant encouragement and care.

Ann E. Berthoff has supported this work long before anyone else would even consider it. She has provided me with a model of a teacher and scholar who still gets excited about such things. I want to thank her for carefully and dialectically reading so much of my work over the years, and for all the accompanying written comments, done voluntarily. Ann Berthoff has been an exemplary teacher of the entire field of Composition, one who warned us of theoretical pitfalls long—years—before we fell into them, but a teacher who nonetheless was willing to lend a helping hand to pull us out of these pitfalls after we had ignored her sage advice.

I want to thank Louise Wetherbee Phelps for suggesting and supporting this book idea from the start, Patricia Stock for helping me find a publisher, Carol Lipson for helping me put together my leave request, and Syracuse University for granting me a one-year research leave to finish this book and to continue my research on Lev Vygotsky.

Many thanks go to Peter Stillman for being patient with a writer green to the publishing business and for offering some very helpful suggestions for improving this book.

I also want to express my appreciation of and support for my fellow writing teachers in the Syracuse Writing Program, the best teachers of writing in the country.

The readers of the manuscript have offered helpful suggestions and have been very supportive. Thanks to Steve Mailloux, Patricia Stock, Nancy Mack, Mike Murphy, Cheryl Burghdurf, Jayne Shoup and Bron Adam. Your incredibly diverse viewpoints have taught me much and have improved this book.

Becky Madge has gone way beyond the call of duty by helping me to translate the text from various computer programs. David Susman was a Mac lifesaver.

I want to say thanks to Rob Faivre who has been a research assistant for two years and who has done everything from tracking down references to helping to type and put together the final manuscript. You have helped to preserve my sanity, no small thing over the last year.

And finally, thanks to Andrew Holleran who at a critical moment early in the writing process said a few kind words to me that motivated me to start writing again and get this whole project off the ground. Your kind words and good example have taught me much about "vir bonus dicendi peritus." Thanks too for helping me to envision the shape of my next book.

Introduction

Composing Theory:
How Theory Can (And Can't) Help the Writing Teacher

As nearly as I can recollect, my first experience with theory was in the seventh grade when I was on a reading spree, checking out every book the public library had on or by Albert Einstein. I had become fascinated with Einstein because I was a child of my age, a child of Sputnik and the years that followed, in which the scientist, and especially the physicist, was hero. But I also was interested in Einstein because he always seemed to be mischievous in a gentle kind of way. I came from an authoritarian, ethnic, working-class family where teachers were always right simply because they were teachers, and I appreciated Einstein's refusal to fit easily into that sort of system, while I, of course, was doing whatever was necessary to fit in. Einstein became an emblem for me of the person who beat the system at its own game by simply circling around it. As I was reading through some book about Einstein, I came across a little story. The story told of how Professor and Mrs. Einstein had visited California in the early 1930s. While there, the Einsteins were taken to one of the new marvels, a huge telescope on the top of a mountain. They were shown the workings of the instrument and were told how the new device would reach many times farther into the universe than previous telescopes, allowing scientists to probe the secrets of the universe. Mrs. Einstein was reported to have responded, "Oh, you mean that the telescope will do what my husband does on the back of an envelope?"

1

There was a simple elegance and a stubborn populism that I read into this little story about the experts and their expertise that appealed to me then and still attracts me now. Theory as this book uses that term begins with this sense. I have been interested in composing theory for nearly twenty years now, but I have been primarily interested in it from the teacher's point of view. There are many books out on the market these days that are about theory, but very, very few of them view theory from the teacher's perspective. This book is unusual in that it shuttles back and forth between theory and practice on a regular basis.

My interest in discovering how theory was answerable to practice, if it indeed was answerable at all, began when I was a junior in college and was introduced to the work of James Moffett and the ideas of Northrop Frye in two different courses that I simply happened to be taking during the same semester. While Moffett and Frye come out of very different universes of discourse, they were both theorists, and I was taken with their explanations of "structure," whether that structure was in the student or in a field of study. When I returned for graduate work, I took a summer seminar that furthered my theoretical education. In that seminar, I encountered Mina Shaughnessy's *Errors and Expectations* (it had just come out) and Lev Vygotsky's *Thought and Language*. Two more different books I cannot imagine. Yet as a teacher I found that Shaughnessy and Vygotsky did share a belief that surface manifestations of language could be better understood by searching for and studying the deeper psychological and linguistic processes that produce them. This was a revolutionary idea to take back into the public schools where error policing seemed to take up entirely too much time and energy, with very little positive effect. So theory for me from this time forward was a political as well as a pedagogical device. It might give me ideas about what occurred when my students wrote and what I might do to intervene to help them to write better, but it was also and as importantly a way of countering the reigning arguments of the local authorities who believed that my job as English teacher was primarily to impose linguistic order.

Years passed. I discovered Russian and Eastern European language theory. I also had my first run-ins with poststructural theory. I believe that theory and practice need to be answerable to each other. "Answerability" is a concept that Mikhail Bakhtin developed to study the relations between art and life. Theory and practice, like art and life, need to be in a kind of dialogue with each other, though at the same time the differences between the two must be preserved. Further, we must allow for the moments when of necessity silence passes between them. This book tries to present one sort of theory that I have found to be helpful, the theory of language and mind that comes out of the work of Lev Vygotsky, the great Russian psychologist of the 1920s. Almost every one of these essays takes up Vygotsky's ideas in one way or another. But I also have tried to present this theory as I have experienced it, as a process, as a *thinking through* of certain questions and positions concerning language that may or may not immediately connect with my teaching practices, but which nevertheless interest me as a teacher. These essays in very rough chronological order track my tries at theory. They begin with the classroom, the composition course, the composing context, and they end with my profession, my discourse community, the society of Composition, as Stephen North calls us. The essays enact the process of theorizing and therefore are exploratory. Sometimes I have changed my mind about a key issue. Sometimes I have returned to positions that I had earlier abandoned. That's the way life, and the life of the mind, is. I don't expect my students to take a position in their writing and never veer from it; why should I hold myself to such preposterousness? Over a ten-year period I thought hard about writing and what composing theory means for composition, but I also have always kept at the back of my mind the issue of what composing theory does for composition. This book in some small way records that journey, at the same time documenting some of the concerns and debates of the profession.

Composing theory is relatively new and almost completely underdeveloped. There are many historical and sociological reasons for this, but surely no small reason is that composition teachers, and English teachers generally, have been so busy simply attempting to keep up with paper grading and with class preparations that they haven't had the luxury of possessing the time that theory requires for its elaboration. It is pretty easy to hit the high points of composing theory in a brief paragraph or two. Such a précis might begin with a review of James Moffett's *Teaching the Universe of Discourse* (1968), move on to Richard Young, Alton Becker, and Kenneth Pike's *Rhetoric: Discovery and Change* (1970), linger over James Kinneavy's *A Theory of Discourse* (1971), consider Ann E. Berthoff's critique in "The Problem of Problem Solving" (1971), look at Frank D'Angelo's *A Conceptual Theory of Rhetoric* (1975), note John Warnock's "Who's Afraid of Theory?" (1976), observe Nancy Sommers's "The Need for Theory in Composition Research" (1979), and examine Louise Wetherbee Phelps's *Composition as a Human Science* (1988). This summary would reveal that theory began in composition as a means for ordering the chaos (Kinneavy), untidiness, and amorphousness (Moffett) of the field. Tracking theory through these sources and over twenty years, the traveler would arrive at the concept of theory in composition as a means of disrupting systems, generating new questions and practices (Phelps). A dialectical philosopher like Lev Vygotsky might note that composing theory has unfolded historically as a dialectical contradiction. The very impetus to composing theory seems to have been institutional, disciplinary control, while present theory would appear to seek to break out of such restraints. What began as a move to control ends as a call for release. What started as a search for an underlying order has (re)turned full circle to the dialectical other, to a quest for generativity and chaos. Then, theory disciplined composing. Now, composing theorizes such disciplining as well as the discipline. Such a fast trip through theoryland, of course, is akin to "If it's Tuesday, this must be Belgium," but it is perhaps more shocking to see what little is left out by such a grand tour. To be sure, the great compositionists have always been great theorists, people like James Britton, Janet Emig, Ann Berthoff. James Britton introduced the work of Lev Vygotsky to English teachers. Janet Emig blended creative writing accounts with psychological theory to view composing as process. Ann E. Berthoff taught us of the great heuristic of language as seen by Peirce, Richards, Langer, and Freire. But these and all of the others in Composition who have drawn on theory have been unable to detail their vision. No matter how committed, composition theorists have had to face an institutional apparatus of departments, editors, conference chairs, and publishers who have for the most part been uninterested in and sometimes hostile to theory.

This is significant, because when we move to literary studies we find dozens of presses and journals that have been cranking out huge amounts of theory for decades now. To write a book on composing theory is still, by comparison, a rather exotic affair. And to forward Russian (or Eastern European) language theory is the apex of exotica. I do so knowing full well the dangers. On the one hand, there will be some teachers who may wonder why I am dillydallying around when the class is waiting, why I spend so much time on aspects of theory that never directly feed back into ideas for the classroom. I am sympathetic to this response and have tried to answer it by placing in the first section of essays, "Composing Context," a lot of practical course plans and assignment ideas that have been generated by composing theory, as well as including some examples of student writing generated by these assignments. I have tested these ideas out at four very different universities over the last ten years and have included the results that seem to work best. Beyond this, I would have to say that my take on theory reflects my personality and my own broader interests beyond my classroom. I am a teacher, but I also have intellectual interests that go beyond my teacherly commitments.

On the other hand, I am less sympathetic to the inevitable responses from poststructural Theorists, High Theorists who will find easy prey throughout for Critique. I refer such to my final essay, "The End(s) of Theory." I could say more, but I won't.

Composing as Intersectionality

I have composed theory that starts from Jim Corder's rich definition of rhetoric as *intersectionality.* Corder (1984) develops this notion at some length in "A New Introduction to Psychoanalysis Taken as Version of Modern Rhetoric" and I have simply appropriated his notion of rhetoric and used it to think about composing. Corder describes what I am here calling *intersectionality* as follows:

> Every utterance belongs to, exists in, issues from, somewhere (its inventive origin), emerges as a structure, and manifests itself as a style. All the features of utterance—invention, structure, style— cycle, reciprocate, and occur simultaneously. *Each of us is a gathering place for a host of rhetorical universes.* Some of them we share with others, indeed with whole cultures; some of them we inhabit alone, and some of them we occupy without knowing that we do so. *Each of us is a busy corner where multiple rhetorical universes intersect.* Ordinarily, we keep some consonance among these multiple universes, and hold order and relation among them. But not always. Sometimes the traffic within a single rhetorical universe stalls; sometimes the traffic from one universe collides with that from another. (141, emphasis mine)

Corder's idea is broad enough to leave room for various views of writing found in widely divergent contexts. It fits well, for example, with Bakhtin and Vygotsky's view that language is dynamic and shifting, takes on multiple functions, is dialogic, and is simultaneously social and individual. Composing as the intersection of universes of discourse is also highly reflexive and recursive, always including itself in the process. So any composing, any writing, is a creating of that composing itself, as well as the text in the strict sense. Composing can be seen as the intersection of context, text, self, and society. But then too composing is simultaneously the active (if partial) (re)constructing of these discursive universes of context, text, self, and society. One obviously could choose other discursive universes that pass through the intersection, but these dimensions of writing will be sufficient for me to work through those aspects of theory that most interest me and that most contribute to my work as a composition teacher. Any time I write, I create these four discursive universes. Each universe entails the others, and the composing event itself. The reflexive dimension of this makes it a little difficult to follow in a linear fashion, but that is precisely the point. Life—and even writing—isn't linear.

I have sorted out my essays, then, according to this framework of composing as the intersection of context, text, self, and society.

- "Composing Context" looks at the classroom as discursive event. What does it mean to say that the class, the composition course, is composed? Using ideas from Lev Vygotsky, I design theory-based college composition courses at the freshman, the intermediate, and the graduate levels. I look at course design evolving across time by examining early and later versions of the intermediate and graduate courses. Further, I theorize ethnographic writing and portfolio assignments. This is a pragmatic section in which I have purposefully kept the distance between theory and practices, between reflections and actual syllabi and assignments, short.

- "Composing Text" extends my reflections on the writing event, using Vygotsky's insights on inner speech and literacy development. These essays capture the way I think through theory. They also provide an elaboration of one theory, as well as a thorough introduction to its keywords and sources. Vygotsky's theory in the 1920s dealt with many of the issues we now are only beginning to address.

- "Composing Self" asks the question of whatever happened to expressive discourse and the "self" in composition. I argue for a retheorizing of the "self" and argue against a reduction of "self" merely to the social, to places in academic discourse communities, or to subject positions. Student experience is valuable. It needs to play a central role in our courses.

- "Composing Society" analyzes the field of composition studies as a Self by attending to keywords, keysources, and keyconflicts. In a time when "discourse community" and "academic discourse" have become hegemonic discourses, the disciplinary apparat has yet to say much about our discourse community. True, there have been some histories, but few have taken up those events central to composition's emergence in our lifetimes. This section of essays suggests some ways to begin this project with our graduate students. I end with a cautionary tale about the dangers of too quickly buying into the kind of poststructural language that dominates literary studies.

Composing theory can generate ideas about language and teaching language. It can suggest some new ways for thinking about ourselves as writers and teachers. Composing theory provides a conceptual framework, leaving sufficient flexibility to allow us to grow or to change our mind about some aspect of writing and teaching. Theory, as Y. Lotman says, is a "thinking device" that takes the form of a certain kind of language and that is used to mediate our worldview and our practices. This sort of theory guarantees nothing. It is heuristic. It is not a science that searches for universal laws. Nor is there even any guarantee that theory will contribute to practice. Sometimes it simply cannot. It won't settle anything finally and absolutely. Perhaps theory's biggest contribution to my life as a teacher has been that it has made me clearer about what my students and I already know, making it possible to go into the classroom with patience and more enthusiasm for the very act of teaching. Theory, of course, is still, these many years later, a means for arguing against the prevailing expertise and authority. The irony now is that Theory of the poststructuralist variety has too often become that authority. Real dialogue requires that all participants *begin* as equals and until I see evidence that literary theorists are willing to learn as much about composing theory as composition theorists have learned (or "should" have learned) about literary theory, I am suspicious of all calls for a "dialogue." I have tried since 1982 to become conversant with literary theory. I have to confess that sometimes I have felt that I am "through" with that kind of theory in the same way that Sylvia Plath's persona is "through" in her poem, "Daddy."

The sort of theory that I do can help the composition teacher because it returns us to the wonder of our world, the wonder that scientists experienced when they turned their new telescope to the skies, but also the wonder that Mrs. Einstein encountered when the Herr Professor, writing on the back of an envelope, explored the farthest reaches of the universe.

References

Berthoff, A. 1971. The problem of problem solving. *College Composition and Communication.* 22:237–42.

———. 1981. *The making of meaning.* Portsmouth, NH: Boynton/Cook.

Britton, J. 1970. *Language and learning.* New York: Penguin.

Corder, J. 1984. A new introduction to psychoanalysis taken as a version of modern rhetoric. *Pre/Text* 5:3–4.

D'Angelo, F. 1975. *A conceptual theory of rhetoric.* Cambridge, MA: Winthrop.

Emig, J. 1971. *The composing processes of twelfth graders.* Urbana, IL: National Council of Teachers of English.

Frye, N. 1971. *Anatomy of criticism.* Princeton, NJ: Princeton University Press.

Kinneavy, J. 1971. *A theory of discourse.* New York: Norton.

Moffett, J. 1968. *Teaching the universe of discourse.* Boston: Houghton Mifflin.

North, S. 1987. *The making of knowledge in composition: Portrait of an emerging field.* Portsmouth, NH: Boynton/Cook.

Phelps, L. 1988. *Composition as a human science.* New York: Oxford University Press.

Plath, S. 1975. Daddy. *Contemporary American Poets,* edited by A. Poulin. Boston: Houghton Mifflin.

Shaughnessy, M. 1977. *Errors and expectations.* New York: Oxford University Press.

Sommers, N. 1979. The need for theory in composition research. *College Composition and Communication* 30:46–49.

Vygotsky, L. 1962. *Thought and language.* Cambridge, MA: MIT Press.

Warnock, J. 1976. Who's afraid of theory. *College Composition and Communication.* 27:16–20.

Young, R., A. Becker, & K. Pike. 1970. *Rhetoric: Discovery and change.* New York: Harcourt Brace Jovanovich.

Part One

Composing Context

Theory and practice are involved in each other in ways far more complicated than the usual pairing of these terms in discussion among composition teachers and scholars would indicate. Both theory and practice arise out of some broader, richer, and more dynamic life activity. The essays in this first section try to work through theory-practice relations, by seeing the construction of a course, the coauthoring of a composition class by teacher and student, as one of the four major kinds of composition that go on in our professional lives. While I only mention the ideas of Lev Vygotsky in these essays in passing, his theory is a constant backdrop to my teaching. I begin with teaching, with the composing of the context, the setting or environment in which reading and writing occur and grow, because I think the class context is the most important.

We all have worked with teachers who know a lot, are "theoretically smart," but who are fumblers in the classroom. We also know classroom-wise teachers who are efficient because they have given up thinking about things, because they have opted to create activities that "work," that provide an almost guaranteed "answer." It is understandable that both types exist in the fragmented and alienating work setting in which most teachers find themselves, but I think the majority of teachers see the dangers inherent in these "pure" examples of theory without practice and practice without theory.

These four essays talk about the context of the composition course. They provide a record of my attempt as a classroom teacher since 1979 to bring theory and practice into some principled relationship with each other. To work in the spirit of a theory, to use theory, as a way to puzzle through classroom enigmas, as a mediation of thought, as an instrument for envisioning the class and its relations to the student's experience and the world, is composing of the highest sort. Aristotle somewhere said that teaching is the highest form of understanding. I would only add it is also the highest form of composing.

I use theory as a way to think through what happens and doesn't happen in my class. And I see my classroom experience as a means to interrogate, to test out, to try my theory. To see a role, an important role, for theory in good teaching is not to privilege either theory or practice, but it is also not simply to add theory and practice together and argue that a "balance" or some comfortable mixture of both is needed. "Dialectic" used to be a word that described the kind of profound tension and incommensurability that often exist, and that should exist, between theory and practice, but "dialectic," with the exception of Ann Berthoff's use of the concept, sounds wooden, smelling of philosophical dead ends and dry academic disputes, not at all evoking the dense, tension-filled, dynamic, and historical event that calls into question all our categories, even the very category of "dialectic" that Vygotsky meant when he used the term. Too often dialectic comes to mean some simple addition of theory to practice or the monolithic imposition of theory onto practice (or conversely, the building up of theory through reflection on practice, a sort of pretend science for teachers seemingly incapable of the real thing).

For these reasons I generally do not use the term "dialectic" to describe theory and practice relations, partly because I don't think the term always leaves room for the possibility that theory does not necessarily connect with my teaching, not in any conscious, short-term way. I do theory of a certain sort; I teach in a certain style. What connects them is that they are separable in principle, but that they are also *answerable* to each other over time. Like the relation between art and life, theory and teaching should not be reduced to each other, but they are involved together in a whole set of changing relations over time. They have histories.

History is perhaps *the* connecting concept. Theory and practice cross and recross *over time.* So these essays are about a "history" of a composition course, the things I do in it, how I distinguish beginning composition courses from advanced ones, how I try to get a historical perspective on student writing through portfolios, but they are also about the changes my thinking has undergone in a decade.

In "Creating the Introductory Composition Course," I think of the course as an emerging discourse event and argue that the same standards we apply to our students' writing when we grade their essays, we ought to apply to the composition of the course as a whole. If we believe that essays benefit from having a thesis statement or a theme, then the composition course ought to also have such a theme, open-ended enough to involve the students and their worlds, but also somehow coming back at the end to the reality that this is a course on writing. Students leave such a course with a diverse set of writing experiences, but also with an evolving set of writing understandings (a theory) and a collection of modeling experiences. Perhaps these modeling experiences—the teacher showing the student what it is *like* to see her- or himself as a practicing writer—are the most important things we teach. I have always believed that I teach students myself; that is, that I teach them the attitude I have as a working writer. I hope to pass on to them the excitement and pain that I get from writing. And I have to confess that I am very suspicious of a composition course in which the teacher does not talk about her or his own writing experiences and their attendant frustrations and pleasures. I also wonder about the composition teacher who doesn't share at least some of her or his own writing. Teaching is partly a silent witnessing of a complex and beautiful event unfolding.

"Using Ethnographic Writing to Construct Classroom Knowledge" shows my roots in cultural anthropology and folklore in the way that it takes the ethnographic method and uses it within a Vygotskian framework to create a writing research project that I have found to be very successful and stimulating. The anthropologist and folklorist whom I worked with for over four years as a doctoral student had no problems with my use of ethnography and in fact were very supportive and encouraging of the ways I adapted ethnographic methods, though some compositionists have criticized, even calling this ethnography. In response I would argue that the ethnographic practices I appropriate come out of a specific worldview (Vygotskian) and a specific moment in history (postmodern), that may well put it at odds with other ethnographic research methods. The results have convinced me that it is possible to ask students to have a real writing experience in a class and begin to understand that they are knowledge producers, not simply knowledge consumers. There are dangers, of course, that the ethnographic alternative that I detail can be inappropriately or badly used, that it can be made into a formula, that it can become just the latest incarnation of the Five-Paragraph Theme that still exists in far too many college and high school composition courses. But it doesn't have to be. I have used ethnographic writing at four very different colleges. It is flexible and adaptable. I have gotten some wonderful writing from this approach. That's the bottom line for me.

Some of this writing is reproduced in the third essay in this section, "Using Portfolios for Reflection Not Evaluation." I have included some of the texts produced by a student who took my introductory composition course and who did some interesting work. I try to bring together Steve Lisauskas's writing with a new idea that I have been thinking about only recently, that we must reinvent our *categories* for thinking about writing. The two categories that I theorize are "text" and "writer." I borrow a set of terms from folkloristics to think about writing because I think these categories better describe what happens as a writer, in this case Steve, writes over time, but also because they are provocative and suggestive. More often that not, composition teachers and scholars have thought of the writing subject as being a unified, monolithic, singular being, clearly bounded and centered, and the written text as something that the writer composes many discrete examples of over the course of a class or a lifetime. But if we reverse those notions so that we see the writer as plural and the text as that singular discourse composed over time within the course but also in her or his life, we get a theory of composing that makes us rethink the whole idea of reading and evaluating student texts and collapses the false dichotomy set up by the terms "product" and "process."

In the fourth in this series of essays, "Creating the Advanced Writing Course," I make the case that an advanced course ought to be more than simply a rehash of what went before in the earlier composition courses. I think students are justified to question the value of having to take another course in composition, one of the perennial themes that arises almost the first day of class in the advanced courses I have taught, if that course is just more of the same. But by the same token, any advanced writing teacher knows that entering students often need more practice in beginning composition activities. In this essay I have tried to work through that tension, applying the ideas I developed in the preceding essays, but also making the case for teaching composition as composition, that is, as both writing practices and disciplinary practices. The advanced composition course, like the advanced physics course or the advanced literary theory course, ought to have as part of its content the ideas at work and in process in the field, in other words, the ideas we composition people find important enough to fight over. I try to detail how I introduce my students to the field of composition by getting them to try out some very different writing techniques and theories put forward by experts in the field, but also by having students read briefly in the history of composition. This is tricky, because I also believe a large part of the advanced writing course needs to be opened up so that students can work individually on the writing they want and need to do. But by carefully selecting the issues and the readings, I have discovered that I am able to introduce students to the field in ways that interest them. I have taken up in this essay the idea that Jerome Bruner and, long before him, Lev Vygotsky formulated: that students learn by doing, and that any subject can be taught effectively in some intellectually honest form to any person at any stage of development.

In the last essay of this section, "When Words Fail," I try to show the ways I have worked with new teachers, especially incoming teaching assistants (TAs) from the English department, introducing them to both the discipline of composition and to teaching practices. In the composition practicum course required of new TAs who will teach the freshman writing courses, I have found the most evident example of the limits of my teaching and of my need to be constantly gentle and patient with myself about what I seem (or do not seem) to be accomplishing. We simply don't always know what is going on in teaching, and that's not all bad if we believe and act on the belief that at bottom we do make some difference. This essay tells a little story about one such experience that I had while teaching the composition practicum course and how it was a rewarding, if difficult, situation. What would be a challenging course in any circumstance becomes an immensely trying experience because new teachers resort to the only models they have, the writing courses that they took. But most TAs wrote well enough that they didn't have to take any college writing courses, so they often return to murky memories of "hard" high school or college teachers and, clutching these models, try to impose their will on freshmen who, also new to the university scene, are not exactly thrilled to be in a required composition course.

The composition practicum course, the graduate teachers often feel, takes away attention from the courses which they are taking— the ones they came to graduate school for. After all, aside from a bibliography course, the practicum is the only *required* graduate course. The college composition faculty are among the very few college faculty who have to teach the *required* graduate course. In fact, it is not that unusual for composition faculty to teach *only* required courses at both graduate and undergraduate levels. This matters. In Vygotsky's theory of language and self, *motive* is always at the heart of discourse. The motives of students in the required graduate practicum are always mixed. At first glance one would think that theory would be the perfect bridge to use in the graduate course, but my experience has been that studying composition theory more often than not simply presents graduate students with the perfect discourse for poststructuralist critique, which, I am convinced, I can now intelligently respond to, but which once again takes the students and me far away from what is happening in our own classrooms, once more implicitly reproducing the ideology that scholarship, research, and theory is somehow more important than the mere activity of teaching. My response to this has been to begin with activities, with practices that are theoretically grounded, and get the graduate students to do some of these things themselves. They become much more sensitive, for example, in asking their students to exchange papers and do peer responses when they are being asked to do the same sort of thing (often for the first time in their academic lives) in the practicum. This is no panacea for what in the end often turn out to be unbridgeable differences of ideology and worldview between me and the teaching assistants, but it does get things going in the right direction, that is, in the direction of the classroom and composing context.

Chapter One

Creating the Introductory College Composition Course

Theory—the word too often conjures up notions of the impractical, the superfluous, even the sophistic. Too frequently, compositionists have opposed theory to practice and have opted for practice, for "what works." But what do we mean when we assert that an activity "works"? How do we gauge apparent practicality? How do we evaluate the success or failure of a writing activity or of our own teaching? The moment we begin to ask such questions, to reflect on our reflections, we are involved in theory.

Theory is not the opposite of practice; theory is not even a supplement to practice. Theory *is* practice, a practice of a particular kind, and practice is always theoretical. The question then is not whether we have a theory of composition, that is, a view, or better, a vision of our selves and our activity, but whether we are going to become conscious of our theory. To what extent will theory play a role in composing our writing courses? How will we use theory to think about what has gone on in our teaching and what might occur in our new classes? When will theory help us and when will it distract us from our students and their very different rhythms of growth? How, in fact, can theory help our students become better writers?

Lev Vygotsky, the great Soviet psychologist, believed that theory was too important to be merely the pastime of harmless academic drudges. Vygotsky believed that theory was inevitable and important. "But facts are always examined in light of some theory and therefore cannot be disentangled from philosophy," Vygotsky wrote (1962, 11). Vygotsky argues that "deliberate avoidance of philosophy is itself a philosophy and one that may involve its proponents in many inconsistencies" (1962, 20).

Vygotsky saw theory as basic, as a necessary part of the dialectics of development, as an instrument that helps us to bootstrap ourselves and our students into new zones of development. Vygotsky knew that students as well as teachers need to "learn" theory.

Over the last decade, I have reconstructed my freshman composition courses in light of Vygotsky's thoughts on theory and writing development. What might a composition course look like if we took theory seriously, if we believed as Vygotsky that theory is central to our own development as well as the development of our students? An account follows of my ongoing attempts to use theory to think about course design as well as the composing of the daily class in writing. I have discovered theory to be useful in at least four ways. (1) Theory has helped me to excavate my own *assumptions* about writing. (2) Theory has aided me in crafting a more coherent and unified *course structure*. (3) Theory has encouraged me to try out some *new methods* of teaching writing. (4) Theory has helped me to relinquish control and to emphasize the classroom community through *group work*.

Assumptions

Theory can help both teacher and student to look more closely at beliefs and to put them to the test. Vygotsky argues that theory often "leads" writing development. Students can often voice difficulties before they can solve them. Voicing conflict often becomes the first step in resolving it and transforming the conflict as well as the limit situation. Ailita Markova (1979) has created a course syllabus that begins with theoretical notions about language and moves on to try out and test those notions in writing and speaking. Of course, Jerome Bruner's spiral curriculum made an important place for student reflection, yet Bruner attended less to the relationship between teacher and student reflection. Vygotsky through his theory of the zone of proximal development shows that it is critical for teachers as well as students to reexamine assumptions, to rework their theory or vision of composing since this inquisitiveness and willingness to reflect on the teacher's part is shared with, modeled by, and subsequently internalized by the student. Among the more important assumptions that a Vygotskian with a penchant for Bakhtin brings to a writing course for questioning are the following propositions:

- Writing is more than a product; it is more than a process; writing is a relation, a social relation that is first shared between two or more people in community and is subsequently internalized, individuated, and made concrete by the individual.

- A composition course has content. This content is twofold (double-voiced). The primary objective of a writing course is to encourage students, through a variety of experiences and by means of reflective writing assignments, to arrive at a more explicit and conscious "theory" of writing that can guide them to understand their own writing process.

- Such a "theory" already exists when students come through the door, but it is usually implicit, tacit, untested against personal writing experience. Students often have internalized a former teacher's theory of writing or a theory from textbook versions of the writing process that does not fit at all with actual writing experience. Student theory is often plural, contradictory, heteroglossic.

- Because students are rarely conscious that they have a "theory" of composing that is already quite developed and sophisticated, the teacher needs to assist in providing secondary content that can help students to get at the "primary content." Writing and theories of writing, according to Vygotsky, have their roots in social relations, in community. (Consciousness is a sort of co-knowing.) The study of community provides the course with its logical content. It seems appropriate to study communication through the examination of the life of the *community* in which we are immersed. (Vygotsky and Luria call this method of studying one type of content with another type of related content the double stimulus method. They used this approach extensively in their study of psychological functions.)

- The dialectic between these two kinds of content helps to create a zone of proximal development in the individual student that can "lead" writing development.

- One way to bring these forms together in the classroom is through the course theme and structure.

Course Theme and Structure

A theory or vision of composing helps us to see some of the inconsistencies in our practice. Writing teachers, for example, expect students to write unified compositions made coherent by a theme or thesis, and yet the composition course (not to mention most composition textbooks) often lacks unity and coherence. We complain about student writing that is choppy, that jumps from one topic to another unrelated topic without transitions, but we find nothing strange or inconsistent about jumping from one mode to another over the semester, or doing some sentence combining and then discussing Orwell's "Politics and the English Language," curious as to why students don't seem to see the connections. If a composition course is going to be more than a hodgepodge, and if student reflections on the writing activities in that course are going to be more than a hodgepodge, compositionists need to attend more closely to the arrangement of assignments and discussions. William Coles (1978) and Paulo Freire (1973) show us the value of creating a theme that ties the course together and of selecting activities to reflect the various facets of that theme.

A theme provides the course with an evident structure that teacher and students keep returning to, a kind of *refrain* that can help the class to *broaden* its activities, to extend its inquiry. This course theme needs to be flexible enough to open into a variety of related topics and readings which are of interest to the students. The theme, however, also needs to be somehow implicitly linked to writing, which, after all, is what the course is about. By the term's end, it should be apparent to all, if it hasn't been up to that point, that the course theme has turned to, but also has always in some sense been about, *writing.* A teacher and the students need to carefully choose a theme for the course that is open-ended, that is a question to be investigated, without any preformed correct answers decided upon in advance. The class then investigates this theme, coming to its own conclusions, which may well be different or even opposed to the teacher's view. There are dangers in composing a course around a theme. When I have worked with teachers and asked them to try out a course theme, I have sometimes discovered (to my horror) that the theme so tightly structures the choices of readings, writing assignments, and class discussions that the students have no place left within the course to write on their *own* topics. I was shocked to discover that some of the juniors and seniors in my advanced composition course, having taken two previous writing courses built around course themes, never had a chance in three years to write a single paper on their own topics, rather than one dictated by the theme. This situation is as bad as a composition course that has *no* coherence or continuity.

So extremes must be avoided. Using a theme to pattern a course and *suggest* new activities should not make the course any less a composition course. There are dangers that the theme may well make the course so content based that aside from writing a lot, the student would hardly know whether the course was a literary theory, political science, sociology, or minority studies course. Writing courses *do* have content and form unique to composition, and a course that ignores this unique set of knowledges and practices is little different from the so-called composition course I took in 1970 that was simply a basic introduction to a new critical reading of canonical literature. Selection and use of the course theme, then, is a delicate matter.

I have used the themes of *Working in the USA, The Community and the Individual, Education and the Educated Person, Culture and Consciousness,* and *The American Dream.* Each theme has its own merits and its own available literature (everything from Studs Terkel to Bruce Springsteen). I have sketched out the structure of one freshman composition course I taught that focused on the theme of *Community and the Individual.* The various moments of that course are diagrammed in the chart "The Uses of Theory: Course Structure."

Five out-of-class, formal papers address this theme from various related perspectives complementing journal entries on related topics. I try to avoid the difficulty of moving students from expressive to transactional writing by having students engage in both, simultaneously, from the beginning. The order here is derived from Vygotskian theory (Vygotsky, Leontiev, Markova, Davydov) which (unlike Piagetian theory) asserts that development goes from the "abstract" to the "concrete," from the general to the particular, from the whole to the part, from the community to the individual, from the unconscious to the conscious. Assignments, then, move from the other and our misconceptions and stereotypes of the other, to the individual student and that student's unique "theory" of writing. The course ends with the students and their reflections on the writing they have completed over the term.

In addition to formal writing assignments and journal entries, an important place is made in the course for metawriting, that is, writing that reflects on writing, that examines writing experiences of student and professional writers. Students are encouraged to write about their own writing histories. They are asked to reflect on what they have been told about writing and how this information fits with their own experiences. Early in the term and then again during the last week of classes, I ask my students to write informally about their theory of writing and their writing history. Here are the assigned journal entries I gave students one term.

- Journal 1 . . . Discuss your theory of writing.

- Journal 2 . . . Discuss the highlights of your history as a writer.

- Journal 3 . . . Define through reason(s) and examples *Good Writing*. What is it? Why? What are its chief traits or characteristics in your mind? (Don't give me some other English teacher's view.) Who are good writers? What have they written? What might they do?

- Journal 4 . . . Write about your hometown. Where is it? What is it like? How do you feel about it now and/or before? Why?

- Journal 5 . . . Introduce me to you by writing about yourself. More specifically, describe one characteristic of yourself that is least evident to outsiders but a very important part of you. What would most people be surprised to find out about you? Why would this be the case? You might use the formula "Most people think I am _____, but in reality I am _____ (the opposite)." Or "On the outside (or on the surface) I appear _____, but inside (or down deeper) I am really _____." Again the audience is me.

- Journal 6 . . . Write on whatever topics are of interest.

I also try to do some of this writing myself to model a writer writing, as well as give the students a sense of the informal way I am using the word "theory." Here is one informal writing piece that I did.

Literacy Autobiography

I guess reading various parts of the Bible in my youth was important to my growth as a reader, possibly as a writer. I was more religious then than now and read the Bible to find "truth," not as literature, but as revelation, as the voices of generations of believers (and God I suppose) across the ages. It seemed to me a very uneven, and because of that, interesting document. Everything in it. Lists. History. Recipes even. And sure, philosophy, religion, ethics, all that too. Reading parts of the Bible often taught me more about reading and questions of interpretation than almost any other reading experience I have had. That in turn has had to have important effects on the way I write, though it is harder to point to them.

I have "always" it seems written journals or letters for myself (and sometimes for others). Remember 7th grade and writing that spy novel? Some novel, if you could call it that! And those journals going back to 1969. Not anything official. Not diaries. Not great ideas. Just me. Wondering. Wondering what I was going to do. Where? Why? Wondering who I was. What I felt. Why.

Writing this sort of thing really helped me grow. Almost like a baby playing by himself in the corner, talking to himself, or talking to himself right before sleep. I think I even remember doing that and certainly journal writing has been that for me. Babbling till I . . .

Other writing? I suppose I have to add the dissertation, not because it's any good or anyone would (or could) EVER read it. (It's basically unreadable. More babbling!) But because it was the longest single text I ever wrote and tried to stay on one subject. 300 pages originally. Boy was it a bear. A bear to get started. A bear to keep going. A bear to stop. I think at the end I could have written another couple of hundred pages if life hadn't thankfully intervened and the job in Texas hadn't stopped it.

I see this gets down to the fast and slow types of writing. Fast (letters, journals). Slow (dissertations, Bible reading). The times and seasons of a writer's life. Writing that is formal or informal, slow or fast. Who am "I"?

I'm in between/made up of all these (and other) writings I guess.

The exploratory and informal quality of this piece of writing on my own literacy experience is typical of the kind of writing that I ask students to frequently do throughout the term. But there are other occasions for writing about writing in addition to such reflections on process. For instance, students are expected to write responses (questions, agreements, disagreements, clarifications, and elaborations) to teacher comments on their papers. This has proved to be particularly revealing. Students are also expected to read the papers of peers and write evaluations and suggestions for improvement. All of this *metawriting* serves to help improve "content" while making students increasingly aware of their own theories of writing.

The *Community/Communication* theme allows the class to consider the way language comes out of community but also fashions and (re)creates community. The theme is broad enough to be adapt-

---

The Uses of Theory: Course Structure

Paper Assignments	Relation to Theme	Freire's Process
I. Stereotyping the Other Dispute some widely held and accepted belief about a group of people. You may use the form "Most people think that (group) are ____, but really they are ____ (the opposite)."	Community— what it is not.	Investigation

The Uses of Theory: Course Structure *(continued)*

Paper Assignments	Relation to Theme	Freire's Process
II. Mini-ethnography Report on the way of life of a specific community you have observed and participated in. Student Reports are then gathered to produce the class "textbook" to be read, discussed, and analyzed.	Community— what it is from the *insider's* perspective.	Investigation/ Reduction/ Coding of Thematic Universe
III. Inductive Analysis of Ethnographies Respond to the findings reported in the class textbook, using citations and quotations to support your conclusion. What patterns emerge? What patterns are repeated? omitted? Why? What can we conclude about community? about the community of our writing class? Why?	Community— what it is from the *outsider's* perspective.	Decoding and Discovery of Generative Themes
IV. Utopia How might you pose a problem you see in your community? How might you redesign some aspect of the community to improve the situation? Why? How?	Community— what it might become.	Problematization
V. The Student's "Theory" of Writing Using your experiences in and out of class, write up your "theory" of composition using a central metaphor. You may use the form "Writing is (or is like) _____ because . . ."	Communication in Community	Praxis

able to most any setting. I have more recently been using the theme of *Working* with even better results, since students generally come to class with some work experience and they often see their reason for being at college to be primarily to get a good job. By using the *Working* theme, I have been able to discuss the intellectual work of the university, and even specific disciplines and professions represented at the university, while at the same time encouraging students to think about the writer's work. Here is the explanation I gave to one composition class that I centered around this theme:

Working

The Writing Studio I course develops the student's ability to use writing as a mode of learning, thinking, and critical reading.

To address these concerns this term, we will be focusing on the theme of work. What exactly do we mean by work? What role does work play in our lives? What, if anything, does work have to do with our life at S.U.? What do our conceptions of work tell us about the world we live in? What does "the world" tell us about possible conceptions of work? What do Americans at the end of the twentieth century have to say about work and working?

And of course, what does any of this have to do with the world created by words? with the writing processes? These are just a few of the questions we will be thinking about.

Reading and writing assignments, revolving around this theme of work, will move through three phases.

1. WORKING IN THE WORLD This first thematic moment will be concerned with definitional and experiential questions— what we think about work, what others think about work, and how we have experienced work in our lives and in the lives of our family and friends.

2. WORKING AROUND S.U. During this moment we will consider the work of education, especially the student's work. This is a logical point to think, among other things, about how (and why) we often oppose the "real world" to "school."

3. WORKING THROUGH WORDS In this final moment of the course, we will try to synthesize our discoveries about work by investigating the writing processes of working writers. What do successful writers have to say about writing? What is the significance of this? How can we become better at working through the words?

The theme moves from the abstract to the concrete, from others to self, from experience to possibility. The theme should unify our reading/writing/talking activities over the course of the semester. Yet the concept of WORK will be addressed in such a broad and varied way that the student shouldn't be unduly restricted in choosing paper topics.

To give some sense of how a theme might play itself across the course of a semester, I include the syllabus I used one term. These assignments are obviously only recommendations. I have done a variety of other things on the working theme besides these activities, though over the last few years I have settled for dividing the course into three parts—an introductory section in which students do a great deal of informal writing and talking as well as some fairly challenging reading. The second moment of the course tends to be the time when we meet in individual and group conferences of five to seven students rather than in the large class. The students are doing ethnographic writing at their own sites at this time. In the last third of the course, we gather again in the large class, discuss the findings of the ethnographic writing, and try to begin to see what we can conclude about writing itself. This is often paralleled by reading from working writers about writing. Here then is the syllabus that I used in one freshman writing studio.

SYLLABUS, CLASS POLICIES, PROCEDURES   Dr. James Zebroski
Writing Studio I — Honors
Writing 109
Fall 1990

REQUIRED MATERIALS
Texts: —Photopack at Syracuse Copy Center
        —Working Studs Terkel
        —Writing Studios: A Description for Students
        —By-Line: Ernest Hemingway E. Hemingway (ed. W. White)
            Scribners 1967
        —Looseleaf notebook with paper
        —Portfolio folder (regulation size)
        —Plan on a class set of photocopies of papers

WRITING STUDIO I
This class will be run as a workshop. Unlike many of the other courses you will be taking this term, the writing studio course will NOT be a lecture course in which you sit and take notes. Instead you will be expected to show up and DO things in class time, including participating in discussions, working in small peer groups, writing informal papers, working on and refining longer more formal papers, keeping a daybook, and reflecting on your own reading and writing processes.

The writing studio course is especially concerned that you learn to write better by developing you abilities to (1) use writing to discover new ideas, (2) use writing as a way of reflecting on literacy as social process and cultural practice, (3) use writing as a way of communicating your insights to others.

Attendance, then, is required. You cannot participate if you are not here. What's more, by coming to class you will be able to work with others to build a class community.

There are no MAKE-UP ASSIGNMENTS.

Papers must come in ON DEADLINE.

Formal Papers must be TYPED (wordprocessing is encouraged). Plan for this now.

PLAGIARISM is a serious offense and can result in failure. You are responsible for understanding what plagiarism is and for avoiding it.

A final PORTFOLIO is a course requirement for each student. Keep ALL papers and writing done throughout this course so that you can compose your portfolio at term's end. I will explain the portfolio assignment in more detail later. For now you need to know that in order to do well on Paper 3 and compose a good portfolio you must carefully keep and keep track of your writing this semester.

CONFERENCES and out of class FIELD RESEARCH will be required for each student.

Letter grades will be determined according to the following breakdown:

Formal Writing (Paper 1, 3 = 10%, Paper 2 = 20%)	40%
Informal Writing (daybook)	10%
In class Essays (2x 10%)	20%
Portfolio	20%
Class Participation (quizzes, in class writing, peer groups)	10%

WRITING 109 — ZEBROSKI — FALL 1990 — DAILY PLAN

Sept. 11 E. Fromm "Work in Alienated Society"
13 K. Marx "Estranged Labour"
18 Survey on Work. Assign Writing Product Inventory.
Student Paper on Working in McDonald's
20 H. D. Thoreau "Why I Went to the Woods"
Formal Paper 1 Assigned.

25 Louise Erdrich selection from Tracks.
Woody Guthrie "Pastures of Plenty" and "Deportee".
Joni Mitchell "The Arrangement"
27 Writing Product Inventory due in class.
Work on Paper 1 in class.
Sign up for required conferences. Bring drafts and daybook.

Oct. 2 Individual Conferences. NO CLASS
4 DRAFT of PAPER due in class. Peer evaluation day.

9 NO CLASS. FALL BREAK.
11 PAPER I final draft and packet due in class.
Discuss Spradley "Ethnography and Culture"
and Paper II. Begin ethnographic fieldwork.

16 Group Conferences meet in 005 HBC during class.
18 No Class. Voluntary individual conferences scheduled
throughout the week. Continue fieldwork and ethnographic
writing.

23 Group Conferences. Ethnographic writing continues.
25 Individual Conferences. Ethnographic writing continues.

30 Group Conferences. Ethnographic writing continues.
Nov. 1 Individual Conferences. Ethnographic writing continues.

6 DRAFT of PAPER II due in class. Peer evaluation day.
8 Paper II DUE IN CLASS. Reflections on the process.

13 Discussion of ethnographic essays.
15 In Class Essay on ethnographic essays.

20 By-Line: Ernest Hemingway
"American Bohemians" "A Silent, Ghastly Process"
"Old Constant" "Refugees from Thrace"
"Bullfighting: A Tragedy"

22 NO CLASS. THANKSGIVING BREAK.

```
      27  BLEH  "Marlin Off the Morro"  "Notes on the Next War"
      29  BLEH  "Monologue to the Maestro"  "The Great Blue River"

Dec.   4  Joan Didion "On Keeping A Notebook"
          Donald Bateman "Dialectical Reflections on the Process
          of Writing"
       6  Donald Murray "Teaching the Other Self"
          Cinthia Gannet "Musings on Murray"

      11  Evaluation forms. In class essay.

       *  Portfolio due by Monday December 17, noon.

      THERE IS NO FINAL EXAMINATION SCHEDULED IN THIS COURSE
```

Method

The search for a more conscious theory of composition has led me to use new methods. Students do a miniethnography in this course. Ethnography is writing about a people and their way of life. While often associated with cultural anthropologists and folklorists, ethnography bears a strong resemblance to what writers (Hemingway, Didion), "new journalists" (Tom Wolfe, Norman Mailer, Truman Capote), historians, and travel-book writers have always done, whether they were conscious of it at the time or not. So why ethnography in a freshman composition course?

First, it allows students to produce good writing. Ethnography has gotten more students to write down rich, interesting, and concrete detail than any other method I have tried. Ethnography moves students to the concrete (to life) in a way that writing "Be Specific" thousands of times on student papers never has. Ethnography also has helped students listen to the voices of people around them in a way traditional research papers rarely do.

Shirley Brice Heath (1983) has demonstrated the usefulness of ethnography for both students and teachers, and has suggested that we all learn ethnographically, that is, by placing ourselves in both the insider's and the outsider's position. Ethnography emphasizes the double-voiced nature of discourse since the report the students write up must communicate the insider's point of view (gleaned from observations and interviews at the site) to the outsider (the other students in class who will read the report and respond to it and to other reports in the following paper).

The student ethnographer has to observe closely, take profuse notes, carefully separate her language in the notes from the language of the people, and distance herself enough from the scene (from what seems "common sense" to the insiders) to find something significant. The student ethnographer must decontextualize and abstract, but within a real context and for a real motive. Finally, the student ethnographer has to write this up using accurate and appropriate quotations in a coherent manner.

Even the problems that the ethnographic assignment raises are good problems. Students have to decide whether to tell the people at the site what they are doing, dealing with important ethical questions, discovering that language is not a neutral, nonideological medium that somehow comes detached from human beings and human motives. Rather the student discovers that even the decision to be neutral and not to tell the informants is a decision with consequences, that involves those people and their words even if they are not conscious of it.

Student ethnographers also discover, often for the first time, that they have too much to write about. They feel the tension that every writer feels when trying to condense the richness and ambiguity of life into an inevitably reductive discourse, to lose life's diversity, to simplify the complex. Students experience this limiting side of language at the same time that they begin to experience its potential, to get satisfaction from creating a "piece" of language that somehow mysteriously represents the whole of life. Somehow, they discover, writing can be more real than reality. Students also experience the heuristic nature of language, discovering revelatory insights about self and subject in the process.

Finally, students engage in the writing process in a deeper way. Unlike other papers, the ethnography requires student observation, note-taking, and reflection over a long period. You can't sit down the night before and crank out ethnography. It doesn't work.

This method, which I developed by using theory to think through the problem of vague and lifeless freshman writing, has been one of our most popular activities. Students feel a bit uncomfortable early in the fieldwork, but so do most anthropologists (their name for it—culture shock). But in the reflection papers that students write at the end, they consistently endorse the value of the project. The most surprising student response to the assignment is that most of them do not find the extensive hours spent in fieldwork (often five to ten hours a week outside of class) to be burdensome. In fact, they are already involved in many communities—either through work or internships or extracurricular activities—and they welcome the opportunity to try to make sense of their world in some

deeper way. My most successful assignment then, is the fruit of my
search for a more developed theory.

Group Work

Vygotskian theory asserts that group work is important to writing
development. While it doesn't always *appear* to work well, group
work is a central component of the Vygotskian classroom. It is
critical to provide occasions for students to work frequently and
regularly together in small groups, especially because our individualistic, competitive culture militates against this kind of sharing.
Students may have had twelve to fourteen years in classrooms without small-group experience. Thus it is often rough going; many
times group work doesn't succeed. I have recently been trying out
dividing class time (usually one-and-a-half hours) into three small-
group meetings. I, too, participate in these half-hour mini-classes. I
have had very good success with these half-hour seminar groups of
five to seven students. I get to know them well, they come prepared
because I lead the group, at least at first, and they feel more involved
in talking about readings or writing assignments. These groups also
offer a nice change of pace to the large and long classes as well as
to the (sometimes intimidating) individual conference. When we
return afterward to the large class, there is usually a marked and
positive change in energy and participation. *Those classes that have
shown the greatest individual writing development have been those
classes that have made the best of group work.* In these classes
things will often seem disappointing until past midterm and then
suddenly, sometimes in one class session, the class comes together
and seems to have developed a sense of community. Students will
comment on this phenomenon to me, and the students in particular
small groups often become close friends outside of the classroom.
At this point, I try to relinquish control and let the groups play a
larger role. Theory helps me to understand why this happens.

   Group work requires more involvement from students. It provides more chances for interaction in a supportive atmosphere. It
thus helps activate the zone of proximal development. As Vygotsky
demonstrated, what the student can do in cooperation with others
leads what she will in the near future be able to do individually.
This developing individual, in turn, returns to the group (and to the
larger class) with new insights and ideas and confidence which then
help move the group and class to higher levels of energy and development. Group work, then, not only helps the teacher to deal with
overloads, to vary the routine, and to encourage student responsibil-

ity: it also provides the very mechanism that helps lead the individual student's writing process to new levels of development.

Conclusion

Theory is an instrument that my students and I use to think about writing. We come through the door with highly developed and complex, though usually unconscious, understandings of writing. My freshman composition course asks students to think more consciously about that theory. In fact, it asks them to compose and revise a theory of writing.

One of the last papers asks students to reflect on the term and to write an essay about their writing process, using a metaphor. This is an enjoyable essay for me to read since the metaphors are hardly ever the same, but it is also a good activity for students to finish with, since it asks them to synthesize *their* experience, to come up with a vision of writing that is new and particular to them. The following list suggests some things students might consider.

What is a "Theory" of Writing?

What is a "theory" of writing? It is difficult to answer this question since what one views as being the essence of a theory of writing will of course determine what one thinks is important in writing, to the writer, concerning the written. Thus if I were to give you my sense (completely) of what a theory of writing is, I would be in some sense telling you what the theory of writing is. There is a world of difference between the view I have and the view you have. The point of this assignment is to deal with what view you have, whether implicit or explicit.

The only point to make is that some things *are* expected of course writing, including unity, synthesis, proof (reasoning plus evidence), etc.

Some questions that you might need to consider to clarify your theory of writing:
- What is the root metaphor of writing? (What is writing *like?*)
- How might one define writing?
- How might one define "good" writing? bad writing?
- How can one explain one's writing process?
- How does one's writing (and process) relate to other writers (and their processes)?
- What are the important external influences on writing and writing development? Why?
- Discuss writing block. How might one explain it? What is it like? So?
- What significance (if any) does writing have? So what?

- What are the parts of the writing activity? What are its components? What different kinds of writing are there? Why? How can you explain their origins?
- What are the "ethics" of writing? Of communication? What is the relation of ends to means in writing?
- What is the distinction between style and taste?
- What is the history of writing? (Social as well as personal)
- What is the psychology of writing? What goes on inside the head as/after/before one writes? What is the relation between the mental, psychological process and the written, external product?
- Where does writing arise from? Where does it go?
- What are your reactions to the theories posed by:

Hemingway?	cummings?	Quintilian?
Faulkner?	Young, Becker, Pike?	Hitler?
Emig/Lauer?	Kinneavy?	Williams?
Zebroski?		Woolf?

Theory, then, provides both teachers and students with a way of framing their experience. Theory also gives us a chance to envision ourselves and our world in new ways. Ernst Bloch argues that hope is the principle. We are but paltry imitations of our destiny. Theory can help bridge us, slowly and hesitantly, to a newer world.

References

Bakhtin, M. 1982. *The dialogic imagination: Four essays.* Trans. M. Holquist. Austin: University of Texas Press.

Bruner, J. 1960. *The process of education.* Cambridge, MA: Harvard University Press.

Coles, W. 1978. *The plural I: The teaching of writing.* New York: Holt, Rinehart, and Winston.

Freire, P. 1973. *Education for critical consciousness.* New York: Seabury Press.

Hammersley, M. & P. Atkinson. 1983. *Ethnography: Principles in practice.* New York: Tavistock.

Heath, S. 1983. *Ways with words.* Cambridge: Cambridge University Press.

Markova, A. 1979. *The teaching and mastery of language.* White Plains, NY: M. E. Sharpe.

Shor, I. 1980. *Critical teaching and everyday life.* Boston: South End Press.

Spradley, J. 1980. *Participant observation.* New York: Holt, Rinehart and Winston.

Vygotsky, L. 1962. *Thought and language.* Cambridge, MA: MIT Press.

Chapter Two

Using Ethnographic Writing to Construct Classroom Knowledge

When you teach four sections of introductory composition each semester, three of which are the research paper course, what can you do to keep your own sanity and teach students something about real research? Teaching the one-shot, traditional research paper has simply not worked for me. For my students the research paper is some occult art that only depraved English teachers practice (and force their students to commit) and the resulting products are correspondingly appalling, regardless of well-intentioned scavenger hunts in the library, pre-paper note cards and drafts, and attempts at discovering student preferences, which understandably enough are to do the same paper using the same sources that they did in high school.

So I have given up the research paper and have thrown my lot in with ethnography. Ethnography is writing about a people and their way of life. The resulting papers have been specific, surprisingly interesting to me and my students, and more often than not, authentic language acts that have engaged students with real research issues. Through ethnography I have avoided the whole problem of plagiarism—who do you know that teaches ethnography as the research paper?—and in the process have had students coming to me to inquire earnestly about things like quotes within a quote and the extent of personal voice in the papers. Finally, I have focused the course less on me and more on the students. The ethnographic research project begins from the assumption that knowledge is a process of creating understandings of one's world through language. Students are knowledge makers and the composition class-room becomes the site where the community of writers create such knowledge. When the teacher and the students view knowledge as socially constructed, as a process that is in fact going on all the time, classroom relations can potentially be transformed. In the end, I am less bored because I never know exactly what the papers will be about from term to term—they are surprisingly varied—and students are less bored because they can try to make sense out of some aspect of their life.

Actually ethnographic writing is not only what anthropologists do but bears a strong resemblance to what many novelists (Heming-way and Steinbeck), "new journalists" (Joan Didion and Tom Wolfe), historians, and travel-book writers do, whether all of these folk are conscious of it or not. Ethnographic writing is writing about a people and their way of life, their lived experience. The people in the community or group being studied (called the "site") become the experts, and the teacher and the writer become their students. The writer tries to understand how these people view their world, how they construct meaning in shared ways. The writer tries to find the right words, the appropriate language to capture this and report it to readers outside the site. Ethnographic writing focuses on the other and the other's world. The ethnographic writer often tries to *make strange* (or defamiliarize) the automatic, the reflexive, the ordinary, the everyday, but also tries to *make familiar,* to rationalize and to systematize the seemingly bizarre, the strange, and the chaotic in culture.

The ethnographic writer often—

- gives a reader a glimpse of the daily activities at the site.
- investigates group motives.
- provides the words of the people through direct quotation.
- provides telling dialogue.
- selects out themes that seem to pervade the community and unfolds the themes.
- tries to understand how all the activities work together as a whole to create community.
- tries to discover overt and hidden conflicts that pull the community apart.
- studies in specific detail how people act, talk, think.
- looks at what people do, say, and make.
- tries to understand how people in their everyday life create meaning, produce knowledge.

- studies the relations between discourse, knowledge, and power.
- does a lot of purposeful hanging around and directed eavesdropping.

I use ethnography to involve students more directly in research processes, to encourage students to perform the complex cognitive activities that writing development requires.

In other words, ethnographic writing encourages—

- specificity in writing.
- writing for discovery (Murray calls this writing for surprise).
- critical thinking—synthesizing, examining the unsaid and assumed of a group.
- reflective thinking, that is, continual rethinking of observing/writing/thinking processes.
- the processes of gathering information—primary research.
- the processes of synthesizing huge amounts of information.
- the processes of revision.
- writing for multiple audiences.
- breaking formulas, blurring genres.
- studying language as a dynamic, forming activity.
- writing on topics close to students.
- writing as experts who produce rather than consume knowledge on their topic.
- making connections between home and school.

I have taught ethnography as one of five paper assignments in a course—a miniethnography of 800 to 1000 words and perhaps four or five visits to the site—and as the major paper of the course, of 2000 to 3000 words. It is flexible and can expand or contract to suit your interests and purposes.

Phase I—Creating the Class Context

I have found it very important to integrate the ethnographic writing assignment into the broader course and its goals and activities. Even when the ethnographic assignment is going well, it challenges students. Students spend several weeks reading and writing about the theme that the ethnographies then take up to investigate. For example, when students look at the theme, "Working in the USA," they begin by talking about experiences of family and friends with working. We read about work and working.

In one recent freshman composition course, I asked students to write informally in their journals about their own experiences working, or if they preferred, to write about the working experience of someone they knew well (a relative, a friend). We then discussed these jobs. A few students shared horror stories about abusive employers, but many students said that though they hated their jobs, this was an exception that proved the rule, an individual peculiarity, that most people liked their work—or should. Even if they didn't, it was probably their own fault for having a bad attitude or not having enough ambition to move to another job that they would like.

I then asked students to closely read the classic "Estranged Labor" by Karl Marx, which enumerates the ways the social system fragments work, and we examined a section from Erich Fromm's book *The Sane Society*, titled "Man in Capitalistic Society," which looks at the psychological consequences of such social alienation. By this point the class was buzzing, and resisting. The ideas proposed in the readings bothered students. Rather than try to resolve the tension, I tried to clarify the issues at stake and to distinguish differences of opinion.

We then read Thoreau's "Why I Went to the Woods," selections from Studs Terkel's *Working*, and listened to Woody Guthrie's "Pastures of Plenty" and "Deportee." (In other courses and at other schools I have also used more popular songs by performers like Bruce Springsteen and John Cougar Mellencamp.) Someone in class recommended we try out a survey among students in the dorms to find out whether their experiences supported the arguments of Marx, Fromm, Terkel, and others, or supported the arguments of most students in class. Each student did a sample and brought back the results, which we tallied up on the blackboard and then copied down and later printed up for every student. The survey for the most part seemed to support the class's view, but there was some qualification. Only at this point, after having carefully spent several weeks setting up the context, did I introduce the ethnographic writing assignment.

I explained that ethnography is writing about a people and involves the writer in close observation and participation in a cultural scene. It also requires regular note taking and keeping of records. In many ways, ethnography is what any student does when she or he tries to learn something whether it be a tennis serve or organic chemistry. It is also what any worker does on the first day on a job. I tell them, "You watch, you try to understand it *from the perspective of the insider*, you ask questions to test your observa-

Work Survey   9/18/90

Range of Jobs	Total/Like/Dislike	Why? Mitigating Facts
	+ −	
office	128 − 84 − 44	− long, boring, not
camp counselor		appreciated by bosses,
[fast food]	+ −	only in for money.
trucker driver (ice clearer)	154 − 117 − 36	
TV cameraman		+ people worked with
sales		fun, outdoors, money,
bartender	+ −	responsibility.
movie translator	203 − 142 − 61	
construction		+ children work, like
technical		hours.
ad manager	**TOTALS:**	
(radio station)		− no mental stimulation
recreational jobs	485 − 343	
babysitting		+ social aspect
	about	(brain power)
	/	\	
	500 − 350 − 150	− repetitive, boring, no
		interaction with people
		+ praised by boss,
		outdoor work,
		well-liked.

Comments

1. At first people aren't sure, have to think, need prompting. [Follow up.]
2. When asking whether you like job is *key*.
       In the job -vs.- *after* the job.
3. Bosses are positive, their job is also. (small companies)

recorder: Heidi Haslett

tions, you take note of—mentally or in writing—what you need to know but might forget, trying it yourself. Since this is a writing course, we're going to add a step and you'll write it up for yourself and for the class." I sometimes ask students to read the first chapter of James Spradley's *Participant Observation* (1980) to clear up any lingering doubts they may have about the whole process.

Phase II—Doing Ethnography

Students, once they get the idea, do not have too much trouble
determining a site; in fact, if a problem arises at this stage, it is
sometimes because students have too many possibilities and can't
narrow it to one. Students have done ethnographic writing on all
kinds of sites, including these:

- barber shops
- nursing homes
- clinics
- emergency rooms
- firefighters
- church groups
- self-help groups
- emergency medical squads
- athletic teams
- video parlors and game rooms
- commuter cars (car pools)
- maintenance workers
- upper class majors (architecture students, art students)
- day care centers
- businesses of all sorts— fast food restaurants, stores, bars
- farmers and farm families
- hang-outs, cafeterias, coffee houses
- radio stations
- fraternities, sororities, clubs, dorms
- libraries
- youth rehabilitation centers
- sites of regular pick-up basketball games
- hike and bike running trail
- student union and people who work there
- other groups—"Dead heads," punk rockers

Neither do students mind spending considerable amounts of
time at the site, since they are usually already involved (sometimes
too involved) in work or internships or out-of-class activities that
often become the cultural scenes they study. What students *do* have
trouble with is *me*—I purposely refuse to tell them exactly what to
do and what to look for (a) because I don't know anything about
their site and what you determine to be important in ethnographic
research will be determined by what happens at the site, (b) because
I want students to become the experts on their subcultures and
communities, to produce knowledge, and (c) because it makes for
varied papers if I shut up.

This is the hard part, trying to defuse their high anxiety while
still not caving in and giving a preset formula. I hold lots of conferences and I give them these instructions in writing:

The Ethnography

The major research project of this course is the ethnography. An ethnography is a report about the way of life of a particular people. This report will *synthesize* your observations, interviews, and other data gathered at the site.

Because you will have so many diverse and varied observations, and because these observations will only be known to your reader through the discourse you create, the final report will need to focus and organize the information very carefully. One way to do this is through the *thesis statement*. What is the single most important and significant point that the reader (or the outsider) will need to know about the group? That idea, expressed in a single sentence and used to unify all parts of the paper, is the thesis.

Concrete examples as well as many (appropriate) quotations accurately attributed and reported, will be included in the ethnography. This means that you will need to visit your site several times a week and that you will need to keep detailed, extensive, and accurate fieldnotes. Fieldnotes using the double entry notebook approach will be checked on _____.

You'll need far more notes than you will eventually write into the report.

Be sure to separate carefully *your* language about the scene from the language of the *participants* in the scene.

Keep in mind that the final report is written for the class. So explain whatever they will need to know but won't.

That is about as explicit as I get unless I have a real blocker. After students have been doing fieldwork for a while, the problem disappears only to reappear as "I've got *so much stuff,* how can I get it all down in one paper?" and that is a good kind of problem to have. When students have accumulated ten pages of notes and reflections for each week at the site (three weeks a minimum), I ask students to begin to look for recurring patterns that they can focus their final reports on. I give this sheet of possible thesis statements only as a list of suggestions for where students might start in the difficult job of writing up this mass of notes and quotations.

Possible Thesis Statements

1. The first thing that an outsider notices about _____ is _____.

2. To most people (a)_____ is (a)_____, but to a member of the _____ community it is (a)_____.

3. The most important *characteristic* an outsider would notice about _____ is _____. (Or role, rule, quality, process, object, activity / event, etc.)

4. In the _____ minds, they are _____.

5. In all human societies some people _____; in the _____ community this is no less true.

6. In many human communities _____ is *so:* in the _____ community it is not. (Or true, accepted, encouraged / discouraged)

7. The _____ community is most concerned with _____. As they see it _____.

8. The _____ at the _____ community aren't really _____ unless they _____.

9. At one level, the _____ community is _____; but at another level, it can be seen as _____.

10. In the _____ community, there are many stages in _____ing. The entire process of _____ing can take as long (or as little time) as _____ and can involve _____.

11. There are _____ kinds of _____ in the _____ community.

12. Many people think that the _____ do _____; but in reality they don't. They do _____.

13. To the _____ people, the single most important _____ is _____ (because _____).

14. The _____ people think that _____ is like _____ (because _____).

15. For you to become a _____, you need (most importantly) to _____, _____, and _____ (because _____).

16. To be a member of the _____ community, you have to know _____, you have to do _____, you have to say _____. (be at, believe, think, etc.)

To help the process along I do check fieldnotes regularly, mostly just to make sure students are getting to their sites and are getting notes down; if anxiety is high, I give the class examples of previous student ethnographies although I have usually regretted it later— they need to find their own forms and not simply mimic someone else's.

I show students that this tension and chaos are a "natural" part of writing processes and that they are not alone, that in fact, this tangle of materials provides a rich, generative set of themes. I provide this handout on "Unity in the Ethnographies" about two-thirds of the way through the research project.

Unity in the Ethnographies

Let me start by saying how pleased I was that some of you are asking me about unity, that is, how to bring your notes together to form an ethnography with a theme. It is completely natural that you are feeling uncomfortable about this at this point. This is a good kind of problem to have since it indicates that you have lots of notes and are trying to understand them in a deeper way rather than simply stringing them together to get the assignment done.

Keep in mind that unity (and how to achieve it, especially in writing), when our very lives tend toward fragmentation and disunity, is one of the key issues of the twentieth century. You are dealing with a problem very comparable to that which Hemingway, Faulkner, Woolf, T. S. Eliot, Joan Didion, Tillie Olsen, Richard Rodriguez, Loren Eiseley, to name just a few of my favorites, and many others have pondered over the last eighty years. So—you are in good company.

Keep These Points in Mind:

- You will not and should not use all the material you have collected through fieldnotes and participant-observation. The idea is to select the best and most important and most detailed information.

- You can do well on the ethnography even if your efforts at unifying are not completely successful. Keep in mind that the significance and specificity of your report is more important than your ability to unify the pieces.

- You are having problems unifying, in part, because you are writing a long piece and a complicated project, not because you are a bad writer or are not smart. Writing creates more writing. Every good ethnographer (or novelist, or dare I say it, true writer) faces the same problem. You want to hear the story of my 300 page dissertation that had to be cut, for financial reasons to 160 pages? Or about my chapter three that was supposed to be 50 pages and wound up being 120 pages? Talk about getting out of control!

- You are having problems unifying in part because that is the way language works—which raises the question of who told you it was ever neat and why?

- You know more than you think you know. Remember, a good part of your paper will be describing and explaining things to the class that you already take for granted and that are not even written down in your notes.

- No one knows what you do not know. If you write a paper that interests your classmates (and yourself), who in class is going to know that you have not achieved perfect unity and that you perhaps changed things in the writing? No one and everyone. No one, because you are the sole expert on your site. Everyone, because almost all of them are having the same problem too.

SOME STRATEGIES: Pick and choose and find out what works best for you. It may be something different entirely and we, your fellow writers, would benefit from hearing about it!

- CALM DOWN. PUT IT ALL IN PERSPECTIVE. You'll survive and may even learn some important things in the process, even if you are unsuccessful this time. There will be other occasions to apply in this course what you have learned. I am not going to hold a good attempt to solve these problems against you.

- Consider the examples of PAST STUDENT ETHNOGRAPHIES that you read and discussed in peer groups. What held together the ones that seemed to work well? Can you "steal" that idea and apply to your paper using my past student's attempts as models?

- FREEWRITE. Peter Elbow has popularized this approach. Go off by yourself with your coffee or cola and all the materials you will need—notes, pens, watch, paper—and close yourself off and don't let anything or anyone interrupt and distract you and force yourself to write through as much of the material as quickly as possible. Start anywhere and write anything, just keep moving. Do some shorter things (maybe fifteen minutes at a time) and pick one idea from each piece that seems important and freewrite from that. Don't stop and don't listen to that voice saying this is bad. Keep alert for a center which seems to connect to most everything you have or wanted to say. When you feel that center—it usually comes at the end of a freewrite or several freewrites—then stop, put it at the top of a new page and use that center as your theme. It may even be possible to use some of the texts or pieces of them that you generated in previous freewrites. If all else fails, you can pick and choose and cut and paste and work inductively, determining your theme from the common connection between materials used.

- LIST the five or six or seven most important things for an outsider to know about your site and the people there. What ties these items together?

- SLEEP ON IT. Study your notes and do some writing about the problem right before you go sleep. Sleep on that problem. Listen for the answer to the question when you wake up or shortly thereafter. Allow yourself some quiet time alone for this early in the AM. Be careful. Insights from this method sometimes come at the worst possible moments, when you are not ready for them. I usually get insights in the shower or during shaving. So be ready with pencil and paper always at hand!

- WEB OUT all the key material on one sheet of paper (write small or get or make a big sheet) so you can see it all. Leave the center open and just start putting down stuff and drawing connecting lines. Where do all of these spokes on the wheel lead? What is at the hub? (See *Writing the Natural Way* by Gabriele Rico.)

- TALK with a dear friend. First tell them what help you need and then take several minutes presenting a summary of your material and your problems with it. Listen to yourself. Take a minute or two and quickly jot down what seems to pull this stuff together at this time, then ask your friend to talk to you about what he or she thinks is pulling the topic together or what is interesting or surprising or apparent (except that you didn't say anything about it) etc.

- Use key word(s) or a haunting phrase or an appropriate metaphor at certain critical junctures of the text. Repeat or extend that word/phrase/metaphor in the title, in the first sentence (or paragraph), in the last sentence (or paragraph). Form a circle by tying the first thing in the paper with the last thing in the paper. Look at the first and last sentences of great novels and see what they do.

Phase III—Follow-Up

We do quite a bit of debriefing after the written assignment is completed. Students usually have a lot to say and want to share it. The day the written assignment is due in class, I have students do some written reflection using these questions:

1. In a short paragraph, reflect on your work as ethnographer. Do you think this assignment was valuable? Why /why not?

2. List several things you learned (or relearned) about language (and writing) by doing the ethnography.

3. Briefly recount your experiences. What was observation like compared to write-up—easier, more difficult, just different?

4. What was the hardest thing about the ethnography? Why? Easiest?

5. Describe your ethnographic experience in terms of an appropriate metaphor and briefly explicate that metaphor.

Students often note that it is really difficult to reduce life to language and to condense that richness to words on a page. I agree and tell them it is impossible, but that in the process of trying, writers create completely new worlds. They don't transmit information about the world so much as they create new worlds. Writers produce knowledge in the process of transmitting it. That is a pretty heavy idea for a freshman research paper course, yet it has been a very rare class in which this issue has not come up spontaneously after doing ethnography.

I then have students follow up the assignment by reading the reports that have been duplicated by each individual student (I tell them it costs about five dollars on the first day of class) and collated into a class book. This book is then given several possible titles by groups and we as a class vote on our favorite—a fun and useful way of getting students to try to abstract, synthesize, and consider the audience. Generally after we discuss the reports, I have students pick out several examples from the text and write up the next paper with only student quotations and bibliographic entries. I try to get them to synthesize the perspectives on "working" reflected in these ethnographic reports, comparing them with the views we read at the term's beginning, those of Marx, Fromm, Thoreau, Terkel, Guthrie. I sometimes provide students with this list of possible things to look for in the set of student ethnographic texts.

Some considerations when writing paper III— analysis of the ethnographies

What papers deal with physical activities?
What papers deal with fraternities/sororities, professional clubs or organizations?
What papers deal with mental activities? aesthetic activities?

What papers deal with positive experiences? for the people at the site? for the researcher?
What papers deal with negative experiences?
What is the explanation for the positive (or negative) nature of the experience?
What papers deal with conflict? How is it approached? Is it positive? negative? neutral?

What is the relation between the site and the author? between positive attitudes and experiences and the subjects of the study at the site? Do men tend to choose similar sorts of sites? Women another? Why? Why not? So what?

How is Syracuse University characterized in the papers? Why?
What would a student going to Cornell or Yale or Brown University or SUNY Albany think of SU (or SU students) after reading these papers? Why?
What about SU that is important seems to be missing? avoided? Why?
What do SU students seem to value? think important? unimportant? avoid dealing with?

How is the world outside of Syracuse portrayed? What kind of world is it? Why?

What emotion seems to be most conspicuous in the papers? How can you account for this?
What emotion seems least conspicuous? Why?

As a simple snapshot of the USA in late 1988, what do these papers seem to show?
What is America about these days according to the papers?
What might an American who was 19 in 1968 think about these papers? Why?

What might an American who was 19 in 1958 think about these
papers? Why?

What might an American who was 19 in 1998 think about these
papers? Why?

What worldviews are expressed in these papers? What are human
beings like? What kind of world is it? What is the place of the
student in this world?

Who, outside of these papers, might benefit from having people
believe this? How does language help create such a worldview?

By this point most students have learned some things not only
about their ethnographic site, but also about working. Most importantly they have written their way through this, using writing to
raise questions and to discover new things about their world. Writing has helped students to sort through massive amounts of information of varying significance. Writing has been an instrument for
communicating what they discovered to fellow classmates and to
the members of the culture they studied. Writing has been a means
for the students to discover what they think and for them to position
themselves. Ethnographic writing, then, has become an instrument
for the making of knowledge. In the composition classroom, both
the students and the teacher compose not only texts, but they also
compose knowledge. From here it is possible to move to the traditional research paper, if that is deemed necessary, because research
for these students is no longer copying what other people say, but
rather is a naming of the world.

References

Elbow, P. 1981. *Writing with power.* New York: Oxford University Press.

Fromm, E. 1955. *The sane society.* Holt, Rinehart, and Winston.

Marx, K. & F. Engels. 1978. *The Marx-Engels reader,* edited by R. Tucker.
New York: Norton.

Murray, D. 1985. *A writer teaches writing.* Boston: Houghton Mifflin.

Rico, G. 1983. *Writing the natural way.* Los Angeles, CA: Tarcher.

Spradley, J. 1980. *Participant observation.* New York: Holt, Rinehart and
Winston.

Terkel, S. 1975. *Working.* New York: Avon.

Thoreau, H. D. 1965. Where I lived and what I lived for. *Walden.* New York:
Harper.

Chapter Three

Using Portfolios for
Reflection Not Evaluation

Over the last ten years I have experimented with using various forms of the writing portfolio in my undergraduate composition courses. I began with a simple idea of portfolios as a collection of papers, but through further reflection, have made portfolios into one of the key parts of my composition course. Drawing on theory from folkloristics, I have thought through portfolios and now see them as a primary means for encouraging students to reflect on their emerging writing history and to begin to see themselves as practicing writers. All the practicing writers I know are almost obsessive about keeping *everything* they write. I know I am.

The Practicing Writer as Text Collector

I have boxes and boxes of little pieces of paper with a phrase or a citation or a metaphor or sentence or two, scrawled on them at various moments—as I take a walk or when I go to work or when I am doing my dishes or wash, or even when I am working on another piece of writing. Writing for me is not something that is turned on or off like a light switch. It doesn't start at 9:05 in the morning and go till 11:20 a.m. and is then over. Writing continues all the time on little pads I smuggle into my pants pockets and quickly scribble on throughout the day. It goes on in dull department meetings where I write not so much to remember anything but to keep awake. I write notes in my own classes as my students discuss a short story or essay, and I often interrupt conferences with students to jot down notes about their writing, but even more so, insights that talking with them has given me about composition. When I am not teaching I write about possible ideas I might try out in the classroom. I write in the margins of books and magazines and papers. I often copy down passages that make me laugh or inspire me on index cards, and post these little cards on the wall or on the bulletin board in my study. I tape emergency reminders on my bathroom mirror to help me to remember to pay the rent or to phone to reserve a taxi for the next morning to take me to the train station. I write letters to friends, family, and professional colleagues to keep in touch and to explore who I am, and I write almost daily in my journal simply because I have since 1969, and it is important for me to keep in long-term contact with myself, even if it seems I have nothing to say that day that is very interesting. Unless my fingers are moving across a page producing and preserving a word, an image, an impression, I don't feel like that event is real. I feel strange on the day I don't write anything and I feel downright uncomfortable if I go three days without writing something.

Now like the writers I know I keep all of this stuff, no matter how insignificant it may seem. I don't really expect that I will someday go back and pull out a text that I suddenly need and remember I composed six months (or six years) ago. Sometimes that does happen, but more often I dump my boxes and take a day or two to reread the papers, try to decipher their faded scribblings, and reorganize them in some seemingly useful order, discovering in that process a text I can use in current work, but which I forgot I even wrote. Even when I do remember that I wrote something that might contribute to a present writing project, the odds that I will ever be able to find it quickly are pretty slim. I have wasted hours and even days looking for a piece of paper I know I wrote a great idea on and then afterward, finally, reluctantly give up, realizing I will probably never find it. And even when I do find the text, my memory of the text was almost always more interesting and useful than the actual document.

So why do I keep closets and file cabinets full of the writings if I only inefficiently use them, if at all? For the same reason that I write journals. Because I have always done so. But also because in some way all these papers, official and unofficial, scribbled and word processed, elliptical and complete, *are* me or some hard-to-pin-down part of me. I have no more respect for the final products that I have written up and have gotten published in books and journals than I do for the humblest piece of scribbling found in one of my boxes on the closet floor. Sometimes the published pieces are especially embarrassing because in their revision and reworking they have been overworked, losing the spontaneity and vitality of these scribbles. If there is a hierarchy among my own writing, then my journals are at the top. Yet these journals are the biggest bunch of uneven, ragtag texts one could conceive of.

But that is just the point. The idea that a writer's production is even and high quality is false. Perhaps machines optimally run that way, but writers are not writing machines. Ray Bradbury (1990) in his recent collection, *Zen and The Art of Writing: Essays on Creativity*, puts it this way:

> Run fast, stand still. This, the lesson from the lizards. For all writers. Observe almost any survival creature, you see the same. Jump, run, freeze. In the ability to flick like an eyelash, crack like a whip, vanish like steam, here this instant, gone the next—life teems the earth. And when that life is not rushing to escape, it is playing statues to do the same. See the hummingbird, there, not there. As thought rises and blinks off, so this thing of summer vapor; the clearing of the cosmic throat, the fall of a leaf. And where it was—a whisper. . . . In quickness is truth. (13)

The collection of writing is the writer's track of this scurrying, a history of where she or he has been, an intimation of where she or he might go. To throw away my papers would be to throw away myself as a writer, something one day perhaps I will need to do, but something that would devastate me if I were to do it right now. By asking students to collect their papers and occasionally to look back at them, I try to communicate this process of being a writer. Portfolios have ended up being one of the most important ways I model being a writer to beginning writers. That is why I use portfolios in my composition courses these days, though it took me more than ten years to get to this point. In the next section I want to sketch out a history of an idea—how the portfolio assignment had its origins in administrative fiat and eventually evolved into the opposite—into a form that questions the administrative uses teachers are being asked to make of student writing.

The Evolution of the Portfolio: From Evaluation to Reflection

Portfolios began for me when I was a graduate student teaching freshmen, as a command from the department to require students to turn in the final draft of each of the formal papers done. The rationale given to the graduate teaching assistants was (1) keeping a theme folder cuts down on plagiarism, (2) keeping a theme folder preserves evidence in case there is a later question about the final grade given in the course. There were, I now suspect, other reasons, for demanding an end-of-course theme folder that was turned in and became the property of the English department at the term's end. One possible reason for this fiat was that keeping theme files gave the administration a quick means (like presenting TAs, fait accompli, with *the* list of textbooks from which they may select to use in the course, collecting syllabi and doing infrequent class observation) of monitoring what teaching assistants did in their composition classes, making sure they were towing the department line, promulgating the official composition program ideology. It was a way, then, of regulating and standardizing the teaching of composition. Another reason for requiring student theme folders was that this provided administrators and high-level, favored graduate students in composition with a pool of student texts that could legally be appropriated and used in decontextualized research. In other words, in the guise of contributing to ongoing program assessment, favored graduate students could quietly build their careers on the work of other less favored TAs and their freshman composition students. From the beginning, there was a politics of portfolios.

There even was a political dimension to the housing of these texts. I can still remember going into the room where the theme folders were kept. The theme file folders, row after row, piled on racks that ran from the floor to the ceiling, were held for a year or so before they were disposed of and a new set of theme folders (and TAs and undergraduates) arrived to take their place. The room was right next to the main departmental office where the secretaries were and the battery of administrator offices could be found. It was a room someone like me would frequent often since it contained one of the few working public typewriters and ditto machines in the department. One could look up from one's typing and see row upon row of theme folders, since there were probably fifty to a hundred composition instructors at this large state university. My own name, of course, was among them, as were the folders from the last two or three courses I had taught. Arranged alphabetically according to the instructors last name—mine were easy to quickly spot—the theme folders somehow always seemed more to me than a simple administrative convenience. They were far more sinister, even spooky, a graveyard of composition. This was the end. This was what it all came down to as far as the department was concerned. A collection of theme folders full of official papers whipped out of unwilling students and marked with grades and marginalia that were them-

selves, I bet, policed. I didn't need Michel Foucault to tell me about
the techniques of discipline and punishment. There they were, all
around me, the fruits of disciplining, in neat, ordered rows.

This seemed the least of my worries at the time, of course.
Turning in theme folders never really bothered me any more than
turning in final grades. In both cases, I learned to make compromises
that protected my students. I graded higher than many of my colleagues, my rationale being that I challenged my students more. I
wrote more comments on my students' papers than my fellows
because I saw myself as writer who, skeptical of the immediate
impact of corrections, opted for longer discursive comments that
students could unconsciously use as a model for their own writing
and their talk about their own language. Fellow writing teachers
complained of the elliptical, seemingly incoherent logic of student
writing, but the typical comments I saw teachers writing on student
papers were far more elliptical and mystifying.

So, comfortable with the folder collection idea and sensing that
it contained in embryo some seed of a truly useful writing activity,
I began collecting student folders when I graduated and went to
other universities to teach in departments in which there were no
demands for a collection of theme folders. Collecting student texts
was like keeping my own writing. It was something I just did,
something that provided me with some security, with some sense
that I was accomplishing things in my teaching, that here was the
proof even if my students themselves went on to other courses and
graduated to jobs, careers, families, and by this point, grandchildren.
My students might go on to other things, but in some sense they
always remained with me—in my thoughts, in my memories of the
course, and in these folders of their writing.

As I continued to think through the structure of a composition
course sifting through various activities, I discovered that it was
important at the beginning and end of the term to get students to
think, briefly, about their writing histories. This assignment included a listing of important writing they could remember—it could
be nonschool writing or things from elementary and secondary
school—and a brief discussion of why these pieces were important,
whether they had a good or a bad influence on the student's attitude
toward writing. I received all kinds of interesting responses to this
query including students easily recalling a picture book they made
in fourth grade, a teacher in ninth grade "anonymously" reading the
student's paper out loud to show how bad it was, and *the* research
paper they put so much work into junior year. But I also heard about
a last letter received from a dying grandmother, which the student

still kept and reread and treasured. I heard from the one or two students in almost every class I taught in composition who wrote poetry or short stories or kept a diary for themselves over several years.

I wanted to get students to see that what we defined as "good writing" was a function of social context and situation, that, for example, if "good writing" was always efficient (simple, direct, clear), then the phone book was a far greater piece of writing than the Bible. I also wanted my students to see that what we defined as "writing" was also a product of a culture's view of writing. I wanted them to see that they were already doing huge amounts of "unofficial" and varied writing. To these ends, I asked students to write on these issues—what is writing? what is your writing history? what is good or bad writing?—on the first day or two of class, but then also at the end of the course, factoring into this second set of reflections what they had done over the term. This logically led to an expanding of the student theme folders as one place to collect not simply official, finished papers, but drafts and peer evaluations of drafts, generative texts, and journals. When I introduced the ethnographic writing project, field notes, summaries, and reflections were also added to the folders. All of these texts were brought to class the last day and I asked students to list on a sheet I provided all the texts included in the folder, putting them into chronological order. Students were often surprised by the amount of writing they had done and were capable of doing. In one freshman class, I made a record of all the writing that students had done with approximate word counts. I was feeling the pressure of the administration to be a rigorous teacher, and more importantly, to account for it. Numbers, as meaningless as they may be, always seem to make administrators happy so I wrote down this list.

Reading logs and journals (10 entries × 200 words per)	2000
Paper I	500
Paper II (Ethnography)	2000
Paper III	750
Paper IV	750
Fieldnotes (20 pages (low) × 100 words per (low))	2000
Reflections on notes (8 × 400 words per)	3200
Peer Evaluations (4 × 400)	1600
Short in-class writing, quizzes, reactions (8 × 200)	1600
TOTAL WORDS WRITTEN FOR FRESHMAN COMPOSITION	**14,400**

I am not proud of such accounting five years afterward, but I include it because it accurately presents my sense at that time of being a teacher under the gun, of never satisfying my superiors no matter what I did or how much I improved. It's that kind of political pressure that is presently making portfolios one more means of extracting conformity from teachers and students. As long as we are all clear about this source of the current interest in portfolios, it may be possible to negotiate some compromise portfolio assignment that will not only contribute to teachers' instruction and help students see their writing in a broader perspective, but that also allows administrators to make substantiated claims about the conformity and, supposedly by implication, the fairness and rigor of the composition courses. Still, what I fear is that too many teachers and administrators will avoid facing the blatant political nature of portfolios and that the portfolio activity will, like the word count list above, be one more tool for squeezing ever more work out of powerless students. I got through my freshman course in 1970 by submitting about seven final papers in a theme folder, about 3500 words in all; the poor students taking freshman composition from me in 1987 have to submit somewhere closer to the 15,000 words. The difference between what is required of a student in 1970 versus 1987 has more to do with changing social and economic realities than it does with either the advance in composition scholarship that has occurred over the last twenty or thirty years or in the improved teaching of composition.

I think I was even a bit shocked by the tally. I was interested in some of my fellow teachers who were abolishing grading individual papers, and instead were grading the portfolio twice a term. This supposedly led to more improvement in student writing, and more time that the teacher spent in conference and in the classroom teaching rather than cycling through endless sets of themes. Teachers found that it could also reduce student anxiety about grades and expectations. Some argued that it was a more fair, because more developmental and contextual, approach to student writing. Finally, a few teachers even argued that if one were efficient about it, portfolio grading could reduce the time spent marking student papers.

Bi-semester portfolio grading never worked for me. I found that it actually increased student anxiety and made them simply more careful about showing their grade consciousness. I use grades more to motivate than to indicate any ironclad "objective" criteria during the first half of the course. Portfolio grading when done only two or three times a term reduced my ability to reward students, as well as to give students a sense of where they were in the course at any one point. I wanted my students to know how they were doing, so they could decide to slack off in composition if they needed suddenly to attend to chemistry or philosophy or political science or one of the other content courses they were taking. When portfolios were graded only two or three times a term, the students seemed to be always on the line, always under the gun, always ready for inspection, since one never knew precisely how all of this was going to count in the final grade. Portfolio grading seemed to make the class even more teacher-centered.

At this point I was torn in my thinking between the argument that grading individual papers was atomistic, acontextual, antidevelopmental (and not a little out-of-fashion) and my felt sense as a teacher of almost twenty years that this would not work for me. I was especially bothered by the idea that the writing portfolio would become an embryo career portfolio that advertising executives or design artists or journalists might create to get jobs. I have no problem with students thinking about work and their careers, but I do not and will not teach only to that career. That gets just a bit too close to organizational indoctrination for me. If I were to use portfolios, they had to play a primarily instructive, not evaluative or careerist function. I was determined to find a way of refining the portfolio into a useful learning activity, or drop it. This is the point where I began to think through the idea of portfolios by drawing on folklore theory. Folklorists had interested me since graduate school, partly because the ways folklorists talked about language and texts were so different from the usual genre classifications that I never felt comfortable with in literature courses in the early 1970s. So I went to folklore theory to discover some new ways of thinking about texts and textuality.

Portfolio Theory and Textual Variants

Portfolios have been radically undertheorized. While they are popular as a substitute for testing, portfolios as evaluative tools shift power from the teacher to the administration or the state. If we use portfolios at all, we should use them first for instructional reasons. Render unto Caesar. . . .

How do I think of the student text? What counts as a text and why? Is a student text, the formal paper she or he turns in at the end of the two- or three-week cycle? That formal paper is usually 500 to 1000 words long, has been revised a couple of times, and is the end product of half-a-dozen shorter writing activities, two or three class readings, and a conference or two. But this formal paper, which I evaluate for five types of things—in order of importance, (1) *significance* of the content, (2) *specificity* of examples, (3) *unity* of the text, (4) appropriate *development* of the parts of the text, (4) *language* matters including mechanics, diction, and style—has no absolute boundaries. Formal papers in my classes are closely related to informal writing like journals or notes or peer evaluations. Common sense tells us that the boundary of the text is connected to the self. So peer evaluations may contribute to the rewriting of the text but are not part of that text because they arise from another person, another self. The formal paper can also be distinguished as a text from other texts because it is individually evaluated, and occurs over a relatively short stretch of time.

Yet if we reflect on these commonsense propositions, we notice that concepts external to the text define a text. Time defines a text (deadlines,units of study, courses of academic credit). Or the singular self who writes (and the other singular self who grades) defines a text. Or the final evaluation (this counts) defines a text. The idea here goes something like this: The student, a self, a relatively distinct and singular entity, comes into the composition course, a relatively discrete academic unit, at the beginning a term and writes on demand of the composition teacher, also a singular self, producing many relatively independent texts, some of which are run-throughs and some of which count and are graded as relatively independent entities. Revision in this scheme is the production of more relatively independent texts, using the sage advice provided by the teacher. The teacher at the end of the term adds up the discrete grades on papers and revisions, and comes to a conclusion about the final grade. We see then a singular self (teacher) evaluating plural texts (the papers) of another singular self (the student) who perhaps has had the help and advice of other singular selves (students). Plagiarism is the breaking of the boundaries set up in this scheme. It is the blurring of the singular self by "counting" a text that belongs to one person as a text that belongs to another person.

But process theory of the 1970s should raise questions about these very matters. If I teach writing as a process, can I really see a student text as a singular product? Can I see the process as a singular and linear thing? And if a text is defined by external criteria, what happens if we question those criteria?

Some wag might well ask at this point why one would want to raise such questions. My response would be why not? History and anthropology show that other societies have not thought about language this way. There is no necessity to do so. In fact, the mechanistic tone of this scheme bothers me. Language is far more dynamic. These categories are products of institutions and societies, rather than useful ways of thinking about and through language. It all sounds a bit like working in the mill, doing piecework. And not by chance. Even the idea of plagiarism is a relatively recent phenomenon, the product of the copyright laws that themselves seemed to have originated in merchant sixteenth-century Venice in the new printing press publishing houses. The Bible is full of what we define today as plagiarism but which the peoples of that time and culture defined as a helpful speaking in the spirit of a widely regarded and highly esteemed master. And does the existing arrangement of clear, policed boundaries between self and text help us to teach writing better or more easily? I can't be sure of that one way or another until I at least try out some other ways of thinking about and organizing writing texts and contexts.

Folklore helps me to think about texts. Long ago, folklorists discovered that they could not use the same conceptual apparatus to study folklore as they used to study elite art or mass art. One cannot find an example of the single authoritative text in folklore. In fact, Barre Toelken (1979) in his book *The Dynamics of Folklore* argues that this dynamic variation of expressive culture within a tradition is the mark of folklore.

> Few folklorists would deny, for example, that folklore scholarship is based almost entirely on the study of variation . . . The most heavily used critical tools in folklore, the type and motif indexes, are founded on the proposition that no single text can be called *the* tale or song. It is axiomatic that folklorists need more than one instance of a tale or motif or ballad or popular belief to even know whether in fact they have before them an item from tradition . . . Structural and comparative studies are predicated entirely on the observation that certain units are continually recombined within the frame of a genre or type . . . . (33)

By focusing on textual variants, the folklorist begins to unfreeze our notions of language. A study of text begins to move toward an examination of change rather than stasis, of relations rather than components, of differents rather than sames. And the folklorist through this conceptual framework privileges egalitarian values, rather than centralized authority. Toelken, for example, argues that the old model of the degeneration of folklore across time reveals elitist values. He notes

> Some students of history, even scholars of oral history, see variation as almost synonymous with error or degeneration. Actually,

it is a matter of hypernaivete for any student of tradition to expect
generally exact duplication in tradition, much less to make value
judgements on that basis, especially where there is no concept of
a fixed text. (39)

Toelken, like Bakhtin, is arguing for the necessity but also the inevitability of diversity within tradition and traditional cultures.
Toelken goes on to say, "Just as there is no single cat that can be
called *the* cat and no single dog that can be called *the* dog, there is
no 'Barbara Allen' that can be called *the* or *the original* ballad" (41).
Similarly we might wonder if there is any single student "Text A"
that is *the* "Text A." Instead of spending their time shoring up
discrete categories and searching for "the original," folklorists study
the ways that variants of a text or folklore item circulate through
contexts, arise, and fold back into history and culture. The motif and
type index is a gigantic network, a mapping of themes and structures
that records all known motifs as they have crisscrossed textual variants and cultures through history. By looking up possible motifs in
the index, one can discover the references to accounts that folklorists have made of the other folklore items that reflect similar motifs
and types.

Circumstances have forced folklorists to develop different ways
of thinking about texts and textuality. Student texts are not necessarily folklore, though that is an interesting idea that few if any
compositionists have taken up and investigated; instead, the categories that folklorists use to talk about texts are suggestive. They show
that there is no inevitability about having to think of textuality as a
matter of a singular writer producing plural, discrete products.

Instead of a singular writer producing plural texts, why can't we
think of a plural writer producing a singular text?

Joan Didion (1968/1990) in her book *Slouching Towards Bethlehem* argues that a writer keeps a notebook not simply to keep a
factual record of events, nor to collect materials that will necessarily
or frequently be used in later writing (she calls this a delusion), but
to keep in touch with the self. Because . . .

> It all comes back. Perhaps it's difficult to see the value in having
> one's self back in that kind of mood, but I do see it; I think we
> would be well advised to keep on nodding terms with the people
> we used to be whether we find them attractive company or not.
> Otherwise they turn up unannounced and surprise us, come ham-
> mering on the mind's door at 4 a.m. of a bad night and demand to
> know who deserted them, who betrayed them, who is going to
> make amends. We forget all too soon the things we thought we
> could never forget. We forget the loves and the betrayals alike,
> forget what we whispered, and what we screamed, forget who we

were. I have already lost touch with a couple of people I used to
be. . . . . (139)

Notice "one's self" rather than "oneself" in the second line of this
passage. Didion here is relating her motive for writing to subjectivity, but a subjectivity far more dynamic and plural than the one
implied by the singular model that structures most composition
courses. It is as if the self—which does exist in this passage, it must
be emphasized—is a plural community of voices. The present self
includes but also is different from the other people the self used to
be. Writing is a means for connecting these selves, for keeping in
touch with these selves, for maintaining contact with the voices who
speak the self. Remembrance enters into this dialogue. Preservation
of difference is at stake in a kind of ecology of the subject. Didion
says "It is a good idea, then, to keep in touch, and I suppose that
keeping in touch is what notebooks are all about" (140). Writing
tracks the various selves, our various voices as they track in and out
of consciousness and in and out of our lives. Notice the complex
pronoun frame in this passage. "It" shifts to "one's self" which is
followed by "I." "I," after a brief touching of "it," bumps into "the
people we used to be" and now "I" transforms into "we." William
Coles wrote a book titled *The Plural I;* Didion seems to be writing
the singular "we."

The student is no less a collective of voices than Didion or I.
Perhaps we might think of the writing the student does in the
composition course as a collection of some variants of the *lifetext*
that any human being is writing. The student is constantly writing
in other courses, but also outside of academics. Students do a great
deal of writing for unofficial, uncredited purposes. If we think of all
this writing in and out of the composition course as the text, then
we might construct the portfolio assignment as a collection of some
of the variants from that lifetext. And the principles for composing
a portfolio? The same we use for constructing any text. A portfolio
would not simply be a representational sampling of three of four
papers that share little else but the name of the self. A portfolio
would be constructed to state a thesis, provide evidence and reasoning that proves this thesis or conveys an image or impression. The
selection and ordering of materials would be critical. The connecting tissue of written commentary would give the reader a running
account, perhaps a narrative, that would temporarily frame this
collection of textual variants. In other words, the portfolio is no less
an artistic construction than any other text in the composition
course, and the teacher would look at the portfolio for the same sort
of things that she or he would look for in any "shorter" text.

When I began using the portfolio in this way as a culminating assignment in my writing courses, I asked students to compose portfolio as both a reflective and an evaluative act. Here is the assignment sheet I have used to get the students started:

**Composition
Zebroski**

Your final assignment of this course is to *compose a writing portfolio.* This portfolio will present a view of your progress in the writing you have done in this course across time. It is a kind of history of your writing.

The portfolio will include:

1. *selected* and varied pieces of *writing* carefully arranged in a thought-out order; these texts should give the reader some sense of the variety of writing you have done and the wide range of writing you are now capable of;

2. brief *annotations* attached to each text; these annotations briefly tell what the text is and why it is important as evidence of your writing development;

3. a short *paper* (two pages double-spaced) that analyzes your writing development by citing the texts included.

The short paper should not be a simple narration of the term, though you may do that to set up the point you are to prove. Rather the paper should interpret the texts, analyzing the rhetoric of the texts and giving the reader other information not included in the texts that is important in the evaluation of writing development across time.

Writing development is NOT usually one long story of progress. Rather it is often periodic, going backward in order to go forward at a later point. Risk-taking is crucial to growth but often creates errors or inadequacies. Your job is to spot some of the patterns of growth in your writing over this term, both to give some rational basis to your evaluation in this course, but also to suggest where you may grow next in your writing abilities.

This collection of texts (and texts about texts) should reflect your growth in writing. This is why selection, annotation, and arrangement are so crucial in putting the portfolio together.

Your portfolio should be presented in an appropriate folder. The order it should be read in, should be clear. Keep in mind that what counts here is (1) insight into your own writing process(es) rather than just summary of what you did; (2) evidence of *varied* writing; (3) *lots* of such examples, though not simply dumping everything you have done in a folder; (4) a clear point (or metaphor) all this material is leading to.

In the final section of this essay, I want to look briefly at one student's portfolio.

One Writer Writing: Stephen Lisauskas's Portfolio

Steve was the one who came back.

I have taught for nearly twenty years in a variety of settings across the country and the one thing that has always disturbed me as a teacher is that our educational system makes it very difficult for the teacher who is aiming at some long-term development ever to see the results of her or his labor. Fragmentation of subjects and grade levels, and the mobility necessary to find and keep a good job, make it very unlikely that the teacher of college composition will see much of her or his students after the course has finished. True, I do sometimes run into former students on campus as they are going to class, and I enjoy these chance meetings, but they happen rarely. Even more rare is the encounter with a former student who has graduated. I once attended an N.C.T.E. convention and was approached by a former freshman composition student who had graduated and had now become an English teacher. It was a moving experience for me. But normally students, understandably enough, get involved in the next set of courses they are taking and the teacher gets involved with the next set of students circulating through composition. When I first began teaching, I used to dread the end of the term because it would mean that all the close relationships I had built up would be ending and I would miss my students. As I have gotten older, I have either matured or hardened—maybe they are the same thing—and I see the end of the term not so much as the last that I'll see of my students but as a temporary and necessary parting. Students do come back, of course. Graduate students come back to visit and ask advice, undergraduates for written recommendations or help with some writing or reading assignment. They usually feel obliged to have a reason to stop by to chat.

Steve was different. He stopped by my office the semester after he had taken my freshman composition course and for a long while, as we sat and talked, I wasn't sure what he was after. It turned out he wasn't after anything. He had returned simply to talk about his writing and he asked me if I would write some comments on a piece he was particularly proud of—not because this piece was going to submitted to a new teacher, not because the essay was going to be published anywhere, but simply because the essay, both the topic and its form, were important to him.

I didn't know quite what to say at first. I hadn't had a student come back just to work more on his writing for a long time. Steve had always seen writing as more than simply a pass into an academic discourse community. It was a way for him to construct his world. We met again and I pontificated grandly about his essay and about the life of a writer, and he seemed truly interested, although he is an engineering major. I had been thinking about the motives for writing and teaching writing at this time and Steve once again made it clear that the best motive for writing was to generate the texts of self and world. Everything else was gravy, as they say.

Steve's portfolio included the following texts:

- Three short, handwritten entries reflecting on "working" from his *journal.*

- A one-page (single space: ss) *informal* piece on Steve's writing and reading history.

- The first *formal* essay that synthesized the readings on working and compared what we had discussed about "work" with the "work of schooling," titled "Liberalism Can Set the Estranged Worker Free." (5 pages ss)

- The second *formal* essay which was a piece of ethnographic writing about the weightlifting room, titled "Respect: King of the Bodybuilding World." (3 pages ss)

- An untitled final *reflective essay* examining and citing the texts included in the portfolio and reviewing the progress over the term. (2 pages ss)

Facing Pocket

- A paper titled "The Misinterpretation of Signs of Gender and Race in *M. Butterfly*" for the English and Textual Studies introductory course (ETS 141) Steve was taking that fall. (1 page ss)

- Another paper titled "Cry Not Lest Ye Be Beaten," a response to the book *This Sex Which Is Not One* by Luce Irigaray, again for ETS 141. (1 page ss)

- "How the Delinquent Functions as a Method of Social Control" a response to Foucault's *Discipline and Punish,* again for ETS 141. (1 page ss)

- The "metaphor" essay which sums up Steve's view of writing and his writing experience. Untitled. (2 pages ss)

- "Why?" which was a revision of "Respect" and done voluntarily. (2 pages ss)

Two index cards attached to each text briefly described the text, its context and function, and then gave a short reflection and evaluation of the text, which placed it in the writing narrative of that term.

It would be easy and enjoyable to explicate in detail this portfolio text, but this could easily fill a book. At some later time, I hope to do this. But in this next section, I will simply reflect on some of the themes and motifs that seem to be circulating through Steve's lifetext and portfolio. Even glancing at the portfolio contents, we can see that Steve takes up questions of *work* (school work or disciplinary work in this case) versus *play* or leisure. He also includes issues of *language,* to a great extent because he is taking a reading and a writing studio at the same time. The theme of *commitment* also makes its way through Steve's lifetexts and his writing texts through abstractions like "liberalism" and "respect," but also through ultimate questions like "Why?" There are no ironclad, clear-cut boundaries between Steve's lifetext and his composition work, rather we see variants of texts circulate in and out of Steve's life and his writing class.

1) *What is work*

Work is, like ~~much of~~ most everything else in life, what you make of it. If you enjoy ~~you're~~ your work then it isn't work.

Those who do not like their job truly work. Given, all labor is work, but those who enjoy ~~w~~ their work do not work. It sounds like double talk but it really isn't.

~~Athlet~~ Professional athletes do not work. Their job is not work it is play. Your job is your profession, not necessarily work. Work is over/used. It now describes your job, which may not be work at all.

2) *What is the Opposite of work*

The opposite of work ~~for some~~ is, yet ~~it~~ is not always, play. For some, work is work and play is play. For others, those who enjoy their work, the opposite of work is ~~play~~ "work".

For those who enjoy their jobs, work is fun and it is not laborious. It is not work. For those who hate their job, play is the opposite of work because it is fun and work is not.

Just as work is what you make it, so is the opposite of work. It all depends upon who you talk to.

3)

Working in a supermarket was true work. It was boring and so very repetitious and throwing cans in a bag takes little intelligence and is very stifling.

When I began to move up and get more freedom, it became fun. I was able to do different things and the change did me good, it broke the ~~monotony~~ monotony.

Even when I was just a lowly bag boy though, I began to enjoy it. The people I worked with were fun and we enjoyed ourselves. Even though we weren't supposed to, God knows everyone hates

their work (or you are suppose to hate it) we enjoyed it, we enjoyed being with each other.
   The work was what we made it. If we just did the job, it was deathly boring, but when you tried to relax and have fun, it ᵂ became what we made it, not work but fun.

With these short journal pieces, Steve begins the course by writing through the question of what is work, and then speculating at a later time on the opposite of work. This writing gets the student to begin theorizing her or his own thinking, by showing that all writing is a positioning. By putting some time between writing on the two topics that are related (X and its opposite), the student also begins to sense what seems contradictory in her or his thinking. However, I try to show them that the difficulty that they experience is not simply individual failure. The students must see that language does not sit still and that language is plural. There is no easy one-to-one correspondence between words and things. This writing activity begins to move the student toward experiencing that difference. Finally, such writing problematizes the concept of a singular writer completely in charge of what gets written. With Joan Didion (1968), the student wonders, "What kind of magpie keeps this notebook?" (138). One way to answer it is to see the writer as a plural compendium of voices who composes variants of those voices.

Steve writes journal entries typical of those I got from the other students in class. There is a hesitancy, indicated by the restartings and crossing outs, which I encourage. There is also a generality that I later try to get students to transform with specific examples. The third variant here, about Steve's actual working history, is significantly longer and specific. In these first jottings we have the initial shaping of the extended argument paper with (1) a thesis, (2) qualification, and (3) proof with reasoning and evidence. As James Britton says, the expressive and informal writing forms the matrix out of which emerges transactional writing.

"Respect: King of the Bodybuilding World"

You enter a room filled with racks and plates. All you can hear is groaning and screaming. A dungeon, a torture chamber? No, a weight room. This community thrives and grows but does so without the co-operation which causes most societies to thrive. This society is successful because of respect and safety. If one is to survive in this society one must learn how to gain the respect of one's peers and how, in the society's eyes to be safe.
   To even begin to be a member of this, the bodybuilding society, one must recognize that respect is what runs the gym. The most highly respected members of the society are the "leaders", those who are looked to for inspiration. When one needs that extra boost all one need do is think of this person and what makes them

respectable (which will be discussed later) and that inspiration may be what gets you through to the end.

The respect that one gets in this society is due to a combination of factors. One of these factors is being able to do the exercises. Perhaps the most important thing that contributes to respect is the ability and will to work hard, to push for that extra rep (a"rep" is a repetition, one lifting of the weight). The size of the person's muscles is a factor, but is not all that important to those who are in the culture and know what is going on. The size does signify that somewhere along the line hard work was done and the person is respected for this. A small person who works hard is much more respected than a huge person who just sits around. The amount of weight does not matter. "You may be lifting 10 pounds and I may be lifting 100 pounds, but as long as we are both working at the limit of our strength, we are essentially doing an equal amount of work." (Schwarzenegger, Arnold *Arnold's Bodybuilding for Men*, p. 13) This attitude, that it is not the quantity but the quality, is prevalent in the gym.

This respect, which makes the hierarchy in the gym, also makes it easy to gain entrance into the community. Anyone who is willing to put in the time and effort to lift will be "allowed" to enter. If you go to the gym but don't work you will still be allowed admittance to the gym but not to the society. You must work to be truly accepted. By going to work-out, you have already gained some respect because you are trying to be a bodybuilder. This will give you instant access to the society. All you must do is go and work-out, it's that simple. If you are willing to work, you gain entrance, no problem.

Being accepted is one matter, staying accepted is another. You must have the stick-to-itiveness to go and sweat under the iron. You must also learn the "gym talk", the slang that is used in the gym. This is easy enough to pick up in the gym. All the words are either self-explanatory or are shortened forms of other words. There is nothing complicated in it. After all, you must keep things as simple as possible. Don't make anything more complicated than it has to be. Don't reach over or under things, this is too complicated (and dangerous). Just wait or move the obstruction. Do things in a simple way. If you begin to get fancy problems will arise and injuries can result.

O.k., you're in the gym, you're now an insider. With this vantage point you can see bodybuilding's most common question, Why? Why do I put myself through this, why do I torture myself for countless hours a week? Some, like Andre Tan (a bike racer) lift for training, to keep in shape. "The only motivation I had to lift was for training" he says. This is very common, it is what lifting is used for in all sports. Some do it because they enjoy the pain (myself included). You have to experience it to believe it, otherwise you will think that we are crazy for enjoying the pain. For us "small guys", there is added incentive to train. Some feel that they must prove themselves to others (or to themselves as I do) while still more do it just to improve themselves. Whatever the motive is this can be said, no matter the differences in size outside the gym, all people, whether huge or tiny, are the same under the iron. We are all going through the same thing and we are all being challenged to our limit. We are all weak. This is the bind that ties all weight lifters from here to Siberia (this binding tie is what makes the bodybuilding community tight and allows easy access. "Anyone who will put themselves through what I put myself through will be respected and also accepted."). We all feel the same things and are all inferior to the weight we lift. The weights will eventually overcome and defeat us. We can no longer move them. They win, but only for the moment, we will defeat them in time only to be defeated by a heavier weight, which we will, in turn eventually defeat.

Any lapse in "coolness" will result in the lowering of the person's status. This may result from dropping weights accidently or dropping whole barbells as done by one of my friends. This "faux pas" can result in alienation. This alienation will only last a short time because the other members will just forget it, it was a mistake, big deal. Other "faux pas" can occur by not doing the movement as prescribed. This can be done by using new scientific training techniques recently invented. I have used one such technique to test for the reaction I would get. This lift is much more difficult than normal and isolates the muscle group better (it puts more stress on that muscle group). By bending to the side while doing a front dumbell raise (lift arm up in an arc with the arm fully extended, stop when your hand gets to eye level) you better isolate the muscle but this movement is not "culturally accepted". By doing it, I have been given many strange looks and have been laughed at. On two occasions I have been approached by friends who, fearing for my safety, want to teach me the "right" way to do the exercise. After explaining it to them, they tried the exercise and agreed that I was right. They do not do the exercise even though it is better because they do not wish to risk a momentary loss of respect by doing this exercise.

The last thing that one may observe the weight room being based on is safety. One cannot lift if one is hurt and no one wants to be hurt. It is therefore easy to surmise that safety is very important. This is the reason for doing as exercise in the prescribed manner. Any change in position or arch in the back when not called for (as in the bench press for example) can result in serious injury down the line. Also, never touch a weight in motion. If you do, you can hurt the lifter, someone else or yourself. The highest form of safety is "the spot" in which someone else watches you and encourages you. If the weight begins to overcome you then the spotter must help you lift the weight. The spotter is there to make sure you don't get hurt. His only role is to insure safety and give encouragement. It is a simple thing not meant for complicated meaning and does not sustain complicated explanation or analysis. It is all, and only, what it appears to be. Asking for a spot may seem like a weakness but in reality it shows your intelligence. As Kevin Kalvitis put it "I don't think any less of someone if he asks for a spotter. I think he is smart."

Other safety tips include NEVER bounce the weight up and down and NEVER ever bounce the weight off of yourself. If you do you could end up with some nice broken bones. Also, it is better if you don't walk between a lifter and a mirror he/she is using. If you do, you may break the lifter's concentration and cause him to "loose the lift" (make his muscles die out, many times the only thing keeping the weight moving is pure concentration).

To be a "weight lifter" all you need to do is to lift weights in an intense, safe, intelligent manner. Doing this will get you respect which will put you on the way up the ladder of status in the gym. You will be accepted as "one of the boys" and will be well on the way to becoming a "native" in the bodybuilding society.

The heart of the writing studio for Steve turns out to be the two variant texts "Respect" and "Why." The "Respect" text was a response to the ethnographic writing assignment that I give students. Steve decided to fulfill that assignment by writing on a topic near to him, the weightlifting room. I ask students to do more than simply describe the scene in this activity, and at several points in this text Steve tries to connect what one does in the weightlifting room to why in the world one would want to do it. This again is a fairly typical paper in that it is mixed. There are attempts to get the reader's attention (the "you" of the first paragraph), to unify the paper (". . . respect is what runs the gym . . ."), to deal with academic perspectives on the scene (use of local language, e.g., "reps," discussion of hierarchies,use of quotations), and to use concepts we have discussed in class like alienation and culture. Steve notes in his end of the term reflection that the paper has its problems. But I would add that Steve, unlike many student writers, seems better able to use contradiction. A key section of this text that will appear in its variant "Why" is the assertion in paragraph six, that ". . . no matter the differences in size outside the gym, all people, whether huge or tiny are the same under the iron . . . We are all weak. This is the bind that ties all weight lifters from here to Siberia . . ."

Steve's writing at this point turns poetic:

We all feel the same things and are all inferior to the weight we lift. The weights will eventually overcome and defeat us. We can no longer move them. They win, but only for the moment, we will defeat them in time only to be defeated by a heavier weight, which we will, in turn eventually defeat.

I like this. The text reminds me of Joan Didion's writing except that we read only a single essay by Didion in Steve's class long after this text was written and turned in, although I was teaching Joan Didion's work in my other class at the time. I do not regularly encounter such a dialectic view of the world in the writing that my freshman do. But I think this is in part because I am not always successful in creating the circumstances in class in which student writers can write on subjects that are near to them. I think one of the reasons that Steve writes so well in this passage is because this is important to him. If I insisted on writing only on academic topics using only academic discourse I doubt I would have the chance of getting something like this. When Steve returns in this text to the academic assignment, his writing is not as good, which doesn't mean, of course, that we should dump the academic discourse, but that we need to bring academic discourse into some relation with expressive discourse, school into some dialectic with home, "scientific concepts" into some relation with "spontaneous concepts," to use Vygotsky's words. We also need to recognize that this is more than just a paper on weightlifters. It is part of a lifetext. What are the weights but a metaphor for what the first term of college must seem to the newcomer?

"Why?"

You feel a searing fire rip through your chest, you look up and can only see a bar above that inferno. You can't see the blazing lights above you and you can't hear the noxious music blaring from the stereo in the corner, all you can do is think of this bar above you, and the weight on the ends of it.

Welcome to the wight room friend. You've just been "benching" (performing the exercise known as the bench press) and that fire you felt is one of the biggest highs in the sport of weight lifting. Can you believe that? People spend hours a day feeling that fire and some are even addicted to it. There are a few people who don't like it but they will learn to "worship the burn", soon they will love it.

Wanna hear something else you won't believe? Everyone in the weight room is exactly equal. "What?!!!" you say. "You must be kidding, that guy in the corner is benching 550 pounds and you are only lifting 120 pounds. You're crazy!" Guess what, you're wrong.

Everyone, from the biggest guy in the gym to the smallest, youngest lifter is the same. It doesn't matter how much less I bench than that guy in the corner because we are both working to our maximum and our body says that the weights are *exactly* the same.

If you don't believe me listen to Arnold Schwarzenegger, who is possibly the greatest bodybuilder in the history of the world, "You may be lifting 10 pounds and I may be lifting 100 pounds, but as long as we are both working at the limit of our strength, we are essentially doing an equal amount of work." (Schwarzenegger, *Arnold Arnold's Bodybuilding for Men,* p. 13)

If you are still skeptical you should look around you, I'm sure you can see both immense and miniscule people building themselves under the iron. If you watch them for a while you'll see that both the giant and the mouse eventually succumb to their respective weights. We are all weak, no matter what the magnitude of our strength may be. This is the tie that binds all lifters from here to Siberia. We all feel the same things and are all inferior to the weight we lift. The weights will eventually overcome and defeat us. We can no longer move them. They win, but only for the moment, we will defeat them in time only to be defeated by a heavier weight which we will, in turn, eventually defeat.

You may see a 260 pound powerlifter squatting 800 pounds and you may see me squatting 100 pounds but the weight is only for book keeping. It matters little. The whole essence of weight lifting is to keep bettering and challenging yourself. This means using a heavier weight when you have defeated a lighter one. Both the powerlifter and I are inferior in the same way and we are both striving to get better. The only difference between he and I is the size of our bodies and this is of no real consequence. To you it may seem that the powerlifter, one of this planet's most incredible phenomena (after all what a sight it is to see a mere human pick up over 1000 pounds) is almost super human. It may seem that the powerlifter is undefeatable abut nothing is further from the truth. Come to the gym and you'll see the lifter get beat by something so simple as metal plates. You'll also see me, a twig in comparison to even a bad powerlifter. I'll be along side the powerlifter getting defeated just like he is. The same weights (but obviously not as many) will defeat me too. These weights make us equal, they bind us together because we are both trying like hell to beat these damn weights and we can't, yet.

To those inside the gym, it is a place of extreme beauty. I would rather spend an hour and a half working out than go to the art gallery. What makes this place so beautiful? It is a kind of poetry written in the weight room, written by each and every person in there.

It seems hard to believe that a building that has all these torture devices can be more beautiful than an art gallery but it is true. Watching the lifter move the weight, struggle against it, groan, strain and fight with every last ounce of strength is something rare these days and is something to behold. A single human is trying to fight something as unstopable as time or the flow of a raging river, the lifter is fighting gravity and the weight that the metal plates have. There is no way to win but still the lifter tries, there is no giving up. The lifter knows that he will progress from a one weight to another, heavier one and that there is no end to his struggle but still he fights. He struggles with all his might to hold back something that will not stop for anyone. The true nobility of the human race is revealed here and also the drive that lets the race dominate the planet Earth. All macho attitudes are lost while lifting. No one has room to be a tough guy when he is pouring all that he has into beating his opponent. The true person is released here also, free from all restraints that society imposes, free from all stereotypes. That is why both the powerlifter and I are equal. Society says we are different and stereotypes me as a pencil neck and him (or her) as a monster but in the gym we are ourselves and we are equal. We are both fighting an invisible, unstopable foe and neither of us will ever win. There are only small victories and there always exists another goal. We are at home in the gym and we reveal our true selves here. The poetry is written in our sweat, our efforts and our tears. Our victories come as a crescendo of joyous trumpets and our defeats are beaten out by heavy brass drums. Beauty is in the eye of the beholder and I behold it in the weight room.

Our equality is beautiful, it is poetic. It is paradise on Earth. Many people have asked for equality, which they rightly deserve. We can all be equal only in paradise, where your soul is judged, nothing else. You must pay to get into paradise, you must go through hell to get there. It is worth it, my friend and it is right in front you, it is all around you. All you must do is seek it and you too can find your paradise, you can be equal to Goliath and you can begin to write your own, timeless poetry that will stay with you forever. The sweat shop that we call the gym, the weight room, is so much more than it seems. The sum here is greater than its parts. All you must do is workout and a cornucopia of benefits is yours for the taking. Why do we workout, because it is heaven.

In the variant of the "Respect" text, the "Why?" text, Steve has thrown out much of the academic discourse specific to the ethnographic assignment, extending the metaphors, making the language even less formal. Let me stress again that this was a text he composed on his own. That he chooses such language and eliminates certain topics says much about his appropriation of academic discourse that is related in complex patterns to Steve's lifetext. Something new has appeared, however. The text is framed by religious iconography. Steve does use some minor religious motifs in earlier work ("God knows everyone hates their work . . ." in the third journal entry; also the language of the title of the ETS paper, "Cry Lest Ye Be Beaten"), but here the "inferno," heaven and hell, appear early and stay late. The hell of weightlifting is part and parcel of it being " a place of great beauty" (paragraph 7).

Steve notes:

> I would rather spend an hour and a half working out than go to the
> art gallery. What makes this place so beautiful? It is a kind of poetry
> written in the weight room, written by each and every person there.
> (paragraph 7)

At the beginning of the term, in his literacy autobiography, Steve
mentioned that one of the real turning points in his reading history
occurred when ". . . I set aside my prejudice and wrote something
that turned out to be a poem. . . . I was amazed . . . in that split
second I realized that poetry was the greatest form of writing that
exists." Steve connects poetry with other kinds of writing here. His
earlier insight into poetry is transferred and extended in the "Why?"
essay where Steve recognizes the artistic quality of certain moments
in life. Over several years, we can observe a movement of motifs and
understandings, a circuit from life to poetry to life again. In the
eighth paragraph of the "Why?" variant text we can track Steve's
tying together of weightlifting with school, of art with everyday life,
of body with the spirit, of heaven with hell.

> A single human is trying to fight something as unstoppable as time
> or the flow of a raging river, the lifter is fighting gravity and the
> weight that the metal plates have.

This whole topic is defamiliarizing for me, for though I realize
that lifting weights and engaging in sports and other physical activities plays a large, if unspoken role, in my students' lives, in their
lifetexts, I do not know this world directly, and I would quarrel with
some of what this passage says about that world. It still is macho,
after all, to try to "beat your opponent." I am not sure that the
human race is "noble" and that that should give "the race" free reign
"to dominate the planet Earth." But my quarrels arise because there
is some common ground created in the text, more because I value
the text even if the precise meanings are not, perhaps cannot be,
communicated. The emphasis on equality appeals to me. The
strangeness of the setting is not eliminated, but it is put into metaphoric, even theological, terms that I can encounter. And there is a
streak of fatalism that I find attractive and unusual here. So I am
ready to temporarily defer my quarrels and first say what impresses
and moves me in this text.

The text concludes with the "true self" being born in "paradise."
The invocation of Goliath certainly matches the differences between
the other "monster" weightlifters and the persona of the text, but it
also curiously if unintentionally brings to mind David. David was
Goliath's opponent, but he was also a poet, a psalmist, a lyricist.

Steve has entered here into a broader and deeper cultural text of which he is unaware, but this text is already teaching him. He is already coauthoring with the other voices of his language and culture ". . . timeless poetry that will stay with you forever."

The religious motifs come out into the open in the final reflective essay for the term.

> My writing has progressed quite a bit this semester. It was an egg waiting to hatch, and I think it has. I believe I have made some serious gains in my writing and I hope it shows.
>
> In the beginning, God said: "WHAT IS WORK?"
>
> Steve replied "Duh, I don't know." And so it was written. Steve danced around the topic and didn't answer the question. He cited no specific examples and didn't say anything new and revolutionary. Steve was still a high school writer. God, being kind and just, said "Well, this was Steve's first quest for me, we'll let it slide." Steve was thankful.
>
> Later God said to Steve, "WHAT IS ESTRANGED LABOR?"
>
> Steve replied with Paper 1. It was much better than "What is Work". The paper had a good beginning and made some good points. These were steps in the right direction. Steve made some major errors, he made some points and didn't qualify them. Steve's paper lacked general unity too. God was not pleased but being the kind soul that He is, he gave Steve an A-B+, Steve was grateful.
>
> Steve also made errors when asked to write about his history in writing. Being a meat head, he didn't explain himself and didn't qualify his statements (again). Steve also showed his naive view of writing, which has since changed. He once thought that once written, the writing belongs only to the author. Not so he learned, it belongs to everyone and has a different meaning for every person. This was a major step up the evolutionary chain of writing for young Stephen.
>
> Lastly, God said: "STEVE, WRITE ME AN ETHNOGRAPHY ABOUT ONE OF EARTH'S CULTURES."
>
> After searching high and low, Steve settled in the weight room, his second home (his first home is his home in Massachusetts and his third home is in Syracuse).
>
> God was quite pleased with some of the things that Steve said. Some things were beautifully written while others were, well, lacking. He needed to fill out some parts and he needed to say something new and surprising. Poor Steve, he even got "preachy" in his essay, not good.
>
> If one good thing can be said about Steve it is that he learns from his mistakes, or as least tries to. He did repeat some mistakes a few times in separate essays, but he is learning to not repeat them again. Steve had been doing some work on the side for a professor of ETS 141 (honors).

Steve's writing for X was pretty good. He proves his points and doesn't "Fiddle and Diddle" too much. He did have trouble conveying his point on one occasion, which is a really bad thing, but he'll learn. One other time he got really aggressive on one topic ("Cry Not Lest Ye Be Beaten") and lost any semblance of his good ethos. He alienated his audience pretty badly. he has since learned from this experience and he swore never to let it happen again.

Steve, being the motivated sort, wrote one final, extra paper for God. he was disappointed with his performance in the ethnography so he wrote a paper about the weight room to do justice to his second home. It can be found in the right flap, all the way in the back.

What has Steve learned this semester? Let's ask him.

"Hey Steve, what has Wrt. 109 taught you?"

"I think it has taught me a lot. I've learned that if you say something, back it up with fact, make sure you qualify it and use specific examples. NEVER alienate the reader if you can help it and NEVER loose your good ethos. I made those mistakes this semester, but I won't make them again. Let's see, what else . . . Oh! Make sure everything is unified. Make sure the paper flows nicely and the title, beginning and the ending all must be related. There must also be specific order, just don't lump things together. This one always kills me, make sure you say something to surprise the reader, say something controversial. If I say something obvious I'm going to bore the reader to tears."

"I've really progressed as a writer, I'm no longer a High-School-English-Class-Writer, I'm a college writing studio writer."

Very good Steve, congratulations.

In a fun parody, Steve writes the teacher (me) as "God"—it is time for final grades after all—and takes on the persona of God's lowly (and suffering?) servant. This may seem to reflect some oppressive classroom relations, and obviously there are conflicts between my attempt to understand Steve's lifetext and coach him to write better in the first half of the term, and my ultimate institutional function as the judge of final things who marks papers, final grades, and individuals. The sense of the apocalyptic that arises in Steve's later writing reflects well the feel of the last weeks of the semester on campus in the dorms, though tempered with a sense of humor. I don't think Steve would have taken the trouble to do this parody if he didn't trust me and feel that I would not punish him for it. So although it may seem to suggest oppressive relations between teacher and student, the last reflection shows, if not relations between equals, at least a separation of the teacher's role of judge from the teacher's role as coach. Further, it suggests an acceptance of the teacher as a person beyond institutional roles. That is, it suggests a plural self. And it is somehow fitting that "Steve" is put into the third person throughout this text. The plurality of self is not simply a characteristic of the teacher, but now of the writer as well.

In these four texts, then, we see a composing of a portfolio, but also of a self. The motifs circulating through these textual variants are both personal and cultural, secular and sacred. They might be seen as embodiments of some wider cultural motifs that I can phrase as proverbs. The first, "Work hard and you shall surely succeed," is perhaps *the* American motif. It constantly circulates through popular culture and even elite culture elaborates on this motif if in no other way by denying it. The second proverb is like it—"God helps those who help themselves." The variant texts Steve produces and circulates through his portfolio are part of this broader cultural text. And these cultural texts have long and illustrious careers in U. S. folklore. We need to investigate further the ways that folklore crosses into Steve's writing and that of other freshman writers. Too often we teachers simply mark these motifs as cliches and stereotypes without understanding how and why the student is appropriating them and how they are part of complex networks of social knowledge making and transmission.

Still, Steve oscillates between acceptance of this proverbial wisdom and a recognition of the inevitability of defeat. Steve needs, as any freshman needs, to believe in a success ideology, and yet Steve, like any freshman, is constantly being confronted with situations where hard work does not pay off, where helping yourself does not call down divine favor. I would argue, following Bakhtin and Vygotsky, that it is precisely that tension, that struggle, that generates Steve's text and allows him to rewrite himself, to wring himself out of the words of others. Where that will take him, we—he—cannot be sure. I ask that each student include a short introduction to the portfolio, just as they might write an introduction to any single paper, any composition. Steve's portfolio introductory essay works out of the "hatching" metaphor, but it also shifts to other tropes. The portfolio assignment has been a way for Steve to reflect on his growth as a writer and in that reflection to become a new writer, a new self. The last words are Steve's:

> My final, extra papers are, you could say, the culmination of my writing studio knowledge. They are interesting and different, to say the least. They are solidly written and I tried to put all my mistakes behind me and not repeat them. I think I did pretty well on them. For once I feel good about my writing.

> The seed was sown in the fall and now the plant has grown. The winter is a time of death and hibernation but my writing has come

to blossom in the shadow of the season's gloom. Because only a .
strong wind can make a strong tree, my mistakes have been quite
beneficial. They strengthened my writing and now the wind, which
has made me stronger, will keep me growing in other writing, will
spread my fruit so it may be enjoyed by all.

References

Bradbury, R. 1990. *Zen and the art of writing: Essays on creativity.* Santa
Barbara, CA: Capra Press.

Britton, J. 1993. *Language and learning.* Portsmouth, NH: Boynton/Cook.

Coles, W. 1978. *The plural I.* New York: Holt, Rinehart and Winston.

Didion, J. 1990. On keeping a notebook. *Slouching towards Bethlehem.* New
York: Noonday Press.

Toelken, B. 1979. *The dynamics of folklore.* Boston: Houghton Mifflin.

Chapter Four

Creating the Advanced Writing Course

Writing Through the Questions

I can vividly remember the second semester that I taught the advanced writing course at Syracuse University. It was January 1991 and it was a Wednesday evening class that met for three hours one night a week. After the break at about 8:15 p.m., students came into class disturbed by the news hot off the wires that the U.S. was bombing Baghdad. Desert Shield was dramatically mutating into Desert Storm. The class was divided even at this early point about the Persian Gulf War. We hardly had a sense of our self as a class, and I had just spent the first half of class going over the syllabus in that ritual of first days sacrificed to the god of bureaucracy. And here we were already in the middle of arguments about the necessity and wisdom of going to war.

A rhetorician of the classic mode might well have taken advantage of the situation to make the case for the inevitability and importance of rhetoric. I didn't. I didn't know exactly what to do. I was so disgusted with the war and with what had passed as the public discussion of it, I was so assaulted by the media blitz—then only beginning—that raised memories of nationalist propaganda in all the modern wars, I was so disturbed by the "fact" proclaimed constantly in the media and increasingly pounded into every American's head over the next two months that I, as a resister of this jingoistic escapade, was in the tiniest of minorities, not a position I was new to, that I simply wanted to get on with the teaching of my writing course. I let the students, mostly juniors but with a large number of graduating seniors as well, talk at some length about their views and feelings concerning the war. It was apparent that they were disturbed, as were most Americans, and needed and wanted to discuss what was happening in their lives. I decided to forgo for a time the script for the night to allow them to say what they needed to say. But after we talked about an hour or so about current events, I drew the discussion and the class back to matters of writing and assignments for the next meeting.

The same class ended in a curious way at the end of that spring semester. We had been through thick and thin—war, victory, armistice, but also writing theory and expressive writing and writing in the disciplines. We had gotten to know each other pretty well—I thought. Students were giving presentations that last night of their final writing projects. Some had studied writing done in their field. Some had written case studies of individual writers. One student had written up accounts of the writing done by a friend who was writing for a newsletter of the Syracuse Peace Council. I was happy with way things had turned out and with the variety and quality of these projects. I felt the class had finally clicked and we not only had done some interesting writing, but we had also developed a class community. That was one reason I was so disturbed to see one of my male students come into class wearing a T-shirt that said among other things, "Bash Gays Not Seals," picturing a crow, the emblem of the fraternity to which he belonged, with a club in its hand over a prostrate male figure. The student who had done the story on the friend who wrote for the Syracuse Peace Council noticed the T-shirt almost as immediately as I did and made a comment directly to the student wearing the T-shirt that had been mass produced and worn by members of his fraternity (this was no individual action) that the T-shirt disturbed her. There was a little talk, but then the class settled down, the rest of the students came into the room, and I asked individuals to do their reports on their writing projects.

So what account can I give of my behavior? Am I a cryptofascist? A naive teacher who thinks he can be politically neutral? A frightened, untenured faculty person overly worried about every move he makes? A minority person (a son of the working class) in a world (the high middle class) not of his making, where positions are remembered and used against you at a later time? How do I answer for my words and deeds? The politically correct reader, given only this information about my actions (or inactions) in my own classroom, might put forward objections to my approach as well as to my deeds. In both cases I avoided the intensification of the issue in the public classroom arena, perhaps giving students the wrong idea that

I was somehow "neutral." And I suppose one reason I am writing about this here is that I too have some questions about what I did in my advanced writing class. Some questions. Enough questions to share my worries about the politics of writing and teaching, but not enough doubts to believe that given exactly the same situation I wouldn't do pretty much the same thing.

Heresy, some might charge. A proper understanding of the teacher's role in a college classroom, others might respond. Neither, I'd argue.

I am not so politically naive as to believe that what I do is not political, indeed, I am implicated in the political forces at work in our society every day, not simply on those days when they reach the surface and make their rather dramatic entrance in my class.

Then my answer has much to do with how I teach any composition course, but especially how I approach the advanced writing course. I suppose there may be some truth in each of the above characterizations of my deeds. I haven't worked out a complete and pat answer on all of this which is why I am writing about it. And that precisely is my point.

Writing is not simply a way of presenting (or even discovering) a political position, or even the position itself, but more importantly it is a way of working through the positions. I am less concerned that my students learn and repeat through writing the proper politics than I am interested in teaching them to use writing to work through the questions of their lives, which, of course, are effects of political and social forces. But writing through the questions requires an entirely different theory of writing than students usually possess when they come into my classroom. More than instruction on the political position or a political theory, students need to be invited to create a theory of writing that will match the complexity of their lives with a complexity of writing practices. And more than even this, students must have writing experiences that illuminate a more complicated theory of language. So my response to political critique is to say that more than a specific political position, my students need to develop their own (1) *theory* of language/writing, (2) writing *practices*, and (3) *experiences* with theory and practice in order to write throughout their own position.

Advanced writing, then, is about advanced understandings which enable advanced performances, all connected with the writer's experience. Until students see language as more than the wrapper in which real life comes packaged, mere instruction on political issues will have little effect other than to take up class time and expend energy that might more usefully be applied to other things. If rhetoric is about knowing when it makes a difference to engage in rhetoric and how to go about discerning the moment when it is fitting to make an argument because people are open to being persuaded, then I am not certain that the beginning of a war (or of a class) is always the best moment to get "political" in the narrow sense of that word. The counterargument obviously is if not then, when? If not us, who? And that is what I want to discuss more fully in the rest of this essay on the advanced writing course.

The Question of Motives

The problem with the advanced writing course is that too often we teachers have no advanced concept of writing. This is understandable of course. Who has time to develop fully elaborated and nuanced theories of language and composing when one is barely able to keep up with, or recover from, the paper load, not to mention nosy and noisome administrators who too often poke into our professional lives giving us even more busy work to do? Still, I believe the only way for the advanced writing course to have a prayer of succeeding is for it to be truly advanced. Students are smart. They pick up almost instantly on our misgivings. They are B.S.-seeking missiles (to pick up on the martial discourse above), and they have little trouble exploding our facades of expertise, especially if they have survived three or four years of the undergraduate courses. It is a mistake for composition teachers to offer the advanced writing course as simply more practice, more of the same. A student understandably enough will argue back, "I have already taken two (or however many) required writing courses at this university. Why should I be required to take another course if it simply is a rehash of the same old stuff? Especially when I have all these major courses to take. I am not a writer and I am not interested in writing. Why am I here?"

And they are right, of course.

Like almost every composition course offered at university in the U.S., the advanced course is usually required. It is required by different administrative units than the first (or second) course. Usually the freshman composition course is required by the university (as is the second in the series when it is offered). The first course more often than not is a theme-a-week writing course, where essays are read and discussed and modes and aims are embodied in student theme topics. The second course is usually a research paper course. (In the dark ages when I took composition courses as a freshman, it was a literature criticism course, a sort of reward for getting through the tedium of McCrimmon's *Writing With A Purpose* [zillionth edition] in the first course.) In contrast to these university requirements, then, the upper division course (there are many monikers for this course—I have seen it taught under the rubric of "Advanced Composition," "Intermediate Writing," "Composition and Rhetoric," "Informative Writing," among others) is required by the specific college or department in which the student is majoring. The reasons that each unit gives for requiring the course are varied and, not infrequently, contradictory. Some faculty in other disciplines think it is important for students to get more practice in writing since they may be called on to do writing in their career and this is the last chance they have to get it right. Some faculty go so far as to require students to take the course so they can work on their resumes and letters of application (when there is no business writing course offered). In stark contrast to this career-building course, other faculty see writing as a liberal art and want their students to take the advanced course because it is so very different from the "straightforward," task-oriented discourse of their field and profession, because it gets their otherwise goal-oriented students to ask broader questions. (It is fascinating to me that some of the faculty in the business school often take this stance, so much at odds with many of their majors). Occasionally, the English (or other liberal arts) major takes the course as an alternative to writing about literature or writing intensive literature courses. According to the in-house S. U. Writing Program journal *Reflections,* as of spring 1991 Writing 305 is required at Syracuse University by Management and Human Development (Retailing and Consumer Studies Programs), the School of Education (Physical education, Health education, Elementary education, and English education) and is offered as one way of fulfilling the College of Arts and Sciences requirement for continuing skills writing course. This is important; the point is the *motives* for each of these constituencies are radically different and the only thing that all students have in common when they walk into my class is that they are there because they have to be.

I don't think Syracuse is unusual in this regard. Most of the advanced writing courses I have taught (or taken) have been radically heterogeneous (verging at times on being incoherent), populated with students who had very mixed motives for there. On the one hand, they had other, seemingly more important things to do—courses in their majors, internships, fieldwork. On the other hand, they often acknowledged that their writing abilities were not very good, so while they were arguing that they shouldn't have to take a course that was a simple rehash of earlier writing courses—more of the same—they often could not do the things advanced writing students should be able to do. How to deal with this unevenness,

how, in fact, to forge a community out of constituencies who seemed
to have nothing in common except their inability to get out of the
requirement—that became the question for me in teaching the advanced writing course.

Theoretical Principles for the Advanced Course

I began my teaching of the advanced writing course with some
theoretical principles from the introductory courses, which I tried
to extend and reshape to fit the strange circumstance of this course.

1. A COMPOSITION COURSE IS A COMPOSITION. The corollary
    of this principle is that whatever we hold to be true of writing
    and hold our own writing and that of our students to, we should
    enact in the discourse of the course. I want to spend consider-
    able time unfolding this principle since it is central to my
    courses and teaching.

    If the composition course is a composition, and if "unity" is
    a concern when we teach writing, then the course should enact
    unity and, like a well-written essay, should have a theme around
    which the parts revolve. If good writing is "heuristic" and ex-
    plores ideas that unfold in unexpected ways, then a good writ-
    ing course should not begin with all the answers, but instead
    should generate then pose questions which students and teach-
    ers can together inquire into. If good writing often requires "col-
    laboration," and always comes out of community, then the
    writing class itself should be a community, a joint effort cowrit-
    ten by students and teachers, opening up significant spaces for
    students to pursue their own interests, to write about things that
    matter to them, and that in the process make community even
    stronger. If good writing comes about because the writer is more
    conscious of her or his "theory" of writing, then the writing
    course ought to be about the investigation of writing processes
    and theories of process.

    In some ways the idea that "a composition course is a com-
    position" is the primary insight from which much of my teach-
    ing comes. It is so important that I take up the topic in greater
    detail at the end of this essay. In the meantime, I want to note
    that the view that "the composition course is a composition"
    brings into relief the whole ethical dimension of writing and
    teaching. What I am arguing is that writers (and writing teach-
    ers) should practice what they preach, and if they won't or can't,
    they should change what they are preaching. In other words, as

different as my students are from me in expertise, in experience, in motivation, not to mention age, they are persons and my dealings with them need to be regulated by ethical principle and the most important ethical principle for me is the Golden Rule. I am a hypocrite if I expect from my students what I do not in some sense expect from myself.

This ethical impulse is not peculiar to me, but in fact is a very old and honorable tradition in the teaching of language, especially language production like speaking and writing. Quintilian in Book XII of *Institutio Oratoria* takes up the view that was even unpopular, or at least not apparent, in his time two thousand years ago, that good rhetoric is a matter not just of language or effects or correctness, but of ethics. Quintilian contends "For I do not merely assert that the ideal orator should be a good man, but I affirm that no man can be a good orator unless he is a good man" (357), which we may translate for our purposes into " a good person writing well." Good writing necessarily requires a good heart and a good purpose, and good teaching of writing requires a harmony between my view of writing and my actions in the classroom.

But we do not have to go back two thousand years to find a similar ethical impulse behind language instruction. We often forget that Mikhail Bakhtin, when he wasn't exiled off doing accounting for a kolkhoz in Central Asia, was a language teacher at a small teacher preparation college in the Russian provinces. Surely his concept of "answerability" and his belief that one has no "alibi" in life or in language, that in fact, language has to do with "response-ability," had a great deal to do with his commitment to students and the teaching of literatures and languages. And finally, closer to home, we need to recall that one of Janet Emig's earliest contributions in 1964 to the then still embryonic field of composition studies was her analysis of the discrepancy—no, it was stronger than that, the contradiction—between the standard composition textbook accounts of writing and those of almost all practicing (whether professional or amateur) writers.

Here are the other theoretical principles that I brought from the teaching of the introductory composition courses to my advance writing course.

2. STUDENTS NEED TO BE GIVEN CHANCES IN A WRITING COURSE TO CONSTRUCT THEORY. This means in practice that I ask students to do some intelligent and critical reflection on their own writing experiences and those of others. I believe

that reflection or metawriting, when it is done at the appropriate or fitting time, plays an important role in developing student writing processes. Part of this reflective process demands that students read accounts of other writers and position themselves in relation to these accounts.

3. INDIVIDUAL AND COMMUNITY ARE IN A DIALECTICAL RE-LATIONSHIP AND ALL WRITING TOPICS AND PRACTICES NEED TO BE APPROACHED WITH THIS DIALECTIC IN MIND. There are no such things in my writing courses as "expressive" versus "transactive," or "personal" versus "academic" discourse, done in isolation. I begin my courses with both sorts of writing and we do both sorts of writing throughout the course to its end. What is key is how one sort of writing illuminates (or occults) the other sort of writing.

4. A COMPOSITION COURSE MUST BE DEVELOPMENTAL. Teaching, then, must always begin where the student (but also the teacher) is. The first part of the course is when students and teacher get a sense of each other and actually do the construction of the rest of the course. Further, this means there is an important place for student experiences and interests, put forward in *their own terms.* (I have more to say about this below.)

The additional theoretical principles that I have discovered in my teaching of the advanced writing course are sometimes in tension with each other and these earlier principles.

1. "ADVANCED" IN ADVANCED WRITING MEANS ADVANCED WRITING THEORY, PRACTICES, AND EXPERIENCES. The advanced course, I believe, needs to make a distinctive, qualitative contribution. It can not simply be more of the same. This principle is sometimes in conflict with the idea that I must start where my students are. They are for the most part *not* advanced in writing theory, practices, or experiences.

2. AN ADVANCED WRITING COURSE IS NOT A GENERIC WRITING COURSE. I don't know if there is any place in the undergraduate college curriculum for a writing course that deals only with the principles and practice of a kind of generic "academic discourse," but if there is, it isn't in the advanced course. This raises a question about the kind of writing we should practice and study in the advanced course. After a good deal of thought, I finally concluded that if the upper division X course (whether X is chemistry or political science or marketing or physical education) is about bringing the student into the disciplinary community of X-ers, then the advanced writing course should

be no different. *The advanced composition course has as a goal the introduction of the student to the discipline of composition.* In the old days, this was much clearer, since the upper-division writing course was about writing about literature (which of course was what the discipline of English was about). Some will no doubt argue that this is a self-serving move, and I admit that it is to the extent that any upper division course in any discipline is self-serving, that is, it is about getting students to *do* science or art or a professional practice. One counterargument to my proposal is there is a difference between the acculturation of declared majors who have chosen "of their own free will" to go into a field (any undergraduate faculty adviser knows immediately how shaky *that* claim is) and the innocent students who are required to take the advanced course but who have *not* chosen to go into that field.

And this is precisely why I make the disciplinary materials and practices only about half of the course, the rest being devoted to the writing on whatever project (within or external to Composition) students choose. At this point, *after* we have done some reading and writing in Composition, I am very willing, even delighted, to let students pursue their own interests. But I cannot and will not present advanced theory, practice, and experience in any other realm than writing as I have known it in Composition, and so if I am to do an *advanced* course I have to begin with what I know well and care deeply about.

3. STUDENTS MUST HAVE THE OPPORTUNITY IN THE ADVANCED WRITING COURSE TO DO A LARGE AMOUNT OF WRITING ON WHATEVER TOPIC THEY WANT. This principle is in need of qualification. Topics are always in a sense negotiated between teacher and student so there is no absolute freedom in choosing topics. On the first day when I set forward the requirement that no writing or talk in our course can advocate violence against any other group or individual or endanger a group or individual (no one has the free-speech right to yell fire in a theatre unless there is a fire)—a policy in keeping with many hundreds of years of decisions about "free speech"—I am already limiting the possible topics on which a student may write.

But what I am addressing here, then, is not any notion of absolute freedom of choice, but instead a tendency I have increasingly noted in Composition over the last few years which de-emphasizes or even denigrates so-called "expressive" writing and writing by students on subjects which may well be important to them, but in which the teacher, as representative of (and enforcer for) academe, has relatively little interest. It seems almost as if we are "permissive" teachers if we allow students to pursue some of their own interests. We seem to be projecting our feelings of disciplinary inferiority onto our students and feel (wrongly in my judgment) that we are being "rigorous" if we exercise the academic version of "toughlove," which at bottom seems to get down too often to, *do it my way.* I know best!

I think there are a variety of reasons why this teacher-centered curriculum has become increasingly acceptable. I think it is sometimes a by-product of one of the principles I put forward earlier, that a composition course needs to cohere (like any discourse) and that a course theme provides a way of unifying readings, discussions, research, and writing assignments across time. But a course constructed around a theme is not, to my way of thinking, a curricular version of the Five-Paragraph Theme with its rigid thesis and supports.

This structuring of the student right out of the writing course does not have to be the alternative to what in the old days used to be called a rap session. "Sequencing" assignments doesn't have to be seen as the opposite of the student right to choose. Ideally, a course theme or a sequence of writing assignments is broad enough, and arrived at in a sufficiently collaborative manner, that students can connect it with those portions of their lives that they want and need to write about. But I have some doubts about how real students' choices can be in a course as minutely worked out as the Basic Reading and Writing Seminar described by Bartholomae and Petrosky. In the volume *Facts, Artifacts, and Counterfacts,* I find only one essay that hints at some negotiation between teacher and student concerning topic and that is Nicholas Coles's wonderful "Empowering Revision." Perhaps the other people teaching that BRW course do make room for significant amounts of student writing on topics of their own choice to go on and it simply is not apparent in the presentation. But my experience at Syracuse where I introduced the idea of a course theme and sequencing of assignments leads me to conclude that too often there is a tendency for the theme after a certain point to constrict the writing choices open to students. One easy way of dealing with that is simply making spaces available in the course that aren't structured by the theme and sequence, where students can write on other topics. Still, the tendency seems to be to make these parts of the course less important than "our" part of the course.

When I began teaching the Advanced Writing course at Syracuse, I was shocked to hear from the students who were the first to have gone through all of the new writing curriculum courses from the start that they had never really had the chance in those courses to write a significant proportion of the writing that they did and got graded on, on topics of their own choosing. If I had to write only on topics that other people suggested (as I too often have to do at work) I think I would not really enjoy writing and I think I would certainly have a distorted view of the uses and potentialities of writing. So at the moment I heard these horror stories, I decided to devote a third to a half of the writing done in the advanced course to topics of the students' own choosing.

This obviously is in some tension with my other principle that an advanced course ought to be about the discourses of the field of Composition. How can we enter those discourses in some deeper and more profound way when I also am committed to opening up a large portion of the course writing to students? Knowing that as an adult and as a teacher I tend to monopolize the conversation even when I try not to, I consciously decided that if I am to make a mistake, it will be on the side of the student topics. And after some trial and error, I believe I have found some compromise between these two positions that works for students and teachers. These are the materials and practices that I want to discuss in the next section of this essay.

The Advanced Course: Materials and Practices

The first time I taught the advance course in composition at Syracuse I tried to get too much crammed into the course. This isn't unusual. I tend to start out with many ideas for activities and discover midway through the term that I could have asked students to do about half of them with better results, but of course, I never know precisely which ideas to keep and which to drop until I try them all out, so the first run-through of a new course almost of necessity differs from its later revisions. As long as I recognize that this will happen, even if I am not exactly sure which assignments will work or not work so well, which readings I'll keep and which writing projects will be dropped, the course turns out alright. I simply have to keep reminding myself from the start that plans can be changed and projects can be altered or dropped altogether and that the "first draft" of a course—and by that I mean the pilot of the course, the first run-through with students, not the first syllabus writing or course planning—will be revised in later drafts of the course. So I am including in this section of this essay short discussions of both the first draft and the second draft of my advanced composition course in order to give a sense of the revision process rather than present one version as the correct one.

When I taught the advanced course I handed out the following statement of philosophy and objectives, along with the course syllabus.

Writing 305 Studio III
Advanced Studies in the Art of Writing
Dr. James Zebroski

"Rhetoric... the political effectivity of trope and argument in culture"
—Steven Mailloux in Rhetorical Power

What goes on in the Writer's Mind? How is that related to what eventuates as the written word? What are the relations between the composing processes and the composed product? How will understanding these relations help the practicing writer with her/his writing?

For the past thirty yeast composition scholars have been very interested in pursuing these questions. A large body of work—accounts of professional writers, descriptions of persons practicing writing in nonacademic settings, experiments on and ethnographic descriptions of creativity in action—has been accumulated. A variety of answers have been given to these questions. While there are no "universal" generic answers, there are rules of thumb that apply across specific contexts.

The Paris Review interviews with professional writers began this line of inquiry in the US in the late 1950s and early 1960s. What professional writers said about their work habits and writing processes seemed to contradict the dogma presented in college writing textbooks. Rohman and Wlecke in 1964 were among the first to do more formal scholarship on this topic. And since then, under the rubrics of "invention," "heuristics," or "pre-writing," hundreds of writers and writing teachers have looked into the writer's mind. Among the more prominent are R. Young (1970), J. Emig (1971), P. Elbow (1973), L. Flower (1979), S. Perl (1979), A. Berthoff (1982), D. Murray (1982), G. Rico (1983), M. Rose (1984), and K. LeFevre (1987).

In this Writing Studio III, we will look into the writer's mind, using the very processes (reading and writing...) that we will be investigating. This course will fall then into two major parts. First, we will master a body of materials on this topic in composition and the arts. Second, we will add our own conclusions to this corpus of scholarship, conclusions derived through a variety of our own individual investigations and research projects.

                    *   *   *

"A thought may be compared to a cloud shedding a shower of words." (Lev Vygotsky, 251)

"The relation of thought to word is not a thing but a process, a continual movement back and forth from thought to word and from word to thought... thought is not merely expressed in words; it comes into existence through them. Every thought moves, grows, and develops, fulfills a function, solves a problem." (Lev Vygotsky, 218)

                    *   *   *

To focus on the relation between thought and word is *not* to ignore or to marginalize the broader social, political, and historical context from which mind and word arise. This course will not merely be a look at the psychology of composing. Because this is a *rhetoric* course, we will always be concerned with the rhetoric of mind and with the rhetoric of talking about mind. We will always be concerned with the *uses* of language and the ways that language both creates and limits our ways of knowing. We will simultaneously be aware of the ways that knowledge is made possible and delimited by power, by the political and social arrangements and structures through which we have our being.

All our discussions will consider the relationship between three dimensions. These three dimensions of rhetoric are variously labeled in the materials we will be looking at.

the written	the writing	writing practices
composed product	composing process	discourse community
text	textuality	context
language	knowledge	power
sign	inner speech (sign image)	social relations
word	mind	society
writing	thinking	forming

Thus one of the purposes of thinking about language in terms of knowledge and power is that it allows us to see that a question or an issue is always raised in an ideological framework. We might speculate, for example, on just why "creativity" has been such a hot topic since the 1950s. Why has invention arisen as an especial concern for compositionists in the last thirty years? Maybe this interest in creativity and the creative process reflects a concern with the US position in the world economy and specifically in the race for space between the US and the Soviet Union in the 1950s and 1960s. Maybe it has something to do with the invention of the atomic bomb and thermonuclear weaponry and the threatened extinction of the entire human race if we are not careful. Maybe our concern with creativity reflects an obsession with the individual subject, in fact, with the ideology of individualism that arises when a person feels her/his life in mass society is meaningless and replaceable. Surely there is a link between capitalism's spread and success this century and the need for an ideology of self help and self creation (the self made man). The burgeoning of creativity studies arises in and from all these and more contexts.

Ideology and power arise and are exercised through signs, through language. There is no use of language that can be severed from these issues. Therefore a language use course is the perfect place for us to study these relations and perhaps effect some change.

*   *   *

"The word is a direct representation of the historical nature of human consciousness. Consciousness is reflected in a word as the sun in a drop of water. A word relates to consciousness as a living cell relates to a whole organism, as an atom relates to the universe. A word is a microcosm of human consciousness." (Lev Vygotsky, 256)

*   *   *

We will begin this course with shared readings and move toward individual research projects. I see the sequence of activities in this course moving something like this:

1. We introduce each other through writing and talking, attending specifically to previous writing studios taken at Syracuse and the place of them, and this course, in the broader writing curriculum.

2. We read selections from Ann E. Berthoff's Forming/Thinking/Writing. We do some of the writing activities she suggests. We view Berthoff's work as giving a *humanistic* perspective on the writer's mind.

3. We read selections from Lev Vygotsky's Thought and Language to get the psychologist's (the *scientific*) perspective on the writer's mind.

4. We compare Berthoff and Vygotsky with our own experiences writing and with what compositionists have said. This will give us the *writer's view* of the *writer's mind*.

5. The major part of this course will involve individual student working on and then sharing with the class the research project on some aspect of the writer's mind.

6. We compare these accounts and these investigations with those of contemporary writer Joan Didion through essays selected from <u>Slouching Towards Bethlehem</u> and <u>The White Album</u>.

*   *   *

REQUIRED MATERIALS

Texts: Ann E. Berthoff. <u>Forming/Thinking/Writing</u>. 2nd edition. Boynton-Cook/ Heinemann. 1988.
Lev Vygotsky. <u>Thought and Language</u>. 2nd Edition. MIT Press. 1986.
Joan Didion. <u>Slouching Towards Bethlehem</u>. Washington Square. 1968/1981.
Joan Didion. <u>The White Album</u>. WSP. 1979.
(Texts are available at Orange Bookstore)

Also, later in the course, a photopack from Syracuse Copy Center
<u>The Writer's Mind: Select Readings in the Rhetoric of Composition</u>.

Looseleaf notebook with paper for Daybook
Portfolio folder (regulation size)
Plan on paying for a class set of photocopied papers after midterm.

WRITING STUDIO III

I am counting on the fact that most of you will have been through the earlier writing studio curriculum at Syracuse University. This course will pick up where those courses left off. I will expect that you will know of and have experience with studio practices such as responding in writing to complex texts, working with peers on drafts of papers, working in small discussion groups, putting together class photocopied texts, working on collaborative writing projects, editing and proofing complex written texts, putting together writing research projects.

I plan to run this class as a seminar. Since we will meet once a week for three hours, you must attend and come to the class prepared. This studio course is especially concerned that you refine your *writing process* by using writing (1) as a *heuristic*, to discover ideas and feelings or memories not otherwise accessible; (2) as *reflection*, as a mode of observing and transforming your thinking processes; (3) as *cultural practice*, as a sign activity that is the product of a specific ideological and historical moment; (4) as an enactment of *style*, as the development of your specific and unique persona/self.

Attendance then is required. There are no makeup assignments.

Papers must come in on deadline. No late papers.

Formal papers must be typed. Wordprocessing is encouraged.

Plagiarism is a serious offense and can result in failure. You are responsible for understanding what plagiarism is and for avoiding it.

A final *portfolio* is a course requirement. Keep all papers and writing done for this course so that you can compose a good portfolio at term's end. I will explain this assignment in more detail. Till then, keep careful track of *all* writing in this course.

Conferences and out of class field research will be required.

Letter grades will be determined according to the following breakdown:

Daybook	10%
Research Project	30%
In class essay	10%
Short Papers (2)	20%
Portfolio	20%
Class Participation	10%

ASSIGNMENT DUE DATES

Sept. 5   Discuss James Berlin "Contemporary Composition: The Major Pedagogical
           Theories" and literacy autobiography. Place and function of SU WP Studio
           Curriculum. Its Philosophy. Observation Writing Activity.

Sept. 12   Double entry Daybook (1) Continue "Observation" Activity (2) Glossing one
           section from Berthoff FTW C: 1, 2, 3. Also read (don't gloss) FTW C: 8
           (3) one other activity from Berthoff reading—your choice.

Sept. 19   Vygotsky T&L: Author's Preface. C: 1 (all). C: 4 (only pp. 80-95)

Sept. 26   Vygotsky T&L C: 7 Begin Paper I in class.

Oct. 3   Photopack The Writer's Mind: Select Readings in the Rhetoric of Composition
           Bateman: "The Psychology of Composition." Emig: "Writing as a Mode of
           Learning." Flower "Writer-Based Prose: A Cognitive Basis for Problems in
           Writing."

Oct. 10   The Writer's Mind Murray "Teaching the Other Self." Gannett "Musings on
           Murray." Bateman: "Dialecticaal Reflections on the Process of Writing."

Oct. 17   In class essay over readings. Assign Research Project. Peer evaluation of
           Paper I drafts in class.

Oct. 24   Paper I DUE. Individual conferences. Research project plan.

Oct. 31   Individual Research Groups Meet with Zebroski in his office at scheduled times.
           Students work on their own research projects.

Nov. 7   Individual Research Groups Meet with Zebroski.

Nov. 14   Drafts of Research Project due in class for Peer Evaluation.

Nov. 21   No Class. All Final Papers for the Research Project DUE by HIGH NOON
           (the day before, Tuesday, would be fine)

Nov. 28   Joan Didion Slouching Towards Bethlehem and The White Album.
           Discussion of selected essays from both books.
           Assignment of Portfolio and Portfolio Paper (Paper 3).

Dec. 5   Final things... A short in class "quiz"... class evaluation forms required...
           Final problems with portfolios and portfolio paper.

The portfolio and portfolio papers will be due by
There is no final exam in this course.

In this short essay on Studio III, I tried to do several things. I wanted to lay out, in more elaborate fashion than the syllabus would allow, the theory from which the course came and give students a sense of the structure and plan of the course activities, but I also in some way felt it important, since this was one of the first pieces of my writing that students would read, to enact the view composing (and of the concept of "good writing") that we would study. I settled on what would later evolve into and be called a "patchwork quilt" form that alternated key quotations from some of the readings that we would be doing with more discursive sections, raising questions and sketching out the parameters of the course materials and practices.

I had hoped that Steven Mailloux's concept of rhetoric as "the political effectivity of trope and argument on culture" would provide a helpful framework for the course. I wanted to be able to talk about issues of "invention" in writing, something I discovered was woefully lacking in my advanced students' previous coursework in composition, but I also wanted to problematize the concept of "creativity" and the sort of "self" and "society" such a concept came from. My view then (and now) was that the "political" was not something that should be parceled out as a separate issue; rather I wanted to investigate how the political underwrote our conceptions of language across the last forty years. The point of this activity would be both to introduce students to "process theory" and "process practice," and to make it clear that "process" was a product of a specific culture and a specific historical moment. I did not want to reduce language (or self) to the simple working out of political forces, nor did I want to pose language (or self) as some sort of independent reality. I wanted to place language (and language theory) next to political and historical context and see what, if any, connections there seemed to be between the two. Following Mailloux's idea, we as a class were to examine the conversation that had gone on for a good part of the twentieth century about creativity and about how mind works—and specifically about how the writer's mind functions—and measure this conversation against our own experiences as writers. I was perfectly open to the possibility that my students might well discover that their experiences with writing simply did not work the way the scientists (Lev Vygotsky) and humanists (Ann E. Berthoff) and practicing writers (Joan Didion) of this period said they worked.

My idea was that students would begin by writing and discussing their previous writing experiences both in and out of the other writing courses. I thought one way of getting into this discussion was to talk about previous writing and English courses in the terms that James Berlin sets out in his essay "Contemporary Composition: The Major Pedagogical Theories." I thought that we could then compare those experiences with the accounts of writing given in Vygotsky, Berthoff, and Didion. I thought we could actually do some of the assisted invitations to explore the composing process in Berthoff's text, as well as compare what she had to say about language and writing with her (and our) actual performance of composing. Finally, I wanted to talk about the disciplinary notions of writing process and creativity, and investigate them in their own fields. What passed as creativity in political science or marketing or teaching and how did it compare or contrast with the idea of creativity we had explored through our readings and writings in this advanced course?

The texts we were to read were difficult, complex texts, and I knew that before we began, but I thought that by having students work in small groups to read selected sections and then report to the class on those sections, we might deal with that complexity in some authentic ways. I had used snippets from Vygotsky's *Thought and Language* (1962) in my sophomore rhetoric course and found students, when working on the text in groups, did a great job of understanding what Vygtosky had to say about writing. By including larger chapters from the book and allotting more time to it, I thought we might extend this reading of Vygotsky.

It was too much, though I was impressed by the students' acceptance of the challenge. They were confused a bit, but as a group kept at it. The problem was that reading the texts required far more time than I had planned into the syllabus, so when I taught the course again the next term, I dropped these texts and replaced them with shorter and simpler articles, either manuscripts of friends or essays from NCTE materials, that were reproduced in a coursepack that became one of our textbooks. The idea of introducing students to composition process theory was right, but it would have to be at a more elementary level if the course was not going to be taken over by disciplinary materials. It is curious, though, that as troublesome as using these complex texts was in my balancing out the course activities, it was the Vygtosky and Berthoff books that students mentioned positively a year later when by chance I would meet them walking across campus or jogging in a nearby park. They seemed to have gained a sense of confidence from having made it through the texts in some intellectually honest fashion and it was this that moved them to speak to me of the course long afterward. Teachers need always to be careful of labeling an activity a "failure" because we often simply don't know what may be troublesome in the short run, but have the most dramatic, positive effects in the long run.But I knew I wanted to revise the readings so they would be more focused and accessible,though I was also convinced that the basic concept of introducing "advanced" students to my discipline was sound, as long as I also made room for students to pursue some of their own interests in writing.

The other major revision that I made when I prepared to teach the advanced course again dealt with the reality that my students had extremely varied experiences in their previous writing courses, and I couldn't count on them having a common vocabulary or a common set of experiences to talk from at the start of the advanced course. Even if they did have some common experiences, often they had difficulty remembering them. As they entered the course, they could not be termed advanced writers. How could I give them more practice writing in a way that would jog their memories of previous writing experiences while at the same time providing a common set of experiences for the class as a whole to share and generalize from? How could I use these common writing practices to deepen students' understandings of issues at stake in composing and composing theory? These were the questions that, together with the problems encountered with the readings, shaped my decision to revise the early assignments and readings.

Writing Studio III   Dr. James Zebroski
Spring 1991   The Writing Program
                                                                    & English Department

REQUIRED MATERIALS: Office Hours:
                                                                      H.B.Crouse 005
Textbooks at Orange Bookstore: 443-4964

Wild Mind: Living the Writer's Life. Natalie Goldberg. Bantam, 1990.
Slouching Towards Bethlehem. Joan Didion. Noonday. 1968/90.
The White Album. Joan Didion. Noonday. 1979/90.

Also, later in the term, a photopack from Syracuse Copy Center (The Writing Process: Select Readings in the Rhetoric of Composition) will be used (plan for about $5 for this).

Spiral notebook for this class only for Writing Practice Notebook.
Portfolio Folder.

WRITING STUDIO III—ADVANCED STUDIES IN THE ART OF WRITING

I am counting on the fact that most of you will have been through the earlier writing studio curriculum at Syracuse. This course will pick up where those courses left off. I will expect that you will know of and have had experience with studio practices such as responding in writing to complex texts, discussing content, form, and political/rhetorical effects of texts that you read,working with peers on drafts of papers, working on collaborative writing projects, putting together research projects and longer papers.

I plan to run this class as a seminar. Since we will meet only once a week for three hours, you must attend and come to class PREPARED. Preparing for a once a week class is very different from preparing for a course that meets two or three times each week. You need to make sure you do the assigned work throughout the week before class, because if you try to do it hours before class, or even the night before, you will find that there is too much to keep up with. A certain internal discipline is required.

Unlike most other courses you have taken, this is NOT a lecture and exam course. You simply cannot "get the notes" or read the textbook instead of coming to class. The theory of knowledge by which we operate is totally different. We MAKE KNOWLEDGE IN CLASS through individual and group processes. You cannot participate in this knowledge making if you do not regularly come to class.

Further, I want to add that I take my teaching very seriously. I prepare for class and I want it to go well. And to be honest, unlike many teachers who are just as happy if you do not show up, I take it as a personal insult it you do not show up. Whether you mean it or not, frequent missing seems to say my class isn't important and my teaching isn't good. That bothers me a lot. This term I will allow 1 1/2 class cuts. (This is generous I think considering each class is a week's worth of instruction.) After this many cuts, you will receive a written warning and further cuts will result in lowering the participation part of your grade.

If you have to miss a class, you should consult with class members about what we did and what assignments were made. I would encourage a buddy system and a phone number exchange, so that you can call other classmates if you need to get assignments. I do *not* have the time to individually tutor each student outside of class if s/he misses class. I expect you as adults to take responsibility for this on your own.

GOALS:

This course will achieve the following goals:

1. Give the student extensive writing practice.
2. Give the student experience with "writing as process."
3. Provide the student experience with varied kinds of writing, including informal/formal, personal/public, memory/research, heuristic/informative/, and reflective writing.
4. Provide the student with the chance to develop and analyze her/his own writing style.

TOPIC OF INQUIRY:

This course has been constructed around the concept of "WRITING AS PROCESS." Everything in the course in some way relates to this idea. The course moves through a series of thematically connected activities. These include: (1) introducing students to the experience of "writing as process"; (2) examining the work of one professional US writer through twenty years as a case study of "writing process" through a specific historical moment (1960-1980); (3) historicizing and critiquing the limits of the concept of "writing as process" as it developed in the field of composition and rhetoric; (4) asking students to create new concepts like "writing as process" to use to make sense of writing in their own world and lives.

This course is theoretical and you will be asked to read complex texts that are about writing and philosophy of writing. But it is also a rhetorical course in that students are asked to position writing and concepts in that context (and by implication develop new positions for themselves). This course requires that you be able to raise questions about the prevalent concepts of writing, language, society, self, and mind. Sometimes students find that difficult or offensive or boring. You need to know from the beginning that this questioning is central to this course. I believe you cannot write well if you cannot question well. If such continual question raising bothers you or will take up more time and energy than you have this term, you might consider another section or taking the course another term.

POLICIES:

* Attendance is required; there are no make up assignments.
* Writing assignments must come in on deadline. No late papers.
* Formal papers must be typed.
* Plagiarism is a serious offense and can result in failure. You are responsible for knowing what plagiarism is and for avoiding it.
* The final project/portfolio will require that you reflect on writing from across the term (and across courses and your undergraduate writing experience). To do this project you must collect and keep ALL writing from the start.
* Conferences and out of class research will be required. Seminar groups meeting in my office will replace class at designated times.

ASSIGNMENTS AND GRADING:

Letter grades will be determined according to the following breakdown:

WRITING PRACTICE NOTEBOOK	20%
FORMAL PAPERS (2)	40%
IN CLASS ESSAY	10%
PORTFOLIO and FINAL PROJECT	20%

CLASS PARTICIPATION   10%
(including peer evaluation sheets, short pieces
of writing, quizzes, short oral reports, class
discussions and seminar groups)

ASSIGNMENT DUE DATES:

Jan. 9   Introduction to the course.

Jan. 16 Wild Mind (Sections 1-21: pp. 1-82). Bring in any five writing practices
from Goldberg. Be ready to talk about writing practice. To turn in: (1) One
page response to "Composition" and (2) One page listing of topics you'd be
interested in writing about.

Jan. 23 Process reports (written and oral). Last questions on Wild Mind. Five more
writing practices due. In class work on Paper I.

Jan. 30 Draft of Paper I due in class: Peer evaluation groups. Discussion of "The
Writing Process" and Heuristics. Have read Joan Didion Slouching Towards
Bethlehem: "The Second Coming," Preface, "Some Dreamers of the Golden
Dream."

Feb. 6   Paper I DUE. Meet in seminar groups to discuss STB: "Slouching Towards
Bethlehem" and "On Keeping a Notebook" (131-141).

Feb. 13 Seminar Groups: STB: "Notes..." (11-48), "Los Angeles Notebook" (217-224),
"Goodbye to All That" (225-238).

Feb. 20 Seminar Groups: The White Album: "The White Album" (171-186), "Georgia
O'Keefe" (126-132), "On the Morning After..." (205-208), "Quiet Days..."
(209-223).

Feb. 27 Seminar Groups: Photopack essays on process.

Mar. 13 Large class discussion of Didion and process. Work on Paper II. Prepare for
in class essay.

Mar. 20 Bring draft Paper II. Peer evaluation day. In class essay on Didion and process.

Mar. 27 No class. Redefined day. (Friday). Paper II DUE.

Apr. 3   Work on project/portfolio.

Apr. 10 Project/portfolio

Apr. 17 Project/portfolio

Apr. 24 Project/portfolio DUE in class. Short oral reports. Course evaluations.

First, I decided to narrow the focus of the course from "creativity" and "the writer's mind" to "process," which helped me to drop a lot of the readings and make room for more writing. I also made more room for reading and discussing Joan Didion's *Slouching Towards Bethlehem* ([1968], 1990) and *The White Album* (1979). The first term I taught the advanced course I was disturbed by my students' dismissal of "process" as being just a subjective, touchy-feely approach to writing, devoid of any intellectual substance. The world of writing for them was either serious, anticreative (i.e., "boring"), and nonpersonal, or it was emotional fluff, expressive, and "free." I wanted to complicate their idea that expressive writing was simple and unstructured, and I also wanted to broaden their concept of writing (and good writing). I wanted my students to consider the possibility that writing might be more than an isolated activity that we rarely do unless our boss (or teacher) insists on it. I wanted my students to think about the possibility that we may be composing all the time, and it's that view that writing is a regular and "natural" part of what we on a daily basis do that differentiates a "writer's life" from a "nonwriter's life." My students had trouble seeing themselves as writers because they viewed writers as being people who got paid for "good" writing, rather than as seeing writers as people who write on a regular basis.

I decided to use Natalie Goldberg's *Wild Mind: Living the Writer's Life* to give my students, who had been indoctrinated into the notion of writing as equalling academic writing and academic writing as being a pass into the discourse community of your choice, an authentic (and for most of them, their very first) experience with so-called expressive writing. We did many of the exercises in the book and read and shared the results. Using this book and its activities as the first thing in the advanced course was a brilliant move since it was fun, it got the students' interest, and yet it still opened up the whole question of what counts as process and creativity in our own lives and why. This first section of the course ended with the "The Patchwork Paper" in which students selected pieces from the large number they had created when they worked through the Goldberg book. Here is the assignment sheet that I gave to students.

Formal Paper I—The Patchwork Paper*

Perhaps you have heard of a patchwork quilt in which a bigger textile is made from smaller oddly assorted patches that have been stitched together. One community patchwork quilt that you may have heard of or seen is The AIDS Quilt in which friends and families have put together hundreds of individual panels. Each individual panel records the name and some representative words or symbols of a loved one who died of AIDS. The AIDS Quilt is a way for the friends and family of a loved one to remember the departed person as an individual, but it is also simultaneously a way for the larger community to make a positive statement about its own commitments.

Patchwork quilts are a traditional American genre. They embody the values of the US. From many individual pieces are composed a work that is the sum total of, but also much more than, the individual parts. From many, one. A respect for the uniqueness of the individual is matched with a commitment to the broader community. Traditionally, a patchwork quilt is also frugal, made of odds and ends left lying around and carefully saved, after fancier clothes are made. (Rag rugs are an even more humble version of this valuing of frugality.) Quiltmaking was frequently an activity an individual did during the long winter months (or during odd moments) when outside farming chores were impossible. Further, quiltmaking was often a social activity, like spelling bees or cornhusking bees. If you saw the film *Witness,* the Amish community volunteered their labor to help a family, the men of the community raising a barn, the women cooking the meal and making a quilt.

In your first formal paper, I want you to put together a patchwork text similar to a patchwork quilt, frugally but also artistically composed from the humbler materials lying around from all your writing (and reading) so far in this course. Also like a quilt, you may add new materials which extend a theme or connect existing texts.

Obviously, the materials you have so far generated are varied and you don't have to make use of all of them or only them. Rather I want you to select a theme (or design) and select from your materials to illustrate and flesh out that theme or design. Arrangement—the order in which you place the texts, and the connecting texts you use to border and cross these texts—is crucially important. Also crucial is selection. One point you should learn from this is that a set of materials can illustrate almost any theme by changing the design or the arrangement of the materials used. When Text A sits next to Text C it creates very different meanings and effects on a reader than when Text A sits next to Text B.

The Writing Process Might Include These Moments—

1. Toying with possible themes or topics that interest you and that can be used for this paper.

2. Rereading your writings after a cooling off period, at one sitting if possible. Put as much time between the generation of the writings and your rereading of them. The idea is to come at your writing in a fresh way. You want to be surprised when you reread the texts by things you didn't expect to be in the texts.

3. Underlining or noting those places that are memorable—good, bad, strange, or of interest. This can be a keyword, a passage, a paragraph or a complete (short) text.

4. Collecting these pieces.

5. Thinking about theme(s)/design(s) again—a theme that interests you and that also can unify the materials.

6. Generating new materials as "Seamtexts" or "Intertexts" to fill out the theme or to take up a new dimension of the theme.

7. Moving between the parts and the whole, between the little texts and the concept of the whole text, do what needs to be done. This may mean

making more texts, cutting existing texts, positioning and repositioning seamtexts.

8. Paying especial attention to the (a) title, (b) beginning text, (c) end text. Great care needs to be taken with these parts.

9. Keeping track of the process in writing practice notebook entry along the way.

10. Assembling the final product. Presenting it appropriately.

Product Requirements—

- LENGTH: 3–4 pages typed (circa 1000 words or more). Final copy must be in standard edited English.

- UNITY: The theme needs to be apparent and interesting.

- ORDER: The order needs to be a necessary order. If I reorder the same texts, it ought to make a big difference in the meaning. (So this is not really a loose collage text.)

- SPECIFICS: General writing won't work on this assignment. Better will be little gems of specifics—whether descriptions, narratives, ideas and theory, or shocking quotes.

- BALANCE: Too many little parts has a negative effect on the reader. But you aren't really doing a patchwork text if there are only a few (2–4) parts. Some balance in length and emphasis needs to be struck. Repetition and omission are very long (or very short) sections should be done on purpose and for a specific effect.

Again, since you will only be required to write a short piece on the process of putting your patchwork text together, be sure you use your writing practice notebook to keep track of what you do and when.

Finally, try to have some fun with this and be creative. I am less concerned with *what* your topic is, than how you put it together. This approach can be applied to anything—a topic like "Who am I" to a topic like "War: Us versus Iraq" or even "Writing."

* I want to thank my fellow writing teacher Rob Faivre for creating and introducing me to this phrase and concept.

I borrowed this idea from a fellow teacher and creative writer (and good friend) Rob Faivre because this patchwork process was more like the process of writing as Rob and I experienced it than were the linear textbook versions. Students had an incredibly difficult time with this assignment. They seemed to have no experience with writing as a generation, selection, rearranging, and revising of texts. They were still, to use Janet Emig's phrase, seeing writing as Sherman's March through Georgia. The patchwork paper gave them another sort of writing experience. It changed their experience of the temporalities of writing and it provided them with a whole new set of strategies for dealing with text. No assignment of revision that I had previously used had made students more sensitive to re-vision than the patchwork assignment. And no other assignment got students to actually understand that arrangement and order was itself a sort of content. The same small texts rearranged in a different order "meant" something else. That was a startling discovery.

Another set of small writing assignments that got students to reflect on their previous experiences in disciplinary terms was to have them first recall and write about an influential (for good or evil) teacher in their life. Here is that assignment, used with the permission of Professor Nancy Mack, Wright State University, Dayton Ohio:

TEACHER REFLECTION ESSAY

Most of you have had about fifteen years of experience with teachers in various classroom settings. At first blink, school and teaching may not seem to have had much outward effect on you. But these informal observations that you have made of teachers at work (over decades) may have a large impact on what you think a classroom is supposed to be like, what constitutes appropriate or inappropriate behavior on both student and teacher's part. This informal classroom experience also influences more subtle concepts of what for you constitutes knowledge and knowing, and even what constitutes appropriate or useful behavior between co-workers, bosses, and workers. Teaching and teachers may well have influenced you in subtle ways you are not aware of.

People tend to imitate uncritically what teachers have done to them. Uncritical imitation means that people do what was done to them without consciously deciding what they want their actions to be. Watch children play school and act out the role of teacher and most probably you will see some pretty frightening things. Your past experiences, unless you reflect on them, will be like ghosts that will haunt you during all your years in school and may well follow you out into the nonschool world, because too often in our culture, "boss" isn't too different from "teacher," and "coworker" isn't radically unrelated to "fellow student." And for the people in class who may be thinking of (or are involved in) marriage (or relationships) someday, somewhere, teaching is obviously related to parenting, and the models of roles in the classroom might surprisingly be connected with spouse to spouse relations.

Thinking through how you feel about your past teacher will help you to decide what type of impact you want to have on your peers, superiors, and, someday sooner than you expect, subordinates.

Your assignment is to write a short (2 page, 500 word) essay about a memorable teacher. This teacher can be any type of teacher during any time in your life. You should think through what you remember about this teacher and how these memories will affect the type of person you will become—at school or at work or beyond these settings, perhaps as a potential parent or spouse. Your memories can be good or bad or any mixture of emotions. Your job is to decide what you will do with these emotions and memories.

This activity was far more valuable than having them read Berlin's essay because it generalized from their experience and in their terms. It began with an emotionally strong experience instead of a taxonomy of categories, and it made clear how mixed people's motives and actions always are. Most students also chose to write on teachers they liked, so it was an upbeat assignment and discussion that nevertheless could lead into a consideration of the kinds of philosophies behind teaching and schooling.

The second short early assignment asked students to examine briefly one of the textbooks of composition that I provided from my collection and discern what sort of philosophy and worldview seemed to motivate the textbook. Here is that assignment sheet.

THE WORLD(VIEW) IN THE TEXT(BOOK) ESSAY

Look at the textbook assigned to you. Read carefully the introductory materials (prefaces, philosophical introductions, quotes from authorities, date and place of publication) and also attend carefully to sections of "creativity" in writing, variously labeled "writing as a process," or "heuristics," or "invention," or "finding a topic," etc. Consider audience and stated beliefs and values of the author(s). Look at the sort of things they ask students to do as well as their view of students. Finally, look at the theory of language the author(s) has/have. What metaphors of language and writing do they rely on?

1. In a developed paragraph, state the essence of the book, especially how it differs from usual writing textbooks and books about writing.
2. In a developed paragraph, state the world view embodied in the text and briefly give examples from the text to support your thesis.
3. In a developed paragraph, give your critique of this text, not simply its limits (all texts and beliefs have inherent limits) but also its potentiality and positive side. Tell why you think this way about this book.

We shared these reports as a class, drawing some conclusions about language and its study over the last several decades. This prepared us to move into the disciplinary readings and look at the developmental history (and "process") of one practicing writer (Joan Didion) in the second section of the course.

I wanted this study of process theory to culminate in some sort of "empirical" research by the students on writing. The idea was that students would learn, then master the concepts and vocabulary as well as develop some sort of historical sense of how the idea of "process" got started, rose, then fell out of favor. Didion's nonfiction books provided a record of one writer writing through this period, and gave an historical framework (slanted to be sure) in which to view "process" and its rise and fall. I hoped that students who understood something of process theory, who had read the work of one practicing writer who lived during this same period, and who received some sense of what was happening in the U.S. during 1960 through 1990 would then be able to apply these understandings to a study of writing in their own discipline or outside of academe. Here is the assignment sheet for the second formal paper, "A Case of Writing."

Writing 305
Zebroski
Spring 1991

Paper II—A Case of Writing

The second major formal paper of this course invites you to do some empirical research, that is, to actually look at a specific case of writing in the ("real") world and see if the writing theory we have read and discussed in this course under the rubric of "process" and process theory is applicable, and to what extent and why. You can decide to examine either products or process or some combination of the two. The requirement of this assignment is to search out writing in a specific discourse community that you have access or can get access to. You will observe and/or collect specific examples of writing and information about writing and you will present some of the most salient of this data and interpret it in a reasonable and informed manner. You are to draw conclusions from the data, not find data that happens to support your view.

This case study can be of either products or processes.

If you focus on *products,* you need to locate three or four examples of varied writing from sources important in the field or discipline (journals, magazines, reports, or memos if in organizations or businesses). You will do a rhetorical analysis of these chosen texts. One way of doing a rhetorical analysis is to apply the canons of rhetoric to generate questions about the texts (and the contexts of those texts). You might then select from these questions to help you read the texts.

Canons of Rhetoric

- INVENTION — Where does one locate new ideas or argument? What counts as tradition and what counts as innovation or *creativity* in the field of discourse?

- ARRANGEMENT — What is the *order?* What this order? How does this form contribute to content?

- STYLE — How does the *language* work? What vocabulary is used? What sort of sentences? paragraphs? Who is the audience and how does this seem to influence the language? What theory of language/use seems to be in effect?

- MEMORY — What counts as tradition in the field? How is *authority* in the field created? How is previous work *cited? quoted?* Why this way?

- DELIVERY — What are the standards and conventions of *presentation?* How is the writing supposed to look? How, for example, is white space used? What would break the accepted conventions of presentation? Why?

But it is also perfectly legitimate to attend to *process.* If you decide to look at writing process, you need an informant whom you can informally interview and perhaps follow around or do a shadow study of. Evidence of process tends to come from three kinds of sources (though, again, this statement as all statements on this sheet is to be read as heuristic, as suggestive, and not as prescriptive): evidence of process gained from direct observation, from what the writer says, or inferred from the products. Each of these sources is partial and open to bias, so (if possible) it makes sense to qualify and corroborate (or contradict) another kind of evidence. The key in presenting and using any evidence in your paper is to present as much, as varied, and as specific evidence as possible. Avoid generalizations from data that you do not include. Present specific examples of evidence, like direct quotations, notes taken during writing process, selections and snippets from real texts.

....

Your objective then is to become the expert on the writing done in a specific discourse community, and to present to a reader who may well not know anything about his discourse course, a rich and comprehensive picture of writing (whether product or process, whether one person or one genre). You need to take some care in deciding which discourse community you are going to study and how you will focus your study.

I found that the best way to read professional essays on process theory was in small seminar group of about six or seven who met with me as a study circle in my office for thirty minutes during the class time. Because the readings had to be done for the seminars to go well and because it was painfully obvious when a student didn't do the readings or didn't show up, but also because students were to be putting a large amount of time into research outside of the class, I eliminated the large class in favor of meeting for shorter but more intense periods in the seminar groups.

Students really enjoyed these groups. They felt more comfortable with me, no doubt partly because I felt more comfortable with them in my office in surroundings that were cramped but familiar and personalized. Students might ask questions about posters I had hanging on the walls, the books on my shelves, the cartoons and jokes on my bulletin board, and they would see the chaos that my writing life is. They also became friends with each other, and would voluntarily gather early, long before the group was scheduled to meet, in the hall outside my office, to talk with fellow group members about the essays assigned for the night, but also about other things going on in their lives—tests in other courses, the war and the anti-war protests being held every week downtown, the huge march against the war in Washington, D.C., but also latest boyfriends or girlfriends and parties attended and anticipated. Students commented frequently to me privately, but also on the written end of course evaluations, how valuable they found these groups. When we returned to the large class for the last third of the course, students came back with a high level of energy and enthusiasm. The small seminar groups made learning fun but they also made it more personal and intense than it ever could be in either the large group or in individual conferences.

Here are the study questions on the essays about process that we read and discussed in the seminar groups. They give some sense of the direction of our talk but also the intellectual depth that advanced students in composition, college juniors and seniors, are capable of reaching.

Study Questions for Writing 305

Joan Didion (1961–1968; 1968–1978; 1976)

1. How is the *form* that Didion chooses a reflection of, an extension of, a part of her writing?
2. What theory of self can be read in Didion's writing?
3. What theory of language can be read in Didion's writing?
4. What can be said about practicing writers and writing practices, using Didion's texts as a case study of one writer's writing over more than twenty years?
5. What traits characterize Didion's texts?
6. How have Didion's texts changed over the last twenty years?
7. What social forces are written into Didion's texts?

8. Consider Didion's writing in terms of the subject position written into the texts. (How are social class, race, gender, and sexualities written into (or out of) Didion's texts?) So?

9. What might be supposed about Didion's writing process from these written products?

....

James Britton, et al. ("The Process of Writing" in *The Development of Writing Abilities*. [London: Macmillan Education, 1975] 11–18.)

1. What are the major stages in the process of writing?

2. What forces seem to be at work in the incubation stage?

3. Why spend so much time and energy studying preparatory phases of writing, when so much school writing minimizes or eliminates them?

4. What are three sources of evidence of process in writing? What are the limits of each?

5. What is inner speech and what is its relevance for writing production?

6. What disciplines does this article draw upon? So? .

....

Donald Bateman ("Dialectical Reflections on the Process of Writing." Unpublished manuscript, 1980)

1. What is a *worldview* and what does it have to do with writing?

2. What is the prevailing worldview in the US, according to this essay?

3. Its characteristics? Significance to composition? beyond composition?

4. What are the limits to "process" according to Bateman?

5. How does the essay attempt to "perform" (and critique) its message?

6. What linguistic forces does Bateman see as involved in the dialectic that produces the writing process?

....

James Zebroski ("New Perspectives on the Social in Composition: Lev Vygotsky's Theory of Process" in *Composition Chronicle* (April 1990) 4–6.)

1. What does teaching/learning "writing as a process" mean?

2. What are the limits of process theory?

3. What has composition turned to, *after process*?

4. What are its (#3's) limits?

5. Speculate on influences from other disciplines on the field of composition; speculate on possible future turns in composition (due to advances in other disciplines, as well as from the resolution of struggles within the field).

....

Conclusion

1. Using the texts (and textbooks) we have examined this term, give a careful "history" of the concept of "process" over the last twenty to twenty-five years.

2. Parallel #1 with historical events in US *outside* of academe; using this broader history, speculate on the reasons for the rise and fall of "process."

3. Track the root (implied but pervasive) metaphors that structure "process" and process theory, and note their effects in the study of writing.

4. Analyze the styles of the texts we examined and note how the style reflects (or contradicts) the content.

5. Track through "process" texts shifting notions of "self."

6. Track through "process" texts shifting notions of "language."

7. Imagine an alternative to process theory or social theory in composition. Elaborate your alternative model. Note its root metaphor(s) and/or notions of "self," "language," "social," etc. Detail its possible advantages/disadvantages over present models, etc.

8. Using all we have learned about "process" and process theory, describe in specific detail your own writing process, determining as you do, the process theorists whose concerns and explanations come closest to your own.

In the final third of the course, I met with individual students in conference and helped them to work on their projects and their writing portfolios. We met as a large class to hear reports of research projects. But mostly, I tried to leave students alone in the last section of the course. They had plenty to do and knew what they needed to do and in fact, were being assaulted by end of the term demands in their other courses. In the next section of this essay, I will discuss some of the final papers students composed for my advanced course. The high quality of these final projects make me feel that I am on right track in theorizing the course. In the next section I try show that forwarding student experience in a writing course, given the present moment and pressures of history, is *the* political question not only in Composition, but also in academe.

The Political Question—Again

I want to return to the question of politics in the teaching of composition raised in the narrative with which I began this essay. The question of politics in the teaching of composition arises in an especially attenuated way in the advanced writing course since the work of the field of composition can best be compared at this point to the work proceeding in literary studies, though clearly the introductory courses are no less "political" than the later ones. But if upper division courses are the ones that give a sense of the field and its conflicts and controversies to the student taking the course, then the advanced composition course, like the advanced literary studies course, is the place where new theories, reading and writing practices, and emerging "devices" for doing things with texts are most likely to be available to the student. And it is in this comparison that students themselves may wonder at the difference between composition and literature as fields of study, for it is very clear that one of the major shifts in literary studies over the last twenty years is the return to the political, the rediscovery of the political effects that anything we write or read or say or do has. It is also very clear that at most places the advanced composition course is either (1) oblivious to these political trends, or (2) imitative of these political trends, or (3) staunchly resistant to these political trends. In this sense the advanced course is reflective of the field of Composition as a whole in which large minorities of teachers and researchers feel compelled either to ape the current fad among the literature faculty to prove their own worthiness among their literati godfathers, or to deny vehemently that they have any connection with those people. The third minority is the group of teachers so busy keeping up with teaching and grading loads that they don't know what the current fads are and could care less. And so one tends to see advanced composition courses that are either little versions of the literary theory courses or that are anti-PC rhetoric courses. Or, most commonly of all, you get advanced courses that are more of the same, that are places where more practice of writing takes place under rubrics of "discourse community" or "process" or stylistic studies in clear, direct prose construction.

I have tried to steer a course through all of these shoals, stopping by, or getting washed up on, none of them. As mentioned above, I have tried to do this by using the concept and practice of rhetoric as Steven Mailloux presents them in his recent book *Rhetorical Power*. Mailloux defines the rediscovery of the political dimensions of discourse that has occurred over the last two decades in English studies as a return to rhetoric and proposes his version of rhetoric as a new currency for negotiating between the contending theoretical parties that crisscross the otherwise fragmented field of literary studies. I feel more comfortable with Mailloux's theory and practice of rhetoric than I do with that of any other literary theorist because his approach provides me with some specific practices that I can begin with in the teaching of composition and that have spaces within them for a historicizing of the theories and practices circulating in my own field. But the fact is, that as much as I find Mailloux's ideas and approach to texts (and rhetoric) consonant with my own, I also find that his work falls short, as it must, of doing anything specific to composition. His book is a reading of the theory and practice of literary studies, after all, not of composition. There is no question that *Rhetorical Power* provides the most valuable discussions that I have encountered of the theoretical issues that have been prominent in literary studies since reader response. It also gives a set of powerful examples of a reader reading texts, demonstrating in its reading practices what a rhetorical hermeneutics is about. I find that Mailloux's definition of rhetoric as the "political effectivity of trope and argument on culture" about the only definition of rhetoric that I feel comfortable with, and it certainly makes a prominent place for the political without reducing everything to the political. For Mailloux there still are tropes and arguments (and history) somewhat distinct from (if only for accidental historical reasons), though nevertheless contributory to, the political. But the fact remains, Mailloux's rhetoric is a *reading* rhetoric; it tells us more about what we do or might do when we read an already existing text, than what we do or might do when we compose a new text. Mailloux's theory also emphasizes the language and power relation, but is all but silent about the language and cognition relation. And Mailloux's text, of necessity, says almost nothing about Composition or about the theoretical disputes specific to Composition. Therefore Mailloux's approach is helpful for me when I introduce students in my advance composition course to a history of a key concept in composition, but it is of less use when I ask my students to compose a text or to compose a context.

So this leaves my advanced composition course with a solid theoretical middle section in which I ask students to historicize a keyword in composition and invite them to attempt to think of new ways of seeing writing. That is political in a fairly explicit sense of seeing the historical contexts and conversations as creating a reason for the emergence of a keyword. But what about the other two-thirds of the course, the beginning and the end? Are these sections of the course apolitical? Is that possible or desirable?

I want to distinguish here between a superficial politicality and a deeper politicalness. It is relatively easy to go into a course and explicitly label one's approach and conclusions as political. And when the choice is between this and teaching a course in language and literacy as a neutral activity, I prefer the former. However, I want to go beyond what too often unfolds as a superficial presentation of political positions to read a deeper acting upon the political dimensions of language. I do not simply want my students to know that writing is always a political (and ethical) act. I want them to experience this on their own terms. That requires that a central place be made in my course for student experience and that that experience not be held up to easy ridicule and critique, but be accepted as a legitimate experience. It is very easy to get students to do the right kind of political reading of texts. It is more difficult to get students to write out of the politics of their own positions. And it is nearly impossible to get students to understand and experience the politicality of language and life. Too much of what passes as a political or social approach to composition (or literature) seems to me to go right back to the days of the New Critics when I was an undergraduate. In the worst of those New Critical classes (I had some very good ones to which these characterizations do not apply) the teacher stood up at the front of the class searching the alternative readings of a text that the students would produce for the "best" reading. While there was some attempt to argue that any intelligent reader of a text could, if given the proper training and long enough time, come to the same sort of conclusions, the reality was (and everyone knew) that the teacher always had the "best" interpretation and the teacher's reading had little if anything to do with my life or even my reading. One scholar at that time critiqued this approach as applied to language study as follows:

> For the last several years curriculum development has proceeded under the banner of inquiry, a somewhat mystical doctrine which encourages the teacher to hide a well-known answer in the soft core of an artificial problem and beseech the student to discover it. When the student uncovers the answer, which he can do with some facility if the teacher asks the right questions, his reward lies in the rich experience of discovery, a vision of a piece of the structure of the discipline he is studying, as well as a good mark for his willingness to play the game enthusiastically. (Bateman 1970, 1)

This was my experience in most of my New Critical literature classes. I felt that I was working through a soft core of a pseudo-problem in order to discover what my teacher already knew. I got quite good at playing this game, but ultimately it had little effect on the rest of my life and intellect, except to leave me with profound misgivings about the professional study of literature. It was because of this experience that I went on in academe, but it is also because of this experience that I went into composition rather than literature.

I suspect that this sort of inquiry is what goes on in most composition and literary studies courses that put forward a political view of language. And I fear that, if I reduce my course to the middle historical, theoretical, and disciplinary section, this will be the experience my students too take from my course. So to counter this possibility, I have consciously added the first and last section of the course where we try to begin with student experiences through the writing assignments in the *Wild Mind* book, and also end with the students' experiences in the final projects and portfolios. I do not hesitate to note political positions implied in student writing and my view of these positions, but I do this after I have established a relationship of trust with the student and after that student has had some time to write out of experience and write the questions of her or his life. "Live the question" advises Rilke to the young writer, and that is precisely what I try to do and to model in front of my students. One of the questions is how is a language act always political? To ask the question is not to reduce everything to this question—there are other questions too, for example, how is a language act always ethical? how is a language act always historical? intertextual? generative?—nor is it to imply that I as teacher have the correct answer. It is to imply that I as a person who studies language and lives one sort of life has an answer, not the answer. And the issue of my advanced composition course is how do I go about, given all of this, helping the students to form *their* answers to these questions.

To some this may seem a soft pluralism. To them, I would point to the middle of my course where an explicit politicizing and historicizing of issues in Composition and language studies occurs. To some this may seem too PC (a patronizing label at any rate). To them I would point to the beginning and ending of the course in the students' experiences. To some, my advanced course may not deal sufficiently with academic discourse, with writing in other disciplines. To them I'd respond that I do not believe there is any such generic thing, and that if there is, there are plenty of spaces within my course for students to bring in the writing of their disciplines. But only if the students want to. And my experience has been that many students, once we get beyond the why-do-I-have-to-take-this-course question, want to write about things outside their disciplines, and outside Composition.

Let me conclude this section with some examples and with a strong claim. I will begin with the claim: I believe that composing a course is as much a composing act as composing a text. And like any composing, it is a complex, multifaceted political and ethical activity. No one can propose a course that deals with political or social dimensions of language in more than a superficial way if they don't first accept the course as a composed discourse act. Yet we rarely find writing teachers thinking about their course as a composition. It is for this reason that in the last section of this essay on the advanced composition course I want to take up this point at some length, to argue that composing goes on in our construction of a course no less than in the writing of a scholarly essay, the writing of a poem, or the inscribing of a journal entry.

Before moving on to that claim and argument, however, I want to push for including more student experience in our college composition courses. While it is very unpopular these days to argue for incorporating student experience and interests into a composition course, the best evidence supporting that argument is the kinds of writing I have received when I have made an important place for it.

One student in my advanced course put together a report, required in another course she was taking, on the needs of the disabled who lived in the local community. Because the student was putting together the report for me as well as for the course in her major, I required her to do more than simply present her quantitative data. I asked her to provide a summary of the methods and an analysis of the problem along with a section on recommendations. The heart of the study for the reader in the profession was the data she collected; the importance of doing a revision of this original assignment in one academic discourse community was to make the report more accessible to a legislator or a legislative committee in Albany considering the state budget. After much work, the student finally agreed that though she did at first have doubts, the opportunity the advanced composition course gave her to revise the report was welcome and actually made her work collecting and analyzing data more valuable. From my perspective this work is political in a nitty-gritty sort of way that an elite reading of an elite text is not.

Another student who was writing a paper for her Women's Studies course didn't want to directly intervene in that paper for my course. Instead what she did was track her process of composing the paper, as well as write reflective essays on why this issue was important to her. My course also made room for her to do her own questionnaire and administer it to survey attitudes on campus toward violence against women. This was not something that was required in her Women's Studies course requirements for the project, but came out of our class discussions of women's issues, her encounter with empirical methods in her library research of the issue, and my ability to provide time and credit for this research in my course.

One student who was very involved in AIDS education wanted to write his paper on some aspect of AIDS. I suggested that he focus on his teaching about AIDS in workshops, rather than on simply presenting scientific information on the subject. The student got very excited about this project. He wrote about how he got involved in AIDS education and described his training as well as some of the workshops that he led. He did an analysis of the rhetoric of some of the state and federal materials on AIDS and noted controversies over, as well as agreements about, the syndrome. The quality and importance to the student of the final product are indicated by his insistence that I send the final text back to him during the summer. He gave me a self-addressed and stamped envelope for this very purpose, indicating that this was an important experience to him. And this from a student who had great difficulty when we started the course because he believed that he was a mediocre writer and really couldn't be bothered in his last semester before graduation with a course that wasn't a major course.

Some students actually wanted to take advantage of the fact that they were taking a writing course in their final semester as an undergraduate to collect and reflect on pieces of writing they had composed during their four years at Syracuse. Both the examples they put together and the analyses they composed were illuminating for me as a person concerned with writing that goes across campus. Students were hard on the majority of their courses that did not require much writing, or if they did, required writing that demanded the student detach her- or himself from experience and interests.

And there were some fascinating papers that had little if anything to do with the disciplines or even with composition. One student wanted to work through some philosophic arguments against the existence of God. This was for her own reasons—she was an environmental science major and was not taking any philosophy or religious studies courses that term, if she ever had. It was just a topic that was important enough for her to commit to writing a fifteen- to twenty-page paper on it. One student was interested in anorexia nervosa, another in Jack Kerouac and the Beats, and they used my course to write on these topics. An accounting major had done some amateur theatre on his own and he decided he wanted to write on some of the plays that he had been in of Tennessee Williams. No other course he took or could take in accounting, but even in the English department, would have allowed him to write on Williams in the way that he did in this paper—as a personal encounter, an experience with the work of one playwright. His paper was excellent, though I have doubts whether it would have been acceptable among any of the constituencies of the English department, whether New Critical or deconstructive or neo-Marxist, since it examined the place of Williams's work in his, this student's, life.

And finally, a student decided he wanted to write his research paper on the philosophy and practice of one of the Far Eastern martial arts in which he had taken courses and had become fairly accomplished. The student seemed to find these martial arts interesting, serving in some ways as a model. He frequently discussed his experiences in the course of training. For example, when I asked this student to write on one teacher who had an important effect on his life, this student wrote on his martial arts teacher showing not only how much he learned form the teacher but also how much he respected him. This student, it turned out, was the same student who came into my last class wearing his gay-bashing shirt. He also provided me with an envelope and his summer address so that I could send his paper back to him. That paper was quite interesting since it got into a discussion of the samurai warrior tradition that was quite detailed. You can only imagine my surprise, after having been disturbed by the classroom incident on the last day and confused about what action I should or should not take, when I was reading his paper and came across the statement that there was a homosexual tradition among many samurai. It was only at this moment that my course reached a deeper level of political engagement because it was only at this moment that my student could read my comment at its most serious, knowing as he did that he had been allowed ample time and place in my advanced course to shape and write on his own interests and experiences, learning as he did to trust my comments on his writing, which came out of my respect for him as a writer and thinker. I wrote something like "I find it strange that you should say this considering what you wore on your shirt the last day of class. Do you see any contradiction here?" Of course, I don't know whether he read the comments or whether he saw the contradictoriness of his position. But I think that it is more likely that that comment had some effect because it intersected with *his experience,* in *his language,* and not on some abstract, teacher-centered plane.

But Am I *Really* Composing?

To teach an advanced writing course, I have been arguing, demands an advanced concept of writing. One way to complicate usefully and enrich our notion of writing (and language) is to make the case for teaching writing as a composing activity. The claim that a teacher (with her or his students) engages in an authentic act of composing when she or he puts together a writing course is not exactly a new one. Ann E. Berthoff so defines composing as to make it an activity of the imagination in which we engage in various ways all the time. She says:

> Composing, putting things together, is a continuum, a process that continues without any sharp breaks. Making sense of the world is composing. . . . writing is like the composing we do all the time when we respond to the world, make up our mind, figure out things again. The work of the active mind is seeing relationships, finding forms, making meanings: when we write we are doing in a particular way what we are already doing when we make sense of the world. We're composers by virtue of of being human. (Berthoff 1988, 3, 5)

Surely in such a generous view of composing, the teacher of writing can find ample room to call her or his own activity of forming, thinking through, and teaching a composition course, a composing activity and the course itself as a composition. Still, Berthoff's major concern lies with the student writing and it remains for us to make a strong claim for teaching writing as composing and to work out the implications of such a claim.

The work of other respected scholars in composition also supports the claim that teaching, participating in, cocreating, and living a writing course is a composing activity of the highest order. William Coles, as early as *The Plural I* (1978), suggests this when in that book he enacts one composition course that is carefully composed through sequential assignments. If anyone in the field has taught composition teachers about the rhetorical canon of arrangement and its implications for teaching the writing course, it is Coles. So too, more recently, Bartholomae and Petrosky (1986) in their *Facts, Artifacts, Counterfacts* argue from the start that their approach is distinctive precisely because "This is a book about reading, writing and teaching and the ways each can be imagined, variously, as acts of composition" (i). But in these cases, and every other major case that I am aware of, there is an understandable if too immediate jump to the business at hand in the classroom, to the students' writing, and what to do about that. I want to push the claim, made in passing in the composition scholarship, that creating a writing course is a composition and a composing itself. It seems to me that this view helps writing teachers to think about their courses in a different way, allowing them to draw on what they already know about writing to apply this in some suggestive ways to the course and curriculum design. Obviously, the essays in this book make this assumption throughout. This insight has certainly allowed me to think about my teaching and my course composing in a different way. And at bottom, I think that aside from making the argument for a prominent role for *student* experience in the composition course, making the argument for *teacher* experience in the composing of the writing course is the second most "political" claim we can make. When I begin to see the composition course as a discourse cocreated by my students and myself, I am less easily persuaded to let a textbook company or national testmakers or legislators or others dictate what it is "I" am to "write." Academic freedom becomes a version of freedom of speech when we see the composition course as discourse. So if we are to think about teaching the composition course as a composing activity, what factors do we usually associate with writing (composing text) and how do these factors play out when we shift them to the realm of course (but also curriculum) construction?

When I think of composing, I am referring to my experiences with writing, which have included factors like text (written discourse inscribed on material, usually, though not always, pages), processes, audience, an aesthetic stance, an epistemic expectation, and a connection with other writing experiences from other parts of my life. I am also referring to the dynamics of these processes, how they never sit still, in fact, how there is a kind of feel or texture to the flow. Finally, I am aware of the socio-historical dimensions of writing, that is, the specific ways that an individual in a culture activates an already existing set of instrumentalities that often come prepackaged with instructions for use, and a history of purposes to which they have been put. But to my mind, this socio-historical dimension of writing also includes the specificity of the moment and of my use of this "collective property." The uniqueness of my subjectivity and my temporality transforms what might be thought of as a "thinking device" that has its own histories, functions, and structures, and makes of it "my writing," something new, something added on to the social edifice of language.

So—text, processes, the feel of the aesthetic, the epistemic expectation, flow, appropriation and transformation of the social—these are the factors that are at work and that I find important when I write. And each of these factors plays a role when I am working out a course, when I "compose a course." Let me take each factor in turn.

Text

If there aren't "written products," it isn't writing as far as I'm concerned. I certainly do not reduce writing to the marks on the page; but they are where I start if I am to name something "writing." And writing is the composing that most concerns me here, but also in my life. I have a problem with some of my literary theory counterparts who insist that reading is writing is reading, that reading is a writing and a rewriting of a text. Yes, I suppose reading and writing are both discourse and both involve what I would call the active construction of meaning (no doubt fighting words for some of my counterparts). In this sense, I suppose writing can be seen as a reading of experience and the cultural "texts" that surround us. But unless I see a written text that is produced by authors, I suspect that the very thing that I am most interested in will get ignored in the shuffle. Historically this has been the case with writing in English departments. So I need to see a produced, written text.

Then a reading selection that one underlines or writes marginal comments on while reading it, involves "composition," whereas reading the same text without making such marks is not composition? That is precisely it, as far as I am concerned. The moment of this final text may well be extended across a long stretch of time and the final product may look rather puny (underlining or checkmarks; big "yes"es written in the margin across from an insight), but in my experience, composing involves some inscribing, some scratching of material surface against material surface, some written products that will remain for a while after. This may all seem a rather subtle, if not esoteric, sort of distinction, but it goes directly to the heart of the question of whether composition courses (and the composition curriculum) should exist independently, separate from literature and reading courses, and as a compositionist I am committed to separate courses that balance out the overemphasis in English department offerings on the consumption of texts, with some attention to the production of texts.

So when we turn to the composing of a writing course, do we find such texts? There are an abundance of written texts in a composition course. They included the syllabus and policy statements about grading and course philosophy. Also there are numerous assignment sheets. There are handouts hot off the presses which good writing teachers are constantly composing at the spur of the moment, not because they are inefficient but because they are dealing with specific issues that have just arisen in class. Only journalists compose more under the gun than teachers. It is not possible to prepare a handout for the next class session that deals with what happened or didn't happen in the last class weeks in advance. And even if that were possible, for many writing teachers who base their teaching on response to student interests, experiences, and needs, the course changes each term as the students change, even if it is the same number in the catalogue. A teacher often tailors what he or she does to the specific chemistry of a class and the diverse student personalities in the class. This is a sign of a quality teacher, not of inefficiency. So it is not unusual to see perfectly good teachers running around minutes before class starts, typing up handouts, photocopying texts they just composed the previous night.

Rarely do administrators see (let alone appreciate) this composing activity, nor do they recognize the huge amount of text that a good teacher writes in a course. If you added up the number of words, even most teachers would be surprised by the amount of written text they generate often under the gun even when doing one rather simple and straightforward activity, "grading papers." Dissertations worth of comments are written in a single class, and over a term or two, teachers produce more written text than scholars do on their own subjects over entire years. This writing for the most part is expected but goes unnoticed, or if noticed, it is simply unappreciated. Grading papers is more often seen by the most sympathetic colleagues as drudgery they prefer not to do, rather than an artistic enactment of a theory of writing, a modeling of a practicing writing for a novice writer, a presentation of a whole new metalanguage for pointing at and shaping emerging written text, as well as a place where contact between teacher and each and every student is constructed, maintained, and individualized. Grading papers is still seen as more of a police action than as an artistic performance, let alone as a legitimate and lengthy composing of text. We can put down on our resumes or end-of-the-year reports "published essays," but there is no place to note the thousands of smaller but even more significant texts we write every term on student papers; somehow that doesn't count unless you do not do enough of it or you do not do it with some minimum of linguistic disciplining. So teachers of writing classes do huge amounts of difficult and quality writing; they compose text in amounts and under conditions they would never dream of inflicting on students. If the production of *text* is a sign of composing, then a writing course with all of its attendant writing is a composition.

Processes

Writing is a set of processes I go through to move toward producing texts. One set of these processes might be called invention (or the creative processes), in which I play around with ideas, rehearse phrasings, and even individual words, that I might use. There is a psychological dimension of things going on here that involves inner speech and the multiplicity of voices that throb through consciousness. I can't imagine calling something composing if these processes don't go on at least in some way. Even copying a text verbatim requires an intonation and an evaluation that is the unique product of a specific consciousness. Even in writing grocery lists, I am re-minded of these processes at work in my attempt to get down some mark of what is flitting through mind and which will soon cease by becoming something else.

I feel these processes at work especially before the course starts and I am playing around with all kinds of possibilities for readings and for writing projects, though these processes do go on all the time throughout the course—when I am in class moderating a class dis-cussion of a reading of a student or professional text, when I am by myself reading student papers and writing comments on them, when I am writing out reports noting and perhaps evaluating a course that I taught. Ordering these ideas and plans and assignments is no less important in course design than in text design. These invention and arrangement processes, influenced by my own expe-rience and student interests, abilities, and motivations, get trans-lated into what works this term for this class. Out of talk with teacher friends come the early textual products like syllabi, unit plans, some of these early assignments and lesson plans. So the processes at work when I write an essay are similar to the processes at work when I compose my writing course.

Audience

Are my students my audience when I teach a writing course? Partly, but they are also my cowriters. They are composing this course too and the feeling I get working with students is often similar to the feeling I get when I cowrite an article with another scholar. It is hard and frustrating, but also, when it works, immensely satisfying. A good collaborative writer has to know when to push and when to give in, how to use the tensions and even conflicts that arise when many different personalities are putting together a single product. To say my students are one of my audiences, then, is not to reduce their role as cowriters. I would also add that administrators and supervisors (as representatives of institutions that are often repre-sentative of a state, or of a religious or philosophical community) form one of the audiences when I compose my course. I too am certainly an audience of my own writing. But perhaps the most important are my fellow teachers, especially a few close friends who teach composition whom I trust, who went to graduate school with me, or taught at my side in the schools or colleges over the last twenty years. When I compose my course, I am often talking with these teachers, sharing what I did, talking about how it turned out, sending them copies of my syllabi or assignment sheets or student papers that I prize or admire or am repulsed by. This "teacher talk" or "deep talk," as Margaret Himley describes it in her book *Shared Territory*, influences my thinking about what I will do in the classroom in profound ways, and if I teach with any audience in mind, it is this one.

Aesthetic Sense

I have always thought that one of the most important insights to be found in Janet Emig's path-breaking *The Composing Processes of Twelfth Graders* was her recognition of the importance of the moment in the composing process when one takes an aesthetic stance toward what one has written, when one, for however long or short a period of time, looks back on the product and enjoys it as a made thing. This contemplative moment is central to writers—whether they be students or teachers or professionals—and yet hardly anything has been said about this moment, and no one that I am aware of, has taken up this insight in research or in textbook accounts of the writing process. Emig describes this moment this way:

> . . . the contemplation of the product—the moment in the process when one feels most godlike. One looks upon part, or all, of his creation and finds it—good? uneven? poor? If he has not steadily, or even erratically, kept his reader in mind during the process, the writer may think of him now and wonder about the reception the piece will experience in the world. (44)

This contemplative or aesthetic factor is often the major motivation for going through the difficulties of writing. I can't be sure of how the piece will be received or how it will function in the world; nor can I count on the excitement of the creative processes as necessarily being an accurate indicator of high quality in the final text. However, I can always plan to leave time for my own aesthetic reception of my text. I can always make time to stand back and reread it with no other purpose in mind than to enjoy. This knowledge gets me through some hard times when I feel I have to compromise my original vision to real world representations and readers. But I too am a reader of such representations, one with high standards developed over several decades of experience with texts. So the aesthetic moment is absolutely crucial for my continued engagement in writing. I often set aside special times—Friday evening or New Year's Eve or my birthday—simply to go back and reread and enjoy journals or essays or poems I have written. In one sense, my writing act has not been consummated until I aesthetically contemplate the product, and during and after the writing process, I often turn to sensing the aesthetic of a single emerging text.

And the writing course? Do I set aside and anticipate the aesthetic moment when I compose my course? Not as much as when I compose a text, I have to admit, usually because by the end of the term I am too tired to engage in the aesthetic act. But I do do it when I go to conferences and reflect on and speak about my teaching, when I write about my courses, when I share my handouts or classroom experiences. And strangely enough, I enjoy the contemplative moment when I am filling in end-of-the-year, required reports about what courses I taught, when I put together longer documents for tenure and promotion. Finally, I am constantly amazed by the course I composed when I can put a little time between it and its aesthetic consummation, when I return to the course materials and my experiences to begin to plan the next version of the course. The contemplative moment occurs when I compose a course and right afterward, but more at the start of the next course when I review my materials and ideas and student papers, beginning to collect my ideas and myself. So I do "contemplate the product."

The Epistemic Moment

There is no question in my mind that my writing and my teaching share a similar epistemic trait. The reason I write and teach is that I always learn something new in the process. I enjoy teaching lower-division courses, especially freshman composition, because the students are constantly asking "naive" questions, which means they haven't been indoctrinated into silence. Their questions, when taken seriously, often bring into sharp relief those very assumptions that I thought the least about. Their questions often set me off on a whole new line of thinking. I end up interrupting my teaching and conferencing to jot down new ideas that have arisen when students comment or ask questions about as often as I do when I am reading an intensely provocative book or when I am in the heat of writing an essay that is going in a totally surprising direction. I agree with Donald Murray when he says the best reason to write is to be surprised. I teach for the same reason. The only thing that cultivates more surprise for me than a set of my journals is a class full of freshman writers.

Flow

The patterns of flow are very different in composing a course and composing a text, but both share a sense of freefall, of kinetic energy. Both composing a text and composing a class context are adrenaline producers. They both frighten and please me in about equal measures. Recognizing the temporalities that emerge and disappear in the classroom are absolutely crucial to successful teaching. Knowing when to push and when to give in, among other things, is the knowledge that separates experienced and novice instructors. Planning for, and adapting to, new temporalities has a determining effect on the shape a course can and does take. And the importance of picking up on, and adding to, the right rhythm can be seen in everything from how long we plan to spend on readings and discussion to how we react when the class discussion seems to take a direction different from what we ever expected. It even extends into matters like the timing of grades. If the teacher gives too many high or low grades too soon in the term, it can have disastrous consequences, since it alters students' motivations and determines the amount of energy they will feel it makes sense to put into the course. Course flow, perhaps more in composition than in any other college subject, is also affected by what happens in other university courses. Because other courses tend to dump content on students at the end of the term, the course flow then tends to be very different (and much more tense) than in the middle of the term. Because composition is perceived to have no content, while most other courses do, course tempo in composition is expected to be more student centered rather than shaped to fit the structure of disciplinary knowledge. I don't accept these notions, though I do accept that my professional colleagues in other disciplines and most students do believe them, so I tend to arrange my course assignments that demand the most attention early in the term, and plan to be finished with the most important course requirements by the time the end-of-the-term craziness begins. I see no value in dumping on students then. Just as I see no value in revising an essay or a poem after a certain point, regardless of the ideology that revision is always good, and the more revision the better. Composing a text and composing a course are both eminently temporal activities. Ripeness is all.

The Social Nature of Composing

There is a history of curriculum no less than a history of literacy. There is a history to my construction of composition courses no less than there is a history to my construction of my reading and writing processes and products. And there is a need when thinking through the composing of a course and the composing of a text to consider both the individual and the social dimensions of these activities, to problematize the ways in which the social gets appropriated by the individual and the individual, with others, transforms the social.

The language I use as I write this essay isn't my private property. It existed before me and will exist after me. Others "own" it as much as I do, more even. But still, I do make some difference, however small, in ways I can only take as a matter of faith. I write and teach partly because I do believe in this difference, and not in mine alone. I believe that students and teachers make some difference when they write, and by changing their conceptions of writing, I am changing eventually some of those writing practices and the English language, through which we all live and have our being.

At thirty-nine, I feel I am only beginning to really feel this English language, to sense how the language moves, works, what part I play in it, what potentials lie buried in it. I feel like a potter who only, after twenty years of intense study, is beginning to understand the smallest things about the clay and the wheel. But it's more than this, because language always lies so close to what once was called the soul. English is no sluggish clay; it is full of the souls of all of the others who spoke and lived it. It's their voices and energies I feel, respect, revere, when I compose a text and teach writing. The ghosts of English classrooms speak through English, and the ghosts who spoke through English since this wondrous language had its dim beginnings in the so-called dark ages, speak through and in my English classroom. My reverence for them and their words is no different when I am alone looking at a page in my journal than it is when I charge into my class and enthusiastically read a student text aloud or write out an assignment or place a comment on a student paper.

And so, as strange as it might seem, composing a course, especially a course in language, is in its most important aspects a form of writing, a legitimate composing process, at least as I experience writing and composition. Composing a course is a different type of writing to be sure, but a writing nonetheless. I believe that advanced composition must acknowledge these connections and obligations, show some deference to the larger issues at stake. Nothing makes me angrier than the trivialization of writing, making it a mere skill or a mere discourse or a mere subject position or a pass for entering some job or career or discourse community. Obviously writing can be all of these things. But to bring these ideas into the advanced composition course is to bring in elementary, not to mention superficial, notions of language. The advanced writing course deserves more.

References

Bartholomae, D. & A. Petrosky. 1986. *Facts, artifacts, and counterfacts.* Portsmouth, NH: Boynton/Cook.

Bateman, D. & F. Zidonis. 1970. *A grammatico-semantic exploration of the problems of sentence formation and interpretation in the classroom: Final report. Vol. I.* Columbus, OH: The Ohio State University Research Foundation.

Berlin, J. 1982. Contemporary composition: The major pedagogical theories. *College English* 44:765–77.

Berthoff, A. 1988. *Forming/thinking/writing.* 2nd ed. Portsmouth, NH: Boynton/Cook.

Coles, N. 1986. Empowering revision. *Facts, artifacts, and counterfacts,* edited by D. Bartholomae & A. Petrosky. Portsmouth NH: Boynton/Cook.

Didion, J. 1990a. *Slouching towards Bethlehem.* New York: Noonday Press.

———. 1990b. *The white album.* New York: Noonday Press.

Emig J. 1971. *The composing processes of twelfth graders.* Urbana, IL: National Council of Teachers of English.

Goldberg, N. 1990. *Wildmind: Living the writer's life.* New York: Bantam.

Himley, M. 1991. *Shared territory.* New York: Oxford University Press.

Mailloux, S. 1989. *Rhetorical power.* Ithaca, NY: Cornell University Press.

Quintilian. 1979. *Institutio oratoria.* Cambridge, MA: Harvard University Press.

Rilke, R. 1962. *Letters to a young poet.* New York: Norton.

Vygotsky, L. 1962. *Thought and language.* Cambridge, MA: MIT Press.

Chapter Five

When Words Fail

"So this is where it all happens," he said.

I remember I was slightly uneasy with the general sense of his words, and as I asked him what he meant, this general uneasiness seemed to be confirmed and amplified. In the fall of 1987, I was new to Syracuse University, excited to be in a new writing program that only the year before had begun to pull away from sole English department affiliation, though it still continued to be staffed by people directly connected to the English department in one way or another. This youthful, second-year English masters student was alerting me on one of the first days of class to the fact that word had (already) gotten around that the 613 course tended to be a "hot spot," often the place ("the site," to speak the language of the locals) where otherwise latent or deflected departmental conflicts tended to come out into the open through the concerns, language, and language theory of the graduate students required to take the course. In other words, English 613, the practicum course, was where the fights broke out.

English 613, like most courses of its type, was (and at this moment still is, though proposals last year were put forward to change this) the only graduate course required of all students regardless of their theoretical proclivities, no matter their scholarly "project," if they desired for whatever reasons—and the reasons often had more to do with making enough money to survive to continue to do the graduate work for which they came to Syracuse in the first place to do—to teach one of the university-required composition courses. Unlike any other faculty on campus, it seems to be the fate of the compositionists to teach, even at the graduate level, only required courses.

Although they would come into class complaining about their undergraduates complaining about having to take a required course that didn't directly contribute to their major, the graduate teaching assistants in 613 frequently conveyed to me by thought, word, and deed their miffedness at having to take this composition teaching practicum course. Usually their discomfort was subtly expressed, but sometimes I inadvertently brought out this voice when I naively assumed that this course was like any other English graduate course since it was worth the identical three credit hours and therefore should have at least a little substance beyond "here's what you do in the next class." I had found in my fourteen years of teaching that theory was the most useful sort of thing that I could study in long run, since theory, the way I thought of it, generated among other things ideas about what I might do in class. I thought that the students at Syracuse would be receptive to the idea that theory could help the writing teacher think through curriculum. I also believed that a framework of theory existed regardless of whether a teacher believed that theory existed or was important. To paraphrase from another universe of discourse, resistance to theory is theory. The assumption that the world is apparent and that language can in a common sense manner reflect that world directly, publicly, trans-parently, and unproblematically was no less theoretical than current poststructuralist theory out of France.

Thinking that students might find it a text that was both practi-cal, full of uncommon sense, and a text that was at least open to a theoretical reading through Vygotsky and Bakhtin, I ordered and assigned Donald Murray's book A Writer Teaches Writing (second edition) and got as one immediate response a graduate student loudly complaining at the beginning of class that it somehow was not fair that I was expecting them first to buy the book—it was $24.00 for a thin paperback, after all—and then, the gods forbid, to read the thing. My public response—since this was raised as a very loud complaint as part of a public class discussion, was "Do you complain to your other graduate teachers about the price of the books they require for their courses?" And I promised to buy several additional copies myself and place them on reserve in the library for graduate students who couldn't—or wouldn't—buy a copy of the book.

The graduate students were already being overwhelmed with coursework and reading, and now this teaching stuff. Crazy Zebroski actually expected them additionally to read books and write papers for 613? Didn't he know that this course was supposed to be the "easy" three hours you get for taking on the dirty job of teaching composition to lowly, if not surly, freshpeople, for crying out loud?

And on top of this, the whole writing curriculum was being re-worked so he won't even tell us what it is we are supposed to be doing. (My feeling about the latter was that if I had told the TAs precisely what to do that wouldn't have made them in the least bit happier.)

We used to come in twice a week, on Tuesday and Thursday mornings, twenty-seven of them and two of us. Denise, an experienced instructor and a Ph.D. in the Writing Program, joined us throughout the semester, agreeing to sit in and help me, and the class as resource person and consultant. She proved to be a helpful coteacher and course confidant who more than anyone or anything else made the composition practicum a good experience for me. This was my first experience with coteaching, which within a few years would become one of the hallmarks of the Syracuse program.

We sat in a very big circle and talked about writing and teaching writing for an hour and a half. We met in a room in an old gymnasium that was being renovated throughout the entire semester, and so it was not unusual for our talks to be interrupted by the pounding or sawing or sandblasting of the construction workers who were scaling the outside of Archbold or invading the corridors within. Everything seemed to be under construction, and there was always pounding of some sort going on. The room also had heating and cooling problems and very high ceilings so it seemed always to be either too hot or too cold and very difficult to hear anyone in there.

What I learned over the next fifteen weeks was that the very word that I brought as a peace offering, as a kind of gift to the graduate student teachers, the word "theory," turned out to be precisely one of the spots where institutional conflicts focused. From the outside of the college, the well-known school of public communication ran articles in the school newspaper questioning the whole direction that the new writing program, which that term was just instituting the first freshman writing studio, appeared to be taking. The very idea of theory seemed repugnant to some persons over there, if the tone and inaccuracies of the articles meant anything. But this was the least of my problems that semester.

There were at this time still a large number of graduate students who had come to Syracuse thinking they would do traditional literature study in a New Critical key. After a short time, it become obvious to them that the English Department itself was turning toward theory of various stripes and they were none too happy about that. And now here they came into the Writing Program and were getting, it must have seemed to them, more of the same. Out of twenty-seven students, four or five were traditionalists who would have made E.D. Hirsch proud. For these traditionalists theory was a denial of the very things they believed in. Theory of any sort meant the world could not be fit into the nice neat categories and simple but powerful narratives that they had committed themselves to. These people often fervently believed in and brought into the classroom the story of the Fall from Grace of English studies. The story went something like this:

Once upon a time there was a Golden Age. For English study this was back in the forties or fifties—back there somewhere—when refined gentlemen and ladies decided to give up their lives to the study of humanities to enrich themselves, their students, and the masses. During this Golden Age, English departments supported this mission and these missionaries. English professors didn't put up with any of this theory nonsense. They spent their time in class wisely. They went over the true classics and the students learned through a close reading how wonderful these works truly were, and how much the general, ignorant public, including our dear students, needed these works for their spiritual salvation. Then the snake appeared in the Garden. (There was a certain vagueness—as there always is, always has to be, in such narratives—about the snake's identity. Some name the snake as Northrop Frye; others, the permissive reader responders; still others, those terrible tenured radicals left over from the sixties.) At any rate, the snake entered the Garden and offered the fruit of theory, which some poor, deluded souls took up. Now all the world has gone down the tube in response. There is no agreement, not only on interpretations of the great works, but even on what the great works are. English departments have lost their way in the wilderness of theory at the very time when our poor freshman can't read or write a line. The blind are leading the blind.

Obviously, when my traditionalist students heard me say "theory," they were not appreciative. One traditionalist reminded me very early on that the college catalogue described English 613 as a course in the teaching of composition and literature, with the stress on literature. In response, I emphasized they were teaching writing, not literature courses, and that the university had just that previous spring approved the new writing studios that made composition the basis for a four-year studio curriculum. Mostly, though, I stayed clear of these students because they scared me. They were angry. Nothing I might say could be heard. So we tended to put up with each other, and I saw that my major task for this group was to prevent them from doing too much harm to their freshmen.

But the 613 course also had some highly developed poststructural theorists in it. These people fell out into various factions. There was a strong group of post-Althusserian Marxists who were active in a Marxist study group for graduate students and others on cam-

pus. The post-Althusserian Marxists used the poststructuralist decentering of the subject (the questioning of the existence of a self
and a subjectivity apart from language, culture, and the subject
positions of race, class, gender, and sexualities) as a tool for doing
ideology critique, that is, revealing the bourgeois humanist discourses that enmesh what we too often uncritically take to be empirically given reality, that is, the ideological production of
subjectivity and positionality in a class society, that is, they tried to
show the rest of us mere mortals how asleep we were and how we
might wake from our dogmatic slumbers and get on with the business (so to speak) of changing the world by changing the subject,
even (gasp) do the work of revolution (this was two years before the
"revolutions" in Eastern Europe, not to mention five years before the
disappearance of the Soviet Union). There were about four of these
sort of people in class and they were very difficult to talk with
because as soon as you said something, if it wasn't in *their* language,
they would critique it. I knew a thing or two about Marxism when
I came into 613, having taken graduate courses on it, read widely in
it, and written a dissertation on the theory of Lev Vygotsky who
lived in a communist society and agreed with many socialist principles. But nothing had prepared me for the sort of activity I got from
my post-Althusserian Marxists. They refused to budge out of their
language and still made it clear how foolish many of the rest of us
were to believe what we did about writing and reading. My major
goal with this group was to read up, to try to learn the lingo, and
then show how much I thought we had in common (which it turned
out, we probably didn't).

But there were other high theory types beside the Marxists. Two
or three people took up deconstruction as practiced by Derrida and
then taken up by the Yale critics. They were far less concerned with
what to do the next day in the classroom since they seemed to be
far less concerned about classrooms generally. There were some
smart people in this group and many of them went on to doctoral
work. I generally had fewer worries about these theorists than the
others because I thought that at worst they were probably teaching
writing the way it had been taught to them. And as it turned out,
some got quite involved in using the changes in the structure of the
writing curriculum to try out some exciting and innovative things
in the classroom. Eventually, one student put together a superb
Studio I freshman course on "Self and Identity," and another went
on to compose the definitive sophomore Studio II course on rhetoric
and discourse communities. During the fall of 1987, I saw these folk
as allies. We seemed to agree that theory was of value and we
seemed to see some connection between it and the writing class-

room. I believed at that time that we could respect each other's theoretical differences and even learn from each other. I did not realize that these theorists too had taken up poststructuralist language and that unless I took it up, there would be little room for accommodation. However, this insight didn't occur to me for three or four years, and I tried during 613 to persuade these students of the value of composition theory. I tried to introduce them to the scholars in composition who had meant so much to me, as well as the whole school of Russian psychology, which I believed could counter the excesses of French theory, since Russian language theory comes out of a historically related, but very different theoretical tradition. Here too I was mistaken.

The next to last of the factions that crossed the 613 practicum were the creative writers. There were about seven creative writing students who themselves, I soon discovered, subdivided into poetry creative writers versus fiction creative writers. Although we disagreed about theory—they were against it; I mean what is more important to the idea of creative writing than the creating self—I got along with the creative writing students because I respected their feel for language. It always seemed to me that what they *did* with language was often the perfect argument *for* theory about language, though they didn't see it that way. Many didn't know much about theory, but had heard about it and were suspicious. And creative writing students always felt that their real reason for being at S.U. was to work at *their* craft and viewed theory, like the Writing Program, as one more set of distractions from their work. In the classroom these students if they got interested in teaching often turned into fine teachers, some of the best in the program. But then if they got too interested in their teaching of writing they were unable to find time and energy to do their own writing, and ended delaying their own degree, a rather draconian sort of tradeoff to my way of thinking, but one implied by institutional structures and demands regardless of what any chair or director or adviser might say to the contrary.

Finally, there were the undecideds, the seven people or so who either could not or would not ally themselves with any one faction, or who would move from faction to faction. These folk had some interest in teaching, but they were generally quiet and seemed to have other outside interests of more importance. The reality is that there was not a single person in the whole class who had even the slightest interest in composition, or even rhetoric, for itself. And here I was trying to persuade the class not only that composition was a legitimate academic enterprise, but that composition theory had an important role to play in the development of our undergraduate writing studio courses.

Words were beginning to fail. We did a great deal of talking in that class, both in the large circle and later in small groups and in individual conferences, but unlike almost any other situation that I could recall, I felt that the more we talked and "clarified" what we meant, the farther away from each other we got. There were simply very few things we had in common. I had thought that theory might be one of them, but there were very few moments when we even shared the same language let alone a common purpose when it came to the concept of theory. Volosinov, in his helpful book *Marxism and the Philosophy of Language,* (1986) gives an account of this sort of situation. He argues that

> . . . the word is the most significant index of social changes, and what is more, of changes still in the process of growth, still without definitive shape and not as yet accommodated into already regularized and fully defined ideological systems . . . the word has the capacity to register all the transitory, delicate, momentary phases of social change. (19)

There were many words like "theory" that were floating around in that 613 and had the same problematic status, that were markers of "transitory social change." These were words no amount of discussion could negotiate since the words came out of different worldviews and differing, if not opposed, universes of discourse. Among them were "studio," "creativity," "self" and "subject" and "subjectivity," not to mention the words the Writing Program was taking up and that were attacked from all theoretical factions, words like "reflection," "contrastive rhetoric," "discourse community." (Later in this volume in my essay "Keywords of Composition: A Discipline's Search for 'Self'" I provide a more detailed account of these historical processes and examine some of the rhetorical effects of the fights we had over words.) We spent a huge amount of time talking about language and the issue of "jargon" (another keyword) and whether there was such a thing and whether "theory" and the theory advocates in the English department and the Writing Program were using and sanctioning it. But so much of our talk depended on "theory" and "theory" disputes, that that in my view would have to be seen as the major keyword of the course.

At the time as I have already noted, I was enthusiastic about theory of all sorts. While not a poststructuralist, I had been reading deeply in poststructuralist theory since 1982. I was self taught in it, and while acknowledging deep differences between Vygotskian (or Russian or Soviet) theory and mostly French poststructuralist theory, nevertheless was sympathetic to it. Both forms of theory shared a common critique of common-sense propositions about language and subjectivity and community. My sense of "theory" is captured in the preface I wrote in a "Suggested Five Week Syllabus" composed the May before for the program document *Studio 1: Working Papers from the Curriculum Group*. I had come up to Syracuse after my academic year in Pennsylvania was over to work with this dynamic group of part-time instructors and teaching assistants who were excited about the program-wide institution of the freshman studio course. This group of teachers put together a book of possible studio courses. Pilots had been run during the spring of 1987, but it was the very autumn that my 613 students and I came into the Writing Program that everyone was going to change over to the new course. In this curriculum document, which was more a collection of descriptions of the many options (in course design, readings, textbooks, writing assignments) teachers might choose from when putting together their first studio course rather than a single, prescribed syllabus, I described my view of "theory":

> My version of this syllabus begins with some ideas about students and literacy that are different from those more traditional freshman composition courses have begun with. I believe that undergraduates are capable of learning to write well by frequent reflection upon their own theories of the world and literacy. Students know more than they know they know—they are very capable, given a supportive and encouraging environment, of making insightful, original observations about their world. (22)

In the week-by-week plan of assignments which asked students do short reflections on their experiences with literacy I elaborated a bit more more on "theory" as I saw it.

> Introduction to course, to this approach, to course requirements OR " How this course will be unlike any English course you have taken before." It seems important to stress that students know quite a lot already, that they have a *theory* (a vision) of what literacy is all about, that the course is primarily a way for them to refine, elaborate, and recreate this "theory" of reading/ writing. (22)

There is a conflict between two theories of theory here. I suppose I wanted to be able to use "theory" in both senses, though neither of these uses of theory were acceptable to poststructuralists. Both passages shift between theory as activity, that is, theory as the reflective process, as a reflection on experience and on action, versus theory as the sum total of those experiences, conscious as well as unconscious, that present the student with her or his stance or view or position. My composition course might said to be theoretical in that I ask students to reflect in their writing assignments about things they have read before or assignments they have written or out of school reading and writing that they have done for its own sake. The course might also be said to be theoretical, however, because the subject matter is the deeper, mostly unconscious discourses (specifically, knowledge of language) that until the course (or education generally) tend to go unnoticed. Students then *do* theory (reflect on literacy practices) and they *have,* compose, and revise theory (they come into the classroom with an already sophisticated set of understandings of literacy).

Throughout, my view of theory is binary. There are deep structures (though I never did, or would have ever wanted to, use that term) and there are surface structures. Reading and writing practices, what we *do,* is in one sense a surface manifestation of deeper knowledge. Knowledge is always more than the behavior. It arises from our action but also from our reflection on our action. In this view, a composition course brings to the surface the deeper "knowledge" for reflection. Students use seemingly empirical methods like ethnographic writing not so much to discover and present the real world that sits statically "out there," but rather to spur on and to stimulate the recovery of some part of these deeper structures, their theory, which is obviously related to, is part and parcel of, the culture(s) the student is a part of. So "theory" the way I was using it at this time is ambiguous. In one sense it is the deep stuff, both the deeper cultural and individual processes, at work in our everyday life. But in another sense, theory is more a translating device that allows the student to move from surface structures (everyday practices and views of them) to deep structures (the theory of literacy that generates possible practices) and then back to transformed surface structures (new abilities to write and read). Reflection is a key, though not the only, theoretical practice that takes what we do, which tends to be fragmented and seemingly chaotic, and translates, or rewrites, these practices into a more sensible version of what we have done. This movement itself subsequently helps us to conceive of and create new practices. Then reflection (and theory) mediates the deep, more comprehensive experiences of life and the practices themselves. Theory is the accounting for surface structures in terms of posited, deep structures, which are themselves never directly and completely available but which reflection usefully suggests.

So at the start of a theoretically-based composition course I might ask students to write short pieces at various times on several theoretical issues, among them "What is your 'theory' of writing?" "What is good writing?" What do good writers do?" and "What is good writing for?" As an example, let's say that a student wrote that "good writing" is writing that is clear, correct, and easy to read. It is writing in which the reader gets the ideas that the writer had in mind to transfer. Then I might ask the student to reflect on her or his own reading and writing experiences. I might also provide selections for the student to read that have to do with reading and writing. I also might ask the student to do some interviewing of people about literacy issues. After this I ask the student to reflect in writing about the writing that had the most dramatic effect on her or him. Perhaps the student thinks about this and writes a reflective essay saying that the Bible had been a very important text in her or his life. Now I might ask the student to compare the earlier account of language with the later account of her or his experience. There seems to be a tension between these two views. Even the most fundamentalist Christian or the most orthodox Jew would admit that the Bible is hardly a clear, direct, simple text, at least not in the same way that a telephone book is. Is a telephone book a clear, direct, simple piece of good writing that people can immediately understand? It would appear so. Then according to the early account of good writing, the telephone book must be a superior form of writing. Well no, that's different. Then what are the differences? And how can you rewrite your view of what good writing is to include what you see as good, even great writing, like the Bible? And finally, after having for a time figured this out in view of the other class members figuring their theory out in view of other writers (who we read in class) figuring their views out, how might this change what you *do* when you write your next long paper in here? Theory in this sort of course was a means for bringing the unconscious to consciousness. Theory was a word reflecting on action for transformation of both. Theory seemed both the view the student starts and ends with, as well as the activity of looking back (and forth) at these experiences and processes in a critical and synthetic manner.

This is an oversimplified example. Classroom practice always went along in much more ad hoc, nonlinear, periodic ways. After all, learning is not simply following the syllogism of life. But from this example we can see that my use of theory was plural, referring to both the activity of reflecting on action with the purpose of transforming future activity and the deeper processes or view or stance that underwrote action. Theory was simultaneously the object we aimed for (deep structures) and the device we aimed at it (reflection or theorizing discourses),both deep process and mediating device. It was also constructivist in that I assumed students always already had (a) theory when they came into the classroom on the first day and that they could, given a supportive context (re)shape this theory in sight of each other in the classroom community and that this would in the longer run influence how they wrote. The point is that in the context of 613, the vagueness (even contradictions) and plurality in my uses of theory were not simply seen as gaps or potentials for future rethinking and reworking, but were viewed as easy prey for the poststructuralist graduate student to swoop in and critique the hell out of. My 613 students were generally kind souls so it didn't get as bad as it could have. I hadn't anticipated that I would be having to rely on the kindness of strangers. At the very least, I was very anxious throughout much of the 613 class; we spent much of the semester discovering that we were unable to meet over the word "theory" since the way I was using it was simply in another universe of discourse from the theory of my graduate students.

This was amply confirmed when Andy, one of the postalthusserian Marxists, decided to read and critique James Moffett's *Teaching the Universe of Discourse* for the midterm writing assignment I gave in 613, after the syllabi for the writing studios had been composed and the initial anxiety about teaching had for the most part (if temporarily) been replaced with the joy and excitement of the teaching honeymoon of the first several weeks. I had asked students to pick a single book from the field of Composition, read it and write a short book review of it. I thought this would get them reading in my field and restore some of my authority in the process, as well as provide me with a sample of their writing and a sense of theoretical position, perhaps suggesting where they might go in designing the writing studios that they were going to teach next term. Andy took up Moffett with a vengeance, and had an easy time dismissing the text because it seemed so hopelessly naive about subjectivity and subject positions. Moffett starts with a self at the center of concentric circles of a universe of discourse and that was a red flag for this student. It wasn't that I wanted students to bow down in front of Moffett's book or any other authority. I had myself in the first chapter of my dissertation critiqued Moffett's theory on a number of scores, some similar to Andy's. But I believed that critique needs to come from within, after one has entered the discursive universe of the work, after one has, to use what no doubt would be seen as a retrograde phrase, willingly suspended one's disbelief. Andy's review had convinced me that he had not first taken Moffett's book on its own terms; it was more an attack than a critique. Andy not only had missed the whole point of Moffett's theory, but he ignored the historical context out of which Moffett's work came and the sort of institutional resistance in the classroom that it suggested, strange things for a self-proclaimed Marxist to do. The student appeared to learn little from this assignment unless it was how simple-minded composition theory seemed to be. I was further convinced that my student hadn't a clue about what I was saying, let alone what his students might be saying. And here we were, people of words, people who studied language, language people. Still words had failed.

One other incident comes to mind. Ben also happened to be a poststructuralist Marxist. He was extremely articulate and generally well liked. He was mostly quiet during class discussions, but when he talked had very specific and clearly worked out points to make. During the course, I individually discussed with students their syllabus, discovering in the process that Ben had his students do two papers during the entire semester. He had students present the papers in seminar and they discussed their readings of very theoretical work. I was aghast. I had repeatedly stressed, I had thought, that a writing course ought to have students doing a good deal of writing, and here was Ben teaching a freshman seminar on textuality, focusing primarily on reading rather than writing. It was hardly a course let alone a studio in writing. Ben conferenced with me, and though I can't recall, I must have said something about this, because I discovered in that conference that Ben simply didn't know what else to do in his class. He pretty much did to his students what was done to him in the courses he was taking. I discovered that the problem was that as intelligent as Ben was in in textual studies, poststructuralist theory, and ideology critique, he had no idea of invention or even a simple notion of "prewriting," let alone of the writing process, which it turned out the field of Composition and the full time faculty at Syracuse were in the middle of critiquing as oversimplified and romantic. I quickly gave Ben a crash course in a few of the dozens of things he might have students usefully do before they turned to a final draft or its revision. I also gave him a rundown of "process" that was more simple than those accounts appearing in the any of the textbooks that I had rejected and that my freshman students had years before surpassed. He seemed truly interested and appreciative. Here my colleagues were bashing process theory daily as antiquated, intent on substituting some version of academic discourse and discourse communities in its place, and my graduate students hadn't a clue of what process was let alone of what one might do in a writing class besides read and write a couple of papers in response to the reading. I had been doing the same thing to my graduate students as they had been doing to their freshman—ignoring their development.

Words had failed. And the more we studied and discussed "theory" of any sort at all in 613, the more we displaced engagement with classroom practices. To raise the word theory meant that we never encountered composing (let alone Composition) on its own terms. We got farther and farther away from the classroom and teaching.

No doubt this is the place where some readers will be gleefully anticipating my bashing of "theory" both in and out of the 613 type of course. I hate to disappoint, but this isn't really the moral of this story. Theory is here. To ignore it or to fight it is only to increase its power. This narrative shows the limitations of my beginning with theory with my graduate students. I assumed that they could come together under the sign of theory. They couldn't. We had very different conceptions of the work of theory. We spoke mutually exclusive languages. I have no question about the good intentions of my graduate students in this course. What I do have a question about is whether focusing on theory first and foremost was useful. We could not come together under the sign of theory, but the attempt to try provided the youthful deconstructionists with fodder for their critique mill and distracted us from those few common experiences that we did share. We were all new to the Writing Program, many of us were new to Syracuse. Almost all of my 613 students had very little, if any, teaching experience and they had few strategies for generating and shaping teaching practices in an actual classroom with real students. By focusing so much on theory, we made little time for teaching practices. This in turn forced graduate students to rely on what they already knew, to model themselves after teachers that they could recall. These teachers had been product centered, if they were concerned with writing at all. The graduate students without specific instruction immediately resorted to these understandings and practices regardless of their theoretical proclivities.

It isn't an accident that the Marxist students, while they paid lip service to the idea of history and revolution, were among the most product-centered teachers of all, hardly possessing any notion of the historicity of writing or of their teaching, resorting to having students do a great deal of reading because they didn't have any idea of what else one might do in a writing class aside from write a paper or two in response to the readings, an approach to composition not unlike the one taken by my freshman composition teachers in 1970. For all their talk about ideology, the Marxist students were reproducing one of the most venerable and elitist traditions in the English department. They were resisting writing in modes that differed hardly at all from the late New Critics who taught me composition. Their teaching of composition functioned to reproduce the hegemony of English department structures. My graduate students, regardless of where the field of Composition might presently be, needed to be educated in writing as a process just to familiarize themselves with practices that compositionists, in similar straits in the late sixties and early seventies, had already worked out. My most up-to-date theorist or my most "with it" creative writer was twenty years behind in the sort of practices he or she could imagine bringing into the composition classroom.

"Theory" failed because it took us away from what we needed to do early in the course, which was to engage these graduate students in the very practices and processes that we were asking them to have their undergraduate students to do. It didn't occur to me until much later how ironic it was to be telling TAs that having their freshmen do peer readings of each others' drafts was of great value in producing, over the long run, better final drafts of papers as well as a stronger sense of class community, when my graduate students themselves had never done "peer response," or if they had, they were even more hesitant and suspicious about it than were their students. How strange to be advocating more invention in the freshman course when my graduate students had never had any experience with invention in their entire academic careers. How bizarre to be touting the values of reflection in our curriculum when the graduate students had never written any reflective writing for themselves for their own courses. In one way, the graduate students were far worse off than any undergraduates because they were less open to any new idea of what literacy might entail. They were sure they already knew. It had worked for them hadn't it? That knowledge, of course, was a product of their own elite educations and positions in society. Still, they were far less open to persuasion and reason than the narrowest undergrad. There was simply too much they would have to bracket if not unlearn. Meeting over theory didn't encourage them to do this bracketing, let alone the unlearning, rather it simply gave them an opportunity to do more of what they were already doing and were quite good at doing: engaging in rather traditional practices of literary and textual study.

Despite all of their education in textual studies, my 613 students were still basically working out of a model of teaching that stresses meaning rather than value, that emphasizes products rather than process. When I imagined that 613 might be a site where we could negotiate the concept and rhetoric of theory in order to rework our teaching practices, I too was falling into the same trap. Basically, both my students and I were starting from a model of teaching which everyone in class whether creative writer, compositionist, or post-Marxist would never dream of accepting as any kind of halfway interesting (let alone useful) account of language. The meaning-centered model of teaching we accepted begins from the idea that teaching is most immediately about getting students to share, represent, and reconstruct the *same* meanings as the teacher, at least at the start. We focused on "understanding" and bringing the student around in part to our level of understanding. Our understandings differed radically—from a cognitive or textual or ideological practice implied by theory to an experiential practice implied by creative writing—but as incommensurate as they might otherwise be, they were still understandings that we wanted the students to get and to be able to enact. We taught in order to get our students to understand and apply the concepts, attitudes, and behaviors that we, as representatives of institutions and the culture generally, possess and that our students need. This model works from a notion of the transparency of learning that these days would be unthinkable if applied to language. As if students given the proper motivation could even understand (directly, immediately) what we were talking about, let alone transfer an identical version of it to their worlds. We were beginning from similarity, from *sameness* in the classroom, rather than starting from *differents* and *difference(s)*.

Teaching and learning are far more complicated than this sender-receiver, meaning-centered model suggests. Words in this model never fail or if they do fail, something is wrong. Words that fail are supposedly the exception, the anomaly, the strange case. If students "get" the wrong idea or perform the inappropriate behavior or misread a text or their own experience, or produce cliche ridden, generalizing writing, then we as teachers have failed or the students haven't tried hard enough, but we never think that the words have failed, in fact must fail. This creates for the new teacher who experiences this failure on an almost daily basis a great deal of anxiety, which further pushes the novice toward simplistic solutions that are often more oppressive, if not fascist, than the instruction the graduate student received when she or he was an undergraduate. So it is not unusual for the new graduate student teaching assistant to come into the classroom enthusiastic about language study and after receiving the first sets of formal papers to be shocked. The teaching assistant had been so clear about what he or she had wanted and the students had seemed so good intentioned and enthusiastic about trying to do these things. So what went wrong? Why these awful papers? The TAs concluded: Either I must be a bad teacher or these must be bad students. Either I have failed or they have failed. I better get more rigorous, get tough, show how important the standards are.

This typically is the end of the honeymoon that the new teacher had initially experienced. How the novice teacher responds at this moment is crucial in setting up the cycle for the rest of the course. Too often working from the meaning-centered model, which puts failure on people rather than seeing words as weak vessels, the teacher hands out low grades and offers negative criticism to assert personal authority. My point is, this reaction comes out of a model that assumes that if meaning hasn't been reproduced, significant learning has not taken place.

But what if we begin from a different perspective that centers on the basic incommunicability of the learning event, that focuses on "meaninglessness" in the same way that current theory focuses on the indeterminacy of the text? What if we shift from a meaning-centered model to a value-centered model of learning?

A value-centered model of learning might begin with the existential act of learning, and life, and the inability of words to ever capture or communicate that act, but also the responsibility to use words to try. Something goes on when I teach and that something is important, valuable, even sacred. But when I insist on putting all of that event into words, I reduce and lose it. At best I create a fiction of life, a figment, a phantom of it. Most of the time, words do fail. Misunderstanding or lack of shared meaning is not the strange case, but the rule, in the same way that misreading is our only way to begin to read a text. We can never truly understand what the other is saying. At best we can sense some tiny atom of it. Temporarily. But that is far less important than that we value it as the word of the other. We can value what the other is saying even if, perhaps only because, we cannot possess it. We begin from differents and difference.

In valuing the other and what the other has to say even when we have no idea what it means, we can begin to build our own meanings, which in turn the other person values and responds to with a parallel set of constructions. Value creates meaning when it exists; but value doesn't need meaning to exist. It is precisely because words fail that we have the best reason to continue speaking and writing them. It is because I value the existential moment of my teaching and the existential being of my students that I continue to use words. Experienced teachers who after many years still love their teaching know all of this already. They know that what happens in the classroom in students is a great mystery. They are skeptical about their own powers to know with certainty. They believe that something does happen somewhere in teaching, but what, precisely, we can never be sure. This uncertainty principle doesn't in the least diminish the value, the joy, and the pain of teaching. The teacher doesn't have to know precisely what is going on to be effective because the experienced teacher knows that more than knowledge, behavior, attitudes—that is, meanings—passes between teacher and student. William Barrett wrote about this sort of knowledge as opposed to the knowledge that relies totally on reason (and meaning).

> Biblical man too had his *knowledge,* though it is not the intellectual knowledge of the Greek. It is not the kind of knowledge that man can have through reason alone, or perhaps through reason at all; he has it rather through body and blood, bones and bowels, through trust and anger and confusion and love and fear; through his passionate adhesion in faith to the Being whom he can never intellectually know. This kind of knowledge a man has only through living, not through reasoning, and perhaps in the end he cannot ever say what it is he knows, yet it is knowledge all the same . . . . (79)

Or to put it more concretely, ". . . existence and a theory of existence are not one and the same, any more than a printed menu is as effective a form of nourishment as an actual meal" (158). We had been consuming the menu instead of eating the meal in my 613 course!

So how will I teach the graduate student teaching practicum differently the next time? Obviously what I have been saying about teaching for value rather than meaning alone does not translate readily into new content or form in the 613 course. I could use the identical assignments that I used the first time I taught the course and teaching for value would not change these aspects of the course. Most of all, my reflection on teaching the 613 practicum course would influence my attitude. Attitude in large measure determines course content and form, and attitude determines the graduate student teaching practicum more than any other course. I hope that I would be less worried about the graduate students "getting" content, coming together over some mere concept like "theory." I hope that I would be less hard on, more gentle and patient with myself. I am a good teacher. On occasion in the midst of teaching, I need to say that out loud, post it on an index card on my bathroom mirror, shout it from the proverbial rooftops. Though it is most difficult, I need to retain my sense of humor, try to be patient, remain calm throughout. It does not accomplish anything if I get bent out of shape and overly anxious, and I do believe that perhaps the most important thing, maybe the only thing, that I can do is to present a role model of the scholar teacher to my graduate students. At least this would be my personal goal in teaching 613 this time around. If in some complex way, I truly teach my self, if the course is me, then the best thing I can do is work on my self and the self's presentation. I have always been attracted to Quintilian (that wily old master teacher) and his theory that a good rhetor (for me, the good writer/ teacher) is, or at least tries to be, first a good person, and only then one who writes well.

Teaching and writing have always been intertwined for me in some complicated way. I can remember vividly being in third grade and "playing school," playing the role of teacher to my sisters' rendition of students, writing out lesson plans and grades. I was very impressed with those secret texts that my elementary school teachers possessed and wrote in—the lesson plan books and grade books, often light green in color, with imitation leather binding. Secret texts of which there was only one copy, a copy never seen by the individual student but omnipresent, always lying on the teacher's desk. Empty books that by the end of the school year were full of Mrs. Greenwood's and Mrs. Gilligan's very own writing. When I played school, I carefully made my own versions of these sacred vessels of the liturgy of teaching. I can also remember writing in chapter installments a mystery "novel" for my seventh-grade busmates to read on our on our ride to Howland Junior High School. Just recently I rediscovered *The Mystical Island,* written in the winter of 1965, featuring a detective named Michael Mahoney, who was a writer for the Chicago Tribune Chronicle, and who was sent by his editor Mr. Whitmore to Honolulu to find out about another reporter who had mysteriously, abruptly disappeared. School and writing, writing and school, a strange and long-running interrelation. School has always been for me the place where I can write and value writing. And writing has always been my real education in the world. So like it or not, this is what I teach—for this I came—what I do is me. This is the attitude that I need to sustain and model for my graduate students, the attitude of a person who twenty years after he began this odyssey, still enjoys what he does for a living.

Out of this attitude, if I can sustain it, comes everything else that is presently important to me: a valuing, preservation, and celebration of difference, a valuing of my students at all their varied zones of development, an appreciation of writing practices and writing theory, a curiosity about the world, an energy that is sensed by my students. Teaching is less about passing on some ideas and practices that I value than about valuing and in that valuing, generating an energy that students sense, that pushes them to generate their own energies. Like Socrates, I believe that I teach a puzzlement, an inquisitiveness about life that I infect my students with and the consequences of which I know not, though I do know, not simply believe, that there are consequences. Beyond value and attitude, however, there are other lessons I have learned about teaching the graduate practicum course. Let me list some of things I would do differently next time around.

Begin With Practices

I would begin with the reading and writing practices that I would be asking the graduate students to be trying out with their own writing studio students. We would read some of the same articles and do some of the same writing assignments. For example, I often ask my freshman to write a short literacy autobiography in which they reflect on their experiences with the written word and recall formative experiences with it. These experiences can be good or bad, and they can be culled from early or later, school or nonschool experiences. If I were to use this assignment with my undergraduate students, I would also ask my graduate students to do their version of this. (See one short draft that I wrote of this assignment that I have included in the first essay in this section, "Creating the Introductory College Composition Course.") We would also go through all the steps in the process for at least one writing assignment— drafting, discussion, reading similar accounts of literacy that other writers have produced, individual conferences with the teacher, redrafting, bringing in drafts for written peer evaluation, putting together a final draft, publishing it in a class magazine, and then the teacher writing comments about each essay. The class might then read and discuss this class booklet as a whole and write something about that. It's a cycle of assignments that I use in my undergraduate writing courses, and it's a cycle that I would transfer to the first third of the graduate practicum.

Get Them Writing and Keep Them Writing

I would not want my graduate students to do *all* the assignments that they give to their freshman, but I do think it important to run through early in the course at least one sequence of assignments. Aside from that, it now seems very important to me to get and keep the graduate students writing. The best teacher of the writing teacher is the writing activity. I am not sure how I would implement this, though I am leaning strongly to requiring my graduate students keep journals and to do some study of writing process, by looking at textbooks (see the "The World(view) in the Text(book) Essay" that I assign in my advanced writing course and have included in that essay). I would also like students to read up on process theory, perhaps doing a short interview with a practicing writer. As noted above, this is less because I am advocating a "process" approach in and of itself, than because this is a part of the history of the field they are entering and it is a part of this history because process offered some practical teaching strategies, which in my judgment can often be adapted to a more social approach to teaching writing.

Focus on Teacher Commentary

The writing that teachers do most is marginalia and end commenting on student texts. I would make an early and important place for discussing this activity and for offering strategies for commenting. Most importantly, early in the practicum course I would be writing comments on my graduate student papers, hoping they would view these as models of such writing. I also would try out a strategy I have used with my undergraduates in which I write comments on a the right hand side of a separate sheet of paper, coding the comments to specific places in the student text. The only marks on the student text are the letters or numbers that correlate with the comment sheet. On this comment sheet, I *begin* with overall comments that are a paragraph or two long and that deal with broader issues in the paper. I follow these more elaborated discursive comments with briefer, but still fairly elaborated comments of a sentence or two, on the half a dozen or so individual passages that struck me. I write all these comments on one half of the sheet, leaving the left hand side free. Then when I return the student papers, I ask students to read my comments and write their own comments on my comment in the left hand margin. I have gotten some fascinating (and useful) responses when I did this. Obviously I would not feel the need, let alone have the time, to do this with every major paper, but it is a good way to set the tone for what you expect, and to model writing for the students. In addition, it provides feedback on what students understand and value when they read your comments. And it gets the students to read the comments closely, rather than simply turning to the grade or being discouraged by corrections scrawled in tiny print all over the student text. It always seemed to me a bit strange for teachers to be complaining about the restricted code that student writers use to relate their insights (how often have we teachers written things like "Say more," "Expand this," "Elaborate") when many of our comments are even more terse and abbreviated. (The worst case of this is the theme graders who simply use letter abbreviations like "Frag.," "R-O," "Sp." Even this isn't so bad if the teacher does it at the *end* rather the beginning of the term. What does this sort of writing model for the students, especially at the term's start?)

Course Structure

Obviously there are limits to how much I can or need to model for my students. A graduate course doesn't have to model everything or even most of what is done in the introductory course. The students are at different levels of development after all. But there is an inter-relation between the way I would structure the graduate course and the way the undergraduate course is structured. I generally think of semester courses in writing dividing into three or four modules. The first,brief module is introductory and upbeat. It gets students in-volved in activities but also begins building class community by getting the students to know each other by name. This brief begin-ning also acts as a buffer so that latecomers to the course don't miss the first important assignments, a capitulation to the bureaucratic nature of colleges.

I try to move to the second module where the course proper begins as soon as possible. If enrollments are stable, then I move to it immediately. I advocate *frontloading* composition courses at any level, because the rest of the university courses write us. As one of the few courses required of all students, composition begins with problems of motivation which are only exacerbated if we follow the schedule that other faculty tend to follow who *endload* their courses with heavy requirements and weighty grades. If anything, I try to have the major work in my composition courses done or at least well along before the rush starts in the other disciplines. I find I get better results and my students have much better attitudes about my course if I open up my course demands toward the end of the semester, allowing the students to attend to the content courses in which the teacher may be frantically trying to cover material because it is going to be on the final examination. Because at semester's end I require only a final writing assignment, worth as much as any other formal writing assignment, I push the heavy requirements in my course to the front of the course. Students have a lot of time before the first round of midterm examinations and papers arrives so I try to take advantage of that free time early in the semester.

So after the first brief preliminaries, I often plunge my students into demanding reading and writing assignments. In the middle section of the course, I abolish the large class and break up into smaller seminar groups, have students work on panel presentations or research projects, meet with students in individual or small-group conferences. In the final section of the course, students pre-sent their research or the work of the panels to the class as a whole, while continuing at their own speed on final writing assignments for the course. This division into modules and frontloading in the undergraduate course would correspond to the structure in the graduate practicum in which we would (1) enact the reading and writing practices the undergraduates were involved in; (2) shift in the second module to smaller groups who read, research, and discuss theoretical and disciplinary issues as they relate to teaching composition; (3) do group presentations and work on final projects. The Syracuse University Writing Program is in a peculiar situation because Writing Studio II is a required sophomore course on rhetoric that is offered, at the request of faculty in *other* disciplines, during the spring. This makes it necessary for us to prepare graduate students in the practicum course *not only* in teaching the introductory course but also the second, sophomore rhetoric course. Therefore the last third of 613 has to be given up to a discussion of rhetoric and a working on the Writing Studio II syllabi for the spring.

The Question of a Textbook

I am at the point in my teaching that no textbook really does a good job of presenting what I do in my composition courses. And textbooks too often are simplistic, monologic, convention-driven. Unlike fifteen years ago when I began teaching college composition, there are today some good textbooks that reflect some familiarity with developments in the field of Composition. But most authors still feel compelled to include materials that may make the textbooks more saleable but which play little part in what I do in the classroom. When I teach by myself, I do not use textbooks very often. The last time I used a traditional composition textbook in an undergraduate course it was as a focus of critique. It was in the sophomore rhetoric course and I thought I would ask the students to examine the rhetoric of the rhetoric book. For example, we read what the composition textbook writer said good writing was, and then we did an analysis of the textbook writer's style itself, using the criteria set out by that writer for determining good writing. This worked fairly well, but it hardly is the standard use to which the textbook is put.

My experience in requiring graduate students to buy Murray's *A Writer Teaches Writing* for 613 makes me hesitant about trying that again. But it is more complicated than the fact that I generally don't like textbooks and I had a bad experience with the one I required in 613. What message do I send as a graduate teacher when all the other courses my students are taking require not one, but often a dozen texts? To be sure, some of the texts are novels and other literary genres, but many others are theory books. In a department committed to theory, what message do I send if I have no text? or a standard publisher's textbook? or even a nuts and bolts, here's-what-to-do-on-Monday-morning text? And what am I saying about my field and disciplinary specialization? Choosing textbooks, or in this case not choosing them, is a political act, no less than writing articles about the professional status of composition teaching.

I have always been convinced that textbooks are far more important as cultural artifacts, ritual symbols whose rhetorical effects are no less real for that than they are as conveyors of subject matter. I also believe that symbols often comfort and support through difficult times, no matter what they say or how they are used. Textbooks say many things, but among them is the assertion that this is school, this is serious, there is substance to this study, there is value to it, there is some agreement about it. I think I probably would decide to use a common text as well as provide photocopies of articles from NCTE publications, which allow photocopy rights for instructional purposes. One book I would seriously consider using, since it stresses the social dimension of composing, using ethnographic-like activities and includes large numbers of student texts which the authors obviously value, is *Texts and Contexts: A Contribution to the Theory and Practice of Teaching Composition* by Judith Summerfield and Geoffrey Summerfield. Of all the books in the field that talk about teaching writing, this one probably comes closest to what I do. It includes ideas for many pragmatic exercises and class activities and the resulting texts that came from these practices, but it also is a theoretical book in the best sense of presenting these teaching ideas in a sensible and smart way. It is indebted to the theory of James Britton, James Moffett, D. W. Harding, M.A.K. Halliday, and many others scholars whose work I appreciate and feel students should know. Unlike other similar sorts of books, *Texts and Contexts* also includes examples of a variety of writing, including letters, journals, dramas, and poetry. I find this a refreshing and needed counterpoint to the overemphasis that academic discourse has received in some quarters of Composition over the last decade. Not that I want to turn the introductory composition course into a literature-producing or -appreciating course, but because to write well—including writing academic discourse well—we need sophisticated views of language and language processes and this sort of theory tends to be narrowed if we read and study only one sort of similar writing—whether it be only poetry or only academic discourse, so-called.

Writing as Value

I want to conclude by reemphasizing my view that not only should I be more patient with myself when I teach my graduate students, but that my graduate student teachers need to be more patient with themselves when they teach the introductory composition student. We can do this if we take the broader view, if we see our job as professing writing as value. Lev Vygotsky makes the case in psychology for this when he contends that the word (language) plays the central role in the development of thinking and that the word as the child experiences it and the word as the adult experiences are different. Vygotsky argues that this difference, this gap, between the experienced person and the novice, the teacher and student, is precisely what makes meaning possible and makes it develop. In *Thought and Language* Vygotsky gets at the social and individual dialectic process that is at work in the child's development of thinking, but which I would argue is also at work in the student's development of writing.

> The linguistic milieu, with its stable, permanent word meanings, charts the way that the child's generalizations will take. But constrained as it is, the child's thinking proceeds along this preordained path in the manner characteristic of the child's own stage of intellectual development. Adults, through the verbal communication with the child, are able to predetermine the path of the development of generalizations and its final point—a fully formed concept. *But the adult cannot pass onto the child his mode of thinking.* He merely supplies the readymade meanings of words around which the child builds complexes. Such complexes are nothing but pseudoconcepts. They are similar to concepts in appearance, but differ substantially in their essence. (120, emphasis mine)

This passage sorts out the kind of things a composition teacher can and cannot do. The composition teacher can introduce the student to the "linguistic milieu," which itself offers various *relatively* stable meanings (one might call these subject positions and discourses, in light of recent literary theory). The composition teacher can nudge students down the path of generalization and conceptual thought, itself a cultural construct, though the student will proceed in her or his own characteristic manner. The composition teacher can supply words (and texts) around which students can build their own words and texts and minds. But the teacher cannot pass on her or his own mode of thinking. The best she or he can do is create a gap between the teacher's word and the student's word, value and preserve the difference between words, between meanings. The teacher needs to recognize that even when the student seems to share a similar concept, it more often differs substantially from the teacher's concept. And that is okay.

In other words, the teacher cannot have the experience for the student. That does not at all mean that there is no experience, or that it isn't valuable, or that it can't be changed or shaped across time, or that the teacher doesn't have some important role in all of this. Vygotsky argues that learning begins from difference acted upon. He puts forward a view of development that privileges multiple points of view, developmental discontinuities, and multiple representations. He contends that the potential for the deepest learning lies in the widest difference, which is one reason why young children learn so much so quickly, because their minds are so different from those of the reigning adults. Children must constantly value what they do not understand and they must continually make the attempt to translate the strange word and world of the adult into their own. And most importantly, Vygotsky knows that good teachers not only live through this indeterminateness, but thrive on it, "going along" with the students because they value them and their language, and within that "going along" moment, work with the students to transform the whole context. In *The Construction Zone* (1989), Newman, Griffin, and Cole, working explicitly out of Vygotsky's theory to conduct empirical research on how learning occurs for so-called high-ability students, but seems not to occur for so-called low-achieving students (who, not by chance, come from different social groups and linguistic communities than the English-speaking, middle-class, white, high achievers), put this in a way that resonates with my experience teaching the English 613 course.

> Within a ZPD [zone of proximal development], objects do not have a unique analysis. An object such as a poem, a chart, or a spoken concept may be understood very differently by the child and the teacher. Likewise the same speech act may be interpreted quite differently. But these differences need not cause "trouble" for the teacher of the child or the social interaction; the participants can act AS IF their understandings are the same. At first, this systematic vagueness about what the object "really is" may appear to make cognitive analysis impossible. However, it now appears to us that this looseness is just what is needed to allow change to to happen when people of differing analyses interact. (62)

Acting *as if* understandings are the same, even when clearly they are not and can, thankfully, never be the same. "Going along" for the sake of valuing the conversation and the speakers, rather than extracting clear meaning efficiently from the talk. A "systematic vagueness" about what the object "really is," in this case about what "theory" is, a systematic vagueness that none of us intended but which was forced upon us all by the social forces at work in our institution. This describes well my English 613 experience in the autumn of 1987.

For a long time after that course, I regarded it as one of my greatest teaching failures. Yet as the years passed and some of the pain healed, I began to hear things that made me think that this "failure" of words was one of the best teaching experiences I had had and perhaps had been a good experience for my students as well. A friend who went to the Conference on College Composition and Communication, which I had missed that year, returned to tell me about Ben, who had gone on to do doctoral work at another well-regarded university, searching for me at the convention to tell me he now appreciated the 613 course more than he had at the time. But even more astonishing, I was talking with a couple of former 613 students who had gone on into doctoral work in other programs at Syracuse. Somehow the conversation turned to the English 613 course and they remarked on how they still remembered and found interesting an invention model that I, out of guilt for not providing more practices and not giving my literature students a better introduction to composition, had *lectured* the class on. I had almost forgotten my quick, twenty-minute run-through of Young, Becker, and Pike's tagmemic heuristic, but not only had my students remembered it four years later, they remembered it fondly, almost nostalgically, and they remembered it in far more detail than I did, telling me about how I had energetically drawn a set of diagrams on the blackboard—one of a pond, they instructed me—to illustrate the heuristic. Of all the things I had thought at the time—or for years later—that my students might take from my course, this mini-lecture, done almost out of desperation on my part, was not one of them. Words had failed, but learning somewhere, somehow, had happened. Learning had occurred because words had to fail. But that failure was coupled with a valuing of difference and was prefigured in a quote from William Stafford, that I placed, for very different reasons at the time, at the top of the very first handout that I composed for my graduate students. It turned out that I needed to practice this bit of advice on myself: "In matters of writing, we must forgive each other much."

References

Barrett, W. 1962 *Irrational man*. Garden City, NY: Doubleday Anchor.

Moffett, J. 1968. *Teaching the universe of discourse*. Boston: Houghton Mifflin.

Murray, D. 1985. *A writer teaches writing.* Boston: Houghton Mifflin.

Newman, D., P. Griffin, & M. Cole. 1989. *The construction zone: Working for cognitive change.* New York: Cambridge University Press.

Stafford, W. 1979. In *Teaching expository writing,* edited by W. Irmscher. New York: Holt, Rinehard and Winston.

Summerfield, J. & G. Summerfield. 1986. *Texts and contexts.* New York: Random House.

Volosinov, V. 1986. *Marxism and the philosophy of language.* Cambrdige, MA: Harvard University Press.

Zebroski, J. 1987. Suggested five week syllabus. *Studio I: Working papers from the curriculum group.* Syracuse, NY: Syracuse University Writing Program.

Part Two

Composing Text

In the first set of essays, "Composing Context," I have shown how over the last ten years I have thought through teaching composition, composing writing courses from freshman year to the graduate seminar by using certain principles that make sense to me as a teacher, writer, and scholar. In this second set of essays, "Composing Text," I think through the notion of "writing" itself, using concepts derived from Lev Vygotsky's socio-historical theory of mind. This is a heavily theoretical section, though even within these essays I am interested in the consequences Vygotsky's work holds for both theory and practice. I do not see this set of essays as somehow opposed to the first set of practical essays, but rather view the construction of context and the composition of text as interrelated sets of activities having their own relatively independent histories that are somehow "answerable" to each other. To teach writing, I have to experience writing. To experience writing, I have to reflect on writing. The essays in this section try to work through a history of experiencing, teaching, theorizing. What happens then when a person "composes text"?

We can think of writing as a social, historical, functional, and temporal set of processes that occurs at the intersection of text, context, self, and society. Composing text selects and arranges these discursive universes. To compose text, "I"—quotation marks are in order around "I" since it too is a composed text, though one at a differing temporality than the marks on the page—select not simply the words that get marked but also the context, the self, and the society that meets those marks and marks those meetings. Writing is not so much a series of nested discourses, but rather the emptiness, the interstices, the intersection between discourses. Writing never sits still. It is dynamic, its functioning limited only by human convention and imagination. I am trying in this view of composing to avoid defining writing as only the marks on the page, the processes of mind, or the dialect used in discourse communities. I need a conception of writing that has room within it to place the representations of Cro-Magnon people found in the caves at Lascaux, Albert Einstein's equations and connecting commentary found in his 1905 special relativity papers, the watercolor and construction paper cutout done by my four-year-old nephew that I have tacked to the bulletin board in my study, the "diaries" that nineteenth-century farmers kept for themselves on the Michigan and Ohio frontiers described by Marilyn Motz, the letters family members send each other, this book, and the processes that unfold these artifacts. Viewing writing as an intersection of discourses helps me to avoid thinking about writing in dichotomous terms, reducing writing to either external convention or internal cognition.

Lev Vygotsky placed the word at the center of his theory of mind, self, and society, arguing that signifying functions transform what are otherwise elementary psychological responses into the higher psychological functions that compose mind. The word in a literal, material way makes us human. The word, for Vygotsky, is central because it is a mediation and a transformation of social and individual processes. In the word, through the word, all the great questions of mind and consciousness intersect. Vygotsky's theory privileges the moment when thinking and speaking intersect and the child begins to learn to talk. From this point on, consciousness qualitatively changes. Thinking comes more under the influence of speaking; speech becomes more intellectual and intentional. Perhaps the only event that approaches this in importance in its influence on mind is the acquisition of literacy, the appropriation of writing practices. Vygotsky was convinced that writing had a slow but profound effect on mind, on the development of inner speech, on the subsequent transformation of the other higher mental functions. He saw the roots of writing early in childhood when, at three or four, children begin to draw and to act out games through gesture and symbolization. He also saw writing in other cultural practices, like the knot tying of the Incas and other native Americans, in the digital counting practices of Melanesians, in the use of objects to symbolize, in the practice of tying a thread around one's finger to remember.

More than any other psychologist or social scientist, Lev Vygotsky privileges language. His view of language is nuanced, nonreductive, and multi-faceted, reflecting Vygotsky's undergraduate work in the humanities as well as his continued interest in the Russian avant-garde's experiments throughout the postrevolutionary period with language practices (futurist and acmeist poetry, for example) and language theory (Russian formalism, for one). Colleagues in English are often aware of the work of Anna Akhmatova, but know nothing of her 1924 recommendation that fellow writers read a newly published dissertation *The Psychology of Art* written by a young White Russian Jew, Lev Vygotsky. So too literary theorists and creative writers may know of the work of Osip Mandelstam, yet have never heard that Vygotsky so admired Mandelstam's work that he not only included in his later work citations from Mandelstam's poetry when it was clearly dangerous to do so and when Mandelstam himself could not get his work published, but also was a close enough acquaintance that he apparently stopped by Mandelstam's apartment and saw a fair amount of Mandelstam and his wife, Hope, during 1933, no doubt an act that enlarged Vygotsky's file at the state police.

It is curious that Lev Vygtosky has received so little attention outside of a tiny corner of U.S. psycholinguistics. Vygotsky's *Thought and Language* (in strangely edited forms, to be sure) has been available since 1962, and yet the uses to which it has been put in composition are rather disappointing. What makes this even stranger is at this very same time English departments are full of excitement about Freud, Jung, and Lacan, and the discourses of subjectivity. Even Mikhail Bakhtin's work has come into favor among radically different constituencies who otherwise hardly talk to each other. In fact, since Mikhail Bakhtin came out of the same milieu as Vygotsky, it is instructive to compare how quickly Bakhtin's work, once made available in accessible English translations, was lapped up by literary theorists and how slowly by comparison Vygotsky's work has been cited, let alone appropriated. Bakhtin's work has become canonical for poststructuralist theorists of all stripes (from neo-pragmatists to post-Marxists to cryptoformalists). Vygotsky is hardly known. The U.S. psychologists, aside from mavericks like Jerome Bruner, Michael Cole, James Wertsch, and Alex Kozulin, seem to think Vygotsky too "soft," too humanistic; the humanists who know of Vygotsky tend to be bothered by Vygotsky's commitment to intelligent empiricism, his use of experimental data to draw conclusions about mind and its development, as well as by the occasional statement about language, which taken out of context, makes Vygotsky seem naive. But this ambivalence on the part of U.S. scholars toward Vygotsky only parallels a similar, and even more attenuated, history of ambivalence in the former Soviet Union where Vygotsky's work was indexed for twenty years and put to official state uses for another twenty.

I am guided in each of the essays in this section by the principle that it is far more important to understand the *worldview* and the broader theory out of which Vygotsky's view of language and mind comes than it is to cite or even agree with any single statement that Vygotsky makes. Some of Vygotsky's remarks about writing are simply wrong. But he says enough interesting things about writing and his theory or worldview provides a distinctive enough approach to understanding writing even in these days of a poststructuralist theoretical boom that Vygotsky ought to be far better known and appreciated among compositionists, humanists, and social scientists than he is. I have tried in each essay to take up some aspect of Vygotsky's theory and, after understanding its context, use it to think through some facet of writing. Long before compositionists were talking about writing as product or process or as products of discourse communities, Vygotsky had worked through some of these conceptual difficulties. If Vygotsky's work had been fully appreciated in composition ten or twenty years ago, we may well have moved through the interminable debate between the social *versus* the individual view of writing much more quickly and productively.

In the first essay from 1983, "A Vygotskian Theory of Writing," I sketch out four insights of Russian language theory that I use to think through writing. Both the appropriation and the "application" of Vygotsky's theory are "creative" in that I take Vygotsky's insights into text less as scientific laws or even hypotheses (though I sometimes use that word) than as texts about texts (and textuality) that interest me as a teacher and a writer. If we take up Vygotsky's idea that writing is a specific psychological function, no different in kind than perception or memory, and this function is a creation of history, both individual and social, then what might we say about writing? Where does this view take us? How, for example, does my assertion that Vygotsky sees writing as a social relation differ radically from Bartholomae and Petrosky's argument in *Facts, Artifacts, and Counterfacts* that sees ". . . reading and writing as a struggle within and against the languages of academic life . . . [in which] the student has to appropriate or be appropriated by a specialized discourse . . ." (8)? Both views seem "social." Why then does my thinking through Vygotsky's theory of language and writing lead to conclusions and to teaching practices so opposed to those that Bartholomae and Petrosky reach? In this first essay I try to sketch out the landscape of Vygotskian theory that will serve me through the rest of these essays (and the book) as landmarks in my exploration of writing and teaching. This is theory, then, but theory from a teacher's perspective. Vygotsky began his career at a teacher's college and throughout his life saw teaching and curriculum as important enough to allot many books and conference presentations as well as a sizable chunk of his professional time and energy to it, so I feel comfortable in this sort of appropriation.

In the second essay in this section, "Writing as Dialogue (and Quarrel)," I contextualize what I take to be an Eastern European, specifically Bakhtinian, notion of writing and place it beside prominent composition theorists like James Moffett, James Kinneavy, and James Britton. Mikhail Bakhtin's work was just appearing when this essay was written in 1983 and the enthusiasm that I felt (and still feel) about Bakhtin was already being tempered by a sense that no one seemed to notice (except Slavicist Caryl Emerson) that there were important historical and theoretical connections between Vygotsky's work and that of Bakhtin, and further, that there were dangers in picking out a few isolated concepts from either theorist and plopping them down inside a traditional Anglo-American communication model of language that both Vygotsky and Bakhtin critiqued. Keeping categories fluid and the worldview prominent, this essay attempts to argue against the domestication of the "baggy monsters" of Eastern Europe by using Bakhtin (and Vygotsky) to propose a kind of ethno-composing practice in the writing classroom. Here is the more elaborated rationale for the practice I advocate earlier in "Using Ethnographic Writing to Construct Classroom Knowledge." I also try in this essay to avoid the easy intellectual move whereby "dialogue" becomes a warm and fuzzy rationalization for eclectic and pluralistic relativism in the classroom and beyond, by adding that "dialogue" for Bakhtin is often a quarreling, a bickering, and a backbiting activity that is not at all as pleasant or simple (or as trivial as) Kenneth Burke's famous (and middle-class) depiction of history as a parlor game, as chitchat at a cocktail party. Even in 1983 I was starting to feel uncomfortable with the ways Bakhtin was being used (and Vygotsky was being ignored).

In "Vygotsky on Composing: Theoretical Implications" I briefly extend the critique of composition theory begun in "Writing as Dialogue (And Quarrel)" and move it into a discussion of the specific uses to which Vygtosky has been put by the few language scholars who have done more than cite him. I briefly note that Vygotsky's ideas have been reified (and fossilized) when they have been appropriated by scholars such as Ong, Barritt and Kroll, Lunsford, and Gee, and I argue that we need to begin from a dialectic worldview to appreciate the richness and complexity of Vygotsky's formulations. I find Vygotsky unappreciated for his steadfast refusal to reduce the "social" and the "individual" to each other, for his insistent use of the dialectic to talk about process in open, nondeterministic ways, and for his complicated privileging of the "interfunctional system" to discuss psychological activities, rather than hard and fast notions of orality "versus" literacy. I also contend here that Vygotsky was clearer about the limitations of his own theories than we often give him credit for being. I think Vygotsky would be shocked by the uses to which certain cognitivists have put his work to create flow charts of the mind—flow charts that Vygotsky seemed constantly compelled to move away from. For example, Vygotsky in the preface to his final work *Thought and Language* (Plenum edition) says:

> In this book we have attempted to make explicit much that remained implicit in previous work. Still, there is a great deal that we once believed to be correct that has been excluded from this book *because it represented simple delusion on our part.* . . . We are only too aware of of the limitations of this first step we have taken in developing a new approach to the study of the relationship between thinking and speech. (40–41, emphasis mine)

And too:

> Among the most basic defects of traditional approaches to the study of psychology has been the isolation of the intellectual from the volitional and affective aspects of consciousness. The inevitable consequence of the isolation of these functions has been the transformation of thinking into an autonomous stream. Thinking itself becomes the thinker of thoughts. Thinking was *divorced from the full vitality of life, from motives, interests, and inclinations of the thinking individual.* (50, emphasis mine)

No better critique of cognitivist flow charts of the composing process exists; no better warning about the importation of certain poststructuralist theories that dissolve the individual (the subject) into the totalization of textuality exists. I try to show in "Vygotsky on Composing: Theoretical Implications" that Vygotsky takes a great deal of care in composing a conceptual system that has an inbuilt flexibility. He also is always careful to acknowledge that there are real worlds beyond all this theory.

Which is not to say that Vygotsky cannot be wrong. One of his key concepts is "development." Central to the concept of development is time. Vygotsky proposes a new idea of development but retains old notions of time. These traditional notions of time allow his theory of development to be taken up in politically dangerous ways. In the final essay of this section, "Writing Time," I take up the idea of time in Vygotsky's work as well as in composing, and argue that to accept a linear and singular notion of time is to give the state (or any ruling social group) the intellectual apparatus that can potentially rationalize the marginalization and eventual destruction of difference(s). When we argue that all is history, that history is linear, that "earlier" formations in history are not as good as "later" formations in history, we make it possible to privilege ourselves as the culmination of history. That enables "later" embodiments of development to call for the elimination (liquidation) of pesky "earlier" formations. I oppose that. I want instead to preserve history, development, and time as key ideas, in order to recognize, appreciate, and preserve difference. To reach the theoretical conclusion that another culture or individual or even life-form is somehow "inferior" because it is "lower" on the historical (evolutionary) ladder has provided the intellectual justification for what is wrongly called "development"—the destruction of previously existing life-forms, environments, cultures, discourses, and people in the name of "progress" (or socialism or profit). I do want to talk about progress—in writing, in life, in history—but not at the expense of a decreasing variety of life.

In "Writing Time," then, I critique Vygotsky and move farthest away from his theory, trying in the process to bring along the concepts that I have found most fascinating and valuable in Vygotsky. In a sense I use Vygotsky to critique Vygotsky, saying in that process what we can conclude about composing text.

This "Composing Text" section ends with a poem I wrote about, appropriately enough, writing the poem. I am not palming this off as great poetry; it isn't. But just as I am suspicious of composition teachers who never show students their writing—both in draft and published form—and who rarely discuss their writing processes and projects (the agony and the ecstasy), so I am suspicious of the writing teacher who has never tried her or his hand at writing poetry. There is no better way for us to see the limitations of even the best of our writing theory than to write even the worst piece of poetry. Maybe we ought to demand that the finishing doctoral student in composition and rhetoric write some poetry as part of her or his requirements and share it publicly no matter how bad. In this little text, then, we see a bundling of some of the important themes of this section—the dynamics of composing, the need for similarly flexible theoretical notions of writing, the intersectionality of composing text, the historicity of discourse, the ever-present dangers of reductionism. Finally, this little text plays on the signified/ signifier "I"—an appropriate bridge to the next section of essays on "Composing Self."

Chapter Six

A Vygotskian Theory of Writing

Vygotsky and Writing

Recent translations of the work of Lev Vygotsky and that of coworkers who carried on his thought and research after Vygotsky's untimely death reveal a school of thought that has few parallels in the twentieth century.[1] The depth and breadth of the Vygotskian tradition as glimpsed through these recent publications belies the common view of Vygotsky as an insightful thinker perhaps, but one who nonetheless, in his published work, was a bit thin on empirical, practical, and theoretical elaboration. The curious fact about the new body of literature reaching American publication is that it is both so theoretically elaborate and so practice and research oriented. On the one hand, Vygotsky had a very clear grasp of the philosophical issues that demand clarification and conceptual analysis. On the other hand, Vygotsky was simultaneously immersed in the practical concerns of the clinician, the teacher, and the teacher educator. His "laboratory" was spread across the Soviet Union in the hospitals, public schools, and universities of a society in transition. Thus Vygotsky concerned himself with the practical kinds of issues that one feels are, if not absent, at least neglected by Chomsky, Piaget, and poststructuralist theorists. In fact, Vygotsky's theory of discourse arises from a scholarly tradition that purposely distinguished itself from both a Western European tradition of language theory and from the dogmatism of the commissars who ultimately suppressed it. Yet Vygotsky is hardly antitheoretical or concerned only with pragmatic issues. He saw the centrality of a theory that leads and develops practice. The characteristic comprehensiveness and thoughtfulness of Vygotskian formulations makes much American work pale by comparison.

Having thus noted the comprehensiveness of Vygotsky's theory, I find it difficult, if not hypocritical, to propose to condense all or some part of it into a single essay. Perhaps if I limit this essay and insist on the interconnectedness of the Vygotskian theory (so that a clear understanding of one part really entails a clear understanding of the entire theory), I will be able to retain enough credibility to encourage the reader to further investigate this more complete body of work her- or himself. It is my experience that a sensitive reading of the works of the Vygotskian school of psychology can be a breathtaking event, not so much because there are no irrelevant or inaccurate ideas to be found there (there are), nor because these ideas are crystal clear and immediately and apparently applicable (they often are not), nor because I am the true believer who accepts Vygotsky chapter and verse (I do not), but rather because such a reading reveals a group of people collectively committed for over half a century to a remarkable enterprise. That enterprise is the attempt, a human and therefore partial one to be sure, to create a single unified theory that, while constantly struggling to avoid reductionisms of all sorts, understands and explains human consciousness and human activity as it is now and as it has developed through the millennia. This theory, not restricting itself to the laboratory and elegant statistical analyses alone, continually tries to immerse itself in the ambiguity, the messiness, but also the richness of human relations and actual life. Vygotsky does not restrict himself to a narrow, disciplinary definition of psychological phenomenon. Rather, for Vygotsky, wherever there is human consciousness, there is the potential for psychological investigation of that dimension of the phenomenon. Language, and sign systems generally, become central to his project since signification is the key process of consciousness. Vygotsky's theory often makes forays into art theory, art history, cinema, drama, language education, anthropology, ethnohistory, folklore, medicine, linguistics, and even philosophy and literature since each of these areas (and artifacts) reveals some facet of human consciousness, some dimension of the mind at work, in process, that would otherwise not be accessible. This theory, to make matters more complicated but perhaps less reductionist, additionally tries to accomplish this grand (if not grandiose) aim in an interrelated and holistic manner.

One of the pervasive themes that runs throughout Vygotsky's work is the unity (but also diversity) of human consciousness. Vygotsky did his work during the 1920s and 1930s, and he is a child of his age. He is a modernist. To the poststructuralist reader, then, Vygotsky may seem outdated, certainly unfashionable, maybe even quaint. The poststructuralist revels in the fragments; Vygotsky is interested in the mosaic the fragments point toward. He assumes there is some larger image and that it ought to be of concern to us. But it is not quite accurate to leave it at that. Vygotsky's work in most ways departs from the sort of high modernism that flourished in Western Europe and the U.S. for over fifty years. Vygotsky condenses these fifty years of Western history into ten years of his own scholarship and quickly works through modernism, ending with conclusions that could well be termed postmodern, though with a difference. In this sense, the trajectory of Vygotsky's project parallels that of contemporary Russian avant-garde artists, painters like Malevich, who anticipated questions that would arise only in the 1960s and the 1970s in the West. To the extent that Vygotsky's education and scholarly project continually cross and recross disciplinary and conceptual borders, his work is often postmodern in practice, in form, and in many of its conclusions.

It is my view that Vygotsky's original interest and training in the humanities and the arts never really disappeared and together with the era he lived in has a great deal to do with the humanities orientation of much of his and his colleagues' work. Whatever the case, I find the ideal behind this theory commendable and a refreshing counterpoint to the trends of overspecialization, fragmentation, and scientism that appear increasingly in our own disciplines as well as in the culture in which we live. It is in these terms, then, that the reader needs to consider both this essay's motives and its limits.

So what are some of the new or neglected insights that Vygotskian theory has to offer us? One can pull out, somewhat arbitrarily, at least four ideas that Vygotsky insists upon and about which recent composition has said little. Vygotsky hypothesizes that (1) to understand higher mental functions one must trace their genesis first in shared social relations, (2) to understand higher mental functions and their sources in social relations one must view both developmentally and, in fact, have a clear conception of the nature of development, (3) to understand the development of higher mental functions and their relation to activities such as writing, one must understand the nature and role of inner speech, (4) to understand inner speech development and its tie to writing development, one must view language dynamically as a realm of clashing forces that entails far more than the currently popular communication model of language can even suggest, let alone summarize. While the last point is not fully developed in the work of Vygotsky proper, I believe it is implicit in it and in the work and reflections of the members of the Vygotskian school. I believe there is sufficient evidence to justify a linking of the work of the Vygotskian school with that of the Bakhtin school. M. M. Bakhtin's work on language and literature is monumental and at least offers one possible model of what a dynamic theory of language might look like.[2]

Writing As Social Relation

Turning to the first insight of the Vygotskian school then, I must stress the centrality of the proposition that all higher mental functions result from the internalization and transformation of *social* relations. At first glance, this does not seem all that new an idea. After all, psychologists for many years has discussed the process of internalization and the development of mental capacities. James Moffett (1968) has made use of a similar idea of internalization in his theory of discourse and subsequent curriculum. Yet Vygotsky is very insistent on the importance and the uniqueness of his insight.

He states:

> In general, we could say that the relations among higher mental functions were at some earlier time actual relations among people. I shall relate to myself as people relate to me. Just as verbal thought is the transferal of speech to an internal level, and just as reflection is the transferal of argumentation to an internal level, the mental function of a word, as Janet demonstrated, cannot be explained except through a system extending beyond individual humans.[3]

And again,

> We may go even further and say that all higher functions are not developed in biology and not in the history of pure phylogenesis. Rather, the very mechanism underlying higher mental functions is a copy from social interaction; all higher mental functions are internalized social relationships.[4]

James Wertsch, one of the prominent Vygotskian scholars in this country, argues for a strong reading of such passages. Wertsch notes that Vygotsky "is not simply claiming that social interaction leads to the development of the child's abilities in problem solving, memory, etc.; rather he is saying that the very means (especially speech) used in social interaction are taken over by the individual child and internalized. Thus, Vygotsky is making a very strong statement here about internalization and the social foundations of cognition."[5]

In essence Vygotsky is arguing that the social act is related to and in fact leads individual cognition (which, of course, itself then reconstructs and redirects the social act). Thus individual consciousness needs always to be viewed as both a social and an individual creation. This is the key hypothesis of the Vygotskian school and therefore Vygotsky avoids talking about the innate or even the universal (transcultural) modes of thinking. Because of this hypothesis he also reaches the conclusion that behaviorism is impoverished. Beginning as it does from an essentially individualistic and reductionist perspective, behaviorism, according to Vygotsky, simply cannot account for the sources of thought nor for the basic novelty of human thought when compared to animal "consciousness." That a child by the age of five can master her or his language and immediate environment bears witness to the fact that individual thought is at the same time a "team" effort, and that the child does not have to start from square one, reinventing those ways of thinking that it has taken the community centuries to develop.

Our concept of logic is one site where the implications of such a view become clear. Logic often seems to be the one mode of thinking that is universal, that goes beyond the limits of any specific culture or age. Logic, according to some developmental researchers, supposedly reflects real relations that first arise between *objects* in the material world and are subsequently abstracted and formalized to be applicable and consistent beyond the sphere of immediate experience. At the very minimum, logic can tell us some things about the clear use of language and the linguistic analysis of concepts—at least this has been the position of most English and American philosophers of the twentieth century. Piaget's developmental theory is firmly grounded in such convictions. Yet Vygotsky contends, and the work of Luria and others seems to show, that universal, formal patterns of thinking like those developed in the study of logic are to a considerable extent culture specific, perhaps even contextually bound. Thus logic, which many writing teachers take to be one of the pillars of argumentation and much writing, if not of critical thinking itself, does not seem to be the universal mode of thinking that we take it to be. Further, Vygotsky and his coworkers are arguing that this is not simply because people, due to cultural or class factors, have not been exposed to logic and trained to think logically, although this may account for some situations. Rather, people in many cultures (or other ages) have apparently been capable of such thought, have often been aware of it, have confronted it, and have chosen, nonetheless, to use other modes of thought. Unless one dismisses entire cultures and many epochs of human history, one has to confront this fact. At the very least, this calls into question developmental theories that claim cross-cultural universality and that view the acquisition of formal logical modes of thinking as characteristic of the highest stage of development. It throws into question some of the criteria—increasing abstracting abilities, decentering capacities, and logical analyses—by which writing teachers and researchers have conventionally gauged writing development. Vygotsky's theory, then, raises questions about how we order our assignments, our course units, and our courses themselves across the undergraduate curriculum.

If this were not unsettling enough, Vygotsky's hypothesis of the social genesis of thinking also raises some serious questions about the related matter of the modes of writing. Rhetoricians have attempted, especially in the last fifteen years, to deal with the criticism that the modes, if they even exist, apparently characterize products rather than composing processes. One way to get around this objection is to identify modes of writing with the patterns of thought. Thus the modes can serve as a stimulus for process, in fact as a writing heuristic. This rather elegant idea has one drawback, according to a Vygotskian perspective. Where do these patterns of thinking come from? One way to end discussion is simply to assert the innateness and universality of such modes of thought. Yet aside from the question of why we need to bother teaching such modes if they exist and are indeed innate and universal, such a solution creates many of the same difficulties that postulating logic as innate raised.

A Vygotskian might argue that the whole notion of the modes of writing, a notion that still organizes most writing textbooks and college writing courses, needs to be seriously reevaluated in light of psychological, sociological, and anthropological evidence. If indeed such a notion proves useful for writing instruction (a debatable proposition), if in reality the modes can be shown empirically to exist as processes or even as products (again, a questionable idea), then the *sources* of the modes of thinking/writing/the written need to be discovered. These sources, according to a Vygotskian view, would be social relations. Such modes would change as social relations change and would exist first between persons. The idea that the modes of writing may actually be related to internalized social relations is striking.

If the modes have their origins in the patterns of group activity that are subsequently internalized by the individual, then one of the important tasks for writing research and instruction would be to trace out such categories of cultural activity. Perhaps, then, to "teach the modes" we need first to teach specific kinds of group processes rather than solely focusing on texts. Perhaps also writing teachers need to study anthropology and possible cultural activities and categories in order to study rhetoric in its most complete form. Interestingly enough, the notion that reading and writing instruction must first and foremost have its categorical and processual roots in the community and in community activities occurs independently of the work of the Vygotskian school in the work of Paulo Freire.[6]

One qualification or at least clarification needs to be made before moving on to some of Vygotsky's other insights. Vygotsky is not arguing that social relations and thinking (and subsequently writing) are *identical.* Rather he is arguing that they form a *unity,* inextricably interrelated and bound up with one another. Social relations are always transformed when they are internalized by the individual. Thereafter, the writing act again transforms thinking processes into written signs. At each transition, there is a transformation, and each transformation is guided, even formed, by motive. The individual to a great extent decides what is important and why, and these decisions are of critical importance in determining what social relations are internalized. The individual reconstructs and enfolds (or unfolds) the social semiotic accordingly.

This clarification answers two objections. First, it deals with the false conclusion that if mind is social, it necessarily cannot be individual and that Vygotsky views human beings as simply Orwellian robots programmed to think in a given way. This is disguised behaviorism inappropriately applied to the social realm and Vygotsky vehemently denies such individual versus society dichotomies and the resulting conclusions. Secondly, the distinction made between identity and unity refutes the proposition that we think only in words or in language. Clearly such is not the case, though a component of our mental world is verbal. Vygotsky does not *identify* consciousness or thinking with language. Even if he did, he doesn't identify internal language with external language. For Vygotsky, inner speech and outer speech are quite different and distinct entities—they are not identities though they are *related.* What is true concerning inner and outer speech differences is also true for speech and writing differences. For these reasons, writing can never simply be a transcription of inner speech or speech. If one attempts to transcribe thought into writing, to reproduce thoughts directly onto the paper, a transformation occurs. The very structure of thinking (at least inner speech) is opposite that of writing. Thus a writer struggles with correlating a *related,* though not an *identical* set of processes.

Writing As Developmental

As can be seen, we are already discussing change—how a change in the context creates a new text, how the movement from inner speech to outer speech or written speech produces a qualitatively new development. This essentially leads into Vygotsky's second insight that higher mental functions must be understood concretely, that is, developmentally. This, of course, entails some discussion of what exactly Vygotsky means by development and of what he and his colleagues see as the nature of development. Vygotsky conceives of development as a dialectic process, as the "movement of movement." Human activity changes with time and these changes have a direction. Later levels of development dialectically depend upon, but also negate, earlier levels. Without getting into the specifics of Hegelian dialectics (what really is required here), I can at least note that Vygotsky sees development as *both* continuous and discontinuous, as recursive but not circular. He views the *solution* of the most critical problem facing the person at one level of development as becoming the source of the *problem* to be solved at the next level of development. The process of development is "contradictory" in that its successes turn into, are the flip side of, its failures.

Perhaps by setting Vygotsky's picture of development next to two views of development that contrast with it, I can more fully illustrate some of these points.[7] The first view of development is that of the "step" theorist. Development in this model is continuous and incremental. It is a slow process that goes forward one small step at a time. It is unidirectional. Development is closely correlated with simple growth and is uniform. When graphed in terms of time and the criteria of development (usually those characteristics that lend themselves to easy measurement and quantification), development takes the shape of a smooth curve that perhaps approaches certain limits. In its simplest form, the step theory of development can be pictured as a straight, upwardly slanting line, since the steps are many and the "stairway," by comparison, long.

The second view of development is that of the "stage" theorist. Development in this model, unlike the step model, is at certain critical points or during certain critical periods discontinuous. The individual makes a leap from a lower stage to a higher one. Development in the stage model, then, is quite rapid at specific points. Emerging developmental abilities come into existence, breaking with the past, forming qualitatively new kinds of activity. Development is nonincremental at these critical points. Yet like the step model, the stage view of development is progressive—that is, one must go through a sequence of stages and there really is no regression. One may get stuck at a particular stage of development and future stages may never be reached, but the overall direction of development is still forward toward increasing mastery of the characteristic processes of each stage. When graphed in terms of the criteria of each stage and across time, development in this model takes the shape of large separated steps or plateaus.

Against the pictures of a smooth line or a progressive series of steps, we can place the Vygotskian graph of development across time. It appears as an oscillating, sometimes broken sine wave in which the dips and crests of each developmental zone alternate. The wave widens and heightens across time. We might label this the "tidal wave" picture of development since there is a cumulative effect here. Because past experiences are continually being reconstructed in terms of new experiences, later levels of development, as in the stage model, are qualitatively different from earlier levels and there is discontinuity. Yet each level depends on and is connected with what precedes it and hence there is also a kind of overall continuity. The bigger the dip, the bigger the crest of the developing wave. The model is both progressive *and* regressive, making a very important place for risk taking and apparent "failure" and "backward" development, which nonetheless often foreshadow the reorganization and restructuring of experience and prepare for the developmental leap that follows. Thus, the tidal wave model connects the two apparently opposed notions of progression and regression in development as related aspects of each other.

While asserting that the height and depth of the crests and dips of the developmental wave are interrelated, the Vygotskian model also notes that these dimensions of the wave have a relation to the rate of development and that this rate varies. This rate of development (velocity of the wave) at times speeds up and at other times slows down. Thus, the wave or a section of the wave itself has a frequency that varies. Differences among individuals as well as within one's life can be seen as differences in this frequency. Most importantly, the Vygotskian model of development relates an individual's general development to the social. The importance of the community to individual development is articulated in this model through the concepts of leading activity and zone of proximal development.

Although fluctuation is always occurring in this model even when things look extremely stable (dialectically such seemingly stable times are tied to revolutionary periods), each community, in addition, designates certain times in the individual's life as special zones of development. Within these zones, new activities (and new kinds of consciousness) are expected of the individual. These "leading activities" initiate a developmental crisis (or turning point) that in time causes the individual to restructure and reconstruct the rest of her or his activity, copying and transforming it onto the new wave. Through the intervention of the community, qualitatively new means of accomplishing tasks are offered for individual appropriation. These new modes of activity, when appropriated and internalized by the individual, allow that individual to restructure consciousness, to pull past experiences and abilities over into new developmental zones, in essence, to think and to act in new ways. James Wertsch comments on these developmental revolutions.

> The most important of these qualitative shifts in ontogenesis is concerned with the introduction of cultural means of mediation into what were formerly "natural processes." The use of cultural sign systems plays an especially important role in this qualitative shift. The introduction of these signs systems into the child's functioning in such areas as memory and problemsolving changes the nature of these processes in a fundamental way. There are a massive disruption and restructuring of the child's mental processes at this point. There may even be a temporary *decrease* in the level of functioning; but after the psychological processes have been restructured as a result of acquiring sign systems, the process (e.g., memory) becomes much more powerful in the cultural milieu in which it will be called upon to operate.[8]

Vygotsky himself argues that the introduction of these "psychological tools" into activity has three kinds of effects.

> The inclusion of a tool in the process of behavior (a) introduces several new functions connected with the use of the given tool and with its control; (b) abolishes and makes unnecessary several natural processes, whose work is accomplished by the tool; and (c) alters the course and individual features (the intensity, duration, sequence, etc.) of all the mental processes that enter into the composition of the instrumental act, replacing some functions with others (i.e., it recreates and reorganizes the whole structure of behavior just as a technical tool recreates the whole structure of labor operations).[9]

We can sense in Vygotsky's words the processive nature of development, its feedback and feedforward qualities, and its dialectic movement.

If one accepts the basic unity of social and individual development, and if one admits the developmental importance, even necessity, of certain kinds of "regression," it then becomes clear that we cannot really discern very much about an individual's development by observing what that person can do alone. In fact, what the individual can accomplish in cooperation with others becomes the leading edge of the developmental wave. It is the developmental distance between these two kinds of abilities that Vygotsky calls the zone of proximal or near development and that he and his colleagues find to be of such critical import.

We have seen how the Vygotskian model of development differs from the step and the stage models, and we have also delineated the relationship between social and individual development. Some members of the Vygotskian school (especially A. N. Leontiev and A. Markova) have specified possible leading activities which include (1) social and emotional activity (perhaps what we might call the phatic function of communication), (2) object activity, (3) play activity, (4) formal learning activity (this does not always mean formal schooling), (5) interpersonal communicative activity, (6) study and vocational activity, (7) vocational and social activity.[10]

It must be stressed that this is not a simple listing of discrete, successive "stages." Although Vygotsky uses the concept of the developmental stage, I have tried to show that he has a unique sense of what a dialectic stage entails. I have found some reason as well as precedent for avoiding the usual static and linear concept of stage altogether, replacing it with the notion of developmental zones. This concept allows for a more dynamic sense of development and additionally helps us to avoid reducing all development during a period to one preponderant cognitive process. Development in this model involves the many diverse life activities the individual is engaged in, affective as well as cognitive, and these activities coexist and, although forming a unified whole, have their own relatively independent histories. Development here, unlike the stage model, does not require that earlier activities end for the individual to advance to higher stages. There is, for example, no need to think that phatic or object or play activity ends when one develops. To some extent their nature may change due to the restructuring of consciousness, yet it does not seem unlikely that many remnants, in fact great streams and currents of earlier activity continue and even grow in later life. What changes are the new tasks life demands of us and the new ways of thinking offered to us by the community to accomplish these tasks.

One final caution about this list of leading activities. The members of the Vygotskian school (and originally Vygotsky himself) are very emphatic about the cultural specificity of such categories and about the need for investigators to study the concrete life of the community through ethnographic research in order to discover such categories. Each community has its own needs, preoccupations, hopes, and dreams. These community concerns, together with the community's view of itself and its destiny, all of which change through history, will play a major role in the determination of individual development. To universalize one set of categories is to tear them out of their historical and cultural context and hence to falsify them to varying degrees.

Writing development will always have to be examined in terms of these broader leading activities. A model of writing development will likewise be accurate only to the extent that it is situated in this wider developmental context. One of the concerns of such a writing development model would be the interaction between leading activities in the individual's life and leading activities specific to writing development. I wonder, for example, if we aren't telling adolescents in our writing classes two opposite things when on the one hand, as members of the community, we "tell" the student that interpersonal communicative activity is the leading life activity of this period, while on the other hand we believe writing to be a completely individual activity and demand that students do their own work in isolation from friends. We insist on the sustained monologue on the paper yet are frustrated when we don't have sustained and interesting dialogue in class.

Before moving on to Vygotsky's remarks concerning inner speech, we need to note that Vygotsky does use a four "stage" scheme to discuss the development of specific activities. He adopts a scheme first proposed by the Soviet psychologist Blonsky that distinguishes "four general fundamental genetic stages through which behavioral development passes."[11] Vygotsky modifies the scheme slightly and settles on (1) a natural or "primitive" (unconscious) stage, (2) the unconscious use of external signs stage, (3) the conscious use of external signs stage, and (4) the internalization of signs stage (unconscious, but at a new developmental level). Writing activity, like other higher psychological functions, might be expected to move through these four general stages. Using these stages, viewing them in terms of wider developmental zones, and situating them in the context of the leading activities of the individual in a particular community and the leading activities peculiar to writing development, we can generate a developmental model that is specifically Vygotskian. I have elsewhere sketched out one possible model of writing development based on these principles.[12]

From such a writing development model comes the finding that *reflection* plays a critical role in helping students to bootstrap themselves into later developmental zones. To an extent "all development, whether it be of the individual personality or of a society, involves bringing unconscious processes to consciousness."[13] The discovery that the writing act itself both generates and solves the identical developmental problems is one such insight. Initially, writing overloads short-term memory and deluges the beginning writer with information. This conflict is resolved by the realization that writing can be used to store, by means of notes, keywords, outlines, thesis statements, and finally the entire draft itself, the very infor-

mation that is being lost. This realization and the subsequent altera-
tion of behavior creates the next developmental conflict since meaning, generated in these auxiliary and prefabricated forms, is being
lost. A certain resulting deadness and lack of insights, frequently
encountered in the writing of college freshman, can be overcome by
the student who experiences and recognizes the heuristic potential
of the writing act. This *recognition,* usually occurring later in development and only after certain conflicts have arisen, permits the
writer to make new connections and to find a new voice specific to
the writing medium. In turn, this very solution of the problem of the
preformed meanings leads to new information overload, in some
ways similar to the difficulties experienced by the beginning writer.
The difference between the difficulties the beginning writer has with
transcription and encoding of meaning and those that the advanced
writer encounters is that the advanced writer has internalized the
writing activity in a more complete way. This results in an important
restructuring of inner speech as discussed by Luria.

> The functional and structural features of written speech have still
> another important feature; they inevitably lead to a significant
> development of *inner speech*. Because it delays the direct appear-
> ance of speech connections, inhibits them, and increases require-
> ments for the preliminary, internal preparation for the speech act,
> written speech produces a rich development of inner speech which
> could not take place in the earliest phases of development.[14]

So the advanced writer shares some problems with the beginning writer; however, the advanced writer can count on the new
developments in inner speech to help solve these problems. The
writing student needs to experience her or his own development
and to make use of these experiences through reflection and metawriting as well as through group processing. In this way reflection
contributes to overall writing development.

Writing and Inner Speech

When we apply Vygotsky's insights into development to the specific
history of writing, we begin to see how critical "inner speech" is in
this whole process. Inner speech is that constantly shifting amalga-
mation of words and images, voices and tones, that seem to be at
the heart of consciousness as we individually experience it. Yet this
private, emotion-filled, silent speech is also a social product, the
result of a long and specific developmental history. Vygotsky and his
colleagues argued long for the need to understand inner speech in

order to understand the development of other higher mental functions and human activity generally. When American psychologists were talking about black boxes and the dangers of studying consciousness (a strange kind of psychology to be sure—one that finds the psyche an improper object of study), when American linguists were talking about collecting a corpus and subjecting it to linear, structural analyses, Vygotsky and his coworkers were investigating inner speech. Since inner speech in its purest form is inaccessible to the direct observations of others, and because the introspective methods of Wundt were found to be inadequate, Vygotsky contended that the most available and fruitful means for trying to track down and study the protean phenomenon of inner speech was the genetic or developmental approach. If we can trace the sources of inner speech in social relations and in problem solving contexts, and if we can observe the development of these forerunners of verbal thinking in the primates and especially in the child, we may be able to draw some conclusions about the direction these processes seem to be taking. From these conclusions then, we can infer and subsequently test out hypotheses concerning the nature and development of inner speech.

Vygotsky's conclusions about inner speech are fairly well known. He remarks that inner speech "is speech almost without words."[15] Yet this is a rather unique kind of "speech." Vygotsky notes that it has at least three unusual characteristics. Inner speech is characterized by its agglutinativeness, its immersion and flowing in and through senses, and its predicativity.

Agglutination is a process whereby words, phrases, or even entire texts are combined and merged into a single new word unit. This new word unit is the result of the combination of several previous units and meanings, and yet also is a new entity. It takes on new meanings and senses, though these meanings are genetically related to the former, separated meanings. What the agglutinated unit reveals is the movement, interference, and fusion of meanings and senses across time. Meanings and senses, these interconnected semantic relations and multidimensional nets of associations, form a critical part of the notion of inner speech and Vygotsky distinguishes them and emphasizes the necessity of tracing their history and development. Vygotsky states that "Meaning is a property of a sign. Sense is the content of meaning (the result of meaning), but is not fixed in the sign."[16] Vygotsky argues that inner speech first seems to be shortened, abbreviated, shoved together into fewer and more compact units (agglutinated), and then these compacted and fused units, themselves also taking on new meanings and senses in addition to their earlier, relatively separate ones, begin to flow in and out of each other (influx of sense), often in extremely specific, individual and context-dependent ways.

What anchors this increasingly amorphous and ever-changing inner speech? For one thing, senses and meanings are not arbitrary, but are built up through experiences that have concrete, sensual qualities. Senses, then, have a history of sensations attached to them. Additionally, the present situation, the context, provides a structure for thought by its very availability. That which is *given* needs to be kept in mind less and less, and we can concentrate more exclusively on *new* information. This is what Vygotsky seems to be referring to when he argues that inner speech is highly predicated.[17] Because inner speech is highly contextual, that is, because an individual knows the subject and the situation about which she or he is thinking, and additionally, because inner speech serves a personal rather than intersubjective function, there is little need for the portion of language that has to be elaborated and developed more completely in external speech or written speech to be unfolded and attended to. This "psychological subject" of inner speech can be dispensed with, or at least its role can be dramatically reduced, while the "psychological predicate" remains. This permits speech to be speeded up when it enters the realm of inner speech, thus allowing more information to be processed before the constraints of short-term memory begin to be felt.

Zhinkin, another Soviet psychologist, puts all of this in the following manner.

> The language of inner speech is free of the redundancy inherent in all natural languages. Natural languages are determined by strict rules, as a result of which the correlative elements are concrete, i.e., the presence of some elements entails the appearance of others. This is also the source of redundancy. In inner speech, on the other hand, the connections are objective, i.e., they have content and are not merely formal, and the conventional rule consists only in the time necessary for a given mental operation.[18]

Before moving on, we must stress that Vygotsky makes a very clear distinction between psychological subjects and predicates, and grammatical subjects and predicates. They are in no way identical. This assertion should make it once again clear that we do not "think in words," but through meanings and senses, though of course it is possible to subvocalize. The Vygotskian school labels the latter *inner speaking* and it is viewed as a psychologically quite different phenomenon from inner speech.

In sum, what we observe at work in the realm of inner speech is a continual process of abbreviation, condensation, and enfolding, matched with the appropriate elaboration and unfolding necessary for utterances or for the recovery of information lost to short-term memory. This process of inner speech takes on a life of its own, relatively independent of external speech, growing and developing according to its own principles and nature. Inner speech, then, is a kind of abstraction of speech activity, as speech activity is a kind of abstraction of a community's experience and activity. A. A. Leontiev, working in the Vygotskian tradition, adds the psychological function of *inner programming* to the model. We might oversimplify and say that inner programming is a kind of abstraction of inner speech. It is the "uncognized construction of a certain scheme on the basis of which an outer statement is subsequently produced."[19] Inner programming participates to varying degrees in the production of utterances. Monologue demands a high degree of inner programming, while dialogue (one might argue, especially dialogue performing the contact function) requires little or almost no inner programming. We might speculate that just as inner speech arises as a means of controlling activity and speech activity for oneself, inner programming arises from the need to regulate inner speech and long-term utterances. Writing development would appear to initiate such a need for regulation of the inner speech stream, and, hence, to require a kind of inner programming.

At bottom, the streams of inner programming, inner speech, inner speaking, and outer speech, find their source in *motive*. The affective-volitional tendency is related to the emergence of a problem or a conflict. This tendency or motive directs the streams of verbalization to varying degrees. One is reminded of the centrality of motive in Kenneth Burke's work and of its ties to scene, act, agent, agency, and purpose. Each of these aspects of motive are both individual and social so there is a constant relationship between the community and our ways of thinking. To an extent, scenes, acts, actors (roles), agencies, and purposes lead double lives, first in their external form in community life and secondly in their internalized inner form. Motives then can be viewed as existing both within a person and within the community. Thus in the Vygotskian theory, the inner, "private" "self" is shown to be related to the most public aspects of community life and to that community's sense of Self.

The model I have just presented is, of course, an oversimplification of years of research and thought of the Vygotskian school. Members of the Vygotskian school are the first to admit that their most elaborate models are sketchy and limited. Vygotsky certainly never reduced consciousness to inner speech nor solely to verbal or cognitive processes. Consciousness clearly involves affect and sensation, both of which are always woven into "words," which themselves are primarily means for talking about *signs* in this theory. Any internalization of speech in an interconnected and holistic model suggests a simultaneous internalization of connected roles, scenes, contexts, and values rather than isolated and fragmentary words. Finally, this model must be understood dynamically. Few if any of these processes are strictly linear, uniform, and harmonious. Actually, it may well be argued that it is the very interference and conflicts among the streams of verbalization that help to create new developmental problems that give rise to new functions and their accompanying new forms. M. M. Bakhtin has been especially clear about the need to see language (and literature and thinking) in constant movement. This view of language complements Vygotsky's view of consciousness.

Vygotsky's insight into the origins, nature, and development of inner speech and its relationship to verbal thinking, as well as his delineation of the internalization (rooting) process, encourages the writing teacher and the researcher to broaden their views of the writing process. As I have constantly stressed, we cannot really create, develop, and test out a nonbehavioristic theory of writing development unless we deal with these inner processes and their growth, as sketchy and as incomplete as such present efforts may be. One obvious area that further investigation of inner speech may be able to illuminate is that of writer's block. When we keep in mind Vygotsky's insights into development and inner speech, however, it would appear to be perfectly consistent if there were developmental reasons for writing block, or at least certain kinds of writing block. More questions than answers arise here. For example, is it possible that we internalize writing block, or does writing block originate due to the turbulence in the internalization (or externalization) process? As conflicts in other arenas often lead development, can writing blocks lead writing development? Can certain kinds of writing blocks in fact be leading activities at specific points of time? Might they indicate a zone of proximal development between what a writer can do alone and what a writer can do with the help of others? What is the consequence of Luria's contention that the development of inner speech requires that we learn to inhibit as well as to elaborate senses and meanings? How does it relate to blocking? What does the development of inner programming have to do with writing block? It would seem to be the case that just as aphasia and other disorders of speech have taught us a great deal about speech production and comprehension, so too writing block might help us to understand written speech activity and its inner aspects.

Another issue that suggests itself when we consider Vygotsky's insights into inner speech is the possible relationship between thinking in the broadest sense of that word and the arts, and hence between verbalization and artistic activity. The filmmaker Eisenstein was interested in just this question and with several others formed a study circle with Vygotsky to pursue such matters.[20] The deeper we get into psychological processes, the farther away we seem to get from a linear and static, perhaps discursive mode. What then is the relationship between inner psychological processes and presentational artistic forms? Do we take the same paths through consciousness when we create a work of art as we do when we speak? Or does art short-circuit this developmental and linearizing process, coming out of consciousness through the back door, so to speak? Are we basically dealing with two very different kinds of processes here—perhaps scientific versus artistic, or linear versus nonlinear, or discursive versus presentational? Or "at bottom" is it essentially the same process, perhaps always taking a slightly different route through consciousness? Concretely, do we teach writing as an art or as a science, or is the very asking of this question and the very splitting of the whole into such dualistic categories the problem itself? Such are the kinds of questions that arise when we really attempt to get at the psychology of writing even through such rough categories as inner speech.

Writing as Dialogue

It seems these issues are at the very heart of the kind of theory of language we have. The Vygotskian school has done some work in this area as have other related schools in various republics in and out of the Soviet Union. Vygotsky's colleague, A. N. Leontiev, with his son A. A. Leontiev, wrote a fascinating if complex article titled "The Social and the Individual in Language," which sets out some of the implications of viewing language as the embodiment of "socially accumulated and generalised experience" that is reflected, refracted, and reconstructed in consciousness. A. A. Leontiev tried to sort out in a more specific way the various dimensions of language in his article "The Psycholinguistic Aspect of Linguistic Meaning." And for over thirty years, Yuri Lotmann and his coworkers at Tartu in Estonia have also been at work on a theory of language that complements and extends Vygotsky's own insights.[21]

Vygotsky had some fascinating things to say regarding language, but Vygotsky's theory is found scattered throughout his works, many of which still have not been published in English. Vygotsky is always interested in seeing language as a function distinct from, but related to, other "higher mental functions" like perception, attention, memory, emotions, imagination, and will. He agrees that language is the central function since it is by means of language that the other functions originate, are constructed, and develop. But he also refuses to reduce these other functions to language. One reason is that for Vygotsky language itself is always in change. Language is dynamic and shifting, both the product of a community and individual, and the instrument for transforming community and individual. A sign or text in one situation will mean something different than the identical sign or text in another situation. This functional and dynamic quality of language is most evident in dialogue. To an extent, because writing as a form of language shares these dynamics with other forms of language, writing is a very special sort of dialogue. Vygotsky implies as much in the final chapter of *Thought and Language*. But it is in the work of Vygotsky's contemporary Mikhail Bakhtin that we find a more fully elaborated model of writing as dialogue.

Unlike Vygotsky's work, Mikhail Bakhtin's work is more widely known among literary theorists and critics. His work has also found its way into English publication much more quickly, and in far more complete form, than Vygotsky's. Using Bakhtin's work as a proxy in this area (until Vygotsky's work is translated into English and taken up by writing scholars) we can begin to understand what it means to assert that writing is dialogic.

Eschewing the simplistic sender-receiver models that dominate so much Anglo-American thinking about language, Bakhtin and his coworkers find the essence of language to be dialogue. Volosinov (some say a pseudonym for Bakhtin himself) argues that dialogue is the basis of inner speech and even of written speech.

> Closer analysis would show that the units of which inner speech is constituted are certain *whole entities* somewhat resembling a passage of monologic speech or whole utterances. But most of all, they resemble the *alternating lines of a dialogue*. There was good reason why thinkers in ancient times should have conceived of inner speech as inner *dialogue*. These whole entities of inner speech are not resolvable into grammatical elements (or are resolvable only with considerable qualifications) and have in force between them, just as in the case of the alternating lines of dialogue, not grammatical connections but connections of a different kind.[22]

And again

> Were we to probe deeper into the linguistic nature of paragraphs, we would surely find that in certain crucial respects paragraphs are analogous to exchanges in dialogue. The paragraph is something

like a vitiated dialogue worked into the body of a monologic utterance.[23]

What, then, does it mean to think of written speech activity as a dialogic act from its conception in inner speech or thought to its expression in a final product? What does it mean to conceive of language dialogically rather than monologically, as we are wont to do?

I am not exactly sure, to be completely frank. Both the Vygotskians and the members of Bakhtin's circle are agreed upon one thing, however—that such a dialogic conception of language will prove to be radically different from the common monologic approach that has dominated Western linguistics.

> This exclusive "orientation toward unity" in the present and past life of languages has concentrated attention of philosophical and linguistic thought on the firmest, most stable, least changeable and most monosemic aspects of discourse—on the phonetic aspects first of all—that are furthest removed from the changing sociosemantic spheres of discourse. Real ideologically saturated "language consciousness," one that participates in actual heteroglossia and multi-languagedness, has remained outside its field of vision.[24]

What we get from traditional language study is only the tip of the iceberg, in a way a superficial abstraction that overlooks the richness, variety, and most importantly the dynamism of language. Bakhtin echoes Vygotsky in a related passage.

> Discourse lives, as it were, beyond itself, in a living impulse toward the object; if we detach ourselves completely from this impulse all we have left is the naked corpse of the word, from which we can learn nothing at all about the social situation or the fate of a given word in life. To study the word as such, ignoring the impulse that reaches out beyond it, is just as senseless as to study psychological experience outside context of that real life toward which it was directed and by which it is determined.[25]

Bakhtin, then, denies the proposition that language is static, monolithic, an arbitrary and conventional matching of sign to referent, or signifier to signified, an instrument used primarily for the sending and receiving of messages between "atomistic" individuals. Bakhtin refutes as does Vygotsky the very view of language that underlies most all of our current models of the writing process.

Bakhtin's view of language is, as one would expect, considerably messier but far more dynamic than the discredited communication model of language. Bakhtin at times sees language as a landscape of interacting forces that penetrate and withdraw, as a battlefield of armies clashing and merging. Language is a multivoiced plurality—even language that seems the most unified and monologic, the language of our own utterance, even the language of our own individual thoughts. Apparent unity in utterance and thought is premised upon stratification, which in turn reflects the dialogic and heteroglossic springs of discourse. A constant conflict is fought between the centripetal forces that want to centralize and unify, and the centrifugal forces that want to disperse, decentralize, and fragment, with the latter ultimately prevailing, at least in living discourse. The truly unified language is the dead one, after all.[26]

What better describes the predicament of the writer? How often do we experience this conflict and take it to be an indication that something is wrong? How often do we think that if only we could eliminate this constant battling in our minds and on the paper, all would be well? There seems to be a profound consonance between Bakhtin's description of language and my personal experiencing of its multivoicedness, of its life. Perhaps we have overemphasized the negative consequences of such battling—might I say of such *bickering,* since that is how I frequently feel about the "noise" that is going on in my mind when I write. It may be that real coherence in a text comes about less because the many voices have been suppressed and silenced than because they have become dialogic, speaking to each other and to "the" writer who is made up of this "community" of voices. Perhaps unity in a text is less a matter of singleness of purpose or form or content (let alone of thesis sentences) than a matter of plurality and an openness to, reflection upon, and participation in, this plurality.

At first glance, I find it curious that this essay concludes by speaking about pluralism and dialogue in the *text* when these are the very issues that confront us, that have continued to confront us, in the political arena. But it isn't that strange after all, remembering that Vygotsky and his colleagues believed that our inner world is always interconnected with our outer world, that our individuality is predicated on our membership in a community (and vice versa). It seems, then, somehow appropriate to end by speaking of the subjective experiencing of writing activity, after beginning "objectively" with Vygotsky's insight into the social origins of higher mental functions. In trying to persuade the reader of the richness, insightfulness, and applicability of the work of the Vygotskian tradition, I hope the reader will also be receptive to the possibility that these qualities of the work testify to the individual genius of so many of its exponents, as well as to the intensity and the richness of that community formed more than half a century ago.

Notes

1. There have been dramatic changes in the Vygotsky corpus available to English readers over the last decade. Most importantly, Alex Kozulin has composed a fine new revision of *Thought and Language* (Cambridge, MA: MIT Press. 2nd ed. 1986) that restores huge sections left out of the first 1962 edition and that provides the reader with extensive and authoritative introduction and footnoting. Kozulin also has recently published *Vygotsky's psychology: A biography of ideas* (Cambridge, MA: Harvard University Press. 1990) which not only elaborates and contextualizes Vygotsky's theory in rich and interesting ways, but shows how Vygotsky's thought bears directly on present concerns in the social sciences and the humanities. His call for a humanistic psychology parallels my call here for a social perspective on composition.

Further, Plenum Press has begun the translation and publication of *The Collected Works of L. S. Vygotsky*. The first volume has appeared, Robert W. Rieber and Aaron S. Carlton (eds), *Problems of general psychology: Including the volume "Thinking and speech"* (New York: Plenum Press. 1987).

Other works of Vygotsky are now available as *The psychology of art* (Cambridge, MA: MIT Press. 1971) and *Mind in society* (Cambridge, MA: Harvard University Press. 1978).

James Wertsch has done important work in both introducing Vygotsky to an American audience, furthering Soviet and US scholarly connections, and publishing otherwise unavailable translations, though his work focuses primarily on psycholinguistic issues. See James Wertsch, *Recent trends in Soviet psycholinguistics* (Armonk, NY: M. E. Sharpe. 1978), *The concept of activity in Soviet psychology* (Armonk, NY: M. E. Sharpe. 1981), and most recently, *Voices of the mind: A sociocultural approach to mediated action* (Cambridge, MA: Harvard University Press. 1991). Also see the collection Wertsch edited *Culture, communication and cognition: Vygotskian perspectives* (New York: Cambridge University Press. 1985).

And finally, although Kozulin raises some fascinating questions about the precise relationship between Vygotsky's work and that of his students, works of the Vygotskian school are available in A. N. Leontiev, *Activity, consciousness, and personality* (Englewood Cliffs, NJ: Prentice-Hall. 1978); A. Markova, *The teaching and mastery of language* (White Plains, NY: M. E. Sharpe. 1979); N. Talyzina. *The psychology of learning* (Moscow: Progress Publishers. 1981), A. A. Leontiev, *Psychology and the language learning process* (New York: Pergamon Press. 1981); A. R. Luria, *Language and cognition* (New York: John Wiley and Sons. 1982).

Also for volumes that contextualize and historicize a broad range of schools and approaches to Soviet psychology, and not just the work of the Vygotskian school, see Alex Kozulin, *Psychology in utopia: Toward a social history* (Cambridge, MA: MIT Press. 1984); Jan Valsiner, *Developmental psychology in the Soviet Union* (Bloomington, IN: Indiana University Press. 1988); and David Joravsky, *Russian psychology: A critical history* (Cambridge, MA: Basil Blackwell. 1989).

2. The periodical *Soviet psychology* has over the last few years been publishing articles on Bakhtin and his theory of language as it relates to psychology. Most recently in the US, James Wertsch in his *Voices of the mind* has drawn together Bakhtin and Vygotsky. Michael Holquist a decade ago was agreeing that "Bakhtin's thought parallels in suggestive ways that of Vygotsky . . ." in *The dialogic imagination,* ed. Michael Holquist, trans. Caryl Emerson and Michael Holquist (Austin: University of Texas Press. 1981), p. xx. Caryl Emerson began the work of teasing out the connections between Bakhtin and Vygotsky in her "The outer word and inner speech: Bakhtin, Vygotsky and the internalization of language." *Critical Inquiry* 10:245–64. 1983.

3. Lev Vygotsky. 1981. "The genesis of higher mental functions." In *The concept of activity in Soviet psychology,* edited by James Wertsch. (Armonk, NY: M. E. Sharpe.) pp. 144–88.

4. Ibid., p. 164.

5. Ibid., p. 146. Let me also note here that to see writing as a social relation and a higher mental function is *not* the same thing as to view writing as a "social action." The latter is now quite popular in composition studies. More often than not, however, US theory dichotomizes the "social" from the "individual," privileging the former, relegating the latter to "soft" or less than "rigorous" composition courses. In contrast, for Vygotsky, it is precisely the ways that the individual is social and the social individual that is at stake and of interest. Development is not either individual or social, but is "dialectic," to use a concept theoretically specific to the Vygotskian paradigm, that in many ways seems to be in conflict with the present faddish "social" view of writing.

So, for example, David Bartholomae and Anthony Petrosky put forward in their *Facts, artifacts, and counterfacts* (Portsmouth, NH: Boynton/Cook. 1986) a "social" view of literacy, but one that is quite at odds with the principles and ethos of Vygotsky's theory. Bartholomae and Petrosky assert ". . . we are presenting reading and writing as a struggle within and against the languages of academic life . . . the student has to appropriate or be appropriated by a specialized discourse . . . he has to invent himself . . . finding some compromise between idiosyncrasy, personal history, and the requirements of convention, the history of an institution" (p. 8). For all its superficial similarity to some Vygotskian notions, this "social" view of writing in fact reinforces the very sort of dichotomy Vygotsky is interested in thinking through, the very sort of dichotomy Vygotsky criticizes Piaget of recuperating in his development theory. Further, such "social" views are at base formalistic, since they come down to language and a rather monologic, monolithic, elitist Western, view of language at that. While welcome as an attempt to break away from the reigning "communication model," such "social" views of writing should not be confused with Vygotsky's hypothesis presented here that literacy arises from social relations.

6. Paulo Freire, *Pedagogy of the oppressed* (New York: Herder & Herder. 1970) and *Education for critical consciousness* (New York: Seabury

Press. 1973). See related empirical studies by A. R. Luria, *Cognitive development: Its cultural and social foundations* (Cambridge, MA: Harvard University Press. 1976) and Sylvia Scribner and Michael Cole, *The psychological consequences of literacy.* (Cambridge, MA: Harvard University Press. 1981).

7. These three models are the author's rather than Vygotsky's. Vygotsky's major root metaphors include the spiral of development, the "geologic" layering of development, and Marx's base-superstructure model. Nonetheless, Vygotsky discusses different models of development and their basic inadequacies in a like manner. For more on developmental models, see R. Murray Thomas, *Comparing theories of child development* (Belmont, CA: Wadsworth. 1979).

8. See note 3 above, p. 145.

9. Lev Vygotsky. 1981. "The instrumental method in psychology" In *The concept of activity in Soviet psychology,* edited by James Wertsch. (Armonk, NY: M. E. Sharpe.) pp . 139–40.

10. In James Wertsch. 1979. *A state of the art review of Soviet research in cognitive psychology.* ERIC ED 186–293. Pp. 43–47. And A. Markova, p. 14, as cited in note 1 above.

11. For Vygotsky, see note 3, p. 156.

12. James Zebroski. 1983. *Writing as "activity": Composition development from the perspective of the Vygotskian school.* Dissertation. The Ohio State University.

13. Ann Shukman. 1977. *Literature and semiotics: A study of the writings of Yuri M. Lotman* (New York: North-Holland.) p. 13.

14. A. R. Luria. 1969. "Speech and the formation of mental processes." In *A handbook of contemporary Soviet psychology,* edited by Michael Cole and Irving Maltzman. (New York: Basic Books.) p. 142.

15. Vygotsky, *Thought and language,* see note 1 above, p. 244.

16. Quoted from A. A. Leontiev, "Some recent trends in Soviet psycholinguistics." In *Recent trends,* edited by Wertsch, as in note 1 above, p. 20.

17. James Wertsch. 1977. "Inner speech revisited." Paper presented to Society for Research in Child Development. New Orleans, LA. March.

18. Quoted by A. A. Leontiev, as in note 16 above, p. 14.

19. A. A. Leontiev. 1969. "Inner speech and the processes of the grammatical generation of utterances." *Soviet psychology.* 7:12.

20. James Wertsch, ed. *The concept of activity in Soviet psychology,* as in note 1 above, pp . 13–15 .

21. A. N. Leontiev and A. A. Leontiev. 1959. "The social and the individual in language," *Language and speech,* 2: 193–204. Also, A. A. Leontiev, "The psycholinguistic aspect of linguistic meaning," in Wertsch, ed., *Recent trends,* as above, pp. 21–64. On the work of the Tartu school, specifically Lotman, see Yuri Lotman, "On the reduction and unfolding of

sign systems (The problem of Freudianism and semiotic culturology)," in *Semiotics and structuralism: Readings from the Soviet Union.* Ed. Henryk Baran (White Plains, NY: International Arts and Sciences Press. 1976) 301–309. More recently, Yuri M. Lotman, "Text within text," *Soviet psychology* 26 (Spring, 1988) 32–51. For one of the few articles that discusses Vygotsky's theory of language per se see Benjamin Lee and Maya Hickmann, "Language, thought, and self in Vygotsky's developmental theory," in *Developmental approaches to the self.* Eds. Benjamin Lee and Gil Noam (New York: Plenum Press. 1983) 343–378.

22. Valentin Volosinov. 1973. *Marxism and the philosophy of language.* (New York: Seminar Press.) p. 38.

23. Ibid., pp. 111–112.

24. M. M. Bakhtin, as in note 2 above, p. 274.

25. Ibid, p. 292.

26. Volosinov, pp. 72–75.

Chapter Seven

Writing as Dialogue (and Quarrel)

We are living today through a renaissance in writing scholarship. Over the last ten to fifteen years, composition has risen from what some termed the ghetto of the English department to become, in many if not a sufficient number of departments, a recognized field of study. Scholarly presses are cranking out volumes of studies on composing, and exciting work is proceeding on many fronts. Yet at the heart of this rebirth in composition is a shared theory of language that has changed little over the past century. This shared view of language focuses primarily on individual information exchange. Reflecting a broader Anglo-American tradition, this accepted conception of language, and hence of writing, emphasizes the most unchangeable and static aspects of the communication process. The focus is on the sustained monologue; dialogue is reduced to the simple exchange of such sustained monologues between sender and receiver. I want to argue that this "communication model" of language is simplistic and inadequate, and that it is, nonetheless, pervasive in the composition discipline and in the research issuing forth. Until the pervasiveness and inadequacy of this theory of language is recognized and transcended, much of the new research in writing, as interesting as it may otherwise be, will tell us what we in some sense already know. To see writing activity in a truly new way, to find more successful ways of teaching composition, we need to reconceptualize our entire theory of language. To accomplish this, we must get outside of our Anglo-American tradition temporarily and examine theories of language premised on quite different assumptions. We need to dialogue with other traditions, with other

179

theories. A particularly rich source of dialogue can be found in the traditions of Eastern Europe.

Recently, poststructuralist theory has been gaining ground among U.S. literary theorists and critics and among certain compositionists who find literary theory attractive. Poststructuralist theory does indeed critique the commonsense notions of language and self that still prevail in our society and that heavily contribute to a ruling ideology. But poststructuralist theory traces its "origin" and performs its critique upon the structuralism of Saussure and others who stand right in the middle of a nearly twenty-five-hundred-year-old tradition of Western language study. There are limits to this critique from the inside, however useful it may be. Poststructuralist theory, in its moves and terminology, in what counts as interesting questions, in its critique of the work of established Western scholars like Saussure, and in its daily life, shows how much a part of that very tradition it still is. This is especially the case of poststructuralist theory as practiced in the U.S. U.S. "theory" is too often simply a glossy, high-tech version of the formalisms we were all raised on and grew to hate.

In contrast, Eastern European language theory arises out of strikingly different worldviews, cultures, and histories. Eastern European language theory is no less theoretical than its Western counterpart. To the contrary, it may well be more theoretical. Yet in many ways, Eastern European language theory decades ago worked through issues only now being problematized by poststructuralism. The language theory that has flourished for over seventy years in Russia, the Ukraine, Estonia, Czechoslovakia, and Poland, is, more often than not, aimed at returning to everyday life enriched by theory, and so seems more pragmatic. Eastern theory has frequently been associated with national ethnic studies and the preservation of nationalities and national traditions. Theory has also contributed to folklore studies, literacy education, second language learning, and remediation of the mentally and physically handicapped. East European language theory at its best tries to create a dialogue between theory and everyday practices, between scholarship and everyday life. Nowhere is this attempt at dialogue so profoundly pursued and incorporated into the very essence of the theory itself than in the work of Mikhail Mikhailovich Bakhtin.

M. M. Bakhtin (1895–1975) is "gradually emerging as one of the leading thinkers of the twentieth century."[1] His monumental work on literature and language centers on the idea that language needs to be viewed in wider terms than the communication model permits. Bakhtin argues that we need to move beyond a monologic conception of language that emphasizes the static, the formal, the atomistic, the abstract, and the individualistic, and instead see language in dialogic terms. As far as composition studies are concerned, Bakhtin's work suggests the abandonment of the communication triangle that has been mainstream rhetoric's common-sensical model since Aristotle, and which has played an important role in some of the most important theoretical work of the composition revival. Bakhtin, more than fifty years ago, anticipated the limitations of this monologic view.

> Linguistics, stylistics, and the philosophy of language—as forces in the service of the great centralizing tendencies of European verbal-ideological life—have sought first and foremost for *unity* in diversity. This exclusive "orientation toward unity" in the present and past life of languages has concentrated the attention of philosophical and linguistic thought on the firmest, most stable, least changeable and most mono-semic aspects of discourse—on the *phonetic* aspects first of all—that are furthest removed from the changing socio-semantic spheres of discourse. Real ideologically saturated "language consciousness," one that participates in actual heteroglossia and multi-languageness, has remained outside its field of vision.[2]

We need only reflect on some of the more recent theoretical contributions to the discipline of composition to recognize the validity of Bakhtin's critique today.

A Dialogic Critique of the Communication Model

James Moffett has offered in his *Teaching the Universe of Discourse* and (with Betty Jane Wagner) in *Student-Centered Language Arts and Reading* one of the most extensively worked out and applied models of discourse that we have. His work has much to recommend it. As much as any available model, Moffett's theory of language and learning is processive. It is concerned with the development of linguistic and psycholinguistic processes in the student over time and it serves as a powerful corrective for much in the field that is still behavioristic, atomistic, and short term. Yet Moffett in these works draws heavily upon the sender-receiver, encoding-decoding model that Bakhtin finds wanting.[3] More recently, Moffett has reaffirmed his basic acceptance of this model.

> Among other things, people are transmitter/receiver sets, which means they are made both to transmit and receive but not *at the same time.* If you want to listen, you have to switch the channel over to receiving and keep still . . . But as every one knows who

has ever tried to stop thinking, it is very difficult indeed. The mind is a drunken monkey, say the yogis. But one way to cure the habit of ceaselessly speaking to ourselves is—homeopathically—to go ahead and speak to ourselves but to say the same thing over and over.[4]

Several things become apparent from this and similar passages. Moffett still relies heavily on the communication model with its technological root metaphor. Also Moffett finds the movement of inner speech to be a distraction and a kind of sickness (to be cured) for the writer. Finally, Moffett views the final goal to be the reaching of silence through the development of the individual's powers to control and focus and eventually eliminate the ongoing verbal stream. The emphasis then is on stabilizing and stopping the myriad of voices that arise in inner speech. Bakhtin's whole approach, in contrast, argues that actual development of individual discourse arises not from the silencing of the alien word, but from a more profound incorporation of the word of the other into one's own discourse. It isn't that we want to control, unify, and eliminate the word. Rather we want to *dialogize* it. To accomplish this we need first to recognize that our words are not ours alone but in fact are always shared. As such, they are always "multi-channeled," "double-voiced."

> Someone else's words introduced into our speech inevitably assume a new (our own) intention, that is, they become double-voiced. It is only the relationship between these two voices that may vary. . . . Our everyday speech is full of other people's words: with some of them our voice is completely merged, and we forget whose words they were; we use others that have authority, in our view, to substantiate our own words; and in yet others we implant our different, even antagonistic intention.[5]

Bakhtin accepts this multiplicity as adding richness and vitality to language, and welcomes it. It is from this conflict and interaction between words, between the voices that populate our inner world, that, Bakhtin argues, a higher level of consciousness evolves.

> In the everyday rounds of our consciousness, the internally persuasive word is half-ours and half-someone else's. Its creativity and productiveness consist precisely in the fact that such a word awakens new and independent words, that it organizes masses of our words from within, and does not remain in an isolated and static condition. It is not so much interpreted by us as it is further, that is, freely developed, applied to new material, new conditions; it enters into interanimating relationships with new contexts. More than that, it enters into an intense interaction, a *struggle* with the

other internally persuasive discourses. Our ideological development is just such an intense struggle within us for hegemony
among various available verbal and ideological points of view,
approaches, directions, and values. The semantic structure of an
internally persuasive discourse is *not finite,* it is *open;* in each of
the new contexts that dialogize it, this discourse is able to reveal
ever newer *ways to mean.*[6]

So Moffett, relying on the communication model of language, moves
toward ultimate "unity" and the resolution of all conflict in inner
speech, while Bakhtin argues that this multiplicity and conflict in
inner speech is "real" and ultimately, if rightly understood and
dialogized, beneficial.

Upon closer reflection, it makes sense that Moffett ends up going
in a direction that is apparently so opposed to that of Bakhtin, since
Moffett, unlike Bakhtin, essentially accepts the communication
model of language. If one accepts this model, one necessarily accepts the relative independence of the categories of the model. The
model distinguishes between and severs the sender-message-
receiver relation, and if one accepts the model and its divisions and
if one additionally believes that the primary function of language is
the transmission of new information, two conclusions follow. First,
monologue becomes the most important and most essential form
that language takes. One therefore begins to view inner speech and
the written text as imperfect monologues that always seem to be on
the verge of being interrupted, broken into, disturbed. Second, unity
and how to achieve it become the foremost concerns of thinker and
writer. Two things can be done to achieve this unity. Parts of discourse (inner or outer) can be broken apart, relations can be further
severed and elements of a "text"—again, I use this term to speak of
verbalization, whether mental, spoken, or written—can be structured in a hierarchy that is in turn subordinated to a single theme,
image, thesis, or motif. Or the parts of a "text" can simply be dis-
solved, the slate can be erased, and silence—that paragon of unity
and monologue—can be achieved. Moffett takes the second route.
Traditional composition programs have taken the first. Both seemingly opposite approaches are in actual fact part of the same relation, which exists because the communication model of language is
accepted. Bakhtin argues that we need to reject this model and move
to a theory of language that more accurately reflects and fits reality.
As we will see a bit later, if we do change our theory of language,
we necessarily change our classrooms, our composition programs,
and our research into composition.

Like Moffett, James Kinneavy similarly accepts the communication model of language as embodied in the communication triangle.

Certainly Kinneavy's *A Theory of Discourse* is one of the great works that the discipline of composition has produced. Aside from being theoretical—itself a major achievement in a field that has tended to be so immersed in the immediate concerns of reading and marking student papers that it has found little time left for theory—*A Theory of Discourse* is detailed, comprehensive, and at times brilliant.[7] It integrates much of our knowledge about language into a single, unified, and elegant conceptual framework. Yet this work too, built entirely on the communication triangle, is oriented toward unity. Kinneavy applies the communication triangle to several levels of discourse, in the process generating from the parts of the communicative process the primary aims of discourse. In turn, these aims of discourse allow Kinneavy to create a typology of discourse that includes expressive, referential (scientific and exploratory), persuasive, and literary genres. There is no question that Kinneavy's theory provides the discipline of composition with a far more logical and consistent framework than does the mixed bag of modes and patterns of development so prevalent in textbooks. There is also little doubt that Kinneavy's approach concentrates precisely on the "firmest, most stable, least changeable, and most mono-semic aspects of discourse" that Bakhtin finds so objectionable. Who is the addresser, the sender, the "I" in Kinneavy's model? This "I" is the individual (or collection—not collective—of individuals) who lives outside of community and outside of history. This "I" is single-voiced. It knows its voice and its mind, and before it communicates it knows its aim and intent. This "I" creates discourse. It exists outside of discourse, transcending the messages it sends, and transcending the world those messages both create and reflect. Bakhtin argues that such notions as this "I" or sender, while appearing to be concrete and to contain common sense, given in reality rather than generated by subjects in relation, are in fact high-level abstractions that are even at their inception culturally mediated. To rephrase J. Kristeva on Bakhtin, this "I" is a scribe that does not "think" with "ideas," but prepares confrontations of points of view, of minds, of voices, of texts.[8] This "I" then is, at least conceivably, already a multiplicity that is either dialogic by nature or hopelessly fragmented if not schizoid.

Of all the neighboring disciplines that have affected composition, linguistics still exercises an important influence. Bakhtin's critique is no less penetrating here. We need only recall Roman Jakobson's seminal "Closing Statement: Linguistics and Poetics" to discover another incarnation of the sender/receiver schema.[9] Jakobson, of course, elaborates and greatly strengthens the model by adding the contextual and contact components to the communication process. He also strengthens the theory by associating functions with each component, noting that any piece of discourse always entails all of these components and hence all of the functions. These functions of language, however, form a hierarchy, in which some functions at a specific time and place predominate over other functions. This move makes the model far more flexible but does not essentially change the model's reliance on the same problematic categories. Jakobson's model still is restricted to ". . . a single monologic context, recognizing only the direct, unmediated relationship between word and referent, without consideration of any second context."[10] Together with James Moffett's spectrum of discourse and abstraction, Jakobson's model was adopted by James Britton and his colleagues in England and played an important role in the investigations reported in *The Development of Writing Abilities: 11–18,* one of the major pieces of research on writing to appear in the 1970s. More recently, the shift in linguistics toward the analysis of more complete texts, while an improvement over earlier concern with language at the sentence level, still reflects a primary interest in language as a stable and stabilizing force. Terry Winograd's work, for example, consciously and explicitly accepts the mechanical metaphor of the communication model and moves into the implications such work on language has for computers, those paragons of unity and single-voicedness.[11] Halliday and Hasan's *Cohesion in English,* which also has interested many composition researchers in recent years relies, a bit less explicitly, on the communication model and the mechanistic root metaphor underlying it.[12] Context in *Cohesion in English,* though mentioned, is rather quickly dismissed as secondary, "exophoric" concern and the focus once again becomes those relationships or ties "within" the "text" that make it one, that make it or help it to cohere. Bakhtin might suggest a necessary second volume, perhaps entitled *Diffusion in English* or *Dissemination in English,* needs to accompany the first. This second study would note the ways that a truly living text can never be stable, static, and "unified" in the strictest sense.

Other examples could be multiplied. I hope these are sufficient to indicate that much current and albeit important and useful work in the discipline of composition is premised upon the communication model, traceable to Saussure, the Anglo-American linguistic philosophy tradition, and the logical positivists. The question is, however, what does Bakhtin have to offer in its place? After all, one reason why this model may be so pervasive, aside from the fact that it fits the character of the economic milieu in which we live, is it serves as an accurate and useful representation of language as we encounter it. As might be expected, Bakhtin's theory of language is considerably messier but far more dynamic than the communication model. His theory does not lend itself to neat diagramming, nor to

reduction to mathematical formulae, nor does it focus on the abstract, the universal, the trans- and ultimately ahistorical—those
qualities of language that appear to never change. Bakhtin, as Michael Holquist puts it, is a "baggy monster" and his theory of language reflects the seeming pleasure and glee he takes in muddying
the waters.[13]

Bakhtin's Theory of Language

Bakhtin sees language—itself too dead and reified a term—as a landscape of interacting forces, a field of energies that penetrate and
withdraw, that converge and break up, that obliterate and wash away
the kind of neat categories and boundaries that the communication
model is based on. Language is a battlefield of clashing and merging
armies. It is a multivoiced plurality. Language is dialogue in a literal
kind of way. It is dialogic because even the most complete
monologic utterance can never be understood in and of itself, always
being part of a wider context. A monologue always finds its beginnings and endings, its very essence, outside of itself. My word only
has being through the alien word, through another's word, that is in
dialogue.

   Language is, for Bakhtin, simultaneously being built up and torn
down (deconstructed perhaps, though the forces Bakhtin describes
are far less mechanistic, individual, and conscious than this term
suggests). A constant conflict takes place in language. This conflict
is fought between the monolithic (and one might argue *authoritarian*), centripetal forces that want to centralize, to unify, to forge
hard and fast boundaries, to screen off discourse from any penetra-
tion by another's intonation, and the centrifugal forces that want to
disperse, to decentralize, to fragment, to violate the boundaries of
authorial voice, to depose and dethrone author-itative discourse. In
living discourse, the latter forces gain the upper hand and in the last
instance prevail, since the completely unified utterance and language is the dead one, the hieroglyph on the monument inscribed
in the unspoken, lost tongue.[14]

   And Bakhtin is not arguing that only certain types of discourse
are dialogic. Rather he is making a strong claim that even the apparently most unified and monologic language is at heart a form of
dialogue and has within it the forces of dialogue.

   The dialogic orientation of discourse is a phenomenon that is, of
   course, a property of *any* discourse. It is the natural orientation of
   any living discourse. On all its various routes toward the object, in
   all its directions, the word encounters an alien word and cannot

help encountering it in a living tension-filled interaction. Only the mythical Adam, who approached a virginal and as yet verbally unqualified world with the first word, could have really escaped from the start to finish this dialogic inter-orientation with the alien word that occurs in the object. Concrete historical human discourse does not have this privilege: it can deviate from such inter-orientation only on a conditional basis and only to a certain degree.[15]

Because we meet our world through signs—through the word—and because those signs are always someone else's as well as our own, we meet the world through dialogue. Thinking is then always co-thinking, that is con-sciousness or co-knowing.

So where do Bakhtin's clashing armies and forces of discourse lead us? For one thing to those utterances that we have in the past assumed to be the most monologic and single-voiced. Bakhtin tells us to look at these apparent monologues and find even here dialogue and a history of dialogue. Turn to the utterance of the individual, for example, and recognize that

> . . . all transcription systems—including the speaking voice in a living utterance—are inadequate to the multiplicity of meanings they seek to convey. My voice gives the illusion of unity to what I say; I am, in fact, constantly expressing a plenitude of meanings, some intended, others of which I am unaware.[16]

Look, for example, at inner speech and discover the "common sense fact" that being of two or more minds (or "voices") is the rule, not the exception, that distraction by the voices is dialectically linked to attention and convergence, that speaking with "one" voice, if it happens at all, occurs rarely and briefly when great verbal currents and streams converge rather than settle down and behave themselves and ultimately evaporate. Study verbal art and note that this view of language is reinforced by folk traditions that have always recognized and made an important place for this dialogic side of language, what we may call "nonsense" or verbal "play"—language that has to be sealed off because it is so wild, disruptive, anti-*author*-itarian and hence institutionally "dangerous."[17] Move to literature and note that the genre that in the last two hundred years has swallowed so many forms is the *novel,* that novel force that has moved us from single to multivoicedness.

I like Bakhtin. He appeals to the rogue in me. At another level, I like Bakhtin because I am a composition teacher and Bakhtin's theory of language explains a lot more of what I see in my classroom, in my students' writing, and in my own writing than any of the other theories of language I have so far encountered. In fact, I have to close my mind and consciously ignore or rationalize away what I see and what I have experienced to *not* accept a Bakhtin-like view of language. Bakhtin's theory of language helps to explain why the composition teacher's understanding of "unity" is so foreign to so many students and why methods for achieving this unity, like thesis statements, topic sentences, outlines, and patterns of development, work so imperfectly. First of all, these formalisms do not fit the reality of any living word, of any piece of discourse, let alone the language my students bring to the classroom. Secondly, even if these forms are abstractions and simplifications of some sort of language reality, they are at the end of the spectrum of abilities, *not* at the beginning. You have to already have "unity" in order to make use of them. If you don't, what results is extremely controlled but dead discourse, unconscious parodies of the vibrant and rich language we desire for ourselves and for our students.

It is when I accept Bakhtin's ideas and admit that language is actually the way I experience it and not the way the textbooks say that I *should* experience it, that things begin to make a little more sense. If I realize that monologues and unified works are far more complicated than I have been led to believe, that apparent unity in utterance and thought is premised on stratification which in turn reflects the dialogic and heteroglossic springs of discourse, I find less reason to be always fighting against the current, advocating to students that they build pretend-dams that must inevitably tumble under the weight of the very language they seek to control. Instead I can encourage students to do what I as a writer have always done—go with the flow at first, and learn something of the dynamics and forces of these streams of consciousness. Then, only after feeling and becoming aware of the potential energy to be found within the very substance of language, put this energy to use, use it against itself and for your own purposes. The writer, after all, doesn't simply approach language from the outside and force her purposes upon it. Instead she moves within language, learns of it, and derives the predominant energies from the resources within.

Streams, of course, can be traced back to springs and springs have their origins in deeper and vaster underground watercourses. I like Bakhtin's theory of language because it acknowledges this, complementing in so many ways the work of Lev Vygotsky and his colleagues in psychology. Both argue that underlying language, and writing as one of language's voices, is the community. Bakhtin and Vygotsky agree that to study *communication* we must study *community.*

> The speech act by its nature is social. The word is not a tangible object, but an always shifting, always changing means of social communication. It never rests with one consciousness, one voice.

> Its dynamism consists in movement from speaker to speaker, from
> one context to another. Through it all the word does not forget its
> path of transfer and cannot completely free itself from the power
> of those concrete contexts into which it had entered. By no means
> does each member of the community apprehend the word as a
> neutral element of the language system, free from intentions and
> untenanted by the voices of its previous users. Instead, he receives
> the word from another voice, a word full of that other voice. The
> word enters his context from another context and is permeated
> with the intentions of other speakers. His own intention finds the
> word already occupied.[18]

What describes the predicament of the writer better? How often do
we experience this otherness within the individual utterance and
take it to be an indication that something is wrong, that we are not
being "structured" enough, that we are not being purposive and
single-minded enough? The writer too often recognizes the multivocality of discourse. (She would have to perform an immense act of
will to ignore it.) But the writer takes this dialogism as a problem to
be solved rather than the "solution" itself. The writer thinks if I
could only eliminate this constant battling, this constant bickering,
this endless quarreling in my mind and on the paper, all would be
well. Quarreling and conflict can't be healthy or natural or normal.
Why can't my mind settle down and behave?

Yet if we accept Bakhtin's view of language, as I think good
writers do whether consciously or unconsciously, we would accept
such dialogue or even quarrel as the starting point. It may be that
real coherence in a text comes about less because the many voices
have been suppressed and silenced, than because they have become
dialogic, speaking with, even at times yelling at, each other and the
"writer" who is made up of this community of voices. Perhaps the
kind of unity we are looking for in a text is less a matter of singleness or purpose or of form or of content (let alone of thesis or topic
sentence) and more a matter of accepting and participating in this
plurality.

Bakhtin in the Composition Classroom

Nice words, but what does it all mean? Bakhtin says, "One's own
discourse is gradually and slowly wrought out of others' words that
have been acknowledged and assimilated, and the boundaries between the two are at first scarcely perceptible."[19] How might we get
students to engage in a variety of discourses that others have created
and at the same time encourage them to move toward their own
voices, toward their own styles in writing? How can we encourage

students, as part of the very writing act, to consciously and reflectively study the multivocality of their own languages, which are internalized from social relations to community?

There are obviously many approaches that work, depending on the teacher, students, and community. Kyle Fiore and Nan Elsasser in "'Strangers No More': A Liberatory Literary Curriculum" offer in a dialogic manner a report of one thoughtful approach that matches a Bakhtin-Vygotskian theory of language-psychology with a Freirean pedagogy.[20] I have over the last five years developed a composition course that makes use of some similar insights, placing them, however, in a more formal and traditional educational setting.

I return once again to the earlier assertion that in order to study communication, we are necessarily required to study community. An examination of the life of the community is the logical content of a composition or any other language use course. Therefore, ethnography—the writing about a people—is an especially appropriate method. Ethnography demands that the student ethnographer do several important things. It requires the student ethnographer to become immersed in the actual life of a community, in all of its richness, messiness, and concreteness. (One abstracts, then, from and within a series of concrete contexts rather than detaching from and arising out of them.) It also requires the student to consciously focus on two differing perspectives simultaneously. First and foremost, an ethnographer attempts to record as completely and as accurately as possible the activity of the community from the *insider's* point of view. At the same time, the ethnographer is "making strange" what to the insider appears to be common sense, "nature," even "inevitable" activity. Thus, the ethnographer is also viewing a community from an *outsider's* perspective. This is made even clearer when the final ethnographic reports are shared with members of the class, a community apart from the initial community studied. The written report somehow has to mediate all of this. The student has to decide whether to include direct or indirect discourse about the community and in what proportion and for what reason. The student also has to integrate generalizations with specifics, reports of apparently individual (and idiosyncratic) behavior with individual but culturally shared and meaningful acts. Finally, the student in order to accomplish all of this has to become an expert, often *the* expert, in an area that has in all likelihood never before been investigated; that is, the student ethnographer has to *create* knowledge rather than simply rearrange or consume it.

All of these skills, once developed in the study of the "external" aspect of the community, are subsequently turned on to the "internal" aspect of community, to the classroom and the collective of developing writers. This writing community, to which the students by now concretely and consciously belong, uses these ethnographic tools in the last third of the term to investigate itself. By examining writing activity in this manner, each student creates, and shares, her or his own "theory" of writing. These accounts, often centered around a metaphor (writing is . . . or writing is like . . .), attempt to explain writing activity as the student has experienced it and now sees it. As many writing teachers have long known, it is only when the student sees her or himself as a *real* writer engaged in and able to control a real and important activity that real improvement can take place.[21]

The results of such a course of instruction have been gratifying. When students are allowed to investigate the living word using ethnographic approaches that extend through history, when students are encouraged not so much to abstract and detach as to immerse themselves in concrete reality and re-attach, they discover that culture is a creation of community. They find out that every individual lives through a multitude of communities. They see that culture and community are changeable, not given in nature. They discover that language is a part of culture and community and that it too is open to change. They listen more carefully to those dialogues and quarrels that populate their heads and their worlds, and they find that they are never alone in this literate endeavor. In other words, they discover that this bizarre cultural activity called writing is only another form that dialogue takes, and that they already have a whole history of dialogue to begin from and eventually to contribute to. They understand that the living word is not "in" here or "out" there, but lies on the borderlines and the frontiers of themselves and their worlds. They discover what Bakhtin knew.

> As a living socio-linguistic concrete thing, as heteroglot opinion, language, for the individual consciousness, lies on the borderline between oneself and the other. The word in language is half someone else's. It becomes "one's own" only when the speaker populates it with his own intention, his own accent, when he appropriates the word, adapting it to his own semantic and expressive intention.[22]

Notes

1. Michael Holquist. 1981. Introduction. In *The dialogic imagination: Four essays by M. M. Bakhtin,* edited by M. Holquist. Trans. C. Emerson & M. Holquist. Austin: University of Texas Press.

2. Bakhtin, p. 274.

3. James Moffett. 1983. *Teaching the universe of discourse* Boston: Houghton Mifflin. Pp. 10–13. Also see James Moffett and Betty Jane Wagner, *Student centered language arts and reading, K-13,* A Handbook for Teachers (Boston: Houghton Mifflin, 1983) pp. 4–24 as well as in chapters about reading.

4. James Moffett. 1982. Inner speech, writing, and meditation. *College English* 44:232–33.

5. Mikhail M. Bakhtin. 1971. Discourse typology in prose in *Readings in Russian poetics: Formalist and structuralist views,* edited by L. Matejka & K. Pomorska (Cambridge, MA: MIT Press). p. 187.

6. Bakhtin. *The dialogic imagination.* Pp. 345–46.

7. James Kinneavy. 1971. *A theory of discourse.* New York: Norton.

8. Julia Kristeva. 1973. The Ruin of Poetics. in *Russian formalism: A collection of articles and texts in translation,* edited by S. Bann & J. Boult New York: Barnes and Noble. p. 114.

9. In T. Sebeok, ed. 1960. *Style in language.* Cambridge, MA: MIT Press.

10. Bakhtin. Discourse typology in prose. p. 177.

11. Terry Winograd. 1983. *Language as a cognitive process: Volume I: Syntax* Reading, MA: Addison-Wesley.

12. M. A. K. Halliday and R. Hasan. 1976. *Cohesion in English* London: Longman. See, for example, *College composition and communication* (1983) 34:399–469, for an entire issue devoted to the investigation of these concerns.

13. Holquist, p. xviii.

14. Bakhtin. Discourse in the Novel. *The dialogic imagination.* Pp. 270–79.

15. Bakhtin, *The dialogic imagination.* Pp. 279.

16. Holquist, p. xx.

17. Susan Stewart. 1978. *Nonsense* Baltimore: Johns Hopkins University Press. This is one of the most theoretical investigations of this important topic. Examples from folklore are richly provided throughout. Also see Barbara Kirschenblatt-Gimblett, ed. 1976. *Speech play: Research and resources for studying linguistic creativity.* Philadelphia: University of Pennsylvania Press. Related work in anthropology is presented in William Washabaugh. 1979. Linguistic anti-structure. *Journal of Anthropological Research.* 35:30–46.

18. Bakhtin. Discourse typology in prose. p. 195.

19. Bakhtin. *The dialogic imagination.* p. 345.

20. Kyle Fiore and Nan Elsasser. 1982. 'Strangers no more': A liberatory literacy curriculum. *College English* 44:115–28. Also see Nan Elsasser and Vera John-Steiner. 1977. An interactionist approach to advancing literacy. *Harvard Educational Review* 47:355–70. Ira Shor has done some excellent

related work reported in *Critical teaching and everyday life* (Boston: South End Press, 1980). Also see A. Brick. 1981. First person singular, first person plural, and exposition. *College English* 43:508–15. Finally, for the theoretical and empirical reasons for an ethnographic approach to the teaching of writing, see the fine and exhaustive collection of works by many of the top scholars working within this paradigm, Bruce Bain, ed. 1983. *The sociogenesis of language and human conduct.* New York: Plenum Press.

21. The work of Donald Bartholomae and colleagues at University of Pittsburgh comes first to mind, although one can argue that this view is one held by most of the "second generation" of composition scholars, that is, those compositionists who have come after Janet Emig's pathbreaking work. For a detailed discussion of a specific curriculum based on this belief, see Donald Batholomae. 1979. Teaching basic writing: An alternative to basic skills. *Journal of Basic Writing* 2:85–109. The difficulty with Bartholomae and Petrosky's work, however, is that it is not clear precisely what the role of student experience is in that curriculum, though the course does assume that basic writers have to see themselves first as writers. In contrast, Paulo Freire's work has always been premised on a belief that student experience is central to literacy learning.

22. Bakhtin. *The dialogic imagination.* Pp. 293–94.

Chapter Eight

Vygotsky on Composing:
Theoretical Implications

A word about my title before I begin. What you are obviously going to get here is Zebroski's ideas, not *the* ideas of Vygotsky. I have been rightfully the butt of a few jokes among my good friends for the title. All I can say in my defense is that one of the Bakhtinian un-author-ized voices that "I" am not yet completely on speaking terms with must have created this title, for the "I" writing this now certainly didn't utter it.

Additionally, I want to note that because of space considerations, I will not be focusing in this article primarily on classroom implications, though I believe there are many. (I have set out some of these implications in the Chapter One essay, "Creating the Introductory College Composition Course.") Nor can I summarize the work of Vygotsky and his colleagues—how does one encapsule sixty years of that community's work or seven years of my own study? Nor will I—and this is the difficult one for me—discuss the fascinating and immensely important connections between the ideas of Vygotsky and those of Bakhtin. Rather, what I want to focus on are a few critical conceptual and theoretical matters and in the tradition of I. A. Richards will begin with a brief analysis of some misunderstandings and their remedies, will move on to a discussion of Vygotskian concepts and their relationship to composition theory, and will end with an exploration of inner speech and writing.

First, the misunderstandings. I have felt increasingly uncomfortable since the publication of *Mind in Society* in 1978 with references made to Vygotsky and the work of the Vygotskian school that have appeared in the composition literature. I feel uncomfortable, for example, when I hear people (Ong 1982) quoting Luria's ethnolinguistic study of Central Asians in the early 1930s (Luria 1976) to show that Vygotskian work supports a strict orality versus literacy dichotomy. The very title of Luria's volume—*Cognitive Development: Its Social and Cultural Foundations*—implies that it is community, and community's motives and functions, that give rise to linguistic forms both oral and written, and that it is changes in the community that create changes and developments in speech and written speech activity. Similarly, I feel uncomfortable when I read articles that imply that Piaget and Vygotsky are identical or complimentary approaches (Lunsford 1980; Barritt and Kroll 1978) when in fact, on the contrary, Vygotsky argues that Piaget overemphasizes the intellectual, the biological, the evenness and universality of developmental "stages," the evolutionary character of development, the centrality of the individual, and the essential independence of thought and language. In contrast, Vygotsky contends that the development of the intellect is importantly tied to the development of emotions, that it is the community that leads individual development (which dialectically reconstructs the community), that development itself is in development and is uneven and jerky and context-specific, and that it is the interrelation between thinking and speaking that is of importance in the development of *activity.* Finally, I am uneasy when scholars argue that writing is necessarily a more decontextualized form of language than speech, and that writing development proceeds from the personal, the egocentric, and the concrete to the social, the decentered, and the abstract. The Vygotskian tradition (Markova 1979), while admitting a dialectic, argues that development moves from the theoretical and social and abstract to concrete, individuated praxis. (Margaret Donaldson's work, especially her wonderful book *Children's Minds,* (1978), provides empirical research that questions this Piagetian view of development and supports a Vygotskian position.) I in fact find that my freshmen are in many ways *more* abstract than I. *I* always seem to be the one saying, "Give me more specifics. I need an example. I really don't see what you are saying here," and *they* always seem to be the ones saying, "Can you summarize that twenty-minute monologue in a sentence or two please?" just after I have explained—I thought—why I couldn't do that.

So what *is* Vygotsky saying? I think first of all that he is plumping for the centrality of community. The word *community,* after all, is not accidentally similar to *communication;* nor is *consciousness,* a term that we tend to associate with the zone of the isolated individual, by chance related to the concept of *co-knowing.* Vygotsky, then, is making a very strong claim. He argues, "All higher functions originate as actual relations between human individuals" (1978, 57). He also stresses that it is the interconnections and *functions*—notice that word—that are of greater interest than the separations. He says, for example, regarding the apparent dichotomy between the inner and outer worlds, "There remains a constant interaction between outer and inner operations, one form effortlessly and frequently changing into the other and back again . . . . There is no sharp division between inner and external behavior and each influences the other" (1962, 47). Yet Vygotsky is careful here. He is not creating an *identity* but a *unity*. Vygotsky notes, "There is a vast area of thought that has no direct relation to speech . . . . Nonverbal thought and non-intellectual speech do not participate in this fusion and are affected only indirectly by the process of verbal thought" (1962, 47–48).

In sum, Vygotsky is more subtle than he sometimes appears in the professional reading of him. Vygotsky traces his roots through Marx, Hegel, Leibniz, Spinoza, and Heraclitus, a very different philosophical tradition than has been popular in Anglo-American circles and perhaps for this reason he is sometimes misunderstood. Yet it is because of this very different ontology and epistemology that Vygotsky's work offers compositionists valuable new perspectives on the writing activity.

My intuition is that Vygotsky would tell us who teach composition that a process approach to writing is certainly better than a product approach, but that over the last few years we have tended to reify process. Vygotsky would say that process is not enough, that we need to bridge the gap between the subjective and the objective *through the social,* which gives birth to both. Writing, then, from a Vygotskian perspective, is more than a product or a process or a set of processes; it is a *relation,* specifically a *social relation* shared by a community with its own history, traditions, and motives, and individuated by each new student in her or his own unique way. To study the development of this writing relation, then, we need to study the student and teacher in the zone of proximal development and the concept of leading activity as specifically applied to writing development.

Charles Read (1971) has shown that in young preschool children, writing can lead the development of reading. He elegantly demonstrates that preschoolers who have learned their ABCs by heart from family interaction (in a play context) can construct sophisticated written text long before they can read such discourse in conventional form. When these children enter school, reading is introduced to them first as a shared, often a group, activity that is, over the years, internalized and individuated (the transition from reading out loud to reading silently is an especially important turning point in this process). These new reading abilities then surge dramatically ahead of writing abilities up through high school, writing lagging behind. (Vygotsky was interested in this lagging of writing development and was considering different reasons for this developmental gap. One of the places this issue arises is in Vygotsky's notebooks.) By the time these students appear in my freshman composition classes, they can often read another student's paper critically and are usually very unwilling to put up with the incompleteness or errors that seem to bother me less and less. Yet while freshmen can often read another's paper critically—sometimes *too* critically—and can sometimes offer another student useful critical suggestions, they can not yet read their own writing and apply the same kind of judgments. Thus reading for my freshmen leads their writing development. Reading pulls writing into new developmental zones, first through the other, then through the self. This is precisely why peer evaluation can be so important, since it foreshadows the student's ability to apply these developments to her or his own text, first in the reading and comprehension of one's own text, then later in the production of one's own texts.

Thus we see development moving forward through *contradiction,* in fact, *dialectically.* Read's children can write sophisticatedly but do not "read"; my students can read fairly well but haven't yet learned to apply these abilities to their own writing. Both sets of students share the reading and writing activity first with another (and in community) and then make that activity their own. Development can be seen to move from the social to the individual, from the general and global, to a more concrete individuated appropriation of the shared social relation. The "solution" to an early problem in development becomes over time the very source of contradiction and the "problem" at a later point of development. Writing and reading activity seem at various points to lead each other into new phases of integration and application, while, like thinking and speaking, taking related but not identical paths of individual development.

Another example of a Vygotskian view of writing development is in the area of writing block. The first generation compositionists—the product people—argue that writing block, while it is clearly a nuisance, is primarily a matter of inspiration (or obviously, the lack of it) and perhaps of bad experiences with writing or of audience apprehension. The first generation of compositionists argue that writing block is essentially a matter of process and is therefore beyond the reach of a theory of textuality. The second generation of compositionists—the process people—respond that it is more complicated than that, that writing block can arise due to overgeneralized rules, misconstrued process models, demands made by the processing of a text. Thus, for the second generation of compositionists writing block is a matter of Textuality when Textuality is writ large as process. The third generation of compositionists—the relations people—would certainly not disagree with the above but would add that writing block sounds suspiciously developmental, that in fact it might be an indicator of what the individual has the motive to do but does not yet have the individuated means to accomplish. Thus the third generation of compositionists would want to broaden the analysis of writing block to see it in a social and historical (Vygotsky calls it a genetic) perspective. The third generation of compositionists would want to view writing block dynamically and as an internal relation connected to other relations and Relations. (See Bertell Ollman's excellent study for a clear and useful discussion of the philosophy of internal relations referred to here.) The writing block may, under certain conditions, be the seemingly backward step that prepares development to leap ahead into new zones. Perhaps if this conflict or struggle were to be shared and a more developed writer were to help the blocker individually through the difficult parts of the process by stressing the usefulness of talking through and verbalizing the conflict and by sharing emotional (almost phatic) support and concrete textual help jointly, the transition and the block could be eased.

Thus a Vygotskian sees writing as a complex, interconnected, uneven, and dialectical *activity*. Activity is the English form of the Russian *deyatel'nost,* a technical term in Soviet psychology that has paradigm-specific meanings and sense, and that plays the central role in Soviet theory. *Deyatel'nost* is akin to *culture* in that it implies socially shared, historically developed ways of thinking, speaking, and acting. Yet unlike the term culture, *deyatel'nost* suggests the interactive, or better yet the transactive, nature of the social enterprise. To concentrate on *written speech activity,* then, is to focus on the Process (capital P) that gives rise to written texts and writing processes (small p). It is also to argue that the activity is structured into actions and operations and that "inner"actions/operations are intimately connected to "outer"actions/operations, i.e., these two aspects are internally related. Finally, to speak of written speech activity is to insist that this activity-action-operation structure is dynamic, forged out of conflict and struggle, and necessarily entails linguistic anti-structure (Washabaugh 1979).

Writing activity, then, has its origins in gesture, drawing, and symbolic play (Vygotsky 1978) and is a *function,* is in fact part of an *interfunctional system.* I "write"—functionally at least—when I leave a series of objects, in order perhaps, on my kitchen counter in the morning—an empty coffee can, a used roll of paper towels, an onion—to remind myself to get to the store and buy these things at the day's end. Vygotsky's work suggests that this is writing no less than the peculiar marking process I went through when creating this paper. (Recent research on the origins of writing in the Middle East substantiate these claims as does Vygotsky's (1978) and Luria's (1977–1978) work at the ontogenetic level.) These activities all *function* as writing.

Now if writing is a function, is interfunctional, can inner speech be any less so? In fact, Vygotsky states, "Inner speech may come very close in form to external speech or even become exactly like it when it serves as preparation for external speech—for instance, in thinking over a lecture to be given" (1962, 47). I would suggest that at least at a certain level of development one has language functions that can take virtually any *form*—written, spoken, or thought—and that it is the genesis as well as the dynamics, interrelations, and movement of these forms that is interesting and that a theory of discourse and a theory of composing must account for in some useful and interesting manner. This functional view of writing explains why we who have been at this writing art for a while find it such a heuristic and generative process, such an important way of making sense of our world, in some way a method for ordering and therefore *creating* our world. Writing for us has been so internalized that it comes to "play" the "role" of a kind of externalized inner speech. We control and regulate our world through this activity, thus in the transaction creating a new world as it is worlding. This also explains why for many of our students the idea of writing successive drafts to discover and to generate meaning seems to be such a wasted effort. *Inner speech is their draft* and writing has not developed to this point, as Luria shows us, it has not yet been internalized to the point (Luria 1977–1978) that it can "play" that "role."

Any discussion of inner speech has to distinguish between at least some of the variety of psychological functions that can be performed. Recent Soviet psychologists talk of *inner speaking, inner speech* proper, and *inner programming* among the many other modifications they make and develop in models of psychological processing. (See especially the work of A. A. Leontiev for a discussion of these current issues and for an elaboration of Vygotsky's original model proposed in the final chapter of *Thought and Language*.) Inner speaking is subvocalized speaking, one of the psychological functions most distant from deeper levels of thinking, yet still too often confused for Vygotsky's inner speech. Inner speech in the strict sense is the intermediate and transactional form of think-

ing-speaking that has its own speeded up movement, its own peculiar syntax, semantics, and pragmatics. It is "highly predicated,"
agglutinated, condensed and full of flowing "senses," saturated with
senses that give birth to meanings, and very idiosyncratic. It is
almost speech without "words." Inner programming is an "uncognized construction of a certain scheme on the basis of which an
outer statement is subsequently produced" (A. A. Leontiev 1969,
12). It is beyond the threshold of consciousness but plays an important role in helping to *prepare* for specific kinds of utterances. Motive flows behind and through all these functions, giving the
psychological processing direction.

I prefer to think of these three functions less as linear steps in
the process of the development of an utterance and instead view
them as currents in a broader stream of discourse/thinking. I believe
that as developed writers we can often sense the struggle and interaction between these three functions during the act of writing. As
Sondra Perl (1983) has noted in her empirical work on the writing
process, we are simultaneously (1) preparing for our written utterance and have a felt sense of where it is or is not going (inner
programming); (2) internally verbalizing in some sort of condensed,
predicated, and peculiar form slightly ahead of the words that are
hitting the page (I'd guess that for most of us we are about at the
line's end as the words begin to hit the page at the line's beginning—
inner speech); (3) noting the words that are hitting the page in order
to monitor and regulate and shape them (inner speaking) in accord-
ance with felt sense and inner verbalization. I find a nice fit between
the case studies and empirical findings that Perl has published and
the theoretical and empirical work of the Vygotskian school.

Now all of this is very interesting and perhaps as useful as much
of the composing research that is being conducted. Yet I think Vygotsky himself in his later years was not completely satisfied with
such models, as useful and important in their own way as they
might be. His last words and deeds suggest, to me at least, a critique
of the very work he so brilliantly created.

Vygotsky's last manuscripts, as far as we can tell, dealt with
Spinoza and the higher emotions. Spinoza had always appealed to
Vygotsky and Vygotsky seemed to return to him and other works
periodically to renew and inspire himself. Vygotsky appears to have
returned to Spinoza to clarify his ideas on emotion, to try to work
beyond the emotion/intellect split (and the related mind/body dichotomy) that seemed to pervade much modern psychological theory and that Vygotsky found so problematic. It is important to recall
that Spinoza creates a unified theory of nature and human con-

sciousness that has an important place for emotion and the development of the higher emotions.

Additionally, we learn from Nadezhda Mandelstam, the wife of the famous Russian poet Osip Mandelstam, that Vygotsky visited them a bit during 1933 or so to share ideas (and presumably poetry). Nadezhda Mandelstam notes that Vygotsky, while "a very intelligent psychologist . . ." was "somewhat hampered by the rationalism of the time" (Mandelstam 1970, 223). Significantly, the climactic final chapter of *Thought and Language* begins with an epigram drawn from one of Osip Mandelstam's poems.

Thought and Language itself ends on a mixed note. This brilliant intellectual exercise finds its terminus in emotion, motive, affect. The book on the development of mind ends with an invocation of the soul by its increasing use of poetry and drama and snatches from novels to demonstrate the psychological principles being elaborated, but also to give the reader the experience being described.

Even Vygotsky's good friends Leontiev and Luria ([1956], 1968) note in their introduction to the first volume of Vygotsky's collected works that Vygotsky never did seem to work emotion, which he deemed so important, into his model of the human mind. There seems to be an inner contradiction that I feel Vygotsky was increasingly aware of in this work. Vygotsky the humanist, the former literary critic, the literature teacher, the copublisher (in his youthful days) of some of Ehrenburg's early poetry—Vygotsky, who, according to his hometown friend Semyon Dobkin, was "for ever citing favourite verses," who from his youth to his last days loved the theatre and poetry (Levitan 1982, 27), Vygotsky, the man who no doubt could see the approach of his final days of life—this very human Vygotsky could feel, I think, the incompleteness of this model and of this theory. This is more than a biographical note; we too should keep in mind these reservations about our models. Putting models of the mind into neat little diagrams and boxing psychological functions into however elaborate a flow chart reduces *our minds* if we take our boxes and ourselves too literally, too seriously.

References

Baritt, L. & B. Kroll. 1978. Some implications of cognitive-developmental psychology for research in composing. In *Research on composing*, edited by C. Cooper & L. Odell. Urbana, IL: National Council of Teachers of English.

Donaldson, M. 1978. *Children's minds.* New York: Norton.

Levitan, K. 1982. *One is not born a personality: Profiles of Soviet education psychologists.* Moscow: Progress Publishers.

Leontiev, A. A. 1969. Inner speech and the processes of grammatical generation of utterances. *Soviet psychology* 7(3):11–16.

————. 1978. The psycholinguistic aspect of linguistic meaning. In *Recent trends in Soviet psycholinguistics,* Edited by J. Wertsch. White Plains, NY: M. E. Sharpe.

Leontiev, A. & and A. Luria. 1968. The psychological ideas of L. S. Vygotsky. In *The historical roots of contemporary psychology,* edited by B. Wolman. New York: Harper and Row.

Lundsford, A. 1980. The content of basic writers' essays. *College composition and communication* 31(3):278–90.

Luria, A. R. 1976. *Cognitive development: Its cultural and social foundations.* Cambridge, MA: Harvard University Press.

————. 1977–1978. The development of writing in the child. *Soviet psychology* 16(2):65–114.

Mandelstam, N. 1970. *Hope against hope.* New York: Atheneum.

Markova, A. 1979. *The teaching and mastery of language.* White Plains, NY: M. E. Sharpe.

Ollman, B. 1976. *Alienation: Marx's conception of man in capitalist society.* 2nd ed. New York: Cambridge University Press.

Ong, W. 1982. *Orality and literacy.* New York: Metheun.

Perl, S. 1983. Understanding composing In *The writer's mind: Writing as a mode of thinking,* edited by H. Hays, P. Roth, J. Ramsey, & R. Foulke. Urbana, IL: National Council of Teachers of English.

Read. C. 1971. Pre-school children's knowledge of English phonology. *Harvard educational review* 41(1)1–34.

Sutton, A. 1983. An introduction to Soviet developmental psychology. In *Developing thinking: Approaches to children's cognitive development,* edited by S. Meadows. New York: Metheun.

Vygotsky, L. 1962. *Thought and language.* Cambridge, MA: MIT Press.

————. 1978. *Mind in society.* Cambridge, MA: Harvard University Press.

Washabaugh, W. 1979. Linguistic Anti-Structure. *Journal of anthropological research* 35(1)30–46.

Chapter Nine

Writing Time

This essay is dedicated to Ann E. Berthoff and Janet Emig

> *Time as such has been, and it seems to me remains, the vital question of our period.*
> —Roman Jakobson

While much of what Roman Jakobson (1985) has said over the years has probably hurt composition studies in this country as much as helped it, we need to keep in mind that it was mostly Jakobson's doing that Luria and then Vygotsky came to the attention of inquisitive U.S. psychologists like Jerome Bruner in the 1950s. As a contemporary of both Vygotsky and Bakhtin, Jakobson gives us some insight into that era's intellectual history, at least until Jakobson's departure before the excesses of Stalin. Jakobson's observation that time is central to our understanding of language and, by implication, any theory of composition, seems accurate and, for the most part, ignored. That which most concerns compositionists—the unfolding of thought-word, the development of a piece of discourse, the dynamics of the reading-writing processes, the growth of writing abilities in the individual and in a community across history, the functions of writing in a discourse community and in that community's history, and its destiny—all involve time. What follows is an exploration, an attempt (very much under erasure, to play the poststructuralist literary theorist for the moment) to reinvent time in order to reconceive of composing.

The New Critical approach to teaching composition (Aycock 1985), which compositionists have too freely lumped together with several other stances and called the product approach in composition, tried to avoid this entire issue by sucking time completely out of the work and by marginalizing any consideration of intent, affect, and effect, thereby avoiding the temporal dimensions of the reading and writing processes as well as the historical implications of canon formation. In an effort to move away from the philological, "historical" tradition of the study of texts, which became prominent and then dominant in the late nineteenth century, the New Critics spatialized and detemporalized the work. The work is no longer seen as the juxtapositioning and unfolding of temporalities (or as Bakhtin would say, chronotopes) but rather is (like) a verbal icon that captures and retains a special kind of cognitive experience (See Wimsatt, Ransom, and Brooks for the particularly American version of the New Criticism. Eliot and Richards, while espousing a very closely related sort of "close reading," seem to me to be more concerned with time and history.)

Process approaches to composition in the last two decades have reacted to the devastating effects that New Criticism had on the teaching of writing. One of these effects was a bracketing of time, a move to detemporalize all textual activities, which itself was but one effect of capital's attempt to commodify labor and time, and to reduce the power of a blatantly historical, Marxist movement in the U. S. (Cowley 1980). Yet "time" too often in process theory is still the conventional, one dimensional string of successive points, even when recursion is looped back into the process. The privileging of space over time, of "three" over many, of "one" over three, is still inherent in a very Western and modernist notion of unilinear time that is mapped against three spatial dimensions (time itself is only a single additional dimension) and subdivided into the holy trinity of the past, the present, and the future (all singular).

In research the result is first the case study of the individual writer, then the case study of the individual writing class, and finally the case study of the community, but all, as useful as they be, still premised on time as diachrony (being opposed supposedly to timelessness, synchrony). In contrast, imagine what kind of research and teaching might result if we truly appreciated the following descriptions of composition in all their temporal richness.

Composition is the supplying at the right TIME and place of whatever the developing meaning then and there requires. It is the cooperation of the rest in preparing for what is to come and completing what has preceded. It is more than this though; it is the exploration of what is to come and of how it should be prepared for, and it is the further examination of what has preceded and of how it may be amended and completed.

I. A. RICHARDS (IN BERTHOFF, 1985)

The composition is the thing seen by every one living in living they are doing, they are the composing of the composition that at the TIME they are living is the composition of the time in which they are living. It is that that makes living a thing they are doing. Nothing else is different, of that almost any one can be certain. The time when and the time of and the time in that composition is the natural phenomena of that composition and of that perhaps every one can be certain.

GERTRUDE STEIN (IN MILLER, 1972)

A word is the search for it.

A. A. LEONTIEV (1977)

Time plays an important role in Vygotsky's semiotic and cognitive theory. Sylvia Scribner, in "Vygotsky's Uses of History," (1985) recognizes that Vygotsky's fuzziness about time created some very serious conceptual problems for his theory. Not flinching at apparent contradictions, ambiguities, and incompletenesses, Scribner does some conceptual analysis, grounding it in close historical and textual scrutiny of Vygotsky's work. Scribner locates difficulty in Vygotsky's apparent insistence that children in modern societies and adults in traditional communities share similar "primitive" modes of thinking. Cognitive development seems to parallel historical development, and history is essentially linear with later modes of thinking being more "advanced" than earlier modes. This seems to be perilously close to the old "ontogeny recapitulates phylogeny" argument.

A. R. Luria (1976) in the early 1930s collected ethnographic data among the Uzbek, a traditional society in Moslem Central Asia. Uzbek society at this moment was in "transition" from a feudal mode of production to more modern modes of work and education. Under Vygotsky's supervision, Luria journeyed to Central Asia to test some of Vygotsky's hypotheses, but also to collect and preserve ethnographic information on a society that had existed for thousands of years with minimal changes but was currently changing its way of life, perhaps forever. Just as Boas and the early anthropologists in this country felt a pressing need to gather and preserve ethnographic information before Native American societies became modernized or disappeared, so Vygotsky and Luria saw a once-in-history opportunity to make some observations on a traditional culture.

The ethnographic information that Luria collected was connected with an apparently unilinear notion of time, development and history. The result was an explosion of criticism alleging ethnocentrism, cultural imperialism, racism. Vygotsky appeared to be saying that traditional Uzbek peasants used cognitively more primitive modes of thinking than newly collectivized peasants, the implication being that Russian (and Western) cognitive abilities generally surpassed the more formulaic, conventional, traditional Uzbek forms. Vygotsky and his colleagues, by avoiding an explicit and radical reworking of the concept of time, seemed to accept the unilinear Western version. To be sure, Vygotsky's work in the early 1930s was being critiqued for a variety of reasons and from a range of perspectives in the Soviet Union, and the apparent ethnocentric, bourgeois, imperialistic nature of this ethnographic study was only one of the more visible reasons his work was being attacked. More broadly speaking, Vygotsky's ideas were viewed as being politically incompatible with the emerging Stalinist apparat (see Joravsky 1989). Still, Vygotsky's fuzziness about time and its cognate concepts (history, development, narrative) led to the intellectual, if not the political, basis for the Party's judgment that Vygotsky's ideas were heretical and that they were dangerous enough to warrant subsequent critique, suppression, and indexing.

In fact, Scribner makes a persuasive case that Vygotsky was not reverting to the old ontogeny/phylogeny argument. Instead Vygotsky seemed to be attempting to broaden psychology, to make it more amenable to considering all the rich and diverse artifacts of human activity as "data." Vygotsky wanted to bring his studies to life, to take psychology out of that brass instrument laboratory and put it into the everyday lives and activities of the people. Vygotsky believed that psychologists could learn from the people, from different cultures and eras. He felt especially strongly that a theory of mind had to learn from the arts. Traditional psychologists, after all, have few problems with the notion of time since they (think they) create situations in the laboratory where time is eliminated, reduced, or decontextualized. Of course teachers and practitioners in all disciplines have long known that the results achieved in such context-stripping laboratories are of little value. Even fellow clinical psychologists have difficulty finding anything of use in traditional experimental psychology. Klaus Riegel (1979) and his colleagues, aware of this, created a whole school of Life Span Developmental psychology that tries to put time back into psychology. Elliot

Mishler (1979) provides an eloquent account of the issues involved here in educational research.[1]

Scribner implies that Vygotsky wanted to integrate these various "levels" into a single theory. Vygotsky's theory-constructing process ". . . begins with and returns to observations of behavior in daily life to devise and test models of the history of higher systems. Starting from behavioral observations of contemporary adults, he moves to observations of primitive adults documented in ethnopsychological records and then, by way of experiment, to behavioral observations of children in modern times" (1985, 137). Susan Wells (1986) draws a similar conclusion about Vygotsky's theory of concept development. She argues that we need to read Vygotsky rhetorically, understanding his account of concept formation less as a stage theory and more as a narrative bound up in other narratives, including Karl Marx's analysis of society and history. Scribner (1985, 141) rehabilitates this temporal aspect of Vygotsky's theory by emphasing Vygotsky's geologic root metaphor (Vygotsky also makes extensive use of a meteorological metaphor) and by elaborating the "layers" of development:

- LEVEL 1: *Phylogeny,* the developmental history of the human species and general human history.
- LEVEL 2: The history of individual human *society.*
- LEVEL 3: The natural and cultural life history of the individual in society (*ontogeny*).
- LEVEL 4: The history of a particular *psychological system.*

Scribner, in providing a multitemporal basis for Vygotsky's theory, answers some of the objections concerning Vygotsky's apparent assumption of the unilinear basis of history. She renews the idea of development by arguing that development occurs on four levels, at various rates and tempos that will obviously depend in the first instance on the local circumstances, particularly the community to which an individual belongs and that community's developmental moment. Then cross-cultural comparisons may be useful as a heuristic, but in such a revised Vygotskian theory there is no need to posit a single line of development to which other cultures must conform, in contrast to many developmental theories (like Piaget's) that seem to privilege a set of constant, "objective," cognitive universals.

Notice, however, that while making a place for four levels and for various rates of change among all levels, Scribner, by privileging Vygotsky's geologic root metaphor still assumes a first and a last "layer," an origin and an end. There is a teleology embedded in her solution to Vygotsky's temporal problems that still suggests a linearity, at least in the physical, if not, strictly speaking in the human universe.

> *Maybe nothing ever happens once and is finished. Maybe happen is never once but ripples maybe on water after the pebble sinks, the ripples moving on, spreading.*
>
> WILLIAM FAULKNER.

If the first two movements of this work are allegro, then this section begins the andante.

Jerome Bruner, in *Actual Minds, Possible Worlds,* notes in passing that "We are natural ontologists but reluctant epistemologists . . . The ontology I would want to argue, looks after itself. It is epistemology that needs cultivating" (1986, 155). To agree with Roman Jakobson and take issue with Jerome Bruner in a single essay risks giving a very wrong impression about one's intellectual family tree. Bruner is certainly one of the very few American psychologists (along with Michael Cole) who from the start recognized the importance of the work of Lev Vygotsky and played an instrumental role in introducing Vygotsky's ideas to the public. Still, Bruner's statement reveals his modernist roots and the reason his work can only, now, be of limited help to us. The notion that epistemology is primary while ontology is metaphysics (a bad word to modernists) and should be relegated to the realm of religion and poetry has been a widespread assumption during this century. The difficulty with Bruner's statement is there is some truth to it. Ontology does take care of itself and when the dominant ideology is positivism, we can be relatively sure that if we do not consciously begin with a contrasting ontological position, we will unknowingly have a positivist framework built into our first epistemological statement.

What follows then is ontology, without apology.

> *Movement, flux, rhythms, pulses.*
>
> *The universe is change, energies in change. The wor(l)d is confl(ict)uence.*
>
> *Time is plural, the act is plural, the word is plural.*
>
> *Mixture is the mother of purity. There is a pristine dirtiness about Time that gives birth to times and temporalities. History is human activity through time. Development is the individual*

act through history. Discourse is the word through the individual act.

That is as succinct as I can make it. Now let me unfold some of the ideas packed into these words in a more discursive manner.

Instead of thinking of time as a river it may be more useful for the moment to think of time as a pond (or the ocean). As Faulkner suggests, the so-called "recursiveness" that the poet senses in life and discourse might be more precisely explained if we simply began with the idea that time is plural, that an act ripples on forever, with decreasing intensity in usual circumstances to be sure, and that we can meet this act (which is also the history of connected acts) in its later life.

So,

1. Imagine that time is plural. By plural we mean that any "moment" (which as David Bohm (1980) astutely shows can be any stretch of time that is convenient for our present purposes—e.g., a moment of a textual work, a moment of an individual's life, a moment of history that may be a century or two, the moment of the existence of life on earth . . .) is "made up" of many temporalities interacting. Our sense of time's singularity comes from these confluences and conflicts of multiple temporalities. The unity of the moment is similar to the unity of white light, which "consists of" a mixture of radiations of various wavelengths along the spectrum. This moment, which is not the dead stasis of the structuralist's "timeless" all-at-once synchrony, is the dynamic unfolding of an infinite number of temporalities.

2. Imagine too that time is social. Human beings in community create various temporalities and even the temporalities they do not create (such as the regular movements of the moon, planets, stars) are only accessible through the social. Carol Gould has recognized this. She has noted how Karl Marx discovered that human activity creates time in both its subjective and objective dimensions. Gould says, "Let me begin with a very strong claim: that for Marx, in the *Grundrisse* at least, labor creates time or introduces time into the world. Thus according to Marx, 'Labor is the living, form-giving fire; it is the transitoriness of things, their temporality, as their formation by living time'" (1978, 361). The commodification of time that has taken place in capitalist society over the last several centuries demonstrates this social (and political) nature of the construction of time. We even talk now of "investing time" and of "spending time," since time in capitalist society takes the commodity form like everything else. Time has become an exchange value through which capital ex-

tracts surplus value. The "weekend," as we know it, is one of the most recent and palpable results of this commodification of time, of capital's increasing control of the working day, and the attempt of labor to retain some control over time and activity.

3. Imagine that time is local. There really is no such thing as synchrony. Time is dependent on the local conditions which are, while related to other temporalities, specific and unique. So, instead of thinking of deja-vu as a chance product of a single human being at one point retrieving once-and-for-all information from "back there" (where, after all, is that information? the memory cells or the memory area of the brain has never actually been found), why not instead see an event more as a field that goes on forever and that a person (or a culture) encounters again and again in various forms? Deja-vu might then be viewed as an event that one encounters in several localities, in its later ripples, to use the Faulkner image. We could then view alumni days as attempts of graduates of a college to encounter the old places, the old stories, the old times, literally. And regularly recurring religious meetings are a community's rendezvous with the its past and future.

4. Finally, imagine that time is multidirectional. Here we encounter the greatest resistance from the investment our cultural forebears have made in the notion of causality. With all of the innovations in the New Physics, it is still tantamount to heresy to tamper with time's arrow, to dispute the second law of thermodynamics, to imply entropy may be limited, itself a local phenomena.[2] Ernst Bloch is one of the very few people who has had the courage to dispute this idea. For Bloch (1970) the future flows into the present and we already have images and intimations of that process. So too David Carr eventually follows the logic of his argument to conclude "Far from waiting passively for things to happen, communities negotiate with the future and understand the present in light of the future" (1986, 172). Consider what it might mean to understand a text or the writing process not only in terms of what it was or is, but also as an anticipation or image of its future.

Some might argue against the "unnaturalness" of the kind of time that I here envisage. But I think this way of considering time is actually more in keeping with our experience in daily life than the conventional "common sense" version. We all have a diverse and rich experience of time even in a culture that attempts to make all times conform. We don't think much of turning the clock back and forth for "savings" time every fall and spring, at least not after a day or two. We fly across time zones and datelines with few problems. Nor do we get confused when we sport. In football, time outs are "normal"; in basketball, overtimes indicate the quality of the game. Even in baseball the perfect game is indicated by endlessness—the game goes on "forever" if no errors, no "outs" are made. The most amateur of gardeners knows that the temporality of the zucchini growing in June is wildly different from the zucchini growing in a wet and warm August. We are rightly suspicious when every car, costume, word in a period movie comes out of the same exact year, the same moment of history—we intuit that reality is much more mixed than this. Looking down a city street, we see a lot more diversity, styles from other times hanging on.

And is it really so strange to be writing several different texts or parts of texts "at the same time"? Do we always start out our reading with the first word of an essay? While the convention of reading in this culture is that it is linear and starts at the first word and goes to the last—and to be sure it can go this way—what prevents us from going faster or slower, from beginning with the bibliography, from reading the last section first and then going to the first paragraph, from rereading innumerable times a word or a book? A bookmark saves a time as well as a place. When we forget the word we are searching for, we often can recall its rhythm, its temporality.

Finally, consider the "fundamental particle" of existence in our society, the human being, the individual: my heart beats at a different tempo from my breathing which, while clearly related to it, surely goes at a different pace from my thinking, my verbalizing. Even my thinking is not a single thing, but changes, moves to different beats and pulses: it condenses and unfolds in a whole universe of specific temporalities. I am plural, social, local, and multidirectional. Why should my concept of time be any less so?

So what does all this mean for composition studies? Obviously this is less the place to provide a new cookbook on what to do come Monday morning than it is the moment to suggest how revolutionizing our concept of time (itself part and parcel of its context, the changing socioeconomic conditions of an anemic late capitalism with potential for transformation) can open up new territories, suggest the vague outlines of a New Composition. I will concern myself in the last section of this essay, then, more with creating a dialogue with the twenty-first century than with diddling around with the niceties of what passes as more acceptable composition research.

Let me conclude with an unholy trinity of implications that result from our temporal re-creation. (1) Rewriting time helps us to put certain aspects of the current poststructuralist debate about the primacy of "narrative" into perspective. (2) A new vision of time moves us toward a new definition of the unity of a work. (3) And a new sense of unity provides us with a different glimpse into the psychology of writing.

One of the noisiest current debates in the humanities concerns the nature of narrative and its relation, if any, to the "real world." To oversimplify to the point of caricature, it has traditionally been thought that narrative (and when we say narrative, we often are also referring to discourse generally and the tropes—metaphor, metonymy, synecdoche, and irony—specifically) is *about* the world, that narrative, whether history or poetry, *reflects* or *represents* the world, condensing and transforming that world into something more manageable, but also more universal, more "true." In this view, the world gives birth to narrative. The relation between the world and narrative is mimetic. One reflects, represents, symbolizes, imitates, refers to, copies, or corresponds to the other. Erich Auerbach's magisterial *Mimesis: The Representation of Reality in Western Literature* (1953) is one of the most eloquent attempts to use this notion of narrative to connect the great literature of the Western tradition with the specific developments in the views of reality held by societies themselves undergoing radical social change (the economic and class dimension of Auerbach's argument has been, curiously, consistently underemphasized). Auerbach sees a correspondence between the sharp (monologic) boundaries between high and low style and the sharp division between upper and lower class. In this argument, narrative first symbolizes and only then transforms (partially, if at all) a preexisting and relatively independent world.

Postmodernism quarrels with this traditional notion. Narrative in this (post)structuralist mode creates, or at the very least gives form to, the world. Thus, our notions of history appear to evolve from the tropes we use to invent the narrative we want, which itself is a function of the power relations we are in (White 1974). Perhaps history is real apart from narrative, apart from the tropes, but if so, it is an absent cause only available through some master narrative (Jameson 1981). Our very self, not to mention our cognition of the world, is a primary narrative act (Hardy 1978). At the very least, our ability to experience time and to narrate events forms a necessary dialectic (Ricoeur 1984).

Both the traditional and the (post)modern argument are premised on a unilinear, unidirectional view of time. When, in contrast, we take Time as primary, giving birth to times, temporalities, the world, and narrative, then "copying" (and whether, for example, the sign is or is not arbitrary) becomes a moot issue. Time unfolds into temporalities that "reflect" themselves and Time. Instead of fighting over whether art reflects nature or nature reflects art, the argument shifts in a new mimesis to viewing the universe in a new way. The universe is seen as the explicate unfolding of an implicate order

(Bohm 1980). Thus any moment in the explicate order is less a reflection of another moment in the explicate order than a "reflection" (if we can even use this term) of the unfolding of the implicate order.

Bakhtin (1986) says, "The word . . . is bottomless . . ." This new argument proposes that we can have the word reflecting the world or vice versa, if we first accept the initial ontological plurality of both, if we begin with implicate order, with the (uni)verse "reflecting" or "projecting" or "unfolding" itself through Time. Thus the wor(l)d rather than word versus world. Word and world are already plural, un(en)folding as temporalities. Tropes rather than external (the dress of thought) or internal (the soul of thought) are in-between; the tropes become the hinges of time, time machines that warp us from temporality to temporality, from "one" point of view to another, from one "turn" in a dialogue to another. Tropes are turnings that shoot us into new perspectives, new temporalities. Erich Auerbach's discussion of "Figura" and types in Western literature and Cynthia Ozick's placing of metaphor at the "center" of our reading of history thus acquire an added significance.[3]

This easily transports us to the concept of unity since unity involves the relations between whole and part, the same question, from a slightly different perspective that the tropes address. We have had problems defining what is whole and what is part precisely because we have not taken time into consideration. But what is whole or part depends completely on time. Whole/part is a changing relation dependent on the temporality one is in sync with. Thus the unity of a textual product depends on the unity (and temporalities) of the process, and the unity of the process depends on the discourse community and its conventions, norms, rhythms, temporalities. Edward White (1985) argues that the holistic scoring of essays works because readers share an interpretive community. I do not disagree, but would add that that interpretive community, among other things, is a matter of shared temporalities. Readers can score similarly because they have agreed to temporarily read at a similar speed. Reading at a similar speed brings certain textual characteristics temporarily to the fore, while suppressing other traits. "Product" people have difficulty holistically scoring because they have been brought up to believe that reading is always a matter of "slow time." Reading for them is always "close reading." Thus, textual unity for them is more fine-grained, "tighter," and "resolved." The close reader reads an entirely different text in a completely different time warp from the holistic scorer.

A plural notion of time suggests that unity in art, in discourse, is less a matter of perfect, hermetic singleness, less a once-and-for-all finishedness and independence (note our writing development theories mostly stress the importance of writing so-called "context-free" and "time-independent" discourse): unity becomes more the juxta-positioning of temporalities, more the creation of multiple openings, more the purposeful crafting and anticipation of incompletenesses. If "Art is nature speeded up and God slowed down" (de Chazal in Winokur), then a unified work has a rhythmic richness, a flow of feeling that an otherwise correct, but fragmented work lacks. The unified work then is dialogic, to use Bakhtin's term. In providing us openings, it requires our participation. Time is wound up in the word. The unified work asks us to unwind these temporalities, adding in the process our own temporalities as well. The dialogic work also anticipates the rhythms of other works, readers, epochs, providing blank measures where the notes and beats can be added.

In the conventional theory of discourse, narration in the traditional sense might be seen as "fast" time while description might be viewed as "slow" time. Argument becomes the flow of the temporalities of an idea through time, while persuasion becomes the flow of the dialogue of those arguments through time. That is if we really must have the modes. For a long time, we have used the word *mode* without due consideration of its temporalities. What began in ancient Greece as a way of talking about music and thus time, has become substantial, more often related to content, to stuff, and stuff's state of existence, to a deadened spatial container/contained, than to rhythms, pulses, transformations, the various temporalities a discourse can assume. Theodore Roethke says, "A poet: someone who is never satisfied with saying one thing at a time" (Brenner 1983, 12). The poet, any maker, realizes the temporal richness of life and is not happy with anything less in her or his works.

Vygotsky in the final chapter of *Thought and Language* contends that thinking develops into words through several intermediate phases including inner speech. The key idea here is *phases.* Thought bringing forth the word is likened to a cloud showering raindrops. The word in essence is not something radically different from the thought, but rather is another phase of thought. Water, after all, is water whether in gaseous, liquid, or solid form. The word is in a different phase, in a different mode from thought. The word is thought at a different temporality. Thought condenses and "speeds up" words. The word is "slowed down" and unfolded thought. And the path from thought to word itself changes each time, thus setting off another related set of temporalities in the very process of "slowing down" or "speeding up." Concretely, we do not always go straight from thought to word, though that sometimes happens especially for the very experienced or for the new writer. But writing mostly slows us down, and though we sense the relatedness of thinking, speaking, and writing, we also have all experienced the tendency of thinking to proceed at a different tempo from writing and speaking. Some of our clouds shower down words; but some of our clouds, parts of more encompassing high pressure systems or hurricanes, move along on their own "levels," in their own "layers," condensing presumably into the ocean of temporality deep within. So what we have are entire systems of very different temporalities interacting when we write. We can think of writing then as a dialogue of "words" in various phases, creating a host of different temporalities.

- IMAGING: This involves the feelings that S. Perl (1979) calls felt sense but it also includes what A. A. Leontiev (1969) calls inner programming, images upon which we temporarily project thoughts, words, even entire texts. This is the phase of *very fast time.*

- INNER SPEECH: Highly abbreviated and greatly condensed signs that have a special "predicated" syntax. This is still *fast time,* though slower than imaging, since it is becoming verbalized, though idiosyncratically so.

- INNER SPEAKING: Contrary to popular belief, this is usually *not* inner speech. Subvocalization takes a good deal more time than inner speech and its functions and therefore its structures are usually quite different. Inner speaking is *slow time,* far closer to speech than it is to inner speech.

- SPEECH: Vocalized and *slower time* than "thinking," but usually faster than writing.

- WRITING: In all its various dimensions writing is usually *very slow time.* This slowness itself is the source of a rich development in inner speech (Luria 1969).

These relations are variable. The interactions/transactions between the phases of the word and its various temporalities make writing a unique, unrepeatable activity.

When a writer writes there is a constant shifting of temporalities, a constant alternation between the various tempos of meaning. The writer dances between the word that is hitting the page at the moment (*very slow time*), the word that is being unfolded in embryo form in inner speech (*fast time*), and the felt sense and imaging of where all this is going or should be going (*very fast time*). Add to this the reading temporalities that occur in alternation with our writing and you have a genuinely intricate dance (Phelps 1982).

Writing then connects and rearranges all of these rhythms of meaning. Writing creates temporalities while also itself being a phase, a mode of time. Time creates times and temporalities. We write time and Time writes us and our texts. Or to momentarily stop with the poem that "began" the writing of this essay two years ago—

WARNING: PHILOSOPHICAL POEM[4]

Writing writes the writer and her world.

Homo scribiens   lives through page ink.
The world writes in-order-to; I in-order-to   to write.
The universe is born when it hits the page.
Writing creates the world in its very world-ing.
Writing this very line now pulls my history
                              through the present
                              and into the future.
Writing insists that I see   this dotted i
is premised on all our history, that, in fact,
I congeal and condense all history in
the very dotting   of this i.
this sentence, which as it starts   out doesn't even   know
where it is
going,
takes me into a future concrete and malleable   as
the period
at the end of this sentence

Notes

1. A wide range of approaches in psychology are opposed to behaviorism and brass instrument laboratories. The split between humanistic psychology and experimental psychology is greater than the divisions between experimental psychology and physiology. Riegel (1979, 1976, 1972) is one of the more philosophical and dialectical psychologists, but also Rollo May's (1983) existential psychology provides a humanistic alternative. Unlike Vygotsky, however, both Riegel and May tend to be more philosophically idealistic than materialistic, finding their modernist roots in the phenomenological reaction to positivism that especially grew prominent following the Great War.

2. David Bohm, a former student of Einstein and an important theorist, is disturbed by the fragmentation evidenced in physics by the acceptance of both quantum mechanics and relativity theory, when these two theories in fact are contradictory. Bohm (1980) provides an eloquent statement about the need to re-envision the universe as an un(en)folding whole that only very partially is revealed by what he calls the explicate, the external and unfolding, order. Bohm posits a far vaster implicate order, that underlies and unfolds the explicate order. The explicate order is unfolded by the

implicate order. The explicate order bears a similar relation to the implicate order, as the surface waves and turbulence have to the ocean.

All of this is not to say that Bohm is not very wrongheaded about some things, particularly when he moves into the realm of mind and language. Still he gives us a way out, for now at least, of some philosophical deadends, most apparent in the (post)structuralist debate with tradition.

"String theory" in the New Physics also provides an exciting perspective on the universe that I find consistent with my concern with time.

I would also highly recommend J.T. Fraser's (1981) theory of time. He has created an all encompassing framework that integrates six major temporalities known to humankind by means of the natural or the human sciences. His theory actually broadens Scribner's theory of history/time.

For more on the new physics and time, also see Calder (1977), Gribbin (1979), Morris (1985), Wilber (1982).

For the human science concern with time, see Phelps (1982), Everman (1986), Hall (1983, 1976), Hayles (1984), Leff (1986), Whorf (1956), and, for useful weirdness, Ouspensky (1933).

3. Auerbach (1973) discusses the figural tradition of interpretation. Auerbach says "Figural interpretation establishes a connection between two events or persons, the first of which signifies not only itself but also the second, while the second encompasses or fulfills the first " (53). One might, for example, see the exodus of Israel out of Egypt as a figure of Christ's resurrection from the dead, itself the first step of the Church's call of the sinner out of sin, in preparation for God's call of the Church out of the world at the end of time. All are "real" events in themselves within time, but each also is a figure or type of the others. History (and any "single" event) from a figural view, remains open, questionable, tentative, dialogic, "deeper," than in the modern view. An "event" in the figural view might be seen as rippling through time, though in the process not making present time any less real, unique, concrete.

So too Ozick (1986) hits upon the close relation between our sense of history, our very ability to understand history and empathize with those gone by and those not yet here, and metaphor, with the bringing together of two unlike points of view. Dialogue might also then be considered metaphoric, involving the irreducible other point of view; metaphor can be similarly considered dialogic.

4. Special thanks to *Ginger Hill,* the literary magazine of Slippery Rock University, for publishing this poem.

References

Auerbach, E. 1953. *Mimesis: The representation of reality in western literature.* Trans. Willard Trask. Princeton, NJ: Princeton University Press.

————. Figura. 1973. *Scenes from the drama of European literature.* Gloucester, MA: Peter Smith.

Aycock, C. 1985. New critical rhetoric and composition. Dissertation. University of Southern California.

Bakhtin, M. 1986. *Speech genres and other late essays,* edited by C. Emerson & M. Holquist. Trans. V. McGee. Austin: University of Texas P.

Berthoff, A. 1985. I. A. Richards. *Traditions of inquiry,* edited by J. Brereton. New York: Oxford University Press.

Bloch, E. 1970. *Philosophy of the future.* Trans. J. Cumming. New York: Herder and Herder.

Bohm, D. 1980. *Wholeness and the implicate order.* London: Routledge Kegan Paul.

Brenner, G. 1983. *Concealments in Hemingway's work.* Columbus, Ohio State University Press.

Brooks, C. 1947. *The well wrought urn: Studies in the structure of poetry.* New York: Harcourt.

Bruner, J. 1986. *Actual minds, possible worlds.* Cambridge, MA: Harvard University Press.

Calder, N. 1977. *The key to the universe: A report on the new physics.* New York: Penguin Books.

Carr, D. 1986. *Time, narrative, and history.* Bloomington: Indiana University Press.

Clifford, J. & G. Marcus, eds. *1986. Writing culture: The poetics and politics of ethnography.* Berkeley: University of California Press.

Cowley, M. 1980. *The dream of the golden mountains: Remembering the 1930s.* New York: Viking.

Everman, W. 1986. Long talking: The infinite text. *New Orleans Review* 13:22–30.

Faulkner, W. 1972. *Absalom, Absalom!* New York: Vintage.

Fraser, J. T. 1981. Towards an integrated understanding of time. *The voices of time.* 2nd ed. Amherst: University of Massachusetts Press.

Gould, C. 1978. *Marx's social ontology: Individual and community in Marx's theory of social reality.* Cambridge, MA: MIT Press.

Gribbin, J. 1979. *Timewarps.* New York: Dell.

Hall, E. 1976. *Beyond culture.* Garden City, NY: Anchor.

————. 1983 *The dance of life.* Garden City, NY: Anchor.

Hardy, B. 1978. Narrative as a primary act of mind. *The cool web: The patterns of children's reading,* edited by M. Meek, A. Warlow, & G. Barton. New York: Atheneum.

Hayles, N. K. 1984. *The cosmic web: Scientific field models and literary strategies in the twentieth century.* Ithaca: Cornell University Press.

Jakobson, R. 1985. *Verbal art, verbal sign, verbal time,* edited by K. Pomorska & S. Rudy. Minneapolis: University of Minnesota Press.

Jakobson, R. & K. Pomorska. 1985. Dialogue on time in language and literature. Jakobson.

Jameson, F. 1981. *The political unconscious.* Ithaca, NY: Cornell University Press.

Joravsky, D. 1989. *Russian psychology: A critical history.* Cambridge, MA: Basil Blackwell.

Leff, M. 1986. Textual criticism: The legacy of G. P. Mohrmann. *Quarterly Journal of Speech* 72:377–89.

Leontiev, A. A. 1977. The psycholinguistic of linguistic meaning. *Recent trends in Soviet psycholinguistics,* edited by J. Wertsch. White Plains, NY: M. E. Sharpe.

Luria, A. 1969. Speech and the formation of mental processes. *A handbook of contemporary Soviet psychology.* edited by M. Cole & I. Maltzman. New York: Basic Books.

———. 1976. *Cognitive development: Its cultural and social foundations.* Cambridge, MA: Harvard University Press.

May, R. 1983. *The discovery of being: Writings in existential psychology.* New York: Norton.

Miller, J. 1972. *Word, self, reality.* New York: Dodd & Mead.

Mishler, E. 1979. Meaning in context: Is there any other kind? *Harvard Educational Review* 49:1–19.

Morris, R. 1985. *Time's arrows: Scientific attitudes toward time.* New York: Simon and Schuster.

Ouspensky, P. D. 1933. *Tertium organum: A key to the enigmas of the world.* 2nd American ed. New York: Alfred Knopf.

Ozick, C. 1986. The moral necessity of metaphor: Rooting history in a figure of speech. *Harpers Magazine* May:62–68.

Phelps, L. 1982. The dance of discourse: A dynamic, relativistic view of structure. *Pre/Text* 3:51–83.

Ransom, J. 1941. *The new criticism.* Norfolk, CT: New Directions.

Ricoeur, P. 1984. *Time and narrative.* Vol. 1. Trans. K. McLaughlin & David Pellauer. Chicago, IL: University of Chicago Press.

Riegel, K. 1972. Time and change in the development of the individual and society. In *Advances in child development and behavior.* Vol. 7, edited by H. Reese. New York: Academic.

———. 1976. The Dialectics of Time. *Developmental psychology: Perspectives on experimental research.* edited by N. Datan & H. Reese. New York: Academic.

———. 1979. *Foundations of dialectical psychology.* New York: Academic.

Scribner, S. 1985. Vygotsky's uses of history. *Culture, communication, and cognition: Vygotskian perspectives,* edited by J. Wertsch. Cambridge, MA: Cambridge University Press.

Vygotsky, L. 1986. *Thought and language.* 2nd ed. Trans. and ed. by A. Kozulin. Cambridge, MA: MIT Press.

Washabaugh, W. 1979. Linguistic anti-structure. *Journal of anthropological research* 35:30–46.

Whorf, B. 1956. The relation of habitual thought and behavior to language. In *Language, thought, and reality.* Cambridge, MA: MIT Press.

White E. 1985. *Teaching and assessing writing.* San Francisco, CA: Josey-Bass.

White, H. 1974. *Metahistory: The historical imagination in nineteenth-century Europe.* Baltimore, MD: Johns Hopkins University Press.

———. 1978. *Tropics of discourse: Essays in cultural criticism.* Baltimore, MD: Johns Hopkins University Press.

Winokur, J. 1986. *Writers on writing.* Philadelphia, PA: Running Press.

Part Three

Composing Self

If I had composed this volume twenty years ago, this section on self and composition would perhaps have been the longest in the book. In the early 1970s there was a great deal of interest in "self" and "expression." Ken Macrorie in *Uptaught* (1969) and *Telling Writing* (1973) had argued for an acceptance of the subjective dimensions of writing in order to produce better texts. Peter Elbow in *Writing Without Teachers* (1973) had put forward a theory of the writing process that made teachers secondary to the student writer. James Moffett in *Teaching the Universe of Discourse* (1968) and *A Student-Centered Language Arts Curriculum* (1968, 1973) had worked out an entire range of writing, reading, speaking, and drama activities that began with the self. James Miller in his volume *Word. Self. Reality: The Rhetoric of Imagination* (1972) advocated a "process theory" of composing that drew on literary sources and understandings of self. Miller's book was one of the first in composition to cite Lev Vygotsky on inner speech, and to view writing as a complex act of both mind and society. Finally, James Kinneavy had, almost as an afterthought, added a whole final section on expressive discourse in his *A Theory of Discourse.* Kinneavy says, "If this book had been written a number of years ago, there would be no chapter on expressive discourse" (1971, 393–394). Kinneavy notes that "Without a doubt, the concern common to all of the groups interested in expression was the reassertion of the importance of the individual, of subjectivity, of personal value in an academic, cultural, and social environment that tended to ignore the personal and subjective" (1971, 396).

So what happened? Why is this section of *Thinking Through Theory* the shortest one?

It would, of course, have been easy to add some new essays on subjectivity in writing. But I have purposely included only those texts that I wrote over the last decade dealing with this. To the extent that my essays in this volume track my intellectual project over the last ten years, and in that tracking make a statement about the interests of the discourse community of Composition, I have decided not to add new essays simply to balance things out because I think it is important for Composition to recognize that it has abandoned the "self" for the "social." And I think this is bad.

I think it bad because it perpetuates "the self *versus* society" dichotomy when everything that I know in the work of Vygotsky and Bakhtin questions and transcends that dichotomy. I think it bad because at this point, ten years after the first essays by Patricia Bizzell, David Bartholomae, and others raised the question of the social, the social perspective on writing is less a corrective to a narrow view of process than the hegemonic view that itself needs correction. Many of my graduate students entering English and composition studies do not have any idea of what process theory is and they hardly have any need for a corrective to balance their overenthusiasm for the private and personal. Rather the danger now, as I see it, is that the "social" turn in composition becomes a return of the repressed, a return to the simple and unquestioned authority of the teacher as representative of institutional power. As I have argued elsewhere, I believe that that view oversimplifies what are very complex, often contradictory, and multiple social and individual processes. It also ignores history, the history of the concrete individuals who come together to compose a writing class, as well as the history of the social forces that flow in and out of the institutional spaces that we call university and disciplines. A return to a teacher-centered classroom may be nostalgic but I am not sure it is productive. In fact, the reason I decided not go into literary studies in 1978 when I began my doctoral work was that I was not then comfortable with the execution of authority that occurred in too many of those teacher-centered literature classrooms in which I had been a student. I felt that there was a great deal of talk about the humanities with little humanistic concern for students. Composition teachers, perhaps because they had no preestablished "content" that they felt compelled to press on to the student at all cost, seemed to have different ways of exercising their and their students' authority. I am not sure how true this is anymore.

So I leave this section of essays short. I challenge compositionists to think hard about where we are and to reconsider the question of the composing self, in ways that refuse to sever self from society.

Some might respond that I am missing the boat in these comments, that, in fact, poststructuralism more than any movement in literary studies in one hundred years has already been rethinking subjectivity. It is true that poststructuralist theory does share a common "critique of the subject." But the poststructuralist theorists whom I know would be the first to say the "self" is not the "subject." Subjectivity is a sort of dwelling where self takes up residence and is constructed, the site where social effects through discourse make a self possible. I have not yet been persuaded that this is relevant— to use the word closely associated with the renewed attention to "self" that took place in the late 1960s and early 1970s—to my interest in the composing self. Aside from the fact that such theory comes wrapped in language that other writing teachers find alienating and that I find to be too much in the tradition of what Michael Wood in a recent television series "Legacy" has called the "barbarian West," the poststructuralist critique of the subject seems to toss something out with the essentialized self: agency. Critique appears to be for nought if after we do it, there seems to be little that "I" or that "we" can "do" about the transformation of social relations. Whether we accept or critique the concept of self, we need to begin with that concept because for historical and rhetorical reasons that is where our students and our culture are at, no matter how much we might want to change that reality.

I have been formed by the notion of self and society that comes out of the work of Mikhail Bakhtin and Lev Vygotsky. No doubt, one reason why I found their ideas attractive long before I understood them fully is that they somehow better described the experience that I had growing up in a working-class, Polish-American family. Self and the social were always closely tied up with each other in that ethnic milieu. I as an individual might well make the decision to go to college, but that decision was always tempered by the fact the I was first in my family to go to college, that I had to do well not simply for me but for them. Failure was unthinkable because I would be letting down not simply myself, but my parents, my family, my church, my class. Individual failure—and success—was also social from that first day I received the letter accepting me at Ohio State and requesting that my father fill out the personal financial statement so that I might get scholarships to go to college. Bakhtin and Vygotsky talk about how the self is formed out of the words of others, like the body is formed out of the bodies of others. But they also insist that the newly-fashioned self goes back to transform those others with other words.

So in "The Struggle for Voice" I try to think of writing as one of the places where self comes into existence and grows. The struggle to write is a part of the struggle to become a self. This essay, then, puts forward the view of writing as dialogic, but at the same time it also tries to *enact* this view by working through some texts of Bakhtin, from which I wring my own composing self.

"Vygotsky's Theory of Self" takes up the social turn in Composition by juxtaposing it to what I see to be Vygotsky's theory of society and the self's emergence from, but also continued circulation through, the social matrix. Central to Vygotsky's view is the idea that came from Marx himself, that the full development of the individual requires the full development of community, that the dichotomy of self versus society tells us more about the limits of the social formation in which we live than it tells of us about the nature of individuality and community. In this essay I take up the "self" and summarize Vygotsky's view of it in six propositions. When we see self as social, composed, porous, dynamic, semiotic, and refined through play, we can begin to revise our conceptions of writing and perhaps as well begin to restore the self to Composition.

References

Elbow, P. 1973. *Writing without teachers.* New York: Oxford University Press.

Kinneavy, J. 1971. *A theory of discourse.* New York: Norton.

Macrorie, K. 1969. *Uptaught.* New York: Hayden.

———. 1970. *Telling writing.* New York: Hayden.

Miller, J. 1972. *Word, self, reality: The rhetoric of the imagination.* New York: Dodd, Mead.

Chapter Ten

The Struggle for Voice

Writing is tough. Tom Wolfe somewhere remarks that writing is like arthritis: it only gets worse with age. Now if you think about it, that is an interesting point. That notion questions the received opinion that we composition teachers sometimes carry around in our heads that "skills" necessarily get easier and surely better with practice. Well, that hasn't always been my experience as a writer or as a teacher. Writing is tough. Often when I sit down to write a paper or even a journal entry, I wonder why I engage in this tiring, complicated, and, if you think about it, rather bizarre cultural activity. Here I am, a grown man "whose most absorbed and passionate hours are spent arranging words on paper" (Didion, 1984, 6).

Now I am not going to play the pessimist and say writers are born. Nor am I arguing that writing always is or should be painful. Rather, I want to put forward what I view as a realist position. From those who expect a lot from writing, a good deal is demanded. The best textbook versions of the writing processes do not seem to fit with my experience. They make writing out to be easier than it is. They rarely if ever talk about the conflict and the emotions that the writer feels, nor do they frequently discuss the satisfactions that true authoring—not filling in the blanks or doing theme writing—brings, that it *has* to bring, for writers to continue to write, for writers to continue to put up with and even intentionally seek out this struggle.

My attempt to make some sense of all this has led me to the ideas of Mikhail Bakhtin and Lev Vygotsky. Their work attracts me because they seem to explain my experience with writing better, without assuming that struggle and conflict are necessarily pathological or dysfunctional.

Mikhail Bakhtin was a Soviet language scholar and literary theorist who was fascinated by the otherness of discourse. For Bakhtin a word or discourse is teeming with the voices of others that are constantly mixing with and struggling against our own emerging voice. This constant but everchanging struggle is part of what Bakhtin means when he says that language is dialogue. Self is plural, populated with the voices of others and my task is to appropriate the word for my own purposes and in so doing create my developing voice, in fact to construct my Self. Bakhtin, then, suggests that self is less a plural "I" than a singular "We."

Lev Vygotsky was a Soviet psychologist who was very interested in the workings of the mind. He investigated inner speech, that verbalized portion of the constant flux that flutters between thinking and speaking. For Vygotsky, these streams of consciousness have very peculiar characteristics. They are rhythmic, pulsating thickenings of everyday speech and activity. Words, sentences, and whole utterances in the world of inner speech are shoved together, taking on in that process entirely new patterns of flow. The "units" of inner speech, if we can even refer to such amorphous phenomena as "units," are collected and combined in ways quite unlike most normal speech or writing. Inner speech tends to move toward maximum abbreviation and collapse—sort of the black holes of discourse.

Now, for the points of connection. Bakhtin is interested in looking at the subjective, personal side of the outer word; Vygotsky is interested in giving a more objective account of the subjective and personal inner word. Both agree that conflict is an inherent, natural part of these very processes. Both agree that self and voice are less monolithic and more plural than we tend to think. And both agree that inner speech as internalized and transformed dialogue is alive with other voices, other people, and other worlds.

How often do we experience this otherness within our own individual utterance and take it to be a symptom that something is wrong, that we are not being "structured" enough, that we are not being purposive and single-minded enough? A writer is always experiencing this multivoicedness of language—she or he would have to perform an immense act of will to try to ignore it—but the writer too often takes this dialogism as a problem to be "solved" rather than as a characteristic of the very language processes in which she or he is immersed. The writer thinks if I could only eliminate this constant battling, this continual bickering, this endless quarreling in my mind and on the paper, all would be well. Quarreling and conflict can't be healthy or natural or normal, can they? Why can't my mind simply settle down and behave?

But for Bakhtin and Vygotsky such conflict is natural, even inevitable; their work suggests that we need to accept such dialogue and quarrel as a starting point, since real coherence in a text may come about less because the many voices have been suppressed and silenced than because they have become dialogized, speaking with, even at times yelling at, each other and the "writer" who is made up of this community of voices.

Voice and Void: Dialogues with Myself

In the second section of this essay I want to dialogue (and quarrel) a bit with Mikhail Bakhtin. If we are to reinvent our ways of thinking about, evoking, and ultimately composing the "self," then we find in Bakhtin's work a corpus of materials that will suggest some alternatives to the conventional views of subjectivity. The critique of the subject has become the major theoretical task of literary theory both in the U.S. and France over the last two decades. Russian theory had worked through many of these questions during the 1920s. Bakhtin, as the most popular exponent of Eastern European language theory in the West today, provides us with the apparatus for thinking through subjectivity in sophisticated ways that avoid many of the pitfalls of other postmodern theorists.

Still, when it comes to reading and theorizing Bakhtin on subjectivity, the established style of thinking and writing will not do. To write in conventional monologic forms about the need to transform our views of self and subjectivity to dialogic, plural, and dynamic forms requires us to at least consider the question of style and to become more comfortable with the idea of experimenting with language forms. Bakhtin's writing itself does not conform for the most part to the canons of scholarly exposition, academic discourse if you will, to which we have become inured. When we try to package Bakhtin in conventional academic discourse (whatever that may be since I have still not been persuaded that such a creature exists), we lose much of Bakhtin or, at best, make him over into that which we already know, so that Bakhtin becomes simply another Fish, or Derrida, or Lacan, or Rorty. Bakhtin argues that the best argument for "self" is its distinctive and unreducible place in the universe of discourse, its "otherness." Therefore, in this section I want to loosen up the form and play out some of the ideas that Bakhtin talks about. The section necessarily takes the form of a dialogue with texts, a consciousness forming itself through another consciousness. In his recent book on that other Russian theory,

Vygotsky's Psychology, Alex Kozulin, coming from the social sciences, takes a similar stand. He notes:

> The genre of this book can be defined as that of a commentary. Once a prominent, if not the only acceptable form of scholarly treatise, the genre of commentary in the last century fell into disrepute and was pushed aside by experimental monographs and systematic surveys of literature. There is a good reason for such a fate. To start with, a good commentary always takes as its subject a corpus of writing of superior quality, and there are not many of those nowadays. Second, the very idea commentary is incompatible with the popular view of human knowledge as a temporalized progression from inaccurate facts to accurate ones, from immature generalizations to sophisticated ones. Commentary always aims at a *dialogue* with a superior text, the outcome of which is a new *reading* of this text and thus, by implication, a conception of the new one. (1990, 3)

Kozulin comes to some of the most interesting, startling new readings of Vygotsky that I have seen in studying Vygtosky's work and life for almost twenty years, and it seems that Kozulin achieves this precisely because he tries out some new writing forms. (One of the most interesting sections in Kozulin's book is the chapter on "The Psychology of Tragedy" where Kozulin actually takes on Vygotsky's voice not only to present Vygotsky's views, but to give us a sense of how Vygotsky's mind might have worked, and how his personality and subjectivity, shaped by his milieu and affiliations, come to shape his theoretical and empirical scholarship.) In a somewhat similar, if less courageous, move, I have put together a series of key quotations from Bakhtin (and his commentators) and have responded to them as a composition theorist and teacher. This arrangement preserves some of the forms that theoretical thinking take, but also captures some of its processive and speculative character. This section models both a kind of thinking and a view (and perhaps experience) of subjectivity.

> *Language is not a prison house; it is an ecosystem.*
> CLARK AND HOLQUIST 1984, 227

The move of the postmodernists is from the abstract, basic-building-block, fundamental-particle view of the universe to a specific and concrete, diffused and dynamic conception. Modernist paradigms tend to be mechanist (or, in reaction, organic) while postmodern theory tends to be more interested in contextual root metaphors. Instead of beginning with the specific and working up, building systems piece by piece, particle by particle, postmodernism is more interested in beginning with theory and working "down" to specifics, though this too is not quite fair since the postmodern project is most especially interested in thinking itself beyond such categories as presence and privilege.

> *As the world needs my alterity to give it meaning, I need the authority of others to define, or author, my self. The other is in the deepest sense my friend, because it is only from the other that I can get myself.*
>
> CLARK AND HOLQUIST 1984, 65

I recall the work of Lev Vygotsky and how he argues that human beings are always both social and individual regardless of the circumstance or situation. We are social even when alone because we have internalized the language and ways of knowing and thinking specific to the culture and to the time in which we live. Vygotsky and Bakhtin do not see any diminishing of the individual in this relationship, nor do they view the social and the individual as opposites in conflict. Rather one cannot be one without the other. Thus inner speech and what goes on in my stream of consciousness is both related to and internalized from social ways of thinking and doing and speaking and still is totally new and unique, a "transformed form" as the Vygotskian A.A. Leont'ev calls it.

> *One conventional idea that must be disgarded, which Bakhtin earlier attacked in 'The Problem of Content,' is the concept of the work of art as a finished thing, a hermetic unity. Insofar as the work continues to live, it must be engaged in dialogue, which is possible only when the work is still open and capable of interaction: the work of art is never finished. Characters in a novel are not like flies, immobilized in the objectlike amber of the text that surrounds them.*
>
> CLARK AND HOLQUIST 1984, 243

> *The unity of the text is less that of a 'one and only' than that of a dialogic harmony of unmerged dyads and multiples, much as the unity of self is conceived by Bakhtin as dyadic.*
>
> CLARK AND HOLQUIST 1984, 245

In my view, this is the most profound implication of Bakhtin's work for the composition teacher. Close attention to Bakhtin's argument completely challenges our view of unity which is perhaps the single most important concept in reading texts, interpreting texts, and understanding texts, not to mention, composing texts. Why else

do we spend so much time on thesis statements? Why else do we
still feel drawn to a New Criticism and "close reading" and analysis
of "the text"? Why else are we so bothered by the "lack of focus" in
student writing and why else are we so concerned with students
finding "the parts," the specifics, that will support the thesis? Look
at our metaphors and our obsessions. Doesn't it all get back to unity?

And now here comes Bakhtin (and others) saying we need a
whole new way of viewing unity.

What a trouble maker!

Bakhtin is trying to show us (as does Vygotsky when he discusses the dialectic of thinking and speaking, of concepts and language) that "identity" does *not* mean "unity." Difference and
plurality can form a new kind of unity, a dialogic unity where the
parts do not "build up to" the "point," (again, think on the geometric
metaphors here, a sort of Euclidean rhetoric in Einsteinian or post-
Einsteinian times) but rather where the parts dialogue with other
parts and the whole dialogues with the parts. Bakhtin's conception
of unity allows, even encourages, texts to be far more "open" and
permeated with meaningful "gaps" and "silences."

The "superior" text then (though Bakhtin's anti-systematic "system" even calls into question such a concept) is the text that is
consciously open at certain points, that unfolds and enfolds rather
than "outlines." (David Bohm's work in the new physics, of all
things, is applicable here.)

> . . . *my point of view will only emerge through the interaction
> of my own and another's words as they contend with each
> other in particular situations.*
>
> CLARK AND HOLQUIST 1984, 245

> *One's own discourse is gradually and slowly wrought out of
> others' words that have been acknowledged and assimilated,
> and the boundaries between the two are at first scarcely per-
> ceptible.*
>
> BAKHTIN, 1981, 345

> *The word in language is half someone else's. It becomes 'one's
> own' only when the speaker populates it with his own inten-
> tion, his own accent, when he appropriates the word, adapting
> it to his own semantic and expressive intention. Prior to this
> moment of appropriation, the word does not exist in a neutral
> and impersonal language (it is not, after all, out of a dictionary
> that the speaker gets his words!), but rather it exists in other
> people's mouths, in other people's contexts, serving other peo-
> ple's intentions; it is from there that one must take the word*

and make it one's own. And not all words for just anyone submit equally easy to this appropriation, to this seizure and transformation into private property: many words stubbornly resist, others remain alien, sound foreign in the mouth of the one who appropriated them and who now speaks them; they cannot be assimilated into his context and fall out of it; it is as if they put themselves in quotation marks against the will of the speaker. Language is not a neutral medium that passes free and easily into the private property of the speaker's intentions; it is populated—overpopulated—with the intentions of others. Expropriating it, forcing it to submit to one's own intentions and accents, is a difficult and complicated process.
                                        BAKHTIN 1981, 293–294

With these quotations, it seems that we get into practical implications of Bakhtin's theory for the compositionist. For student writing (as is ours at another remove) is multivoiced. Problems with diction are the most obvious indicator of heteroglossia and doublevoicedness. But so too, the Engfish-y quality of freshman writing is sometimes a sign of the struggle for voice. And is plagiarism (and our obsession with it) simply a matter of out and out laziness and stealing? Well, sometimes it is, but that doesn't really answer the question of why, when it is so much easier to write something awful and take the safe way out (or *is* it easier and if not, why not?) and get at least passing marks, a few students sometimes still insist on going to extreme lengths to plagiarize. Bakhtin's work suggests that part of the problem here is the conflict that the struggle for voice poses for *any* writer.

And doesn't Bakhtin help us understand why the traditional research paper under the best of conditions is always so difficult to teach and often produces such terrible writing from students otherwise capable of interesting work? What makes it unique, aside from the complications of format—which in the worst papers is often, though not always, quite correct? Bakhtin argues that the scholarly article, the research paper, is a prime example of dialogic relations and interrelations existing simultaneously in a single context (1984, 188). Hence the difficulty in tracking reported speeches and handling the borders, creating "ways to control the traffic in voices," which as Clark and Holquist point out "constitutes the substance of whole disciplines and social institutions" (1984, 233–234).

Thus we discover that the research paper in its traditional form involves all kinds of complicated rhetorical acts and these acts, according to Bakhtin and Vygotsky, flow from the social to the individual, from others' speech to the individual voice (and then perhaps to Voice).

Thus it is fascinating to have composition students write up summaries of an article or of a chapter or of an interview with another person, first briefly summarizing the essence of that discourse—itself a complicated assignment (always the question arises of what to leave out and why)—and then in the same length of discourse, responding to (agreeing, disagreeing, asking for a clarification about a point, adding similar and related personal experiences . . .) the summary. Students initially have a very difficult time raising their own voices and tend to repeat or add to their summaries, thinking summary is a response. After students exert great effort over a period of time, however, the teacher can actually physically "see" the growth of voice as the response sections of the student text get longer and longer. The same sort of growth can be tracked in other situations by using Ann Berthoff's famous "double-entry notebook" (1988, 26–60). Students at first find the second set of reflective "notes on notes" very difficult, and only with great effort over a long period of time do we find the second reflections beginning to develop to the sophistication of the first set.

Also it is my contention that what often passes for writing block is less an information-processing problem or an audience-apprehension problem or even a lack of experience in and of itself, though obviously all of these and more are involved; I think that Bakhtin's notion of language makes it more understandable why even (and perhaps especially) the best of writers experience writing block and often have difficulty getting "it" out and down—which, you would think, would be the simplest of things for an experienced writer. But the more you read and write and live, the more you encounter new voices; then, even more dialogues (and quarrels) take place, if you're still interested in trying to make any sense of it at all, that is.

How often do we experience this otherness within our own individual utterance and take it to be a symptom that something is wrong, that we are not being "structured" enough, that we are not being purposive and single-minded enough? Bakhtin suggests that such conflict is natural, even inevitable, and that we need to accept such dialogue or quarrel as a starting point since real coherence in a text may come about less because the many voices have been suppressed and silenced, than because they have become dialogic, speaking with, even at times yelling at, each other and the "writer" who is made up of this community of voices. Maybe we need to be more open to accepting this plurality and this struggle. And here again I see that I have returned to the issue of unity discussed above, a new vision of how we can simultaneously be many and be one.

> *... Bakhtin is intent in imposing to all reading, all cognition, the status of ethnology, the discipline that defines itself by the exotopy [finding oneself outside] of its researcher in relation to his object—at the same time that he is grounding, better than the ethnologists themselves, the legitimacy of their discipline.*
> TODOROV 1984, 110

Though I might quibble with Todorov's use of ethnology rather than ethnography (at least as that distinction applies in the U.S. anthropological community), this has been one of the more practical conclusions to which Bakhtin's and Vygotsky's theory of mind and language have led. I think an ethnographic sort of inquiry has a critical place not only in research about literacy (as Shirley Brice Heath's 1983 *Way with Words* so clearly demonstrates) but in the writing classroom—at least as a complement to and perhaps even as a replacement for the research paper.

I have been having students do mini-ethnographies, or to be more precise, writing that has a certain ethnographic quality about it, with good results. The students enjoy the writing more, learn more about the writing process(es) in all its (their) vagaries (Now there's a word that feels uncomfortable in my mouth. Label it "diction problem."), and produce more specific and more significant papers.

It seems to me that all of these processes are isomorphic; what professional writers outside the classroom do, what the researcher in my classroom does, what I do before, during, and after each class, and what my students do in their assignments seem to be at least somewhat related. Once again, we are very intolerant when student papers lack a coherence, yet we do not seem very bothered that professionally we live among at least as much fragmentation. (It seems, for example, the zenith of fragmentation for literacy researchers to have more in common with statisticians and mathematicians than they do with other writers and composition teachers and students.) Ethnographic genres, then, seem to offer one of the threads that might help tie these texts and textual processes a little more closely together.

> *It all comes back. Perhaps it is difficult to see the value in having one's self back in that kind of mood, but I do see it; I think we are well advised to keep on nodding terms with the*

*people we used to be, whether we find them attractive com-
pany or not. Otherwise they run up unannounced and surprise
us, come hammering on the mind's door at 4:00 a.m. of a bad
night and demand to know who deserted them, who betrayed
them, who is going to make amends. We forget all too soon the
things we thought we could never forget. We forget the loves
and the betrayals alike, forget what we whispered and what
we screamed, forget who we were. I have already lost touch
with a couple of people I used to be . . . It is a good idea, then,
to keep in touch, and I suppose that keeping in touch is what
notebooks are all about.*

DIDION [1968] 1990, 139–140

*To be nobody-but-yourself—in a world which is doing its best,
night and day, to make you everybody else—means to fight the
hardest battle which any human being can fight; and never
stop fighting. . . . As for expressing nobody-but-yourself in
words, that means working just a little harder than anybody
who isn't a poet can possibly imagine. Why? Because nothing
is quite as easy as using words like somebody else. We all of
us do exactly this nearly all of the time—and whenever we do
it, we're not poets.*

E E CUMMINGS, "Three statements" In Hall and Ulanov
1972, 255–258

And so we see there is ample confirmation here and elsewhere
that the Bakhtin's view of discourse corresponds to the writer's
experiencing of the process.

The anguish of writing, as well as its rewards, springs from these
sources—from the plurality of self and the necessity of other. Joan
Didion in her essay "Why I Write" (1985) emphatically asserts that
writing comes from listening to these voices and letting them have
their say, sometimes their way, and does not come up out of some
preformed, intended, prestructured act of the author.

Another author who teaches composition agrees. Donald Murray
will bring these reflections to a stop (though not to an end), since
Murray gives us a clear idea of where all of this can go in the
classroom as well as in our profession. Murray describes the writing
process in very dialogic and Bakhtinian terms:

The act of writing might be described as a conversation between
two workmen muttering to each other at the workbench. The self
speaks, the other self listens and responds. The self proposes,
the other self evaluates. The two selves collaborate: a problem is

spotted, discussed, defined; solutions are proposed, rejected, suggested, attempted, tested, disgarded, accepted. (Murray 1982, 140)

Let me just briefly list a few of the implications of this dialogic view of writing.

1. A dialogic view of writing anchors our writing processes and our teaching of writing in community. The voices we internalize arise from the communities to which we belong, including the discourse and interpretive communities. Many of the voices that I hear, then, come from the people I know and the books I read. Bakhtin and Vygotsky suggest strong connections between reading, talking, and writing.

2. A dialogic view of writing helps us to see writing block less as a sickness and more as a developmental process. One reason I may have difficulty writing is because a dialogue is still taking place between the voices of the past and my present, emerging self. But also there is a kind of dialogue taking place between my present voice and my future voice. Writing from this perspective is one of the activities that helps bridge me to a newer self. Writing block often foreshadows this development.

3. A dialogic view of writing questions the notion that we can only think of one thing at a time and helps explain why when we write it is often necessary to have two pads of paper in front of us so that we can write down on a second pad thoughts that occur that do not seem to fit in with what is presently being composed on the first pad.

4. A dialogic view of writing explains why we so often need a "cooling off" period after we have composed a piece, why it is necessary to go away from our texts for a while in order to revise them. The writer hears new voices both from the text and from the mind and needs to reconsider the relations between these voices. This is also why a long text that we keep coming back to often begins to fall apart—too many voices spoil the broth to mix voices and metaphors.

5. A dialogic view of writing also illuminates the constant recursiveness of the composing processes, why we often have to go back to the beginning of a sentence and reread it, even before we have finished writing the end of the sentence. Perhaps we feel the words do not "sound" right. Maybe we have a feeling that the words already on paper do not fit at all with what is coming out at "the point of utterance," or perhaps neither fit with our sense of where the text should be going. This felt sense, as Sondra Perl has called it, would seem to be closely connected

with the various voices that are in dialogic relations with each other.

6. A dialogic view of writing helps us to see that different writing acts demand different writing speeds, that some texts are meant to be written quickly while other texts are meant to be written slowly, depending on how fully that dialogue has been worked out.

7. As some new research by Nancy Mack (1986) has demonstrated, a dialogic view of writing helps teachers by suggesting that where the syntax and surface level "structure" of a student text is particularly garbled is probably the place where sense is being worked out and where the voices are still in dialogue. In a Donald Murray kind of writing conference that is often the section of the paper the student will need and want to externalize and to talk about, to dialogue with.

8. Finally, a dialogic theory of writing calls for a reexamination and reworking of one of our most important concepts, that of unity. A dialogic concept of unity is more complicated, but more realistic than most of the textbook calls for unity. Dialogic unity would appear to be more open to the gaps and silences and multiplicity of voices in a text than are our current textbook definitions of unity that are based so frequently on New Critical notions.

References

Bakhtin, M. 1981. *The dialogic imagination.* Trans. and ed. M. Holquist. Austin: University of Texas Press.

————. 1984. *Problems of Dostoevsky's poetics.* Trans. and ed. C. Emerson. Minneapolis: University of Minnesota Press.

Berthoff, A. 1988. *Forming, thinking, writing.* 2nd ed. Portsmouth, NH: Boynton/Cook.

Clark, K. & M. Holquist. 1984. *Mikhail Bakhtin.* Cambridge, MA: Belknap Press of Harvard University Press.

Didion, J. 1985. Why I write. In *Themes and variations: A college reader,* edited by W. Ross Winterowd & C. Preston. New York: Harcourt, Brace Jovanovich.

————. 1990. *Slouching toward Bethlehem.* New York: Farrar, Straus and Giroux.

Hall, J. & B. Ulanov. 1972. *Modern culture and the arts.* 2nd ed. New York: McGraw Hill.

Heath, S. 1983. *Ways with words.* New York: Cambridge University Press.

Kozulin, A. 1990. *Vygtosky's psychology: A biography of ideas.* Cambridge, MA: Harvard University Press.

Mack, N. 1986. *False consciousness and the composing process.* Unpublished doctoral dissertation. The Ohio State University.

Murray, D. Teaching the other self: The writer's first reader. *College Composition and Communication* 33(2):140–147.

Perl, S. & A. Egendorf. 1979. The process of creative discovery: Theory research and implications for teaching. In *Linguistic, stylistics, and the teaching of composition,* edited by D. McQuade. Akron, OH: L & S Books.

Todorov, T. 1984. *Mikhail Bakhtin: The dialogic principle.* Trans. W. Godzich. Minneapolis: University of Minnesota Press.

Chapter Eleven

Vygotsky's Theory of Self

This paper had its origins in a certain uncomfortableness with the rising popularity of the idea that writing is a social act. Suddenly the "social" is "in" in composition studies. It isn't that I don't think that writing is a social activity. Over the last decade I have championed such a view at times and places when it was not nearly so popular to do as it now is. Rather I am disturbed by the potential for trivialization. I am afraid that this potentially powerful concept of writing as a social activity will be co-opted, will be domesticated, will become our latest fad, will become one more instrument for the reproduction of existing social relations. To be honest, I am seeing certain scholars in the field jump on the social bandwagon who I cannot help but believe have an extremely different notion of what "social" means from what I have, if indeed they have any notion of "social" at all that goes beyond vague (and bourgeois) notions of "audience" and "context."

This problem dovetails with the difficulties I have had with the uses to which the work of Lev Vygotsky, the Soviet psychologist, has been put in our field. For about a decade, it has been fashionable in certain scholarly quarters to cite Vygotsky. With few exceptions—the work of Susan Wells and Ann E. Berthoff come to mind as exceptions—none of these scholars has mentioned, let alone dealt with the fact that Vygotsky was explicitly a socialist and was explicitly constructing a theory built on what he saw as socialist principles. Composition scholars who use Vygotsky often do not sense the slightest contradiction between the fact that they are using a socialist theory to try to understand composition and the fact that their goal is to better prepare students for their places in a capitalist society. Those who would quote Vygotsky should first look at Chapter Four of his *Thought and Language*. At the end of that chapter, after he has reviewed "empirical" and "idealist" works in psychology, finding both approaches wanting, Vygotsky puts forth his sociohistorical version of cognitive and linguistic development. Vygotsky states it in this way:

> Verbal thought is not an innate, natural form of behavior, but is determined by the historical-cultural process and has specific properties and laws that cannot be found in the natural forms of thought and speech. *Once we acknowledge the historical character of verbal thought, we must consider it subject to all the premises of historical materialism, which are valid for any historical phenomenon in human society.* (1986, 95, emphasis mine)

In other words, Vygotsky is proposing a Marxist psychology, one that calls into question the very categories and contests the very premises of bourgeois psychology. One of the most important of these categories is the concept of "self."

While Vygotsky does not set aside a specific section of his work where he discusses "self"—itself a significant and, I would argue, conscious omission—throughout his essays and books one can detect a framing theory of "self." One of the reasons Vygotsky has been misread or misunderstood in the U.S. is that too often we project our own notions of self—that the self is individual, clearly-bounded, static, and independent of language—onto a body of texts that come out of a differing, if not opposing, tradition. This becomes readily apparent in the middle 1970s when Michael Cole and other U.S. psychologists urged Alexander Luria, the Soviet neuropsychologist and physician who was a close friend and coworker of Vygotsky in the 1930s, to write his autobiography for publication in America. Because our concept of the genre of autobiography relies heavily on our concept of self, Cole was rather unsettled when he received from Luria *The Making of Mind* (1979), a wonderful and readable book, to be sure, but one that seems to have hardly anything to say about Luria alone and in isolation. Instead the book is about others, especially Lev Vygotsky and the life of Vygotsky's ideas in the development of Soviet psychology and thus in Luria's life. Cole, in fact, felt obliged to add lengthy introductory and concluding essays to the book to supply the personal narrative that U.S. readers expect from an "autobiography" and from a "self." Thus we see two very different notions of "self" at work and in conflict.

Vygotsky and his colleagues propose a notion of "self" that challenges our notions as being too narrow, too small. He believes that life in capitalist society tends to narrow our conception of self and reality, our sense of possibilities. Life in capitalist society tends to encourage the composing of a one-dimensional Self. Vygotsky is not interested in abolishing self nor does he advocate subjecting self to some totalizing absolute. Rather Vygotsky wants to show that self is wide-ranging and multidimensional, that self can be more than our conception of Self. Vygotsky is constantly proposing that if we transform the social relations in which we find ourselves, new visions of self can emerge. (This concept of the evolution of self is all part of the doctrine of "the new Soviet Person" delineated by R. Bauer in his book *The New Man in Soviet Psychology* [1972].)

Let me summarize some of Vygotsky's key ideas in six propositions about self.

1. *Self is social.*

    People are ontologically social. That is, the self only comes into existence through community. The self is made of social stuff, put together in social ways by communities, at least at first. Vygotsky views the self as developing from shared activity to individual processes. The discourse of the self tends to shift from public languages to private languages. A person transforms social relations and social processes making of them the "higher psychological functions" that Vygotsky calls consciousness.

    Vygotsky's friend A. N. Leont'ev says that "One is not born a personality, one becomes a personality by socialization and enculturation. . . . Personality is a product of social activity" (Levitin, 1982, 123).

    Vygotsky's contemporary Valentin Volosinov supports Vygotsky saying, "I give myself verbal shape from another's point of view, ultimately from the point of view of the community [and social class] to which I belong" (Volosinov 1986, 113).

    The self gains a certain stability from its communitarian sources, as well as access to a vast storehouse of rich experiences from previous generations. No one then has to begin from square one. The downside is that the individual is necessarily proclaimed a subject in a certain social structure and through a certain ideology. The general notion of Self in our culture, as well as my specific experience of subjectivity, is steeped in social class. Self cannot be reduced to class positions, but it nevertheless cannot be understood without reference to and close scrutiny of its class sources (which, it must be quickly added, does not in any way deny or diminish the importance of the interrelated discourses of race, gender, and sexuality and the effects such discourses have on the speaking subject).

2. *Self is created/constructed/composed.*

Vygotsky argues that the self is actively created both by others and then by our various "selves" across time. I first claim Voice in order to invent my voice. Kozulin, the editor of the recently published second edition of *Thought and Language,* perceptively comments on Vygotsky's discussion of the development of concepts:

> Vygotsky's discussion of the phenomenon of pseudo-concepts has far-reaching philosophical implications. . . . [I]f the conscious awareness of one's own intellectual operations ("concept-for-me") is only a secondary achievement, which follows the practical use of the operations, then the individual cannot be considered a self-conscious center of activity. The individual appears rather as a "construction" built at the crossroads of inner and outer realities. (Kozulin 268)

3. *Self is permeable, porous, fluid.*

Vygotsky turns to weather metaphors when in the final chapter of *Thought and Language* he describes the various planes that thought traverses on its way to words. The boundaries of self in his account are constantly shifting. One of the effects of using the weather metaphors when talking of self and subjectivity is to suggest the self is changeable, amorphous, fluid, permeable. Just as weather has no true divisions, the self does not stop at the skin. Rather, the individual extends her- or himself "into" other people, acquiring in them in this process a "second life" (Asmolov 1988, 62). So Vygotsky often sees self as dual—when a child gets help from her father to tie her shoes, where does self stop and other begin? Vygotsky strongly implies through concepts like the zone of proximal development that child finds self in parent, that lover finds self in the beloved. But the self also extends to innumerable Others as well ("other" in Russian, *drugoi,* is closely related to "friend," "*drug*"). In many cultures, the "extended" family and close friends, kith and kin, are seen as part of "self." So Vygotsky's theory questions the narrow concept we have about where self begins and ends, as well as when self "is" and "is not."

4. *Self is dynamic and developing.*

Self is never settled in Vygotsky. It is dynamic, multiple, many-edged, developing across time. Vygotsky argues that a person's leading activities, those desires and actions that are just beyond our reach but are necessary for the fulfillment of the new tasks we encounter in our community, are "the source and ultimate cause of [her or]his emergence as a unique and integral human individual" (Tolstykh 1987, 25). "I" am my leading edges, my borders. When "I" cross the frontiers of self, "I" must show my passport, and each time I get it out, that passport needs updating and changing.

5. *Self is semiotic.*

Language speaks the self. Vygotsky takes the German psychologist Wilhelm Stern to task, saying:

> The "person" to Stern is a psychophysically neutral entity that in spite of the multiplicity of its part-functions manifests a unitary goal-directed activity. The idealistic "monadic" conception of the individual person naturally leads to a theory that sees language as rooted in personal teleology—hence the intellectualism and anti-genetic bias of Stern's approach to the problems of linguistic development. Applied to the eminently social mechanism of speech behavior, Stern's personalism, ignoring as it does the social side of personality, leads to patent absurdities. His metaphysical conception of personality, deriving all developmental processes from personal teleology, turns genetic relations between personality and language upside down; instead of a developmental history of the personality itself, in which the language plays a far from minor role, we have the metaphysical theory that personality generates language out of the goal-directedness of its own essential nature. (*Thought and Language* 1986, 67)

In contrast, Vygotsky sees self as semiotic. Self is formed by symbolic action. Vygotsky argues that "symbolic activity produces fundamentally new forms of behavior" (1987, 24). This is so because, among other things, language is "reversible" (Lee & Hickmann 1983). At first language forms the social self, but then the self forms language. As the self speaks language, new linguistic forms arise. Through new words and texts, the self becomes able to conceive of new worlds and new selves. Because language is reversible and can be also directed toward itself (that is, language can be reflexive), both *transformation* and *resistance* become possible.[1]

This thread of Vygotsky's theory, it seems to me, complements the advances of poststructuralism while tempering them, still making an important place for the subject's part in broader historical social change.

6. *Self is refined and developed through play.*

Vygotsky writes a great deal about play. He believes play is important not simply because the child constructs her object world through play, but also because the child constructs herself through play. And what is true for the child is no less true for the adult.

Vygotsky argues that play provides human beings with the means to become more conscious of our world and ourselves, which in turn opens more facts of self to (re)composition.

Vygotsky in *Mind in Society* says:

> In life the child behaves without thinking that she is her sister's sister. In the game of sisters playing at "sister," however, they are both concerned with displaying their sisterhood. . . . As a result of playing, the child comes to understand that sisters possess a different relationship to each other than to other people. (1978, 95)

And further:

> Thus, the essential attribute of play is a rule that has become a desire. Spinoza's notions of "an idea which has become a desire, a concept which has turned into a passion" finds its prototype in play. . . . *Play gives a child a new form of desires.* It teaches her to desire by relating her desires to a fictitious"I," to her role in the game and its rules. In this way, a child's greatest achievements are possible in play, achievement that tomorrow will become her basic level of *real action and morality.* (1978, 99–100, emphasis mine)

In a recent article, A. G. Asmolov takes up the question of how and why self develops in the first place. Asmolov argues that play and especially humor are extremely important in the development of personality. Humor is a kind of play that calls everything into question, including the subject of play, the player. Asmolov, drawing on Bakhtin, contends that "Humorous social acts ensure, so to speak, that culture does not slip into a blind alley in its development, that it does not reach a state of equilibrium, balanced immobility, and death" (57). Humor and play refine and reconstruct self and in the process push community toward higher levels of development. Asmolov says "the individual . . . urges the group more rapidly along the evolutionary path chosen by it, establishing a 'zone of proximate development' for the group, as Vygotsky would have said it" (62). It is in the community's long-term best interest that "I" develop fully as a "self."

The implications for teaching composition that follow from such a rethinking of self/society could be rather profound. All kinds of questions arise about what we teach and why, how writing teachers in fact teach and use language.

I would like to spend the remaining pages reflecting on why the social turn in composition might be arising now and what dangers may potentially lie in an uncritical acceptance of such a move, in an acceptance of a concept of the *social* that may reinforce outward notions of *self* or, perhaps even worse, may push us to submit self to the reigning social order.

Just because we do something as a group or with others doesn't necessarily mean we are moving to a "social" notion of teaching/learning. I worry that some forms of "collaborative teaching/learning" might simply become better instruments for indoctrinating and instilling an acceptable self, a self that submits, goes along, and feels obligated to share and bare its "soul" only to discover that in doing so, the self can be *better* monitored, policed, and ultimately controlled.

I worry that one of the reasons why the "social" is suddenly popular is because it is a more efficient way of exploiting people, of getting more work out of them, of raising productivity and profits, of encouraging an economic nationalism in which we see the primary struggle and contradiction to be between economic nation states, between a "Self" we name "Japan" and a "Self" we call "USA." I worry that the "social" is a way for us to better fit students into an economic order that is the real source of contradiction.

As others have already noted, we have to constantly ask *whose* "social" and *whose* "self" when those concepts are used. Who is benefitting from our profession's "move to the social"? To ask this question is *not* to impute the motives of those who in good will see the benefits of collaboration and community. Nor does it imply that collaboration and group work are in themselves suspect. But it does broaden our focus of attention to include questions of institutional affiliation. To ask who benefits helps us to look closely at how our institutions in a hundred subtle ways structure and move to control our actions, our beliefs, our very selves.

But I do think there is a positive potential here. We can claim the "social" for our "selves." Maybe the turn toward the social in composition scholarship is paralleled by, perhaps partially caused by, our own increasing recognition that compositionists too often are not treated as full-fledged partners, as equals, in the academic enterprise. Perhaps our increasing interest in the social dimensions of writing can lead us to strategies for forming communities of teachers and scholars who resist those undemocratic tendencies that we see all around us. We know what the specific issues are: class loads, part-time instructors who get little for their commitment, students who have to take huge loads and work at the same time, some faculty who treat compositionists as their inferiors, decisions made by small cliques about who gets put on programs and published in journals, who gets the scarce jobs, who gets the even rarer tenure. Who benefits from the results of these actions? These are the influences that construct our professional self. Vygotsky believed that building a new discipline is part of building a self. That is why Luria's autobiography seems to be a history of the emerging discipline instead of strictly individualistic narrative. The more that we have a say in our collective destiny, the more a self can be born and act in freedom. It all gets down to some pretty old-fashioned but no less radical notions: equality, democracy, freedom.

In order to reclaim the idea of the social, then, we must necessarily and simultaneously transform our idea of self. And the only ethical reason for doing either is to construct a more democratic profession and country.

Note

1. For more information about transformation and resistance in the composition classroom, see the work of P. Freire and H. Giroux. Also see C. Mark Hurlbert and Michael Blitz, eds. 1991. *Composition and resistance* (Portsmouth, NH: Boynton/Cook.)

References

Asmolov, A. 1988. Premises of a socioevolutionary concept of the personality. *Soviet Psychology* 51–63.

Bauer, R. 1952. *The new man in Soviet psychology.* Cambridge, MA: Harvard University Press.

Lee B. & M. Hickmann. 1983. Language, thought and self in Vygotsky's developmental theory. In *Developmental approaches to the self,* edited by B. Lee & G. Noam. New York: Plenum Press.

Levitin, K. 1982. *One is not born a personality.* Moscow: Progress Publications.

Luria, A. 1979. *The making of mind,* edited by M. Cole. Cambridge, MA: Harvard University Press.

Tolstykh, A. 1987. *Man and his stages of life.* Moscow: Progress.

Volosinov, V. 1986. *Marxism and the philosophy of language.* 2nd ed. Cambridge, MA: Harvard University Press.

Vygotsky, L. 1986. *Thought and language,* 2nd ed., edited by A. Kozulin. Cambridge, MA: MIT Press.

———. 1978. *Mind in society,* edited by M. Cole, V. John-Steiner, S. Scribner, & E. Souberman. Cambridge, MA: Harvard University Press.

Part Four

Composing Society

In the final section of essays,"Composing Society," I take up issues that directly concern the society of Composition. I am suggesting that issues of disciplinarity are political in a local sense, that knowledge-producing communities require the inquirer to take positions, choose methods, and stake professional reputations on decisions made about intellectual work. But I also am suggesting that our composing society has broader effects and actually makes a contribution to the construction of society.

"Society" itself is a curious word. Unlike "community" there are presently far fewer warm fuzzies attached to the term. This was not always so. Raymond Williams in his *Keywords: A Vocabulary of Culture and Society* notes that the primary meaning of the word came into English in the fourteenth century as "companionship or fellowship" (243–247). "Society" was seen to be a free association of equals. This definition actually opposed later uses that emphasized ranking and then the sovereign power of the state. The meanings of "society" became increasingly abstract and distant from the "individual." It took on senses associated with civil and then national groups. "Society" became problematic, having accumulated many of its present connotations, by the time of the Romantic revolt of the late eighteenth and early nineteenth century. At this point in history, "society" became more clearly the "opposite" of the individual human being. Imaginative literature of this period begins for the first time to speak of the individual in conflict with society, fighting for freedom from social restraint.

All of this shows that there are no necessary historical reasons why we must think of society as opposed to the individual. This is clearly the product of changes that have occurred relatively recently.

In these final essays, I want to argue for reinventing the concept of the social in composition.

The four essays in this section foreground the construction of composition studies, but always in the background is the assumption that transforming the profession, especially the profession that finds its roots in the social movements of the 1960s, in the open admissions programs that made it possible for working-class and minority students to come to college, is always a matter of transforming the broader society and culture of which Composition is a part.

But I have also arranged these essays on disciplinary matters so that they deal directly with the question of how we might introduce graduate students to composition studies. Obviously, we can introduce new graduate students to composition through a study of classic texts (a canon). We might also arrange this entry into composition studies by examining specific knowledge-producing communities as Stephen North does in his book. My essays in this section, however, argue for a third approach. I have been experimenting with introducing graduate students to Composition by having them look at (1) keywords of the field, (2) keysources as they enter the field and are translated and circulated within Composition, and (3) keyconflicts, the perennial battles that seem to go on no matter how much the field tries to move on to other things. This framework of words, sources, and conflicts is flexible enough to appeal to student interests, but also quickly gets into the historical and theoretical dimensions of composing. This framework also gives the student some sort of unifying scheme for pulling together the diversity of materials that she or he finds in composition studies. Such schemes are also useful for the purely practical purposes of organizing doctoral examinations. Generally, keywords imply some intersection of interests, at least temporarily. Keysources allow the student to follow a body of work into and out of the field. And keyconflicts suggest regions of discourse where it is seemingly impossible to agree on basic principles for talking about issues. Significantly, I have cast most the poststructuralist debate in Composition into the third category, though the archetypal example of the keyconflict within Composition is the question of instruction in traditional grammar.

Therefore, in "Keywords of Composition: A Discipline's Search for Self," a paper that I delivered in its original version at the Penn State Conference on Rhetoric and Composition in July 1988, I argue that questions of language are more than simply issues of jargon or discourse communities. When we fight about words, something more is going on. I draw in this essay on the insights of V. Volosinov to propose using such debates about terms in composition studies as a generative process that allows us to study and track another set of generative processes. Volosinov says that such words are the most sensitive indicators of social changes that we have. So tracking keywords in a discipline provides us with an ongoing record of that discipline's hopes and obsessions; it gives us a map of the discipline's making of meaning.

In the longish essay "Vygotsky and Composition: Influences on an Emerging Field" I try to extend Volosinov's notion from keywords to keytexts. When a whole body of work suddenly becomes interesting to a field or to a group of people in the field, one can learn quite a bit about both the group and the new body of work. I use Lev Vygotsky's scholarship as the example in this essay, showing that Vygotsky's ideas reached Composition at precisely the time Composition was emerging from literary studies but also was appropriating work from linguistics and psychology. It turns out that Vygotsky's appropriation by Composition tells us quite a lot about Composition, but also about the processes by which discourse communities contact and then influence other discourse communities. Yuri Lotman's dynamic theory of semiotics describes this process precisely and accounts for some of the seeming peculiarities of Composition as an emerging field.

In the third essay in this section, "The Grammar Controversy: Tracking a Discipline by Looking for the Conflicts," I look at Composition's inability to reach any consensus about "grammar" or even to move the debate to other pressing subjects. I state my position on the grammar issue—I am bored with it—and, fatalistically I confess, try to reframe the discussion so that at least teachers can have their say. Because the grammar question has gone on furiously for at least one hundred years with little consensus being reached, I suspect the grammar debate will still be a hot issue in U.S. society long after I am gone. And so, I position myself with Volosinov who sees grammar study and formalistic language analysis as an attempt to hold language still for political reasons, and move on.

I end this section and the book with a reflection on the question of poststructuralist Theory and its contribution to Composition. I have not yet been persuaded that poststructuralist Theory is useful theory for the composition theory. When I read some Theorists who say that they have no intention (of course, intent implies a subject, itself the object of critique here) of dealing with composition practices (teaching or writing practices) or who assert that Theory has no consequences on practice, then I have to conclude that we are talking about very different kinds of theory. I simply am not interested in Theory that is not interested in me. I believe in peaceful coexistence, itself an affront to some radical poststructuralists, so I won't deny anyone else's right to do that sort of Theory. But in the meantime I find Vygotsky's theory to be fascinating and useful after fifteen years, so I'll stick with that for a while, I think.

Chapter Twelve

Keywords of Composition:
A Discipline's Search for Self

What is happening to the language used by composition scholars and teachers?

Within the last few years, strange words and phrases have suddenly crept, almost imperceptibly, into our conversations. At our professional meetings and even in mainstream journals like *College Composition and Communication* and *College English*, we hear of "discourse communities" and "interpretive communities," of "contexts," "contextualizing," and even "contexting," of "cognition" and "metacognition," "foundationalism" and "antifoundationalism," of "privileging" and "marginalizing," of "theory as cultural practice," "discursive practices," "discursive formations," "reflective practice," of "collaborative learning," "collaborative writing," and the "conversation of mankind."

What goes on here?

Are we finally witnessing the long predicted decline and fall of the English language? Are compositionists abandoning the principles of Plain English to commit social science?

In this essay I want to reflect on Composition's search for words. I shall argue that this apparent squabble over words is a key part of our discipline's struggle for voice and search for self. I shall examine the specific case of the Writing Program at Syracuse University because in many ways the struggles that we have faced there are representative of what the discipline at large is experiencing. Using the theory of language worked out by the Soviet theorists Mikhail Bakhtin and his friend Valentin Volosinov, I will conclude by briefly suggesting some parallels between all this disciplinary "deep talk" and the composing processes that we individually experience, teach, and study.

I came to the new Syracuse Writing Program as it began its second year. I was amazed by all the energy generated by the contagious discussions that seemed to be constantly going on. This "deep talk," as Margaret Himley has described it, was not limited to composition specialists but seemed to be as intense among instructors, teaching assistants, and staff as it was among full-time faculty.[1] Because I was working with twenty-eight TAs, mostly from the English department, who like myself were new to S.U., I was in a unique position to see the broad contours of this dialogue.

What emerged almost immediately was that talk here was serious. It was not just chitchat but a way of discovering, working out, and advocating certain courses of action.

Most of the people new to the program, myself included, were a bit confused by the language being used. We all seemingly spoke the same English language and we all knew the words—or most of them anyhow—that people were speaking. But there was this underlying feeling, this felt sense, that there was a lot of talking past each other even at the very moment when individuals and groups were trying their hardest to make things clear.

No matter what I said, I felt that I inevitably would alienate two-thirds or more of graduate students and faculty, and the other third would probably misunderstand what I was trying to say.

Take the word *reflection*. This is a critical term for the Writing Program since it describes one of the ways our studio courses differ from traditional composition courses. To learn to write means, among other things, to learn to write about one's experiences in various ways. At the university perhaps the central experience for the undergraduate is literacy—writing, for example, that takes a constellation of forms and that occurs continuously, in class and out of class, in formal papers and essay exams and on textbooks, but even more frequently, in notes, marginalia, letters, and doodlings. We ask our students to reflect on this writing through writing, to write about the writing they do, to track the variety of writing they do and the times and places such writing occurs, as well as the functions it serves. Finally we ask students to write about and reflect on their own composing processes.[2] Writing in our studios becomes an instrument for making visible the writing that students do in their college lives.[3]

While I thought that this was a new idea for teaching freshman composition, I was not ready for the sort of uproar that this notion of *reflection* created. My graduate practicum class for the new TAs almost immediately fragmented into three discourse communities that reflected, if I may use that term, the major camps in the English department.

First, there was the community of literary scholars who called themselves the "theorists." The "theorists" were folk who read, among others, Derrida, Fish, Foucault, Heidegger, Barthes. The "theorists" were interested in exploring and extending the new poststructuralist views of discourse that find problematic the common-sensical communication model of language as sender/message/receiver, language as representation and reference.

Second, there were the creative writers who reacted against what they saw as the jargon of the theorists, objecting to their "Parisian aesthetics" and the politics of the third group, the Marxists. The creative writers were suspicious of anything that took time away from the only reason for being there—to write poetry, short stories, and novels.

Third, the poststructuralist Marxists, who, unlike any of the Marxists I had encountered through a decade of study, based their Marxism on the theory of Althusser and constantly talked of discourse in terms of the "subject" and its function of subjecting people through a bourgeois humanist ideology of pluralism and pleasure. These Althusserian Marxists view cultural critique, a political deconstruction of the reigning ideas of capitalist ideology, as their primary reason for being.

Now to return to the word *reflection.*

The theorists were bothered by the stasis that seemed to be implied by the term. "Reflection" can imply mirrors and representations and correspondences and a given empirical reality that exists apart from discourse. It implies a stable world and a language that is an unproblematic, transparent medium that does exactly what we tell it to, a language that straightforwardly and immediately points to its objects in the world. The Writing Program, then, seemed to be calling for a return to old-fashioned, worn-out ideas about language.

The creative writers found the term "reflection" to be jargon, since it seemed implicated in a psychological and sociological consideration of the personal experiences (and mysteries) of writing. They found the very idea of toying with the mysteries of the writing processes repugnant. They seemed to think that the more you talk about and study these processes, the more you were likely to foul them up, and end up paralyzed, unable to write anything powerful and creative. And obviously such "reflection" took time away from what freshman writers needed most, in the creative writers' judgment—reading good literature and writing creatively, expressively forging a personal style.

The Marxists saw the out-of-date bourgeois philosophy of Dewey and the bourgeois psychology of Bruner in the word "reflection." "Reflection" necessarily implies, they seemed to think, an empirical self that is given, rather than constructed through discourse. "Reflection" seems to accept the world as empirical reality rather than ideological function of discourse. It entirely ignores questions of authority and power, by nostalgically reverting to romantic notions of self and creativity.

Now as all of this was taking place, I felt that what the three communities heard in my use of the word "reflection" simply did not overlap with my invocation of the word.

And so it went with an entire set of keywords.

Contrastive rhetoric, for example, a term borrowed from studies in English as a Second Language, is central to an understanding of our Studio II course.[4] In this second composition course, sophomores contrast the various forms that writing takes as it changes functions across campus. "Contrastive rhetoric" provides a border rhetoric, a rubric and a method that helps us to analyze and explore writing and theories of writing in and out of the disciplines. In my mind at least, the construction and use of a contrastive rhetoric differentiates our Studio II course from both a traditional "writing as rhetoric" course that focuses mostly on composition from the perspective of one discipline—English and literary studies—and a straight writing-across-the-curriculum course that frequently has no overarching principle and that lately has come under fire as a possible instrument of indoctrination rather than education.[5] "Contrastive rhetoric" helps us to think of our Studio II course as a place where we study not only the relation between language and knowledge, but where we can also consider the relation between language and power, as these issues arise locally, in the university.

But the theorists were suspicious of the idea of rhetoric as a kind of metadiscipline or metadiscourse. For the poststructuralists "meta" is not "betta"; it is not even possible. You can't get out of language. Why pretend you are offering students a solid place to stand? There is no solid ground. It's all constantly shifting.

The creative writers argued they didn't come here to teach the writing of lab reports or sociology papers to students. What they know best is language used at its best—literature. Rhetoric is an excuse for flabby ornamental language, anyhow, they seemed to believe. More jargon.

The Marxists seemed to think that a contrastive rhetoric implies a belief that we can talk ourselves to salvation without acknowledging the political. It also appeared to them one more act of a discredited formalism.

Discourse community got a big rise, even from composition people. It is, if nothing else, an ugly phrase, one abstract noun modifying another abstract noun. The theorists saw "discourse community" as a typically watered-down version of Fish's interpretive community or Foucault's discursive formation—feeble theory without the density and materiality of sustained, rigorous thought. The creative writers found it too sociological. Use of the phrase "discourse community" proved for them that composition people were committing social science. The Marxists saw "discourse community" as symptomatic of a relativism that holds that all discourses are created equal and acceptable. Such a view ignores the contradictions inherent in capitalist relations of production and elides the conflict that cultural critique reveals.

To sum up my experience as a newcomer to the Syracuse Writing Program, out of necessity I became a translator. To make sense of this world of shifting discourses and alliances, I had to write and talk my way through it. This essay itself is one of the results of this intense dialogue.

It would be easy to invoke an acceptable dichotomy here and argue that the discourses on which I have been reflecting are perfect examples of either straight-out, no-holds-barred *jargon* or paragons of *discourse communities*-in-action. In this usual dichotomous view of things, language is either pure or impure. Plain English or gobbledygook. Value-free or doublespeak. And the world, and our knowledge of it, is either absolute or relative, foundationalist or antifoundationalist. Elsewhere I have analyzed the ideological functions and power relations such dichotomies serve.[6] Let it suffice here to say that Volosinov and Bakhtin, in my judgment, offer us another interpretation, one that I find more interesting.[7]

Valentin Volosinov and Mikhail Bakhtin are Russian theorists of language and literature who collaborated on some philosophical projects during the 1920s in the postrevolutionary Soviet Union. What interests me far more than whether Volosinov is a pen name for Bakhtin and whether Bakhtin actually composed the very important work *Marxism and the Philosophy of Language,* which was first published in 1929, is the sort of world from which this book and partnership came and which is reflected/refracted, embodied/enacted, concealed/revealed in this text.[8]

Soviet society in the 1920s was not by any measure a free, open society. The groundwork was already being laid for the police state that was to come during the time of Stalin. Still we should not ignore the fact that the Soviet Union in the 1920s was for the first time in centuries beginning to open its doors to groups never before allowed within the pale. For example, the only reason we have the work of a Vygotsky or a Luria is because the Soviet Union abolished czarist restrictions on the number of Jewish people accepted into high positions in academe and in government institutes. Vygotsky and Luria were the products of one of the world's first open admissions programs. This they never forgot.[9]

So the very subject of Volosinov/Bakhtin's theory as it is found in the book *Marxism and the Philosophy of Language* is a part of what was going on in the Soviet Union at that moment. The text evokes and enacts the context. It talks about, but is also a part of, the blurring of the boundaries between ethnic, class, and scholarly discourses and their respective communities. It is a text about texts while simultaneously being a text within texts. The same thing can be said about our professional discourse, but also about language generally.[10] Volosinov puts it this way:

> The word is implicated in literally each and every act or contact between people—in collaboration on the job, in ideological exchanges, in the chance contacts of ordinary life, in political relationships and so on.
>
> Countless ideological threads running through all areas of social intercourse register effect in the word. It stands to reason, then, that the word is the most sensitive index of social changes, and what is more, of changes still in the process of growth, still without definitive shape and not as yet fully accommodated into already regularized and fully defined ideological systems. . . . the word has the capacity to register all the transitory, delicate, momentary phases of social change. (MPL, 19)

Volosinov goes on to assert that the intersecting of accents from differing discourse communities is what keeps language alive, vibrant, dynamic. Language is then a sort of sensor system that picks up on social changes that are not yet visible. In fact, it is through language that we as a community and as individuals first begin to conceive of such changes and put forward one view against another. To oversimplify Volosinov and Bakhtin's rather detailed theory, if we find that in our discussions certain words keep recurring and that these keywords frequently get quick, emotionally charged, intense responses perhaps all out of proportion to their relative importance in the specific situation, if then they are "fighting words" or "communing words," God-terms or devil terms[11] we can be pretty certain that they indicate shifting power relations, that some critical issue is being contested in the community through the word.

In concrete terms, then, one reason there may be so much deep talk at Syracuse, according to Volosinov, is the extremely close proximity of discourse communities that are so radically different and that are contending for hegemony within the department and program. It is the very difficulty of translating one set of terms or one view of the world into another that encourages the growth and stretching and struggle that we observe in certain keywords that keep reappearing. It is the very openness of the whole process that makes it generative. It is the very potential for institutional change that encourages continued dialogue. Because all camps believe a lot is a stake and that the institution in which we work is changing and changeable, and that at present no one group is dominant, one feels the need for dialogue.

It is almost as if keywords were a community's version of inner speech.[12] These keywords are compact, abbreviated, shifting, condensations of the larger texts, dialogues, quarrels. Keywords are the means by which a community "makes sense," to use an idea from the work of Nancy Mack.[13] They encode the community's struggles to define itself by being the very means through which the community tries to conceive of, work out, and sometimes resolve these issues.

I want to conclude with the claim that, no less than our students, we are composers. What we find true of their writing processes, we will find describes pretty well our own activity in building a field of study. We not only teach composition, but simultaneously through our professional conferences and journals and disciplinary deep talk, we are composing composition. Keywords provide us with a way of tracking this activity, just as drafts and notes as well as diaries, letters, and documents, give us a way of tracking our concerns, obsessions, hopes, and dreams throughout our own personal lives. I think then that we need to remind ourselves that composing, whether it is the composing our students do for our classes, the composing we do for work and play, or the composing that we collectively, collaboratively do when we construct the field of composition is a messy business. I also want to claim that composing in one plane *requires* a composing in multiple planes. We can create a *text* because we are simultaneously composing a *context,* a *self,* and a *society.* I write this *essay* on a *field* that is creating *me* and my *world.* We ignore the *intersectionality* of composition at our own peril.

In all of these cases we need to recall what we know best—

- Composing is often a struggle.
- Composing often works better when the boundaries and the genres are blurred.
- Composing is always political.
- Composing reflects but can also transform the contexts out of which it comes.
- Composing works best when people feel they can take risks and make mistakes without undue worry of punishment.
- Composing in its deepest and most authentic form only works when composers believe something important, important to both them and to others, is at stake.
- Composing only works when no one person or voice or group dominates or controls.

The explosion of new terms and keywords in our field of discourse, then, is not simply a matter of jargon or of varied discourse communities, but instead is a sign of a collective, generative process of inventing composition, searching for the words that will speak our self.

Notes

1. For more on the concept and practice of deep talk and its centrality to the Syracuse University Writing Program see Margaret Himley's essay "Deep Talk" in her forthcoming *Shared territory: Understanding children's writing as 'works.'* NY: Oxford U.P.

2. For examples of reflective essays that some rhetoricians composed on their writing process, see Tom Waldrep's *Writers on writing.* 1987. New York: Random House.

3. See Louise Phelps "Making writing visible at Syracuse," Writing Program Document, Syracuse Writing Program.

4. Most recently, see Alan Purves (Ed.). *Writing across languages and cultures: Issues in contrastive rhetoric.* Newbury Park, CA: Sage. 1988. Especially see Robert Kaplan, "Contrastive rhetoric and second language learning: Notes toward a theory of contrastive rhetoric" in this volume.

5. The recent panel at the 1988 CCCC "Writing Against the Curriculum" is one example of the sort of critique that I believe we can expect to

see more of in the near future. As the discipline of composition begins to gain more of a sense of itself as a discipline, I think we can expect the whole notion of composition as a "service" course to increasingly come under attack.

6. Regarding the ideological dimensions and the historicity of dichotomies see my essay "Rewriting Composition as a Post-modern Discipline: Transforming the Research/Teaching Dichotomy." In Hepzibah Roskelly and Kate Ronald (Eds.) *Painful Divisions.* Portsmouth, NH: Heinemann-Boynton/Cook, forthcoming.

7. This analysis will draw entirely on Volosinov, V. *Marxism and the philosophy of language.* Cambridge, MA: Harvard. 1986. Hereafter MPL.

8. It is curious how the issue of authorship has dominated discussions of this text in the West for over a decade now. I begin to wonder after so much attention is paid to such a relatively small point, whether it just coincidental that this work appears and its authorship becomes so problematic at precisely the time that the (post)structuralists declare the "death of the author." My view, elaborated in "Is Formal Language Study Possible? Bakhtin on Reported Speech," (unpublished manuscript, delivered in Atlanta at the 1987 CCCC) is that it is more productive, certainly more interesting, to *accept* ambiguous authorship. After all, authorship, authority, voice, and "reported speech" are what the text is "about." It is logical that the text would "do" what it "says." Thus we can analyze *Marxism and the philosophy of language* artistically, as *both* a straight-out statement about language *and* as a reflexive "double" text that performs its script, which is "itself."

9. See Luria's comments on this in his intellectual autobiography *The making of mind* (Cambridge, MA: Harvard. 1979) especially pages 18–19.

10. See Volosinov (115) "Reported speech is speech within speech, utterance within utterance, and at the same time also speech about speech, utterance about utterance." Also "Between the reported speech and the reporting context, dynamic relations of high complexity and tension are in force" (119).

11. For a delineation of the concept of God-term/devil-term, as well as for a discussion of the rhetoric of some modern God/devil terms, see Richard Weaver, *The Ethics of Rhetoric.* Chicago: Chicago, 1959.

12. For a discussion of inner speech, see Lev Vygotsky, *Thought and language.* Cambridge, MA: M.I.T., 1986 (2nd edition, translation by Alex Kozulin). The second edition is a major, welcome, expansion of the 1962 edition. While the original translators had good reason, considering the social context as well as the audience for Vygotsky's work in the early 1960s, for drastically abridging the U.S. version of *Thought and language,* many of the current misconceptions about Vygotsky, including the mistaken notion that his work was simply a more "social" version of Piaget's, can be traced to the elliptical, even cryptic, quality of this dramatically abridged text.

13. Mack uses this phrase purposely to make use of but also to expand Ann E. Berthoff's "making of meaning" by drawing on Vygotsky's concept of the dialectic between "sense" and "meaning." Personal communication with author.

Appendix
Eleven Keywords of the Writing Program

Around 1930, almost immediately after the stock market crash as the U.S. began its long plunge into the Great Depression, the U.S. artistic community, most visibly painting at first, was racked by a struggle among three major camps. Like Gaul, all painting seemed to be divided into three parts—"abstractionists" (including O'Keefe, Marin, Dove, Demuth), American Scene "regionalists" (especially Thomas Hart Benton, but also Grant Wood, Edward Hopper, Andrew Wyeth), and "social realists" (including Ben Shahn, Jack Levine, Soyer, Marsh, Evergood).

The abstractionists were interested in exploring and elaborating the new notions of painting (its forms and functions) that had arrived from the avant-garde of Europe, especially France. Abstractionists were not generally interested in representation and concerned themselves more with "capturing the beauty of form and mood." A painting should "not be compared with anything in the real world . . . it was an original, independent object of art from which a viewer could derive whatever he wished." Reference and representation became dirty words among many of the abstractionists.

The American Scene painters reacted against the abstractionists and their "jargon-filled" theories of art. Thomas Hart Benton described the rise of popularity of some American Scene painters this way:

> We objected to the new Parisian esthetics which was more and more turning art away from the living world of active men and women into an academic world of empty pattern. (Benton in von Hartz, 62)

The American Scene painters "stuck to their paintings of folk legends and uncomplicated views of rural and small town life, and in them many Americans found a measure of comfort in time of profound national doubt" (von Hartz, 63).

The social realists countered that such excursions into nostalgia were inappropriate (even immoral) at a time when the U.S. faced political and economic crisis. People were unemployed and starving, and painting about some pretty mythic time and place, in such circumstances, was no less a political act than painting about a riot between strikers and police or depicting the shabby, everyday world that most Americans were living in. The social realists argued that art is a weapon of class struggle and the only real question is not whether art is political, but whose side are you on.

So what does this have to do with the writing studios?

I find analogous camps in the English department and the Writing Program today. Inevitably, all my attempts to explain how I envision writing and our writing program and what it is doing and trying to do, alienates at least two and often all three groups.

And this is not simply because one group or another is using "jargon." That is a smokescreen that hides the fact that what we really are arguing about here are completely different, perhaps incompatible, worldviews, which themselves provide notions of what counts as being worthy of knowing and doing. Even a simplistic notion of language and how it "ought" to be used necessarily embodies, enacts, and evokes a whole network of such values and understandings.

Take the wonderful notion from Barzun and Strunk and White (not to mention Orwell) that language should always be simple, direct, active, concrete. I find it curious that this very notion of "prose" arises at the same time and from the same people who just loved T.S. Eliot and Wallace Stevens and William Faulkner and James Joyce and Gertrude Stein in "literature." Well, that's different!

And what worldview might such a belief in "pure" language embody, enact, but also conceal? What kinds of things come to our attention, became worthy of our attention when we are armed with this belief? Might there possibly be a fit between the notion of facile language and a facile acceptance of the "empirical," "real," always-existing-never-changing-and-therefore unchangeable, world?

And if you think I am arguing *for* a complicated, Latinate, "inflated" style, you've missed my point.

What follows then is one more attempt to try to "translate" my understanding of the writing studios and our larger purposes into language that is at least somewhat available to all involved. I do so believing that, to a certain extent, the more this writing program moves into new territories and really tries some innovative things, the more we will implant new and sometimes bothersome meanings into old words and create, what many will find, new, startling, and troublesome discourse. And here I show my true colors: I think that's what poetry is about and I believe we are making poetry.

Context

People trained in English are, of course, familiar with the notion of context, though too narrowly construed. Context has traditionally been that which "surrounds" the text, that which immediately precedes and follows a word or passage, usually the Text that comes before and after.

The term has always had a wider application among scholars in folklore, however, often referring to the performance situation, as well as the text, if there actually was a single text, which in folklore there rarely is, variations on myths, legends, proverbs, jokes, and other folklore genres being the rule rather than the exception. One of the important assumptions of folklorists for decades has been the Context determines Text.

The Writing Program has adopted the uses of Context that prevail in folklore, anthropology, and even some philosophy (e.g. Stephen Pepper). The studio courses are "contextual" for many reasons, but most importantly because they begin with the experiences of students at S.U. and make an important place in the course for reflection on those experiences. The studios are especially concerned with determining the intellectual context the student each year finds him or herself in and providing the student with highly specific and appropriate writing activities that will lead the student in higher developmental levels. Thus student views, student talk, student uses of literacy outside of the Writing Program and the English department, are central to the studio approach to teaching writing.

Studio II, among other things, considers how changes in Context change the meanings/forms/functions (see Markova) of writing.

Contrastive Rhetoric

This term, as I am aware of it, comes from teachers in ESL, English as a Second Language, though it is also the type of activity that cultural anthropologists study and do.

In ESL, contrastive rhetoric might be seen as a transitional study of language and contexts in both a native (or primary culture) and in the new (or secondary) culture. A contrastive rhetoric spans the two cultures by discovering how the meanings/forms/functions of language in the primary culture might be translated into the secondary culture.

A contrastive rhetoric is then a sort of conceptual tool or speculative instrument (both phrases emphasize the heuristic, dynamic, utilitarian temporary qualities) that we create to bootstrap ourselves and our students into higher developmental levels.

A contrastive rhetoric then is both the subject of our activity in a literacy course (to a degree, the course is about creating such rhetorics, how we might go about it, what we might do, and why) and an instrument of our activity that we use to do other things—in this case begin our study of writing in other disciplines, professions, contexts.

In the Writing Program, we are trying to use contrastive rhetoric to help students to apply what they have learned and can do in their writing classes to the writing they are doing in a multitude of changing contexts, including writing they do in other courses, writing they do in professions, and writing they do in their lives outside of the world of school and work.

In terms of Studio II, if rhetoric involves accepted modes of invention, arrangement, style, memory, and delivery (the classical canons of rhetoric), then we might investigate with students how these canons change across disciplines. Thus a contrastive rhetoric in Studio II might ask questions like:

- invention: what counts as original in a field or discipline? how is original work conducted? what is considered conventional work and how it is valued? by whom? why? what kind of information is considered valuable enough to be put into writing? what kind of writing? what information is considered important enough not to be put into writing? when? why? by whom?

- arrangement: what are the conventional ways of arranging discourse in the field? why? what are the rules for using a different order? how does inquiry in a field proceed? are there different/opposite ordering principles for doing work in the field and presenting the results of the work in the field?

- style: what counts as "good"/ "effective"/ "persuasive"/ "efficient" writing in the field? what are it marks? how is it recognized (or cognized)? how is it (supposed to be) produced? what counts as "ethical" writing, in all the senses of that word? and so on you can generate further questions, probes into other discourse communities . . . and you obviously can set this up in a multitude of ways, depending on what you and your students count as "rhetoric" (see below). And any set of questions can obviously be negated (e.g. what counts as "bad" style, . . .). And to be sure all of this can be accomplished less systematically and more intuitively, even more inductively, by letting students decide on questions and categories (as small group projects), since it is they, not we, who cross the disciplines.

Development

The unfolding (through time) of activity. Activity is always both social and individual, though we may use the word development to focus more on one or the other. So the capitalist mode of production is developing, the S.U. Writing Program is developing, the writing studios are developing, the writing teachers and students are developing. Although the term has conventionally been applied in Western psychology to the cognitive changes a person goes through during life, development as the word has been applied in the writing Program has far broader applications. I use the word more as U. Bronfenbrenner does when he talks of the ecology of human development that implies that social and individual development are intimately related to (and according to Vygotsky lead) each other.

In terms of the teaching of writing, taking a developmental approach means, among other things, rejection of the idea that learning is a set of skills acquired once and for all in a strictly linear sequence. A developmental stance disputs the view that writing should be taught by beginning with the smallest elements (sentences, paragraphs, themes, research papers, literary analyses, and finally poetry, stories, novels, surprise, surprise).

Discourse Community

A term I first encountered in the work of Patricia Bizzell though today it is fairly universally used among compositionists. The term would appear to be connected to Stanley Fish's "interpretive community," Foucault's "discursive formation," and folklore/sociolinguistics/anthropology's interest in creating "ethnographies of speaking," though I can't prove any of this right now. As far as teachers of writing are concerned, we probably need this term or some equivalent since what it gets at is what so often is left out of traditional composition instruction.

Writing, in all its meanings/forms/functions, radically changes when the context changes. As does oral language. (Hence "discourse" to avoid the oral versus literate dichotomy? or because "discourse" is more fashionable now? Certainly "speech community" or "language community" carry too much Saussurean baggage to be of much value?)

Discourse communities are in a sense the object of study for a contrastive rhetoric. Our students who most usually belong to one culture often (like us) belong to many discourse communities. In a sense, every time they write in a discipline, they are briefly participating at some (perhaps hierarchically low) level in discourse community. At least I would suspect that, though the term begins getting very fluid and tricky if we take it much farther in this direction. Perhaps language development is the result of the conflicts/confluences among the discourse communities an individual belongs to? or wants to belong to? (See Zebroski's "A Hero in the Classroom.")

One critical issue that I want to raise at this point is how far work in composition goes (I'm thinking now mostly about Bizzell, Bartholomae, and Porter) in its consideration of power and discourse communities. There is a tendency to assume that all we have to do to get students accepted into academic discourse communities is to help them analyze different ways language is used and adapt accordingly. I don't believe it is this simple. While in no way negating the value of doing this (of teaching writing as rhetoric—now *there's* a radical notion), we need to recognize that the ultimate decisions about who will be allowed into a discourse community lies with the discourse community, any may have little or nothing to do with appropriate use of language. Language is a necessary but not sufficient cause for gaining admission into a discourse community.

Further, we need to be cautious about transmitting a means/end view of language itself, that focuses so much on adapting ourselves and our discourse that it loses sight of our abilities (and our obligation) to contest and transform discourse and discourse communities.

Finally "discourse community" suggests "discourse analysis," though I think what we are doing is inventing, with our students, approaches to and procedures for discourse analysis. I certainly would *not* want to use any of the methods for discourse analysis that I know exist. I guess I would call discourse analysis that I could stomach, contrastive rhetoric, or, even better, rhetoric, if we keep the phrase sufficiently broad, a big "if" considering our training in English departments.

Genre

This is a term chosen purposely because it is familiar to those of us with traditional literature training but also because it is being newly applied by scholars throughout the "human sciences"—itself a kind of shorthand for the sort of transdisciplinary (even anti-disciplinary) work going on in what traditionally have been called the humanities and the social sciences.

Specifically, Clifford Geertz since at least 1973 has been raiding literary studies for concepts and terms useful to his work in cultural anthropology (his *The Interpretation of Culture,* for example, resulted from an "interdisciplinary" project that involved, among others, J. Hillis Miller).

At any rate Geertz asserts in a more recent essay titled "Blurred Genres" that the truly exciting and innovative work is going on in precisely those fields where there is a blurring of disciplinary boundaries and norms, and an appropriating of concepts by one discipline that have been richly developed in other disciplines. (Of course, this implicitly raises the question some of our students ask or at least hint at, why are there these disciplinary boundaries in the first place, when it seems knowledge of the world is "one." And therein lies a tale about who benefits when our knowledge about the world get fragmented, disconnected, and diffused.)

Genre then is being applied to a lot more than literature and texts on a page. Bakhtin talks about "speech genres" and we have the "genre project" in which we are attempting to delineate and re-create, as a community, the studios.

Genre is a type, a kind, a construct, an act itself, that (dare I say such a thing these days?) "represents" our activity, our practices when we teach the studios, our theoretical notions as we think about the studios for ourselves and others.

Genre implies a history, a constellation of similarities or traits or features that themselves undergo change, that evolve, through time. Genre also implies "style," a related set of *ways of doing* things, ways of acting and being in our world. Thus we can think of the genre of the studios as involving those characteristic (and not so characteristic) ways of weaving "studio texts" and "studio subtexts" together.

Meaning/Form/Function

These are the categories (and most importantly, the *relations* between these categories) that Ailita Markova used to organize her reform curriculum in literacy. This was a ten-year project that was conducted in the Soviet Union in response to the U.S. educational response to Sputnik.

(The irony here is that the U.S. curricular response to Sputnik was influenced in large part by Jerome Bruner's work, specifically his notion of the spiral curriculum. That spiral curriculum, and much of Bruner's subsequent work, was profoundly influenced by

Lev Vygotsky, whose work was suppressed in the Soviet Union from 1936 to 1956.)

Markova sets up a curriculum that teaches literacy across several grade levels. Each course concretely applies and further deepens a "theory of utterance." The first courses, after introducing the theory of utterance, focus more on the meaning-form relation while the later courses focus more on the form-function relation. Students consider the meaning-form relation when they investigate the shapes various discourses take and how any change in form creates a corresponding change in meaning. Additionally, students look at the form-function relation when they consider how form (and meaning) changes in different contexts, when motives and the uses of text change.

It seems to me that there may be some parallels here between Markova's early and later courses and our Studio I and II. Perhaps we might see Studio I focusing more, though not exclusively, on how meaning in writing takes many forms and how various forms (informal writing, drafting, notetaking) shape, even at times, determine meaning. Meaning being, of course, plural, recursive, generating, and not at all limited to text as that is narrowly construed. (The relations between meaning, experience, and reflection are involved.)

Studio II might then be seen as focusing more, though not exclusively, on how changes in form influence function and how changes in function (in different disciplines, situations, contexts) change forms of writing.

Reflection

A key concept in this writing program, being one of the things that I think really makes this approach to teaching writing unlike most of what is going on around the country.

I assume that writing is always active and reflective if it is authentic (and here I borrow from Freire). Most people across this campus accept the fact that writing is an important, often crucial, way of communicating information across time and space—that's why all the interest and dispute—but far fewer, I would argue, see writing as a way of coming to know something, as a way of discovering something that one would not know if one did not write reflectively. Writing *generates* ideas and feelings and relations as well as *transmits* them.

But fewer people still—perhaps only what I would label "writers," those people whose "most absorbed and passionate hours are spent arranging words on pieces of paper"—would acknowledge that writing is a developmental activity, that by using writing reflectively we can actually come to new realizations and bootstrap ourselves into new developmental zones.

Vygotsky believed that and that's one reason why Markova makes an important place in her "Vygotskian" curriculum for reflection. Writing reflectively can be a critical part of consciousness raising, and by that I do *not* mean a changing self-awareness alone, but also what Freire calls "conscientizaçao" an insight into the way the world "is" that leads to praxis, a questioning of the necessity of that world and a move to transform it. Vygotsky and Freire both believe this is what sets the human species apart in its biological evolution and cultural development. And reflection on our action is a key part in all of this.

I could go on to elaborate my notion of reflection in more detail but this is not the appropriate place for what will be a theoretical and lengthy piece. So let me assert here what I hope later to have time to prove—that reflection does *not* require a romantic notion of self, nor is it primarily a self-centered activity. Language in a multitude of ways "reflects" our experience and our activity, and our "reflection" on that language will necessarily, if allowed to unfold sufficiently, involve consideration of our "place" in society.

In an interconnected and interrelated universe any individual reflection is necessarily always already social.

Rhetoric

What to do with this one? Perhaps it would be helpful to simply list some of the various definitions of rhetoric that appeal to me and I hope are relevant to Studio II and the teaching of "writing as rhetoric."

- identification (Kenneth Burke)

- persuasion

- discovering all available means of persuasion (Aristotle)

- understanding and applying Zebroski's Law: IT ALL DEPENDS

- the study of the tropes of discourse

- the study of relations between language, knowledge, power (Foucault)

- the study of the relations between addressor/text/addressee (Kinneavy, Jakobson)

- the study of the relations between text and contexts (Summerfield and Summerfield)
- the study of the relations between meaning/form/function (Markova)
- the study of the making of meaning (Berthoff)

Spiral Curriculum

The Spiral Curriculum is an idea advanced by Louise Phelps via Jerome Bruner (who got it partly from Lev Vygotsky—don't you just love intertextuality) that any subject could be taught to any child no matter the age, in some form that was intellectually honest. Of course, the child would return later on to pursue, to deepen, to concretize and to transform all that had originally been taught in the discipline. That constant returning to a set of themes at later developmental levels is one of the things that sets the spiral curriculum apart from others. Most of us have been educated in schools where it was thought that once you "taught" something and it was "learned"—that was it. Nevermore. Go on to other things. (see DEVELOPMENT.) Bruner made a persuasive argument for the place of overlap and key repetition across time.

Obviously the point when a person comes back to a theme at a higher level will in part be determined by what is going on in her or his life, the changing contexts, the new developmental challenges offered.

Studio

I obviously am not including this term to give a definition or a gloss, since in a sense this entire document is a gloss on the idea of studio and on the commitment to teach writing using a studio approach.

What I do think we might usefully recall here is the connection that we tend, after a while, to take for granted between the teaching of writing and the teaching of the other arts. Studio was chosen carefully because it has those craft associations. We need to keep those associations fresh.

"Using the studio approach to teach writing." I like that line, the sound of it, what it means when we get into the classroom. It means I never have to "lecture" again. It means I don't have to worry about transmitting a hugh amount of largely irrelevant content. It means

that what really counts is what students are *doing* in the deepest
sense, not just what I am saying.

Studio means that my students and I collaborate on projects and
that that collaboration brings their intellectual lives outside of the
classroom together with my current intellectual preoccupations and
interests. My "research" then becomes part of what our "classroom"
is about just as their "education" becomes part of their writing
"research."

"I'm going to my writing studio." Sure sounds different from "I
gotta go teach my comp. class." And I believe that the people who
are really teaching a writing studio are those who believe the difference as one of deeds as well as words.

Theory

- Theory is a view, a vision of the world.
- Theory is a guide to action as well as an action.
- Theory is unavoidable (resistance to theory is a theory).
- Theory is created and can be changed.
- Theory moves (in sometimes strange and subtle ways) into prac-
  tice, and practice invigorates and reinvents theory; the move-
  ment between the two I term Praxis.
- Theory is both reflective and active.

I do not go into the classroom to "give" students "theory." Nor
do I believe everyone has his own theory. I view theory as being the
focusing of a worldview on to a particular concern or set of related
concerns. Such a focusing involves many implicit/tacit/unsaid dimensions. My job is to try to elaborate some of those highly abbreviated, often unnoticed understandings. That is what theory is.

In my judgment there are only three or four persuasive/perva-
sive worldviews in contemporary Western society. (I list them as
positivism, phenomenology, and Marxism; Stephen Pepper in 1942
labeled them formism, organicism, mechanism, and contextualism.)

The studio courses are theoretical because they ask both students and teachers to reflect on their activity and because that activity of reflection becomes a determinant in where the course will go
next.

Students and teachers are usefully entangled in theory every
time they talk, read, write, and wonder about who they are and what
they are doing and where they are and where they are going to go
next and why. Studio II is theoretical in that we ask teachers and

students to theorize their practice, or think (deeply) about what they do (deeply). (See Clifford Geertz again, on "Deep Play . . .") Studio II is theoretical because we (students and teachers) bring one view of discourse to the classroom and begin to contrast that to other views/uses of discourse in other disciplines and in other discourse communities.

References

Bizzell, P. 1992. *Academic discourse and critical consciousness.* Pittsburgh: University of Pittsburgh Press.

Bronfenbrenner, U. 1976. The experimental ecology of education. *Educational Researcher.* 5:5–15.

Geertz, C. 1973. *The interpretation of cultures.* New York: Basic Books.

Hayles, K. 1984. *The cosmic web: Scientific field models and literary strategies in the 20th century.* Ithaca: Cornell University Press.

Markova, A. 1979. *The teaching and mastery of language.* White Plains, NY: M. E. Sharpe.

Ollman, B. 1976. *Alienation: Marx's conception of man in capitalist society.* New York: Cambridge University Press. 2nd edition.

Pepper, S. 1942. *World hypotheses.* Berkeley, CA: University of California Press.

Phelps, L. 1988. Speculative instrument. *Reflections in writing: The genre project—a survey of studio teaching methods.* Syracuse: Syracuse University Writing Program.

von Hartz, J. 1970. America rediscovered. *Modern american painting.* Ed. J. McCoubrey. NY: Time-Life. 61–68.

Zebroski, J. 1989. A hero in the classroom. *Encountering student texts.* Eds. B. Lawson, S. Sterr, W. R. Winterowd. Urbana, IL: NCTE. 35–47.

Chapter Thirteen

Vygotsky and Composition:
Influences on an Emerging Field

Keywords come attached to keytexts. In the last essay, "Keywords of Composition: A Discipline's Search For Self," I proposed that we consider some of the "God terms" and the "devil terms," to use Richard Weaver's lexicon, that occur in our disciplinary dialogues and quarrels to track the broader and deeper social forces that intersect in our composing discourses. In this essay, I want to extend that idea to argue that another instrument for tracking a field, especially a new one, is the keysource. We can learn by observing a keysource, a set of related keytexts, as it enters, then makes its way through the emerging field.

To do this we need, but do not have, a fully developed theory of textual dynamics, an account of both social and individual processes in discourse communities, a description of the ways in which texts get produced, circulated, consumed and reproduced in such discourse communities, and an examination of the effects these processes have on both entering text and recipient context. While the eighties saw the increasing popularity of a cluster of concepts associated with "discourse community," "academic discourse," "collaborative learning and writing," and "social constructionism," in the attempt to offer an alternative to process theory, the discourse community theorists have reified the new conceptual framework. "Discourse community" too often is used to designate a monolithic, monologic context outside of and prior to the writer, the text, and history. Discourse communities are viewed as freestanding, independent groups, unaffected (or at least little affected) by ruling social structures, neither capitulating to nor resisting economic and political forces, having no histories, existing in larger cultures that have no histories. "Discourse community" has become a static concept in which processes are eliminated or at best oversimplified. To avoid the reification of one cluster of concepts associated with "writing-as-process," we have witnessed in the last decade the slow but sure reification of another cluster of concepts associated with "writing-in-discourse community." This has occurred in part because no theoretical work has been done that pragmatically offers the compositionist some alternatives to one of the grand old dichotomies of Western tradition, the dichotomy of the "individual versus society." By seeing the world through this grand dichotomy and embracing the second term, rather than trying to generate new ways of thinking about self, textuality, and society, discourse community theorists have more often than not, and sometimes in contradiction to their own publicly stated individual intentions, simply reproduced the most traditional notions of writing under the sign of the postmodern. They have too often replaced so-called romantic notions of subjectivity with the idea of authority, an authority that it is very difficult to distinguish from the dogmatic authority of those New Critical teachers who taught these theorists composition. Too often some discourse community theorists have asserted that the student writer must submit or the discourse community simply will not accept her or him and that this will obviously have detrimental effects on the student's ability to succeed in college, if not in the workplace. Appropriate or be appropriated. This idea makes an extremely complicated set of textual and social processes into a simple classroom procedure "Do what I say or else." This method is perilously close to the fiat "Be me." If this is the best that discourse community theory has to offer the composition teacher and scholar, a notion of subjectivity as textual effects and a notion of community as the simple and complete submission of these textual effects to the reigning linguistic authority, then perhaps it is time to think again about the social turn in composition.

There are a few exceptions. Joseph Harris in an admirable recent essay, "The Idea of Community in the Study of Writing" (*CCC,* 40.1, 11–21), critiques the uses to which the term has been put, arguing that discourse community is more dynamic than some composition scholars would have us believe. And yet, as helpful as Harris's analysis is in moving us to more nuanced concepts of community, it still avoids recognizing that one of the reasons why our view of community has become reified is that we *still* are dichotomizing the individual *from* the social. It is unclear in this new view of the social that the individual brings to the community *anything* of value; more specifically, it is unclear that our students can teach the university anything new. To the extent that revisions of community still privilege the community in power and the individual is only important in staking out a *position* in that community (rather than transforming it), our models will be partial and elitist.

Charles Bazerman, in his book *Shaping Written Knowledge: The Genre and Activity of the Experimental Article in Science,* comes the closest to at least raising the question of the individual's contribution to the discourse community. His analysis of the history of the experimental article in science clearly shows that that most hegemonic discourse of our time, that God-term, "Science," is itself full of conflict, plurality, heteroglossia, gaps, silences, mythology. Bazerman demystifies science by constructing a history that begins to look at the dynamics of texts (individual and social texts) as they cross the borders of power and knowledge. Bazerman's chapter "Between Books and Articles: Newton Faces Controversy" initiates perhaps the key investigation of our historical moment: how might an individual work to transform the community on her or his own with the support of like-minded others. Bazerman, in fact, concludes his book by recognizing the value of the Vygotskian model of "practical social semiosis" (of "activity," *deyatel'nost*) for a deeper understanding of the ways language, and rhetoric, realize the work of science. Bazerman is acutely aware of both the history of U.S. language study over the last three decades and the critique of poststructuralism. He precisely and shrewdly reviews them both, and concludes that linguistics, sociolinguistics, text grammar, functional grammar, and poststructuralist critique, as valuable as they may be in locating difficulties in the prevailing model of language, all fall short in providing an alternative theory, since they all arise out of Western, Saussurean tradition. *Vygotsky's work does not come out of that tradition, though Vygotsky is very aware of it.* Bazerman, then, presents one of the most powerful arguments in composition for the need for a new theory of language, doing so working in one of the most traditional areas of areas of composition, scientific and technical writing.

In the next section of this essay, I want to make the case for turning to the semiotic theory of the Tartu school in Estonia that is associated primarily with work of Yuri Lotman, in order to temporarily fill this need for a new theory of language. I will argue that, although Vygotsky's vision of language is powerful and gives us hints about how we may escape our present dilemma, we nonetheless encounter difficulties if we simply try to appropriate the existing language theory of the "Vygotskian school," just as we discover problems if we try to create our own sign theory from it. Finally, I will argue that while the work of Mikhail Bakhtin has been very helpful in forging a link between current U.S. literary theory and Russian and Eastern European language theory, we cannot simply appropriate Bakhtin as a kind of popular surrogate for Vygotsky. This leaves us with the option of pursuing a theory that might mediate Bakhtin and Vygotsky, but also Eastern European language theory and Western (especially U.S.) literary theory. Yuri Lotman's theory of dynamic semiotic systems provides us with one possible mediation.

In the section of this essay that follows my argument for Lotman's theory, I will detail the specifics of Lotman's theory that may help us to put the concept of "discourse community" into a more productive framework. Lotman's dynamic model of semiotic systems provides us with a model of social and individual textual processes that is generative in what it brings to bear on the idea of discourse community, but is equally interesting for what it suggests about the one particular discourse community that most concerns me at this moment, the discourse community of compositionists, the society of Composition. Finally, Lotman's theory of semiotic dynamics usefully frames my discussion in the last section of this essay of the effects of the work of Lev Vygotsky on Composition. In other words, I will use Lotman's sign theory to frame Vygotsky's theory of mind and language and to track Vygotsky's theory when it enters the U.S. and then the composition discourse community.

Why the theory of Estonian Yuri Lotman? The simple answer is because Lev Vygotsky never fully spelled out his theory of the sign, although we have many fragments that give us some idea of what interested him about the sign. One is found in *The Psychology of Art* (1971), a book that announced Vygotsky's turn from his training in literary and textual studies to the new discipline of psychology. Yet *The Psychology of Art* is a relatively early discussion of the psychology of language and of the literary work of art, and is not very representative of Vygotsky's later perspective on signifying functions. So when it comes to understanding Lev Vygotsky's theory of language the options for the English-speaking U.S. scholar are rather limited. Vygotsky's complete works have only recently (1982) been published in the (former) Soviet Union and there are still a large number of his texts that are unavailable in translation. There are no doubt also archival texts unpublished even in Russia. Caryl Emerson, in her talk "The Russians Reclaim Bakhtin" at the 1991 M.L.A., comments on the understandable tendency of Russian scholars ". . . to sit on the archives and dribble it out," which would seem to be true regarding Vygotsky's work as well. Still, it is doubtful that any single manuscript is going to appear that details in a complete way Vygotsky's theory of language and in effect does our work for us; his interests, though related, lay elsewhere. This leaves us with three options.

The first option is to turn to Vygotsky's students, to the work of the Vygotskian school, to try to discover a theory of the sign that, while not created by Vygotsky himself, has been constructed with his interests and assumptions in mind. It seemed logical for several years, at the behest of knowledgeable scholars like James Wertsch, to turn to work of A. A. Leontiev in his "The Psycholinguistic Aspect of Linguistic Meaning" (1978) for a Vygotskian theory of the sign and of language. A. A. Leontiev, the son of A. N. Leontiev, heir apparent, with A. Luria, to the Vygotskian tradition, seemed to have worked out this detailed psycholinguistic theory in keeping with Vygotskian principles. However, Alex Kozulin has questioned the legitimacy of A. N. Leontiev's role as the official and legitimate keeper of the Vygotskian tradition in psychology, casting doubts as well on the work of A. A. Leontiev, whose work has not appeared since the early 1980s. So the question of whether we can in fairness appropriate the work of the Vygotskian school as a legitimate elaboration of a theory of language consonant with Vygotsky's intentions remains unanswered.

The second option is to turn to the fragments on language theory that we find throughout the work of Vygotsky's that we do have and expand these texts into a theory applicable to composition studies, but also in keeping, as nearly as we can tell given the limitations, to Vygotskian principles. Such a theory would be more immediately applicable to our work and more answerable to our questions in composition. But it takes a great deal of time as well as an intimate familiarity with the Vygotskian canon in both English and Russian. So far few composition scholars have found the intellectual or financial support required to pursue such a long-term project. One goal in putting together this book on Vygotskian theory in composition studies has been to introduce Vygotsky, in a more complete way, to composition teachers and scholars, and especially to encourage new composition scholars just beginning their life's work to look into the great potential that the ideas, theory, and research of Vygotsky, and that of Eastern European language theorists generally, has for composition and rhetoric in the U.S. Although this may be a preferable option because it will more directly respond to our needs, it is a very long-term option. Practically speaking, this option won't immediately help us.

The third option is to go to work by scholars not in the Vygotskian school but who come out of a similar worldview, scholars sympathetic to the principles that guided Vygotsky. Eastern European language theory is rich and fascinating. There are many language theory scholars who have come out of not only the Russian tradition, but also scholarly traditions in Poland (Adam Schaff), Czechoslovakia (Jan Prucha), the Ukraine (Zinchenko), and Estonia (Lotman, but also Jaan Valsiner in psychology). But the first among equals, the primate of Russian literary theory, is of course Mikhail Bakhtin. His work does provide us with a dynamic theory of language that seems to dovetail in many ways with the work of Lev Vygotsky. Bakhtin and Vygotsky were contemporaries, shared many views, and their theories can be productively and in a principled way joined, as Caryl Emerson demonstrated in one of the first scholarly articles that linked the two, "The Inner Word and Outer Speech: Bakhtin, Vygotsky, and the Internalization of Language" first published in *Critical Inquiry* in December of 1983. I have also pursued this strategy of linking Vygotskian psychology with Bakhtinian language theory in my essay "Writing as Dialogue (and Quarrel)," written at about the same time as Emerson's essay and published in the second section of this book.

After almost a decade, however, I have concluded that there are limits to the extent to which Bakhtin's theory of textuality can be appropriated as a surrogate for the work that Vygotsky never finished. Theoretically, Vygotsky and Bakhtin shared many views, but it would seem, if current translations of Bakhtin's early writing and recent commentary on these texts by Holquist, Morson, and Emerson are correct, that Bakhtin was always more a Kantian idealist than a Marxist materialist. Vygotsky was very interested in the philosophy of Spinoza, among others, something that Bakhtin's anti-systematicity and anti-transcendental position would appear to contradict. Vygotsky too was, I would argue, more of an outsider, though I admit that it is difficult to imagine someone more eccentric and outside of the mainstream than Bakhtin. But Vygotsky after all switched disciplines. He was not trained in psychology; he was self taught in it. Vygotsky was neither a Marxist ideologue nor a bourgeois humanist, neither pure scientist nor pure artist. Vygotsky was originally from the western provinces; Western sources were always important to his intellectual project. Like his Byeloruss homeland, Vygotsky's work was crisscrossed by the oppositions of East and West. He was a product of a borderland that had changed hands dozens of time over the centuries; his cultural roots lay in soil that had been taken and retaken time and again by Russians or Poles, by Lithuanians or the Golden Horde, by Eastern Orthodox Christians or Roman Catholics. Vygotsky grew out of a kind of cultural "no man's land," and all his life, and in fact for many years after his death, Vygotsky's work was marginal, peripheral, suppressed and then made into official dogma.

Most importantly, Vygotsky was a White Russian Jew. Except for Alex Kozulin, no one has commented on how important Vygotsky's Jewishness must have been on Vygotsky's psychology and on his work. Kozulin in his book *Vygotsky's Psychology: A Biography of Ideas,* argues that Vygotsky's Jewish roots were important to his later development:

> The first indication of Vygotsky's interest in the social sciences is related to his activity at a discussion club organized by gymnasium students interested in Jewish history and culture. Although there is no written record of these meetings, one can easily surmise that they focused on such questions as "What does it mean to be Jewish?", "What distinguishes Jews from all other nations?" and "What is the historical destiny of Jews?" One should not forget that in the 1910s the western provinces of the Russian Empire were a hotbed of Zionist activism. (1990, 15)

At the very least, even if Vygotsky were a lapsed, nonpracticing Jew, his subjectivity was formed in the crucible of *minority discourse.* Vygotsky may well have given up, or at least publicly downplayed his Jewish roots, though his writing during college years for *Novy Put'* (*The New Way,* a journal of the Jewish intelligentsia) on literature and the new Jewish poetry suggests otherwise, but there can be little doubt that the Russian cultural climate even after the revolution would never allow him or anyone else to forget those Jewish roots. Vygotsky was member of what in the U.S. would be called a minority group and in the Soviet Union was termed a "national minority," and a sizable one at that. Bakhtin, even though he seems to have been part of an underground crypto-Christian group, or at least his work and name were later appropriated by Russian Orthodox believers, was nevertheless a product of a majority Christian cultural tradition. In the traditional Russian culture in which Bakhtin and Vygotsky grew up, Orthodox Christianity was the official state religion, the privileged and ruling discourse. And while both Bakhtin and Vygotsky lived on into post-czarist times in which the official "religion" became communism, the past no doubt lingered on in unstated suspicions and then explicit charges of cosmopolitanism. During Stalin's rule Jews were persecuted supposedly not as Jews but because they were implicated in a "cosmopolitan conspiracy." Bakhtin, for all his troubles, never had to deal with the stigma of being Jewish and the ever-present threat of the pogrom, something that according to Kozulin, Vygotsky no doubt well remembered from his own childhood in the western provinces "beyond the pale." Bakhtin was the dissident product of a ruling, sometimes elitist, metropolitan Russian culture, a culture it is true that was suppressed by the new communist rulers. Still, Bakhtin was not a provincial, he was not a member of a "a national minority" that had been oppressed for hundreds of years. In fact, I don't think it would be easy for such a Russian Christian to have any real sense of what it meant and means for a person to grow up as a Byeloruss Jew in an anti-Semitic culture. It is difficult for any person formed in the ruling discourse to understand the experience of a person formed in minority discourse. This difference exists not simply at the level of subjectivity or individual experience or of words alone, but at the level of worldview, in the language one uses to construct reality and in the reality that that language then constructs. Ultimately, that for me is the salient point. Vygotsky unlike Bakhtin was a minority person. *Because Vygotsky was a minority person, his language, his worldview, his categories for thinking about the world, the questions that intrigued him, necessarily differed from the reigning order.* I am suggesting, then, that to link Vygotsky's theory with Bakhtin's theory is to stick together related, but incommensurate, worldviews. Care needs to be taken.

Can we have much doubt, for instance, that despite the relative status of his family in Gomel that Vygotsky was influenced by the traditions of Jewish life in Eastern Europe? One wonders if Vygotsky's interest in inner speech didn't reflect his own experience with a kind of language very *unlike* the elaborated academic discourse of the Soviet intelligentsia. One wonders if Vygotsky was familiar with the undercurrents of Shtetl life, the small-town Jewish community found throughout the western provinces beyond the pale. Mark Zborowski and Elizabeth Herzog portray that world in *Life is With People: The Culture of the Shtetl* (New York: Schocken, 1952). Zborowski and Herzog make the following observation about the language of the shtetl.

> In keeping with his own conception of contradictory reality, the man of the shtetl is noted both for volubility and for laconic, allusive speech. Both pictures are true, and both are characteristic of the yeshiva as well as the market place. When the scholar converses with his intellectual peers, *incomplete sentences, a hint, a gesture, may replace a whole paragraph.* The listener is expected to *understand the full meaning on the basis of a word or even a sound.* It is assumed that a truly learned man is familiar not only with quotations from Torah and Talmud, but also with the trend that comment or interpretation would be apt to take. *Accordingly, in speaking or writing, a scholar may pronounce only the first*

*words of a sentence, expecting his hearer to complete it in his
mind.* Such a conversation, prolonged and animated, may be as
incomprehensible to the uninitiated as if the excited discussants
were talking in tongues. The same verbal economy may be found
in domestic or business circles. (123, emphasis is mine)

One wonders why this quotation bears such a striking similarity to
Vygotsky's views on language and inner speech and to Vygotsky's
writing itself. And one wonders how this compares with the language theory and practice of Mikhail Bakhtin.

To extend Vygotsky's work by means of Bakhtin's words is to
level the very sort of differences that make Vygotsky unique, distinct, and of value. As provocative as the similarities between the
two theorists of the twenties are, I have decided that ultimately their
differences are more important. Those differences are not accidental,
nor are they simply the result of working in different disciplines.
Vygotsky differs from Bakhtin in the subject position his discourse
occupies, due in part to his being a member of a minority group with
hundreds of years of marginalization from mainstream culture, and
of development of its own language and traditions. We need to
preserve this difference for ethical and as well intellectual reasons.
Bakhtin's language theory then cannot simply be taken up in Vygotsky's name, without difficulty, without reservation. So this leads us
to other Eastern European language theorists who do not so much
synthesize the crosscurrents at work in Vygotsky and Bakhtin, but
who rather approach textual dynamics from another perspective
entirely. Lotman's theory of language illuminates the issues of textuality that we need to get at, in order to see how Vygotsky's work
has influenced composition studies.

Lotman, like Vygotsky, began as a literary scholar who was interested in the social and individual aspects of the work of art.
During the 1960s and 1970s, Lotman widened his interests beyond
the literary work of art to develop a theory of textuality that stressed
the importance of the cultural and historical context but that was
also a description of changes that occur to texts as they appear on
the horizon, then enter and circulate through a second textual system, whether it is a textual system of the psychological subject or
the textual system of a discourse community. Lotman's theory then
is of sufficient abstractive power to be applicable to the life of any
text, whether artistic or everyday, whether individual or social, as
the text circulates through a variety of intersecting, often conflicting
contexts, and is itself appropriated or ignored. In fact, Lotman's
theory of the dynamics of textual systems helps us to think through
dichotomies like artistic versus everyday and individual versus so-

cial, by focusing on textual transformations across history and contexts.

Yuri Lotman's work, developed with his colleagues at Tartu University in Estonia over the last thirty years, approaches text dynamically, theoretically, and historically.

- What happens when a text from an "alien" culture comes to the attention of a native or home culture?
- What are the various ways a home culture might react to an alien keysource?
- What are the possible effects the home culture might have on the approaching text?
- What are the possible effects the alien text might have on the home culture?
- How do textual and cultural systems evolve across time in relation to each other?
- How might we see textual dynamics as a bridge between individual and social processes?
- What is the historical role of textual and cultural difference?

These are just some of the questions that come up in Lotman's work. In part, Lotman's interest in the textual dynamics of individual and cultural systems is a response to the political climate that developed in the former Soviet Union since Stalin. Faced with a closed society and with an official version of history, the nationalities of Eastern Europe and the Soviet Union found that one of the few sites of resistance was the preservation of local culture, history, folklore, customs. Lotman's theory is not simply a theory; it is in some measure a description of the kind of life one had to live in a closed society where the alien texts might be, as Czech President Vaclav Havel has so emphatically pointed out, rock and roll songs. So Lotman's theory is not just or merely theory. Living in the Soviet Union required that the everyday citizen develop her or his own semiotic theory for getting past the official "truth" found in the official "news" organs like *Pravda*.

Lotman is concerned with the translation of texts across cultures and time. In an early article "On the Reduction and Unfolding of Sign Systems (The Problem of 'Freudianism and Semiotic Culturology')" in Henryk Baran's *Semiotics and Structuralism: Readings From the Soviet Union* (White Plains, NY: International Arts and Science Press, 1976), Lotman uses textual theory to reread an aspect of Freud's theory of the child's development. Lotman argues that one could see the development of various psychological formations like the Oedipus complex, less as a biological imperative than as the result of the working out of textual dynamics between two differing semiotic systems. The child's Oedipus complex could be read then as the result of ". . . the recoding of a text with a large alphabet into a text with a small one." (302).

> The child's contact with the world of adults is constantly imposed on him by the subordinated position of his world in the general hierarchy of the culture of adults. However, this contact itself is possible only as an act of *translation*. . . . the child establishes a correspondence between some texts familiar and comprehensive to him in "his" language and the texts of "adults". . . In such translation of a whole text by another whole text, the child discovers an extraordinary abundance of "superfluous" words in "adult" texts. The act of translation is accompanied by the semantic reduction of the text. (302)

Lotman explains that in this process of semantic reduction, which occurs because of the necessity of translation between two extremely *different* textual systems, the child leaves untranslated or partially translated big chunks of the adult text and these chunks play a role as "spores" or "folded programs" that unfold later when the child has further developed her or his own textual system. The more translation the child does, the greater the number of unfolded or spore texts; the greater the number of these spore texts, the greater the effects on the whole textual system when they are translated at a later date, when to use Lotman's metaphor, the child has a larger alphabet into which to transliterate and translate the adult texts.

The details of Freud's theory and how it might be reread as a the result of semiotic rather than purely biological or psychological processes are of less interest to us here than is the principle Lotman is working out. The principle of semiotic translation between uneven textual systems is one as applicable to the individual as to the culture at large, since one is not essentializing the individual or the social, but instead is discussing the textuality of the individual and the social. In composition, one might speculate that process theory could well use a dose of Lotman's semiotics. What sometimes became a matter of biology, psychology, or even information theory, in the development of writing processes, could instead be read as semiotic development. The differences between the processes of the beginning and advanced writer might well be more due to the difference in textual systems and in the effects of translating among textual systems. We might be able to reread process theory through Lotman.

But more importantly for our purposes in this essay, the principles at work in Lotman's theory seem applicable to Vygotsky's appropriation by composition. Vygotsky's work has been translated from its larger alphabet into our smaller alphabet. There has been a semantic reduction of Vygotsky's text, when those texts have even been translated at all. Vygotsky's work has often not been "translated" but frequently was simply incorporated into composition studies as an easy and faddish footnote. But Vygotsky's alien text has been taken up whenever a shift in the intellectual work done has taken place in composition studies, though taken up in strikingly different ways. In the early days of composition, Vygotsky was taken up as spokesman for a view of language that seemed to imply deep and surface structures. The section of *Thought And Language* that scholars looked especially closely at was the section on inner speech. A decade later in the 1970s, Vygotsky was appropriated to support theories that distinguished orality from literacy, at the very historical moment when sociolinguistics was becoming increasingly important. In the 1980s Vygotsky's work was appropriated for the zone of proximal development concept, since composition (but also the psychology done by Wertsch, Rogoff, Bruner and others) was suddenly interested in collaboration and the social dimensions of writing and learning. This is especially ironic since in 1937 one of the very first U.S. articles to use Vygotsky's work discussed the zone of proximal development as an important idea, as a keytext. The concept was also elaborated at length in the very first U.S. translation of *Thought and Language.* Still hardly anyone noticed ZPD or made use of it for over forty years. It took the rise of the social in composition (and psychology) and the publication of a second book of Vygotsky's selected essays called *Mind In Society,* for this "unfolded program" in Vygotsky that was there from the very "beginning" to even be recognized as a powerful concept and experimental tool. We never deal then with Vygotsky's ideas alone, but rather deal with composition's reading of those ideas. Our uses of Vygotsky's work tell us as much about us as they do Vygotsky.

At the heart of Lotman's theory is the view that this is not only the way things are, but that this is good. Lotman distinguishes his view from that of many modern studies of language and culture which assume the two cultures, two textual systems, react in reciprocal and equal ways on each other. Lotman argues against this model since similarity implies that no truly new message can arise from the contact between cultures. Lotman contends:

> Of considerably greater significance in the overall cultural sense is the process of obtaining texts from a culture at a different stage—

more developed or more primitive. In this case there takes place reduction and complicating [sic] unfolding of the received text, as well as an accumulation of untranslatable texts . . . the result is an abrupt transformation of the internal semiotic order of the perceiving culture, which is accompanied by explosive acceleration of the flow of cultural processes. (306–307)

I wonder if this isn't a good description of what has taken place in composition over the last thirty years. Not only have alien texts like those of Vygotsky been appropriated, but so too have texts from disciplines at far different points in their development and history. Certainly, composition studies has experienced a momentous "explosive acceleration" of intellectual and textual activity since 1960 or so, at the very time when compositionists began to turn to other disciplines. In fact, one might track the origin of composition to the failure of New Critical reading practices in helping the writing teacher of the late 1960s and early 1970s make sense of the texts produced by the huge number of new (often open admissions) college students and to the subsequent search for useful theory and practice in psychology and linguistics, two disciplines undergoing their own self-styled revolutions at the time. Mina Shaughnessy's experience recounted in *Errors and Expectations* is only the best known example of what many composition teachers experienced.

Lotman is clear about the semiotic values he privileges.

Traditional comparativistics, noting empirically the difference between particular national cultures, immediately sets itself the task of determining which of them is "backward" and which "advanced," and assumes that the natural destiny of the former is to come to resemble the latter as soon as possible. However, a glance at the culture of an area(and, in the final analysis, at the general culture of the earth) as at some working mechanism persuades us of the necessity of unevenness and diversity of organization of the sign mechanisms of the diachronic movement of culture as a whole. (307)

In other words, the dynamic development of a culture is dependent on the preservation of other, different cultures, the more of them and the more distinctive they are, the greater the potential for cultural development. Considering the context, this was a rather radical thing for Lotman to say in the Soviet Union in 1970. Lotman is a semiotic ecologist arguing for the preservation, in fact for the nurturing, of cultural and semiotic difference. I am reminded of the 4C's Statement of 1974 on "The Students' Right to Their Own Language."

Lotman in his more recent work has extended his semiotic analysis of culture. In "Text Within Text" (*Soviet Psychology* 26.3 [Spring 1988]), he argues that texts can function in two very different ways, as conveyers of meaning or as generators of meaning. These differing functions of text imply different conceptions of language. A text of the second type, a generator of meaning, ". . . is a semiotic space in which languages interact, interfere, and organize themselves hierarchically" (37). This sounds very similar to the definition of writing as the intersection of discursive universes, including those of text, context, self, and society, on which this book is based. Lotman argues that the text of this second type acts as a "thinking device" (36) and privileges differences between input and output, between writing and reading. "The text is generator of meaning, *a thinking device* which requires an interlocutor to be activated . . . To function, consciousness requires a consciousness, a text requires a text, and a culture requires a culture" (40).

Vygotsky's texts then have served composition well as a kind of alien text, as a repository of alien culture. The widely differing ways that Vygotsky's texts have functioned in composition testify to their alienness, to their strangeness. This is, according to Lotman, precisely what makes them useful generators of meaning. Following Lotman's line of reasoning, one might argue that the greatest value of Vygotsky's work for compositionists has not been any one concept or one set of empirical data that he has provided, but rather his different way of seeing the world of mind and language. *Taking this line of argument even further, one might contend that Eastern European language theory as a whole would be more generative than poststructuralist continental theory because it defamiliarizes the assumptions about language that even the poststructuralists take for granted.*

Lotman's words concerning the introduction of the alien text into a local culture seem to apply to Vygotsky's work and its introduction into Composition.

> Introducing an external text into the immanent world of a particular text plays a tremendous role. On the one hand, the external text is transformed, forms a new message, in the structural semantic field of the text. Because the components of textual interaction are complex and multilevel, the transformation the introduced text must undergo is somewhat unpredictable. But not only is the text transformed: the entire semiotic situation within the textual world into which it has been introduced changes. Introduction of an alien semiosis that is untranslatable into the "maternal" text puts the latter in a state of excitation: the object of attention shifts from the message to the language as such and reveals the explicit code of

the maternal text itself. Under these conditions, its constituent subtexts may begin to function relative to one another as alien messages by transforming themselves according to laws that are alien to them. A text extracted from a state of semiotic equilibrium is capable of self-development. Powerful, external, textual incursions into culture, seen as one grand text, not only lead to the adaptation of external messages and the entry of those messages into the memory of culture but also serve as stimuli for the self-development of that memory, the results of which are unpredictable. (40)

While I am not sure about the sexist connotations of using the "maternal text" metaphors, this passage nevertheless seems to me to be a fairly accurate description of the history of Vygotsky's work across composition since the late 1950s. Vygotsky's texts were first taken up by those composition teachers interested in writing *development* and writing curriculum. Then they were appropriated by compositionists versed in *sociolinguistics* in their attempt to sort out the distinctions between orality and literacy. The *cognitivists* appropriated Vygotsky's texts to argue for writing as processing, and the *social constructionists* have returned to Vygotsky most recently to plump for collaborative learning and discourse communities. The point is that for over thirty years Composition has searched out and taken up a variety of "alien" texts including those of Vygotsky, and that this textual interaction between Composition and texts of other fields has contributed to the cultural explosion in Composition. One of the shifts during this time has been from a simple application of these external sources to problems in teaching composing, to a consideration of the method and mode of inquiry in researching composing. This shift is reflected in Stephen North's book, *The Making of Knowledge in Composition.* Lotman's description of the shift during the process of semiotic development from a consideration of the immediate "message" to a consideration of the "language" parallels the shift North's book makes away from the student writing to the methodological confusion of knowledge making in Composition. Further what better description of North's "discovery" of multiplicity in Composition than Lotman's assertion that this shift of attention ". . . reveals the explicit code heterogeneity of the code of the maternal culture itself. . . . its constituent subtexts may begin to function . . . as alien messages"? What North reads as an effect of methodological confusion at best, or sloppy scholarship at worst, Lotman reads as a regular feature of semiotic interaction and development, the dynamics of textual systems.

In using his theory, then, I find a series of historical parallels which Lotman suggests might be related because they all involve the interaction of textual systems. These parallels include:

- Vygotsky's texts emerging from the White Russian Jewish minority community and entering the "Great Russian" majority culture.

- Vygotsky's texts emerging from a study of history and literature, the humanities, and entering the social science of psychology.

- Vygotsky's Marxist Soviet texts entering (at the height of the Cold War) U.S. capitalist culture.

- Vygotsky's psychology texts entering into Composition at that very time that—

- Open admissions, student protests, federal funding of higher education, make it possible for minority students to go to college for the first time in U.S. history. These new voices in academe enter into the academic discourse community through Composition.

Each of these parallels involve the entrance of an alien minority cultural text into a majority culture. Lotman's theory supports the claim that the appropriation of Vygotsky by Composition tells us some interesting things about the Composition. In the last section of this essay, then, I will flesh out this general theory of textual dynamics with the specifics of history. While the theory comes first in this essay, I actually did the historical research that follows several years ago. I would not argue that empirical historical research can be neutral, but I do want to assert that the historical account found in this last section got me to search for a theory that might explain the concrete instances in Composition where Vygotsky was cited, then applied. Lotman's theory came long after my initial research, and seems to explain it. So let me turn to the history of Vygotsky in the U.S. and then in Composition.

On July 4, 1936, the Central Committee of the Communist Party of the Soviet Union decreed that pedology or educational testing was in error, and ordered Lev Vygotsky's work indexed for being complicit with pedology. From 1936 until 1956 when the first Russian volume of Vygotsky's selected works appeared, Vygotsky's work went unpublished in the Soviet Union though colleagues like Alexander Luria and Alexei N. Leontiev continued to keep Vygotsky's ideas alive in their own studies. It is then somewhat ironic that some of the first serious considerations of Vygotsky's work in print to appear after his death in 1934, came out in the U.S.

In 1937, Eugenia Hanfmann and Jacob Kasanin published an article describing the block-sorting test created by Sakharov that Vygotsky had used to construct the early outlines of a theory of conceptual development described in Chapter Five of *Thought And*

Language. The article, "A Method for the Study of Concept Formation," came out in the *Journal of Psychology* (3, 521–540) with the
note that said the article had been ". . . received in the Editorial
Office on December 14, 1936 and published immediately at
Provincetown, Massachusetts" (521). The publication of this essay
came within two years of Vygotsky's death and within months of the
Communist Party decree suppressing Vygotsky's work. The article
cites Vygotsky's book (*Thinking and Speech,* citation number 8)
giving the 1934 publication date and the Socekgiz publishing concern in Moscow as publisher. This is incredibly fast turnaround in
the academic publishing world, even by present-day standards, and
it suggests to me that the authors had been in close contact with the
Vygotskians all along, at least long before this article made it into
print, and perhaps were aware of the effects that Stalin's suppression
were having on Vygotsky's work. But what is even more remarkable
about this article aside from its easy familiarity with Vygotsky's
work and ideas is that in this article is perhaps the first U.S. citation
of Vygotsky's famous thesis of the zone of proximal development.
Hanfmann and Kasanin (1937) commenting on differences in conceptual thinking note:

> This is an instance of a more general rule pertaining to the devel-
> opment of intellectual functions. Vigotsky [*sic*] (8) has formulated
> it in his thesis of the importance of the "zone of proximal devel-
> opment." He points out that of two children who show the same
> level when tested by the usual school achievement tests, one can
> solve far more advanced problems when given some help, while
> the other is not able to advance his standing by utilizing help. In
> Vigotsky's judgement and experience there is a great difference in
> the developmental level of the two children. (529, footnote)

This is startling since the zone of proximal development really did
not stir much interest in the U.S. until after the 1978 publication of
Mind in Society. For forty years this "spore" text, there from the
start, would be ignored. Many of us would at first think that the zone
of proximal development was introduced in the *Mind in Society*
anthology, though it appeared in this first U.S. article on Vygotsky
and also appeared in a section of the first 1962 edition of *Thought
and Language.* This is a good example of how context and motive
construct text. When Vygotsky's work came into an ahistorical, individualistic, behavioristic setting, concepts like ZPD simply were
not seen, and if they were, they were not seen to be useful or
important. As Lotman contends, an alien text is sometimes accepted
into a receiving context without being translated and lies in that

context as a sort of spore awaiting the time it might be unfolded, read, and translated.

Soon after Hanfmann and Kasanin's first article on Vygotsky, a translation appeared in *Psychiatry. Psychiatry* was a new interdisciplinary journal that included among its editorial board, Edward Sapir, whose work on anthropology and language, Vygotsky knew and approvingly cited. *Psychiatry* in 1939 published a complete translation by Hanfmann and Kasanin of the final chapter of Vygotsky's book *Thought and Language.* The note appended to the translation says:

> This translation of Chapter VII of Vigotsky's monograph on *Language and Thought* published by Gostsdat in Moscow USSR in 1934. Chapter VII is the last chapter in the book and summarizes some of the most important ideas of the author. The translation is a combined effort of Drs. Helen Kogan, Eugenia Hanfmann, and Jacob Kasanin. A number of liberties were taken in changing some of the paragraphs of the text and eliminating others; in each instance, however, trying to preserve the sense of the original. This was necessary, as at times the author's ideas were involved and complex. Certain examples which could only be understood by one familiar with Russian or French were omitted. (29)

This passage prefigures certain themes which were to dominate Vygotsky scholarship in the U.S. for the next fifty years. There is a partial publication of a much longer and detailed work. Certain necessary editorial liberties have been taken. There is a double move to both introduce and popularize what the translator-authors take to be an innovative and useful body of work in the field of psychology, while at the same time there is an explicit mention of the difficulties that popularization of such a "complex" and "involved" theory entails. Finally, the Vygotsky-Luria connection is made in this first translation article to which a biographical sketch on Vygotsky written by Luria is attached. This Vygotsky-Luria connection will continue down to the work published into the 1980s in the U.S. Actually, Luria, as a member of the editorial board of the *Journal of Genetic Psychology* in the early thirties—his name has significantly been removed by the time of the Hanfmann and Kasanin translation of 1939—had had a role in getting English translation of articles by A. N. Leontiev and L. S. Vygotsky printed in that journal. But the Hanfmann-Kasanin translation is the first attempt in the U.S. to publish what was to become the most important work in the Vygotsky canon.

From 1939 to 1962 not much was published in the U.S. on Vygotsky's psychology. Only Raymond Bauer's *The New Man in*

Soviet Psychology, published in 1952 by Harvard University Press, dealt even briefly with Vygotsky in the broader historical context of Soviet psychology. For fifty years after the first translation attempt, the accessibility to Vygotsky's work in the U.S. would follow the ups and downs of U.S./Soviet relations. A thaw in those relations, and five or six years later, Vygotsky's name and then his ideas would begin to filter into American journals. An increase in U.S. and Russian tensions would freeze Vygotsky scholarship in its tracks in the U.S. During the period from 1956 to 1990, there were three waves of interest in Vygotsky in the U.S.

The first wave of interest in Vygotsky's theory took shape after the 1956 thaw in the Soviet Union and climaxed with the 1962 publication of the very abridged version of *Thought and Language.* The first U.S. edition of that text was 153 pages long. The second U.S. edition was 256 pages long. The 1956 Russian edition was 318 pages long. Alex Kozulin, the translator and editor of the enlarged second edition, commented on the U.S. first edition of *Thought and Language* in his book *Psychology in Utopia* (1984):

> Americans, represented by the editors of the English translation of *Thought and Language,* decided that the references to Marx were obligatory rhetoric unessential to Vygotsky's theory. As a result, they dropped all the vaguely "philosophical" passages with references not just to Marx but to Hegel and other thinkers. Of the 318 pages in the Russian original, American readers received 153 pages with fewer words per page than the Russian volume. . . . It seems obvious today that in pursuing a "more straight forward exposition" the editors revealed nothing but the cultural and intellectual gap between themselves and Vygotsky. The Soviets also missed the point in their perception of Vygotsky. (116)

While Kozulin is correct, I think it needs to be pointed out that the editors, especially Eugenia Hanfmann, had stayed with their task of introducing Vygotsky to an American intellectual public unprepared for the density of his thinking, even when it would have been easy to go on to other things. It needs to be once again noted that 1962, the year when the Cold War almost became World War III during the Cuban Missile Crisis, was not too distant from the purges of McCarthyism of the early and mid-1950s. To have one's name on a book with Russian letters on the cover, let alone by a Russian psychologist, may in this light have seemed sufficient enough risk. And the editors' stylistic decisions, while they made it almost impossible for the U.S. reader to get a sense of what Vygotsky was up to, also reflect more about the canons of scientific style in still behavioristic U.S. psychology than they reveal about the editors' understanding of Vygotsky. Kozulin does not mention that the editors also stripped the original Russian edition of its many metaphors, as well as its "vaguely philosophical" language, so if nothing else, by the rhetoric of the psychology discourse community for which they were writing, they were consistent. Still, Kozulin is right about the effects of the translation of U.S. scholars. For years our only glimpse at Vygotsky's theory was this brief, elliptical, translation which borders at times on the incomprehensible. We must keep in mind that one of the major reasons Michael Cole and his colleagues went forward with the translation of the essays that were printed in *Mind In Society* was to correct the widespread notion among colleagues in U.S. psychology that Vygotsky was a neo-behaviorist (if not a mouthpiece for the Soviet government). That this patently false charge was generally accepted by some U.S. psychologists as an accurate characterization of the work of a man who fought the behaviorists in his own time and country demonstrates how little Vygotsky's ideas were understood and how "untranslated" and "alien" his texts were. Yet the publication of the first edition of *Thought and Language* at least was a start.

The second wave of U.S. interest in Vygotsky can be traced from the scholarly exchanges made possible during the days of U.S.-Soviet detente from 1972 to 1975. By 1977 and 1978 this wave crested with the translation of *Mind in Society* and the publication of research by Michael Cole, who had done work with Luria in 1962 during the first wave, and James Wertsch who had worked with Luria during this second wave of interest.

With the 1986 publication of the complete edition of *Thought and Language,* translated and annotated by Alex Kozulin, we begin the third wave of Vygotsky scholarship in the U.S., foreshadowed by the volumes put out by Wertsch in 1985 (*Culture, Communication, and Cognition: Vygotskian Perspectives,* an edited collection from Cambridge University Press; and *Vygotsky and the Social Formation of Mind,* from Harvard University Press). In 1987, Plenum Press published the first of six projected volumes, *The Collected Works of L. S. Vygotsky: Problems of General Psychology.* Alex Kozulin added his interpretation of Vygotsky's work in *Vygotsky's Psychology: A Biography of Ideas* which came out in 1990. Of course, many other works by and about Vygotsky came out during these various waves of interest, but these are the benchmark publications. When such prestigious university presses are publishing such lengthy and expensive, not to mention complex works about Vygotsky's theory, one can anticipate increasing interest in Vygotsky, spurred on perhaps by the loosening restrictions, first of Gorbachev's perestroika, and then of the Russian Federation and the new Commonwealth of Independent States. Lotman might say that the long dormant unfolded, "untranslated," alien texts of Vygotsky are beginning to transform ". . . the entire semiotic situation within the textual world into which it has been introduced" (40). Lotman states "In moments of 'cultural (or, in general, semiotic) explosions,' the most remote and, from the standpoint of a particular system, untranslatable (i.e. 'unintelligible') texts are absorbed" (42). Certainly outside of U.S. psychology, Composition has been one of the first fields to take an interest in Vygotsky and to begin this work of translation.

As I move from this brief discussion of the arrival of Vygotsky's work in the U.S. in the field of psychology to a closer analysis of Vygotsky's influence on Composition, I also want to switch metaphors from the wave model I used above to a geological metaphor that Vygotsky himself used to describe periodicity and mixture of development. After thirty years, Vygotsky is still not a household word in the U.S. Many compositionists have cited Vygotsky, but these genuflections before the icon of Vygotsky have less to do with his theory than with the conventions of academic discourse. The proof that many compositionists do not fully grasp Vygotsky's theory is that we lack powerful applications. There has not yet been a *single* article or essay published in *College English* or in *College Composition and Communication* that focuses solely on Vygotsky's ideas. And this after Vygotsky was first recognized in print in a February 1972 *CCC* review written by R. Mortensen on the U.S. publication of Vygotsky's *The Psychology of Art.*

Vygotsky's primary influence on Composition then has been through the leading theorists of the field. These theorists subsequently have gone on to work with teachers and that has had a major impact. In the second U.S. edition of *Thought and Language,* Vygotsky characterizes the unevenness of psychological development by saying ". . . the developmental scene turns out to be much more complex. Different genetic forms coexist in thinking, just as different rock formations coexist in the earth's crust. . . . developmentally late forms coexist with younger formations" (140). We too might say that there are several coexisting layers of influence on Composition. In the earliest layer that can still be observed coexisting today with later layers, we find that compositionists became interested in Vygotsky's work through the concept of *development.* The second layer of influences came through the contribution that *(socio)linguistic* studies made to Composition in the discussions of orality and literacy, code and class. The third layer of influence comes through *cognitive* perspectives on writing processing. The fourth layer of influence comes through the more recent surge of interest in the *social* dimensions of writing. I have included a chart of these four layers and the primary sources and dates of publication of their work. Each of these scholars, having done work in language theory or in composition proper, cites Vygotsky, putting Vygotsky's alien text to varied uses.

VYGOTSKY'S INFLUENCE ON COMPOSITION

DEVELOPMENT	SOCIOLINGUISTICS AND LINGUISTICS	COGNITIVE PERSPECTIVES	SOCIAL VIEWS
	Bernstein, 1959		
Bruner, 1961			
	Bereiter, 1966		
Moffett, 1968			
Britton, 1969			
	Bateman & Zidonis, 1970		
		Emig, 1971	
		Miller, 1972	
Britton, 1975			
		Britton, 1975	
Warnock, 1976	Shaughnessy, 1976		
Emig, 1977	Shaughnessy, 1977		Elsasser & John-Steiner, 1977
Berthoff, 1978		Barritt & Kroll, 1978	
		Flower, 1979	
		Lunsford, 1980	
Berthoff, 1981			
Moffett, 1982	Ong, 1982		Zebroski, 1982
		Lunsford, 1985	Wells, 1985
			LeFevre, 1987
		Brand, 1987	
			Gere, 1987

I have also attempted to capture some of the dialectic of scholarly exchange as well as the nonlinearity of intellectual history by constructing the double-entry bibliography. This bibliography counterposes developments in the publication of Vygotskian materials on the left with Composition's appropriation of Vygotsky on the right. The bibliography is arranged chronologically.

VYGOTSKY AND COMPOSITION: INFLUENCES ON AN EMERGING DISCIPLINE. A SELECT DOUBLE-ENTRY BIBLIOGRAPHY

I. Proto-Composition

1937   Hanfmann, E. & Kasanin, J. A methodology for the study of concept formation. *Journal of psychology* (3), 521–540.

1939   Vygotsky, L. Thought and speech. *Psychiatry* (2.1), 29–54.

1952   Bauer, R. *The new man in Soviet psychology.* Cambridge, MA: Harvard, 1952.

1959   Luria, A. & Yudovich, F. *Speech and the development of mental processes in the child.* London: Staples, 1959. (1st ed.)

Leontiev, A. N. & Leontiev, A. A. The social and the individual in language. *Language and speech* (2), Oct.-Dec. 1959, 193–204.

1960   Bernstein, B. Aspects of language and learning in the genesis of the social process. *Journal of child psychology and psychiatry* (1) 1960–61, 313–324.

Bernstein, B. Social class and linguistic development: A theory of social learning. In A. Halsey, et al., (eds.) *Education, economy, and society.* NY: Free press of Glencoe, 1961

1962   Vygotsky, L. *Thought and language.* Cambridge, MA: M.I.T., 1962.

Bruner, J. Introduction. *Thought and language.*

1966

Bereiter, C. & Englemann, S. *Teaching disadvantaged children in pre-school.* Englewood Cliffs, NJ: Prentice-Hall, 1966.

II. Early Disciplinary Stirrings

1970 Berg, E. L. S. *Vygotsky's theory of the social and historical foundations of consciousness.* Unpublished doctoral dissertation, U. of Wisconsin, 1970.

*Britton, J. *Language and learning.* Coral Gables, FL: U. of Miami, 1970.

Emig, J. *The composing processes of twelfth graders.* Champaign, IL: N.C.T.E., 1971.

Britton, J. Introduction. Luria, A. & Yudovich, F. *Speech and the development of mental processes in the child.* Baltimore: Penguin, 1971 (new edition).

Vygotsky, L. *The psychology of art.* Cambridge, MA: M.I.T., 1971.

Mortenson, R. Review: 'The psychology of art.' *College composition and communication,* (23.1) Feb. 1972, 93–94.

Miller, J. *Word, self, reality: The rhetoric of imagination.* NY: Dodd, Mead, 1972.

III. Process over Product: The Cognitive Turn, 1975

Britton, J. et al. *The development of writing abilities: 11–18.* London: Macmillan, 1975.

Luria, A. *Cognitive development: Its cultural and social foundations.* Cambridge, MA: Harvard, 1976.

Warnock, J. New rhetoric and the grammar of pedagogy. *Freshman English news* (5.2) Fall 1976, 1–22.

Shaughnessy, M. Basic writing. In G. Tate (ed.) Teaching composition: *Ten bibliographic essays,* Fort Worth, TX: T.C.U., 1976.

Shaughnessy, M. *Errors and expectations.* NY: Oxford, 1977.

*Emig, J. Writing as a mode of learning. *College composition and communication*, (28.2) May 1977, 122–128.

Elsasser, N. & John-Steiner, V. An interactionist approach to literacy. *Harvard educational review* (47.3) Aug. 1977, 355–370.

Vygotsky, L. *Mind in society.* Cambridge, MA: Harvard, 1978.

*Berthoff, A. Tolstoy, Vygotsky, and the making of meaning. *College composition and communication* (29.3) Oct. 1978, 249-255.

Barritt, L. & Kroll, B. Some implications of cognitive-developmental psychology for research in composing. In C. Cooper & L. Odell (eds.) *Research on composing: Points of departure.* Urbana, IL: N.C.T.E., 1978.

Luria, A. *The making of mind.* Cambridge, MA: Harvard, 1978.

Flower, L. Writer-based prose: A cognitive basis for problems in writing. *College English* (41.1) Sept. 1979, 19–37.

Lunsford, A. Cognitive development and the basic writer. *College English* (41.1) Sept. 1979, 38–47.

1980

Lunsford, A. The content of basic writers' essays. *College composition and communication* (31.3) Oct. 1980, 278–290.

Fiore, K. & Elsasser, N. 'Strangers no more': A liberatory literacy curriculum. *College English* (44.2) Feb. 1982. 115–128.

Luria, A. *Language and cognition.* NY: John Wiley Sons, 1981.

Moffett, J. Writing, inner speech, and meditation. *College English* (44.3) Mar. 1982, 231–246.

*Emig, J. Nonmagical thinking: Presenting writing developmentally in the schools. In C. Frederiksen & J. Dominic (eds.) *Writing: The nature, development, and teaching of written communication.* Hillsdale, NJ: Erlbaum, 1982.

Zebroski, J. Soviet psycholinguistics: Implications for teaching of writing. In W. Frawley (ed.) *Linguistics and literacy.* NY: Plenum Press, 1982, 51–63.

IV. Writing in Community: Seeing Composing as a Social Process

1985

Lunsford, A. Cognitive studies and teaching writing. In B. McCleland & T. Donovan (eds.) *Perspectives on research and scholar- ship in composition*. NY: M.L.A., 1985.

Wells, S. Vygotsky reads Capital. *Correspondences: Two,* 1985.

Wertsch, J. (ed.) *Culture, communication, and Vygotskian perspectives.* Cambridge, MA: Cambridge U. P., 1985.

Wertsch, J. *Vygotsky and the social formation of mind.* Cambridge, MA: M.I.T., 1986. (revised edition)

Zebroski, J. Tropes and zones. *Correspondences: Four.* April 1986.

Zebroski, J. The uses of theory: A Vygotskian approach to composition. The Writing Instructor (5.2) Winter 1986, 57–67.

LeFevre, K. *Invention as a social act.* Carbondale, IL: Southern Illinois U. P., 1987.

*Gere, A. Writing groups: *History, theory, and implications.* Carbondale, IL: Southern Illinois U. P., 1987.

Brand, A. The why of cognition: Emotion and the writing process. *College composition and communication* (38.4) Dec. 1987, 436–443.

Phelps, L. *Composition as a human science.* NY: Oxford, 1988.

Bazerman, C. *Shaping written knowledge: The genre and activity of the experimental articlin science.* Madison, WI: University of Wisconsin Press, 1988

1990 Kozulin, A. *Vygotsky's psychology: A biography of ideas.* Cambridge, MA: Harvard, 1990.

I will spend more time examining the first layer of influence, the developmentalists' appropriation of Vygotsky, because the developmentalists have been the most formative to composition studies so far and because they have read Vygotsky in the most interesting ways. We have tended to pass through the linguistic, sociolinguistic, and cognitive phases, and it is not yet clear, how long and influential the social turn will be, but because development deals directly with students, it has become a sort of bedrock and continues to attract new scholars. Vygotsky first came to the attention of language teachers and scholars through the work of the U.S. developmentalist Jerome Bruner. Bruner has had a long term interest in Vygotsky and in Soviet psychology. A doctoral student of Bruner's, Raymond Bauer, produced a dissertation that was published in 1952 by Harvard University Press as *The New Man In Soviet Psychology.* Bruner recalls that he had heard more about Vygotsky through Roman Jakobson who introduced Bruner to Luria at an international conference held in the mid-1950s at the beginning of what would be called the cognitive revolution. The thaw was in progress at this time in the Soviet Union. In 1961 Bruner published his book *The Process of Education,* a recounting of some of the principles of the Woods Hole Conference on science and mathematics education, in which he argued for a spiral curriculum and set the stage for curricular reform not only in science and math, but also in English. In 1962, Bruner wrote the introduction to the first edition of Vygotsky's *Thought and Language* published in the U.S., specifically noting the connections that Vygotsky makes between learning (and curriculum) and development.

Bruner sought out Vygotsky's view that learning and development were dialectically related, that a student could discover the structure of the discipline. At just about the same moment in history the Soviets were in turn reacting to the U.S. educational reforms, themselves a product of the U.S. reaction to Sputnik. Ailita Markova in the Soviet Union, working out of Vygotsky, was charged with a ten-year curricular reform in middle- and high-school language arts. There is a dialectic in theory and practice between Soviet and U.S. research that makes it difficult to clearly and definitively sort out who has contributed what to whom. The "spiral curriculum," for example, draws on metaphors that were used by Vygotsky but had deeper roots in the postrevolutionary culture of the Soviet Union. That one can at this moment find a "spiral curriculum" in writing at Syracuse University testifies to the many mutual influences among scholars interested in development. That post-Marxists at Syracuse, having no knowledge of any of this history, can easily attack the very metaphor of spiral of development further reveals how history itself is contradictory.

What attracted Bruner and U.S. educators was Vygotsky's optimism that instruction counted, that it was a key force in development, that in fact, instruction led and is dialectically related to development. Three compositionists picked up on the developmental importance of instruction and therefore were attracted earlier than most to Vygotsky's ideas, intelligently and creatively reading and applying Vygotsky to composition: James Britton, Janet Emig, and Ann Berthoff.

James Britton was the first compositionist to cite, explicate, and apply Vygotsky's ideas of development to language instruction. In 1969, Britton's book *Language and Learning* came out. In this book, Britton puts forth his theory that language is a representation of the world of the speaker or writer and that that representation helps the speaker or writer to develop as she revises that conception. Britton writes about complex matters of language, representation, and mind in a clear, accurate, and direct manner. In Chapter Five of *Language and Learning,* titled "Language and Thought," Britton zeros in on the work of Bruner and then of Vygotsky. One can almost see Vygotsky rising from Bruner's text in Britton's chapter. Britton synthesizes Bruner and Vygotsky's view of development of thought and language as follows:

As a child's powers of thought develop they might be seen to go through the stages of first drawing level with and then surpassing his powers of speech. Or putting it crudely by the numbers:

1. He speaks a language which embodies powers of organization he cannot achieve in thought.
2. He achieves the ability to organize in thought what is organized in his speech.
3. He extends the range of his powers of organization in thought first by verbalizing more complex experiences and contemplating these verbalizations.
4. His powers of organization in thought come to exceed his powers of organization in speech (205).

Britton delineates Vygotsky's analysis of concept development, echoing Vygotsky's last work (and especially his return to a rereading of Spinoza) that such schema are reductive because they leave out emotion and affect.

The real danger, it would seem to me, lies in imposing a disjunction between thought and feeling between cognitive and affective modes of representation. Psychologists in general have traditionally concentrated upon cognitive organization and tended to regard emotion as itself disorganized and possessing a disorganizing influence. We need to recognize the value and importance of both discursive, logical organization and at the same time that of undis-

> sociated intuitive processes, the organization represented in its
> highest form in works of art. (217)

Britton makes a point that seems to need to be constantly remade.
As Vygotsky says, thinking doesn't think itself. The first English
volume of Vygotsky's *Collected Works,* published years later in 1987,
confirms Britton's reading of Vygotsky. In this text, Vygotsky's six
"Lectures on Psychology" are presented and Lecture Four (following, it must be noted, Lecture Three on "Thinking") is on "Emotions
and Their Development in the Child" in which Vygotsky argues for
the importance of emotion to psychological life and its development. A complex self, or subject, is crossed by motives and emotives
that shape thinking. It is very Western to divide emotion from intellect and to concentrate on intellect, dismissing feeling as disorganizing, as Britton says. We encounter here another grand dichotomy
comparable to the division of the individual from the social in the
importance it has had for modern Western images of the world.
Later, Alice Brand, citing Vygotsky among others, will pick up this
thread and pursue research on affect and feeling in writing. Between
Britton's recognition of this dilemma and Brand's work, the idea of
process intervenes, providing at first, a concept that united affect
with intellect. It isn't simply chance that Britton in this section ends
by mentioning process, specifically intuitive processes, since the
early process theorists would be influenced by the recognition of the
importance of such mental events.

As Mary Kay Tirrell noted in a personal communication, Britton
has never really received the credit he deserved for introducing
language teachers and compositionists specifically, to the work of
Vygotsky in 1969. His uses of Vygotsky are generally thoughtful and
applicable to language development and the concerns of teachers for
curricular design. Britton is well versed in Vygotsky's theory and
does not simply use some flashy quotes to make his own point, but
in fact, tries to work through the point Vygotsky is making in his
chapter on concept formation. Britton is a translator of an alien text
and shifts seemingly effortlessly between high-level abstraction and
homely example, between psychological, sociological, linguistic,
and aesthetic theory and curricular design, between accounts of the
reading, writing, and talking processes, and suggestions for helping
to teach kids to read and write. Britton's use of theory is similar to
Vygotsky's use of theory—as an instrument, a thinking device, that
will help to immerse us more deeply in everyday life by helping us
to think through everyday life. That Britton two years later in 1971
wrote the introduction to A. R. Luria and F. Y Yudovich's English
edition of *Speech and the Development of Mental Processes in the*

Child, a study of the development of language processes in a pair of identical twins with retarded speech, is no coincidence, but rather demonstrates Britton's long-standing interest in Vygotsky's work and his commitment to translating that work into terms that speak to teachers.

Another developmentalist who contributed to this initial layer of Vygotsky scholarship in Composition is Janet Emig. Emig was well aware of Vygotsky when she did graduate work at Harvard during the 1960s. Emig's pathbreaking *The Composing Processes of Twelfth Graders* came out in 1971, and gave writing teachers a rallying cry as well as a new approach to the study of writing. Emig's emphasis on "process" made a whole series of studies on process possible and provided the phrase "composing process" which would contribute to the vocabulary of the everyday teacher who would come say, "we teach process not product." Emig does cite Vygotsky in the bibliography of *The Composing Processes,* but her more elaborated discussion of Vygotsky occurs in her essay "Writing as Mode of Learning" first published in 1977 in *CCC.* Later in 1982 she extended her discussion of Vygotsky in her essay "Nonmagical Thinking: Presenting Writing Developmentally in the Schools."

In "Writing as a Mode of Learning" Emig cites Vygotsky and Luria to show that writing serves a distinct function that differs from speech, that is, writing can represent the world differently than speech because writing involves a sort of 'drawing' or 'imaging' of abstraction. But writing is also a mode of learning because it is engaged, personal, integrative. Emig follows Vygotsky in arguing that, because it has a special relationship to inner speech, writing integrates and connects by requiring, to use Vygotsky's phrase, ". . . deliberate semantics . . . the deliberate structuring of the web of meaning." Emig's essays would later be collected and published as book under that title, *The Web Of Meaning.* One of the least observed passages in this essay but one that has rich potentialities, is Emig's subtle reading of Luria and her recognition of his central concept that writing is temporally distinct from inner speech because it is so much slower, and thus requires the further development of inner speech. Writing is temporal; writing in unique ways transforms time. I have tried to follow out this single line of thought in my own essay published in this book, "Writing Time."

In "Nonmagical Thinking" Emig unfolds the section of *Mind In Society* in which Vygotsky sketches out the prehistory of writing found in gesture, drawing, and symbolic play. Emig makes the case that learning to write goes far beyond the narrow confines of explicit teaching, arguing for a kind of reflective practice in which teachers write as well as create environments where apprentice writers can take risks. Emig ends by distinguishing developmental error from mistake in a manner that is reminiscent of, and certainly consonant with, Vygotsky's definition of development and his interest in studying processes in process (a phrase to be found both in Emig's *Composing Processes* and in Volosinov's *Marxism and the Philosophy of Language,* which was not even to be available in English until 1973) rather than fossilized behavior.

If James Britton has never been fully recognized for his introduction of Vygotsky's works into Composition, Janet Emig 's work has never been fully appreciated for the many insights into Vygotsky and writing that can be found like nuggets throughout her essays. Emig's texts are dense and subtle; they are full of sentences that themselves, given time and the subtle intelligence with which they were composed, could be elaborated into entire essays. Sometimes the reader comes to articles written by other compositionists expecting to find—maybe—one new idea, worked out and expanded upon. In Janet Emig's writing, one more often feels there are dozens of kernel ideas, each illuminating and full of potential for further expansion and elaboration. Emig, for example, does not simply run to the most obvious quotes in Vygotsky that many compositionists cite. The selection of quotations, the reference to dozens of sources and the synthesis of multiple ideas is careful, purposeful, showing a far broader span of reading and understanding of the cited material. Emig frequently uses lists to arrange the rich and multiple insights she is presenting. Emig's five citations of Vygotsky or Luria in "Writing as a Mode of Learning" which is only a six-page article, reveal more understanding of the Vygotskian school perspective, perhaps worldview, than later essays by others that cite Vygotsky more often or in a flashier way. Emig, for example, takes great care in this essay in using the Vygotskian term "function" to discuss speech, inner speech, and writing relations. By doing this, Emig avoids the sterile Great Divide debates about orality *versus* literacy, and immediately sets the reader up for the possibility that any text can function in a multitude of ways, and that therefore oralities and literacies—plural—exist. All of these points can be found in embryonic form in Vygotsky's work, but few readers have been careful enough to see and then use these distinctions and qualifications.

If Emig's writing has yet to be fully appreciated for the numerous insights buried therein because it demands a close reading, Ann E. Berthoff's work has not received the recognition it deserves for putting Vygotskian theory together with teaching practice because it requires a dialectical reading. Berthoff, like Emig, also draws from a large number of sources. Berthoff's reader has to be familiar with the numerous theorists who have influenced her work, not the least being I. A. Richards, C. S. Peirce, and Freire. If Emig's style crystalizes around the insightful sentence, Berthoff's style (perhaps like Emerson's?) plays itself out mostly at the paragraph level. In Ann Berthoff's 1978 *CCC* essay "Tolstoy, Vygotsky, and the Making of Meaning" Berthoff weds the teaching practices of Tolstoy and Freire to Vygotsky's theory of language and mind. She argues from Vygotsky that composition always must begin with the whole, with the complete unit, not the element, of meaning. In a passage that seems to intimate the later emergence of ethnographic writing in composition studies, Berthoff argues for beginning the instruction in writing with the tissue of form creating complexity that is lived experience. Simple exercises or run-throughs will not do; rather it is the complexity of life that needs to be drawn into dialectic with classroom writing instruction, from the very start.

Berthoff in her writing textbook *Forming/Thinking/Writing: The Composing Imagination* presents an entire writing course based on the development of conceptual thinking, which is indebted to Vygotsky's work. Unlike many others who have taken up the term, Berthoff discusses *writing as dialectic process* and uses the term dialectic in ways Vygotsky would recognize and approve. Nor is it by chance that Berthoff making the connection between a theory of language, a teaching practice, and a political praxis, invokes Paulo Freire's work in teaching literacy as a liberating activity. *Forming/Thinking/Writing* is the only composition textbook that refuses to give students formulas and pretend they are the Truth. Berthoff is following very closely here Vygotsky's belief that you cannot directly teach concepts, that mind, language, and learning are more subtle than this behavioristic view would allow.

In her collection of essays published in 1981, *The Making of Meaning,* Berthoff forwards a theory of language and composing that matches and extends Vygotsky's semiotics. For both Berthoff and Vygotsky, language is a dynamic, dialectic, form-giving form. Language is a mediation, a thinking device, a speculative instrument, through which we discover and convey meaning, but which then reacts in that very process upon our own consciousness, creating higher levels of psychic development, higher forms of thinking, and more advanced uses of language. Berthoff's semiotic theory acts as a heuristic for further developing her view of language, the composing process, and the writing course and curriculum. Berthoff, like Emig, defines composing in a broad enough way to avoid reducing it to a simplistic behavior or skill or confining it to the quarters of academe. Berthoff's definition of composing as a continuum, an activity that a person does all the time, as a putting of things together, and writing as a matter of learning how to use the forms of language to discover the forms of thought, and vice versa, is very close to Vygotsky's formulation of psychological and signifying *functions*. And clearly, Berthoff, when she argues that language is not identical to but is dependent on thought, is directly and precisely applying Vygotsky's findings on the relation between language and thought. Berthoff's acceptance and use of diverse examples of writing—lists, entries from a pioneer's pocket diary, notes by students, reflective paragraphs and essays, questions—reveal the same sort approach that Vygotsky and Luria take when they investigate the developmental prehistory of writing in the child and in society, recognizing the complexity of even the "simplest" written forms. Finally, Berthoff's creation of the double-entry notebook assignment is reminiscent of the clever ways that Vygotsky and Luria discovered for observing processes as they unfolded. There are few ways to discover more quickly where students are at in their reading and writing development, but also to preserve an unfolding record of that development, than the double-entry notebook, a dialectical enterprise if there ever was one.

Much more, obviously, could be said about the work of these scholars who championed Vygotsky's ideas in composition. But at this point I will simply point out that Britton, Emig, and Berthoff have had the widest effect of any of the other developmentalists to date in introducing Vygotsky to scholars and to teachers, and unlike some of those who came after them in the linguistic, sociolinguistic, and cognitive appropriations of Vygotsky, they each translated Vygotsky's strange texts in accurate, elegant, interesting, and useful ways.

The second layer of influence reaches back to 1956 and 1957. This linguistic and sociolinguistic appropriation of Vygotsky has been concerned with issues of dialectic, Standard English, orality and literacy, codes, classes, and control. Although he was a sociologist rather than a linguist or sociolinguist, Basil Bernstein makes the first and perhaps most misunderstood contribution here. Later sociolinguists would bash what would be assumed to be Bernstein's view of language codes when in reality what they were attending to were inappropriate uses of Bernstein. Bernstein in 1956 used Vygotsky to begin to make the distinctions between what later would be called the restricted and the elaborated codes of language. Bernstein was more careful than he was given credit for being, in his use of Vygotsky's ideas of inner speech and the enfolding/unfolding of language forms. He also was more a sociologist concerned with the context of social class and its relations to language, than a linguist making universal statements about language. Nevertheless, Bernstein's ideas, drawn from Vygotsky and Bernstein's own research on (and commitment to) the working class, were appropriated by people like Carl Bereiter (1966) to support the repressive practice of "correcting" the oral language of "disadvantaged" children from minority communities to better indoctrinate them with middle-class language norms in the school. Bereiter's *Teaching Disadvantaged Children In Pre-School* makes assumptions about the deficiency of minority language and culture that would push sociolinguists to show through experiment that no language is deficient. In fact, sociolinguists showed that given a certain set of circumstances, so called Standard English can be far less nuanced and linguistically "advantaged" than a minority "dialect." Because Bernstein's work was labeled as inaccurate and potentially racist, and because Bernstein (and Bereiter) appropriated Vygotsky, Vygotsky's work became associated with a linguistic perspective that was seen to be, at best, out of date and overly simple, and, at worst, wrong and potentially racist.

Other linguists of the time turned to Chomsky's work in critiquing behaviorism and in arguing for deep versus surface structures in language generation. Bateman and Zidonis (1970), aware of Vygotsky's work, turned to transformational generative grammar to help student writers become better and more self aware stylists. Shaughnessy (1977) used the concept of surface and deep structures to describe the generation of errors to better understand then control the production of errors in writing. Ong (1982) distinguished oral and literate cultures to account for language differences between some incoming students and the established academic environment. Each of these scholars knew and cited Vygotsky, though not always in accurate or fully elaborated ways.

The third layer of influences of Vygotsky on Composition came through the cognitive studies of writing initiated by Janet Emig. James Miller's *Word, Self and Reality*, cites Vygotsky on thought and language extensively in 1972. Vygotsky's views on inner speech become Vygotsky, as far as the field of Composition is concerned. Barritt and Kroll (1978) place Vygotsky and Piaget together as presenting complementary views of development, something Vygotsky explicitly and extensively argues against. And Linda Flower (1979) takes up Vygotsky's notion of egocentrism to argue for distinguishing between writer-based prose and reader-based prose, something Vygotsky would have problems with. Following this line of thinking, Lunsford (1980) puts Piaget and Vygotsky together to argue for the developmental backwardness of basic writers. Vygotsky was being cited often in these kind of studies in the late 1970s and early 1980s, but rarely is there any evidence in these studies that Vygotsky's work was understood in a broader and deeper way. Rather Vygotsky was appropriated to support positions on writing development and cognition that had already been taken. My friends at the time joked that one could almost predict that researchers of the time would put in the obligatory Vygotsky footnote, more often than not, citing Vygotsky's *Thought and Language,* page 100, on inner speech and writing. Vygotsky seemed to be chanted more than interpreted.

Finally, as social views of writing began to make it into print as a reaction against the individualism of process theory, Vygotsky appeared in more complete citations. Elsasser and John-Steiner led the way with their *Harvard Education Review* essay of 1977. Susan Wells (1985) provides one of the best and most provocative interpretations, in her "Vygotsky Reads *Capital*" in which she actually accepts the fact that Vygotsky was presenting his version of a socialist psychology heavily indebted to the method of Karl Marx. Wells's reading also stresses the gaps in our understanding of Vygotsky as well as the inconsistencies and incompletenesses of Vygotsky's texts.

Bazerman's work (1988) concludes with Vygotsky's theory, arguing that "A more crisply defined, and I believe ultimately more powerful, model of the role of language in human activity, society, and consciousness can be developed out of the work of the Russian psychologist Lev Vygotsky" (302). Bazerman argues that Vygotsky can contribute to a model ". . . of scientific use of language [that] will suggest how the work of science can be accomplished through the unfolding social and empirical activity of individuals coordinated (cognitively and behaviorally) within groups" (302). Bazerman is well aware of U.S. sources of Vygotsky. His conclusion that Vygotsky's work offers composition more than a citation (or an observation or a concept), in fact, offers Composition a new way to look at and approach perennial conceptual dilemmas is itself new to Composition. Bazerman's appropriation of Vygotsky is more comprehensive than those earlier uses of Vygotsky in Composition.

Bazerman's use of Vygotsky in his analysis of scientific writing parallels LeFevre's (1987) use of Vygotsky to examine the social dimensions of invention. She makes the connection between Vygotsky's theory of language and social formation:

> One would expect the predominant ideology of a society and its
> received views about the nature of human thought to affect and
> reinforce one another. Thus it is not surprising that the work of
> Soviet psychologists such as L. S. Vygotsky and A. R. Luria stresses
> a reciprocal relationship between social activity and individual
> cognition, both accomplished by language. . . . Luria bases his
> study on the assumption that consciousness is not something given
> in advance but is shaped by social activity and used to restructure

conditions as well as to adapt to them. . . . mental processes and self-perception depend on, change with, social history and social practices such as education and the organization of labor (19).

By this point, Composition has come full circle. LeFevre's citation of Vygotsky (and Luria) reveals an understanding not simply of a passage or two, but of the assumptions that underlie the whole work. *We have moved from pure citation of Vygotsky, to the quotation of a passage or two that most deals with pressing concerns, to the more complete appropriation of Vygotsky's work as whole, leading to an interest in the assumptions that guided his work as much as any one conclusion from that work.* The next step in this semiotic appropriation comes with Ann Gere's work on *Writing Groups* (1987) in which she actually goes beyond understanding Vygotsky's work to extending his work into areas he only briefly addressed. Using Vygotsky's concepts of internalization and the zone of proximal development, Gere forwards a theory of language development that supports the establishment of writing groups. Gere admits that "Vygotsky along with his contemporary Mikhail Bakhtin, represents a radical departure from the received tradition of language study in this country" (85). And so I end this account of Vygotsky's influence on Composition with Gere's characterization of Vygotsky as "other," as "different," and useful for that very reason. It seems ironic that the first citation of Vygotsky in a U.S. article contained a description of the zone of proximal development, the very concept that Gere and others find so powerful. But development here seems to have taken the form of a spiral in that the most recent appropriation of ZPD seems to acknowledge the importance of the concept and to have integrated that concept into a more complete set of concepts, keywords, and keytexts. What had been a footnote is now the primary text.

In this final section, I will note potential influences of Vygotsky on composition in the future.

The first major area that I believe we'll see an increasing interest in is Vygotsky's notion of self. While there is no single publication to which we can turn that delivers the canonical version of Vygotsky's concept of self, his entire work is informed by a collectivist perspective. Self for Vygotsky is *both* socially and individually constructed by means of signs. There is a curious but extremely significant footnote by Alex Kozulin in the new edition of *Thought and Language.* Kozulin, referring to Vygotsky's discussion of the development of concepts and pseudo-concepts, states

> . . . if the conscious awareness of one's own intellectual operations ("concept-for-me") is only a secondary achievement, which follows for the practical use of these operations, then the individual can not be considered a self-conscious center of activity. The individual appears rather as a 'construction' built at the crossroads of inner and outer realities. (268)

In my judgment, Kozulin here addresses the questions raised by postmodernism that have to do with the plurality and socialness of Self, but avoids the continental poststructuralist quagmire. He questions the Subject but in ways that make more sense in a U.S. context. Such a re-invention of Self gives us a means of doing ideology critique but ideology critique with a human face, that avoids the abstract, objectivist, and ultimately fatalistic language of most poststructuralism that at least I know. Composition theory is built on Anglo-American empiricism and its notions of self, word, and reality. Vygotsky offers an alternative to that empiricism that is more attractive to compositionists than the French critique.

The second major area where I see advances in Vygotskian scholarship is in the psychology of composing. Vygotsky's description of the dynamics of thought and word in the climactic final chapter of *Thought and Language* has never been very adaptable to the cognitivists. This phenomenological description of the layers of mind is full of quotes from literature and teeming with explicit and submerged metaphors. Thought is a cloud shedding a shower of words. Motive is a wind driving along the clouds of thought. Word meaning arises from the ocean of our society to be transformed into the unique, dynamic, and unrepeatable, but still related weather of mind. Consciousness is reflected in a word as the sun in a drop of water.

Simply and only metaphor? I think Vygotsky's descriptions of the dynamics of thought and word, mind and society, rely so heavily on metaphor in the chapter because only metaphor could communicate the sense of flow. Metaphor provided Vygotsky a language for talking about the regularities and unrepeatability of changing phenomena. So he goes to the weather for his language.

Interestingly enough, it is precisely the weather that first engaged a few scientists two decades ago to pursue the *concept* of *change*. These scientists discovered there are regularities but they are always in specific, local, and therefore, ultimately, unrepeatable contexts. From similar questions arising in the fields of biology, ecology, astronomy, and economics has come the new transdisciplinary field of *chaos* science, which attends to those phenomena and aspects of phenomena that are rhythmic, turbulent, irregular. Chaos science, according to James Gleick, author of *Chaos: Making a New*

Science, addresses questions like how do clouds form, how does smoke rise, how does water eddy in a stream.

Vygotsky it seems was (intuitively) doing chaos science forty to fifty years before its emergence, trying to describe mind in strikingly similar ways as chaos scientists use. It is when chaos science and Vygotsky scholarship are put together that I expect we will get a renewed interest in Vygotsky's theory of cognition and his study of thinking, inner speech, and the composing of speech, writing, and art.

Finally, Vygotsky's powerful concept of zone of proximal development is already being applied in early childhood language studies. I expect that we'll soon get such applications in composition research. There is a clear tie between the increasing interest in collaborative writing and cooperative learning and writing groups, and Vygotsky's work on the zone of proximal development and his theory that higher mental functions arise first as social collective activity and through tutoring and mentoring, apprenticeships are passed on to, internalized, and transformed by the individual into acts of mind. Vygotsky provides an elaborated and tested theory for compositionists who want to teach writing as a collaborative process. The more we investigate writing on the job or outside of the classroom in the university or in other realms of life, we find that writing takes a multitude of forms and functions and seems to be more usually a collaborative activity rather than an isolated individual act. Vygotsky's theory of mind and language, as well as his subtle view of the relations between the social and the individual, between other and self, provide an alternative to an empirical notion of a centered and clearly demarcated *self* or of poststructuralist, decentered, disseminated *subject.*

Vygotsky, then, has influenced composition. But his work has come to compositionists in layers primarily through the discussions of theorists and researchers. Vygotsky's influence on composition has been strong, but periodic and subterranean. As composition teachers and scholars begin to view writing as a social process as well as individual process, Vygotsky's work has the potential of becoming more valuable, more widely read. I hope that this will be true. It would be a shame if the work of a man who wanted to learn from the people and to educate all, only continued to be read and admired by the few. Tracking Vygotsky across Composition can tell us much about the forces at work in Composition. Obviously, it can also tell us some things about Vygotsky's work and about the processes of textual encounter, circulation, exclusion, and inclusion. The story is not over. Vygotsky's work has still not been made available in complete English translations. His concepts are only beginning to be understood in composition studies. A more complete rendering of the rhetoric of Vygotsky's reception both in the U.S. and the Soviet Union is needed to complement the increasingly available corpus. But perhaps what is needed most of all is a consideration of the worldview and the culture of present day Russia and the post-revolutionary Russian of Vygotsky. Until we have a wider perspective on the context that shapes and influences the texts, we will tend to see the Vygotsky who is closest to us, when it is the Vygotsky who is the stranger, the Vygotsky of the alien text, the Vygotsky who is different from us, who has the most to contribute to composition studies.

References

Bateman, D. & F. Zidonis. 1970. A *grammatico-semantic exploration of the problems of sentence formation and interpretation in the classroom: Final report.* Columbus, OH: The Ohio State University Research Foundation.

Berthoff, A. 1981. *Forming/thinking/writing.* Portsmouth, NH: Boynton/Cook.

Bruner, J. 1960. *The process of education.* Cambridge, MA: Harvard University Press.

Emerson, C. 1983. The inner word and outer speech. *Critical Inquiry* 245–64.

Gleick, J. 1988. *Chaos: Making a new science.* New York: Viking.

Harris, J. 1990. The idea of community. *College Composition and Communication* 40:11–21.

Lotman, Y. 1988. Text within text. *Soviet Psychology* 26(3):32–51.

North, S. 1986. *The making of knowledge in composition.* Portsmouth, NH: Boynton/Cook.

Ong, W. 1982. *Orality and literacy.* New York: Methuen.

Shaughnessy, M. 1977. *Errors and expectations.* New York: Oxford University Press.

Tirrell, M. K. 1989. Personal communication.

Weaver R. 1953. *The ethics of rhetoric.* South Bend, IN: Regency/Gateway Press.

Zborowski, M. & E. Herzog. 1952. *Life is with people: the culture of the shtetl.* New York: Schocken Books.

The Vygotskian School of Psychology:
A Select Bibliography Focusing on Language and Development

Akhutina, T. 1978. The role of inner speech in the construction of an utterance. *Soviet psychology* 16(3):2–30.

Arutiunova, N. 1975. Signs, linguistic. *The great Soviet encyclopedia* 9:431–32.

Bain, B. 1983. *The sociogenesis of language and human conduct.* New York: Plenum.

Bakhurst, D. 1991. *Consciousness and revolution in Soviet philosophy from the Bolsheviks to Evald Ilyenkov.* New York: Cambridge University Press.

Baran, H. Ed. 1974. *Semiotics and structuralism: Readings from the Soviet Union.* White Plains, NY: International Arts and Science Press.

Bauer, R. 1952. *The new man in Soviet psychology.* Cambridge, MA: Harvard University Press.

Berg, E. 1970. *L. S. Vygotsky's theory of the social and historical origins of consciousness.* Unpublished doctoral dissertation. University of Wisconsin.

Bibler, V. S. 1983–1984. Thinking as Creation (Introduction to The Logic of Mental Dialogue). *Soviet psychology* 22(2):33–54.

Biriukov, B. 1975. Sign. *The great Soviet encyclopedia* 9:430–33.

Cole, M. & I. Maltzman. Eds. 1969. *A handbook of contemporary Soviet psychology.* New York: Basic Books.

Engels, F. 1940. *The dialectics of nature.* New York: International publisher.

Gal'perin, P. 1969. Stages in the development of mental acts. In *A handbook of contemporary Soviet psychology,* edited by M. Cole. & I. Maltzman. New York: Basic Books.

Gellner, E. Ed. 1980. *Soviet and western anthropology.* London: Duckworth and Co. Ltd.

Gibson, J. 1980. Soviet pedagogical research: Classroom studies, cognitive theories of development and instruction. *Contemporary educational psychology* 5(2):184–91.

Gould, C. 1978. *Marx's social ontology: Individuality and community in Marx's theory of social reality.* Cambridge, MA: MIT Press.

Graham, L. 1974. *Science and philosophy in the Soviet Union.* New York: Vintage Books.

The great Soviet encyclopedia. 3rd ed. 1975. New York: Macmillan.

Il'enkov, E. The Ideal. *The great Soviet encyclopedia* 9:115–16.

Ivanov, V. 1974. The significance of M. M. Bakhtin's ideas of sign, utterance, and dialogue for modern semiotics. In *Semiotics and structuralism:*

Readings from the Soviet Union, edited by H. Baran. White Plains, NY: International Arts and Science Press.

Kozulin, A. 1984a. *Psychology in utopia: Toward a social history of Soviet psychology.* Cambridge, MA: MIT Press

———. 1984b. Psychology and philosophical anthropology: The problem of their interaction. *Philosophical Forum* 15(4):443–58.

———. 1990. *Vygotsky's psychology: A biography of ideas.* Cambridge, MA: Harvard University Press.

Lee, B. & M. Hickmann. 1983. Language, thought, and self in Vygotsky's developmental theory. In *Developmental approaches to the self,* edited by B. Lee & G. Noam. New York: Plenum.

Lee, B., J. Wertsch, A. Stone. 1983. Towards a Vygotskian theory of self. In *Developmental approaches to the self,* edited by B. Lee & G. Noam. New York: Plenum.

Leontiev, A. A. 1990. Inner speech and the processes of grammatical generation of utterances. *Soviet Psychology* 7(3):11–16.

———. 1975. Inner form in linguistics. *The great Soviet encyclopedia* 5:224.

———. 1976. Sense as a psychological concept. In *Soviet studies in language and language behavior,* edited by J. Prucha. New York: North Holland Publishing.

———. 1978. The psycholinguistic aspect of linguistic meaning. In *Recent trends in Soviet psycholinguistics,* edited by J. Wertsch. White Plains, NY: M. E. Sharpe.

———. 1981. *Psychology and the language learning process.* New York: Pergamon Press.

———. 1981. Sign and Activity. In *The concept of activity in Soviet psychology,* edited by J. Wertsch. Armonk, NY: M. E. Sharpe.

Leontiev, A. N. 1978. *Activity, consciousness, and personality.* Englewood Cliffs, NJ: Prentice-Hall.

Leontiev, A. N. & A. A. Leontiev. 1959. The social and the individual in language. *Language and Speech* 2:193–204.

Leontiev, A. N. & A. R. Luria. 1968. The psychological ideas of L. S. Vygotsky. In *The Historical Roots of Contemporary Psychology,* edited by B. Wolman. New York: Harper & Row.

Levitin, K. 1982. *One is not born a personality: Profiles of Soviet education psychologists.* Moscow: Progress.

Lotman, Y. 1974. On the relation and unfolding of sign systems: The problem of Freudian and semiotic culturology. In *Semiotics and Structuralsim: Readings from the Soviet Union,* edited by H. Baran. White Plains, NY: International Arts and Science Press.

Lucid, D. 1977. Ed. *Soviet semiotics: An anthology.* Baltimore, MD: Johns Hopkins University Press.

Luria, A. 1969. Speech and the formation of mental processes. In *A Handbook of contemporary Soviet psychology,* edited by M. Cole & I. Maltzman. New York: Basic Books.

———. 1974–1975. Scientific perspectives and philosophical deadends in modern linguistics. *Cognition* 3(4):377–85.

———. 1976. *Cognitive development: Its cultural and social foundations.* Cambridge, MA: Harvard University Press.

———. 1977–1978. The development of writing in the child. *Soviet Psychology* 16(2):65–114.

———. 1979. *The making of mind.* Cambridge, MA: Harvard University Press.

———. 1981. *Language and cognition.* New York: J. Wiley Sons.

Luria, A. R. & F. Yudovich. 1971. *Speech and the development of mental processes in the child.* Baltimore, MD: Penguin.

Markova, A. 1979. *The teaching and mastery of language.* White Plains, NY: M. E. Sharpe.

Marx, K. 1967. *Capital: A critique of political economy—the process of capitalist production.* Vol. I. New York: International Publishers.

Payne, T. S. 1968. *L. Rubinstein and the philosophical foundations of Soviet psychology.* Dordrecht, Netherlands: Reidel.

Pick, H. 1980. Perceptual and cognitive development of pre-schoolers in Soviet psychology. *Contemporary educational psychology* 5(2):140–49.

Prucha, J. Ed. 1972. *Soviet psycholinguistics.* The Hague: Mouton.

———. 1976. *Soviet studies in language and language behavior.* New York: North Holland.

Radzikhovskii, L. 1987. The dialogic quality of consciousness in the work of M. M. Bakhtin. *The Soviet review* 28(2):66–91.

Rogoff, B. & J. Wertsch. Eds. 1984. *Children's learning in the zone of proximal development.* San Francisco: Jossey-Bass.

Sakharnyi, L. 1978. The structure of word meaning and situation. In *Recent trends in Soviet psycholinguistics,* edited by J. Wertsch. White Plains, NY: M. E. Sharpe.

Schaff, A. 1973. *Language and cognition.* New York: McGraw Hill.

———. 1978. *Structuralism and marxism.* New York: Pergamon Press.

Toulmin, S. 1978. The Mozart of psychology. *New York review of books* 25(14):51–57.

———. 1979. The inwardness of mental life. *Critical inquiry* 6(1):1–16.

Vygotsky, L. 1971. *The psychology of art.* Cambridge, MA: MIT Press.

———. 1978. *Mind in society: The development of higher psychological processes,* edited by trans. by M. Cole, V. John-Steiner, S. Scribner, & E. Souberman. Cambridge, MA: Harvard University Press.

———. 1981. The development of higher forms of attention in childhood.

In *The concept of activity in Soviet psychology,* edited by J. Wertsch. Armonk, NY: M. E. Sharpe.

——. 1981. The instrumental method in psychology. In *The concept of activity in Soviet psychology,* edited by J. Wertsch. Armonk, NY: M. E. Sharpe.

——. 1986. *Thought and language.* 2nd ed. Cambridge, MA: Harvard University Press.

Wells, S. Vygotsky reads *Capital. Correspondences: Two.*

Wertsch, J. Ed. 1978. *Recent trends in Soviet psycholinguistics.* White Plains, NY: M. E. Sharpe.

——. 1980. The significance of dialogue in Vygotsky's account of social, egocentric, and inner speech. *Contemporary educational psychology* 5(2):151–154.

——. Ed. 1981. *The concept of activity in Soviet psychology.* Armonk, NY: M. E. Sharpe.

——. 1985a. *Culture, communication, and cognition: Vygotskian perspectives.* Cambridge: Cambridge University Press.

——. 1985b. *Vygotsky and the social formation of mind.* Cambridge, MA: Harvard University Press.

——. 1988. L. S. Vygotsky's "new" theory of mind. *The American Scholar* Winter:81–89.

Wolman, B. Ed. 1968. *The historical roots of contemporary psychology.* New York: Harper & Row.

Woolfson, C. 1982. *The labour theory of culture: A re-examination of Engels's theory of human origins.* London: Routledge & Kegan Paul.

Wozniak, R. 1975. Dialectics and structuralism: The philosophical foundations of Soviet psychology and Piagetian cognitive developmental theory. In *Structure and transformations: Developmental and historical aspects,* edited by K. Riegel & G. Rosenwald. New York: J. Wiley.

——. 1980. Theory, practice, and the 'Zone of proximal development' in Soviet psychoeducational research. *Contemporary educational psychology* 5(2):175–83.

Zebroski, J. 1982. Soviet psycholinguistics: Implications for teaching of writing. In *Linguistics and literacy,* edited by W. Frawley. New York: Plenum Press.

——. 1983. *Writing as 'Activity:' Composition development from the perspective of the Vygotskian school.* Unpublished doctoral dissertation. The Ohio State University.

——. 1986. Tropes and zones. *Correspondences: Four.*

——. 1986. The uses of theory: A Vygotskian approach to composition. *The writing instructor* 5(2):57–67.

Zhinkin, N. 1976. Thought and speech. In *Soviet studies in language and language behavior,* edited by J. Prucha. New York: North Holland.

Chapter Fourteen

The Grammar Controversy:
Tracking a Discipline by Looking for the Conflicts

The Great American Grammar Controversy

In the autumn of 1973 I began my teaching career at a junior high in Central Ohio. I had the good fortune that year to work with a master teacher, Fran Lambrecht. Inspired by the recent work of James Moffett, Fran had been trying some new methods with her ninth-grade English classes. Among the most controversial changes that Fran initiated was her decision not to teach traditional grammar. Fran's students were doing a great deal of reading and writing—more than other students in the traditional courses. But with the exception of a crash mini-course (remember mini-courses?) set up to help interested students cram for the high school placement test that could exempt them from the required tenth-grade, semester-long course in traditional grammar, students received little or no formal grammar instruction. Fran got a lot of flack, especially from the high-school teachers, about her decision to teach reading and writing without traditional grammar. No wide-eyed, free school advocate myself (remember free schools?), I debated the issue with Fran. While I couldn't really see that not having traditional grammar hurt any of her students, I was not quite comfortable with the idea the grammar study should be eliminated entirely. I had never had any troubles with traditional grammar. Wasn't teaching grammar a part of being an English teacher? Fran's response was that we needed a new vision of what being an English teacher meant. And

I will have to admit her practice was convincing; everyone, even her enemies, gave her that much.

The great American grammar controversy is far from dead. Our professional journals continue to publish articles, pro and con. Research studies continue to be called for and data is still gathered and analyzed. When I taught at a state university in Pennsylvania a few years back, the English student honorary staged a debate between one English professor arguing for the teaching of traditional grammar in introductory college composition courses and another English professor arguing against this teaching of traditional grammar. The great American grammar controversy has been around for at least a hundred years, no doubt longer. Harvard University instituted the required introductory composition course in part to get Harvard men's grammar in their written compositions into shape. And for composition teachers correct grammar remains a kind of minimal requirement in demonstrating literacy competencies, a requirement that students can be held to because most authorities are (supposedly) in agreement. The great American grammar controversy does not seem resolvable. It is less a matter of solution, or of persuasion, since positions are firmly entrenched on both sides of the issue, than a matter of higher or lower intensity and volume, of greater or lesser concern to the public. The grammar controversy ebbs and flows, rises and recedes. The tide of controversy comes in or goes out, but it does not disappear. Compositionists seem incapable of ignoring the controversy or of changing the subject.

Why is this? Why, after more than eighty years of research, which seems to show no correlation between the teaching of traditional grammar and improvement in student writing ability, are we still debating the issue? Why do so many writing teachers still insist on devoting great blocks of time to grammar instruction?

After nineteen years, I have heard most of the major arguments on both sides and to be frank, find them boring. Perhaps we need to ask some new questions about this issue in order to see it in a new way. Perhaps the question is not whether or not traditional grammar should be taught, but rather why this controversy still rages on. Why is grammar such a sore spot for us all? Why can this issue still stir our emotions?

In other words, we need to see language and language controversies as part of their social context. We need to discover not whether grammar helps or hurts, but what function the grammar controversy serves in our discourse communities.

I am reminded of the cargo cults that emerged in the South Pacific in the aftermath of the Second World War. With the coming of the war, the native Pacific islanders often had their first major contacts with twentieth-century technological societies. Both the Americans and the Japanese brought with them a massive inpouring of men and materiale, which had tremendous dislocationary effects on the local societies and their economies. Local peoples discovered that there were other very different cultures out there who seemed to have almost magical powers over natural forces and whose material wants seemed to be more abundantly and conveniently fulfilled. When both armies left at war's end, the native peoples were faced with the task of making sense of all that had happened. The desire for a return to the material riches of the war years revealed itself in the formation of religious groups that mythologized the recent past and prayed for the return of the planes carrying their rich cargo.

Now anthropologists didn't argue about whether the cargo cults were true religion, or not. Instead they found it more useful to try understand why at that particular juncture of history, in that particular locale, the cargo cults arose, and what social role they played. The anthropologists tried to understand the cargo cults as one response to social change and cultural crisis, as a sign of specific political, economic, and social forces that came together at one moment in history in response to a challenge from an alien culture. The cargo cults acted for the anthropologists as a sort of barometer measuring the shifting social pressures in formation and at work. So too we need to see the grammar controversy as an indicator of deeper currents, broader social forces. We need to begin, then, where Patrick Hartwell in his recent *College English* article "Grammar, Grammars, and the Teaching of Grammar" leaves off—with grammar as an issue of power.[1]

If rhetoric is the study of the relations between language, knowledge, and power, then the grammar controversy lying on this very fault line provides an almost textbook case study of rhetoric at work in one professional discourse community. The grammar controversy provides composition scholars with the perfect ongoing set of discourse acts to study the forces at work behind the scenes. It gives us the opportunity of tracking the set of forces at work in the territory of composition, by theorizing and historicizing the (re)emergence of this apparently perennial conflict. The method that I want to use to track the grammar controversy comes from the work of Mikhail Bakhtin.

Mikhail Bakhtin was a Russian literary theorist and philosopher, of sorts, who took dialogue as his key concept. In numerous works written between 1920 and 1975, Bakhtin disputed prevailing modernist theories of language in order to forge his own new dialogic conception of the word. Although scholars are not certain of its authorship, the book *Marxism and the Philosophy of Language,* attributed to Valentin Volosinov when it was first published in the Soviet Union in 1929, seems to be Bakhtinian in conception, if not in fact.[2] I am going to concentrate entirely on the text of *Marxism and the Philosophy of Language* because it speaks directly to our grammar controversy, but also because it is a subtle, artistic, innovative, powerful work that has surprisingly not received the kind of attention it deserves. We are dealing here with a work that rivals anything Fish or Derrida or Ricoeur can mete out, a work that anticipates and transcends much of the intellectual history of the twentieth century.

Is the Formal Study of Language Possible?

Volosinov begins with ideology, the sign, and the word. The word is the ideological sign par excellence (9). Volosinov states that

> the word is the most sensitive index of social changes and what is more, of changes still in the process of growth . . . The word has the capacity to register all the transitory, delicate, momentary phases of social change (19).

Further

> . . . it is thanks to this intersecting of accents that a sign maintains its vitality and dynamism and the capacity for further development.

Volosinov is arguing that the words which are most alive in our society are the words where different social forces in community intersect and struggle. Volosinov states it boldly. "The sign becomes an arena of class struggle" (23). Signs and texts that are controversial may also indicate social conflicts over gender formation, sexualities, racial, and ethnic identities. What is being fought out in a word or in a text is more than the issue that is explicitly stated. It is also, simultaneously, a matter of social and individual identity and conflicts between ruling groups and marginalized groups. The charged word or text is valorized precisely because more is at stake than simply the word or text, precisely because it is a sign of forces at work but also in genesis, present but also in formation, in process. Imagine for a moment the word "grammar" in the mouth of a researcher. How would a researcher say, intone, that word? Now imagine the same word in the mouth of a board of education member, or in John Simons's mouth, or in the mouth of a concerned parent, or in the mouth of a literature professor at your college, or in the mouth of a fellow compositionist.

The intonations, the accents, register the various social forces like a Richter scale registers the shifting and stressing of the earth's surface. That the controversy and the word itself are so volatile suggests that there is a crisis, a shifting of power underneath. Volosinov is arguing that to understand a word, a text, we need to trace it to its discourse situation and then trace that situation to the social forces, and social groups, that create it. The word "grammar" is a kind of barometer that measures the tugging and pulling between these groups.

So if we observe a spate of articles suddenly appearing about the grammar controversy, Volosinov's analysis would suggest that some social forces are newly stirring in the community. And if we do examine some of these groups we discover that the grammar issue is rearing its head at a time when some literature professors are increasingly defensive about all these compositionists who seem to be gaining power and students. We find that this is the case at exactly the moment when some textbook companies are sending out two salesmen in person to high pressure composition teachers into considering their traditionally best-selling handbook. We find as the word grammar slips off our tongue that certain researchers, writing in certain traditionally quantitative journals, are increasingly worried that these teachers are getting a bit uppity and actually have the nerve to think they should do their own research in their own way, that in fact some teachers are insisting on the legitimacy and desirability of teacher research, initiated, produced, and controlled by teachers. Outside of the profession, we also find that as the grammar controversy once again arises, the middle class is working harder and harder, for less and less. The middle class is discovering that the college education their children have received at great sacrifice increasingly means that, if they are lucky, those new college graduates can become managers of a McDonald's or a Burger King.

All of these social forces and more are wound up in the single word, "grammar." For the idea of grammar in our culture, with all its associations, is directly connected with our dreams of social mobility, our beliefs in education as a ticket into a higher socioeconomic class, with our hopes for betterment, if not for ourselves, then at least for our children. And, for some, we must note, grammar is directly connected to their hopes of retaining the power and privilege they already have. All of these forces are at work in composition (and English, generally), the most public of disciplines. The field of composition itself acts as a text that registers the public's hopes and concerns, and the grammar controversy is the subtext where the public and professional discourse communities have most consistently and contentiously met.

Before describing in more detail Volosinov's theory of language, let me note that there are some striking similarities between the two trends in language study that Volosinov finds at work in Western and Soviet linguistic scholarship and the contest that we have been describing as taking place during the past one hundred years in the U.S. over whether grammar should be taught in composition (and English) courses. Volosinov distinguishes two antagonistic perspectives on language and after critiquing each, attempts to formulate a third approach that positions his own work outside of the dichotomy that he views as being one source of the problem. In other words, Volosinov is trying to change the questions, he is questioning the questioning, and in doing so is attempting to refocus a very old and increasingly unproductive debate.

My essay is in a sense modeling itself on Volosinov's text. In the great American grammar debate the two antagonistic perspectives have been produced around the question of whether the direct teaching of traditional grammar is of value in teaching literacy. But the issues, in fact, are broader since "grammar" tends to be a code word for "schooling" and the place of authority in the schooling process, whether it is to be maintained and reinforced or whether it is to be questioned and transformed, at least potentially, in the classroom and beyond. So the conflict has surfaced in dozens of guises, on both sides.[3]

Anti-grammarians have often come out of school reform movements that themselves have appeared at times of social change. These movements have included, among many others, the Progressive Education Association, which was very active in the 1920s and 1930s, the National Defense Act response to the Soviet placement of Sputnik into orbit in the 1950s and the accompanying science and mathematics reform (which spread to the humanities in many forms including transformational generative linguistics, which some English educators used to critique the teaching of traditional grammar), the positive reaction of many newer college and secondary teachers to the principles enunciated at the Dartmouth Conference of 1966, those college composition teachers of the 1970s who advocated teaching writing as a process, rather than a product, and in the 1980s, teachers active in the Whole Language Movement.

Over the same years, those advocating the teaching of traditional grammar have tended to call also for a return to "rigor" and "excellence" in the traditional curriculum. Often, though not always, these traditionalists have associated themselves with those who have been harshly critical of the general education system for its lack of discipline (Mortimer Adler), have been troubled by the lack of knowledge of and experience with the great books of Western civilization

(Robert Hutchins), or have been scandalized by the inability of some students to read (Flesch), or have simply believed that incorrect use of language and lax enforcement of linguistic standards was related to society's potential decline (John Simons and Edwin Newman) or that the rise of other languages than English within the U.S. and in the schools was a threat to U.S. sovereignty (the English Only and English First movements).

There are then a set of parallels here between (1) the opposing forces at work in the great American grammar controversy, (2) the forces delineated by Volosinov in Western study of at least two hundred years, (3) the forces at work in U.S. society (and by implication in the Soviet Union of the late 1920s in which Volosinov's book was composed) that are pressuring the academic study of language, in this case the field of English studies generally and composition studies specifically. In describing a comparable set of material forces, Volosinov significantly spends most of his time and energy examining and critiquing the authoritarian half of the dichotomy, though he is always clear that in the process he is arguing for the inadequacy of the entire dichotomy.

Volosinov goes on to distinguish two basic ways of thinking about language. The first trend—he calls it individualistic subjectivism, let's call it the *artistic* approach, for short—sees language as process, as a creation similar to art, as heuristic, changing, concrete, historical. The major concern of the artistic approach to language is the relation between sign and speaker. The second approach to language—Volosinov calls it abstract objectivism, let's call it the *linguistic* approach to language, for short—views language as a stable, immutable, normative, arbitrary, conventional system that history interrupts and disturbs. The major concern of the linguistic approach is the relation between sign and sign. (See 45–63;77–82.)

Volosinov argues against both views. He contends that the language-as-art view tends to be individualistic, monologic, romantic, not to mention politically and socially naive. The speaker and utterance in this view tend to be foregrounded while the community is backgrounded. Still Volosinov, while critical of both views, concentrated his energy on disputing the linguistic view of language that, while existing for millenia, has, since the advent of Saussure, become an extremely popular view among scholars who aim to study native language scientifically. Volosinov spends many pages working through his critique of the linguistic approach to language. He argues that "Linguistics studies a living language as if it were a dead language, and native tongue as if it were an alien tongue" (77). The linguistic view is monologic and abstract. It is language study that is distant from the people. Volosinov provides a historical and political sketch of traditional language study over the centuries. It isn't a pretty picture.

> At the basis of the modes of linguistic thought that lead to the postulation of language as a system of normatively identical forms lies a practical and theoretical focus of attention on the study of defunct alien languages preserved in written monuments. . . . European linguistic thought formed and matured over concern with the cadavers of written languages . . . Philological need gave birth to linguistics, rocked its cradle, and left its philological flute wrapped in its swaddling clothes. That flute was suppose to awaken the dead. But it lacked the range necessary for mastering living speech as actually and continuously generated.

Further,

> The dead language the linguist studies is, of course, an alien language. Therefore the system of linguistic categories is least of all a product of cognitive reflection on the part of the linguistic consciousness of a speaker of that language.

Finally,

> Orientation . . . toward the alien . . . word is by no means an accidental occurrence or whim . . . The grandiose organizing role of the alien word, which always entered upon the scene with alien force of arms and organization or was found on the scene by the young conqueror-nation of an old and once mighty culture and captivated, from its grave, so to speak, the ideological consciousness of the newcomer nation—this role of the alien word led to its coalescence in the depths of the historical consciousness of nations with the idea of authority, the idea of power, the idea of holiness, the idea of truth, and dictate that notions about the word be preeminently oriented toward the alien word. (75)

There we have it. Grammar, traditional language study, and the linguistic approach to sign studies coalescing around questions of authority, power, holiness, truth. Volosinov is throughout this section making a strong claim that not only language but also traditions of language study are rooted in power relations. Using language as well as teaching about language, then, is a political act. It is no accident therefore that ruling class brings forth an alien grammar. Allon White puts it this way.

> Bakhtin recognized that any abstract . . . theory of language always went hand in hand with the language of the dominant social class. 'High' languages are imperialistic. They establish themselves as both standard and prestige by a variety of methods including 'objective' grammars, the prescription of norms, structural theories of

language (and even deconstructive theories) insofar as these systematically exclude the actual speech-use of the majority of people . . . The principal social function served by these theories is to act as sophisticated agents of cultural unification and centralization. . . There is an especially snug fit between linguistic theories. . . and a process of sociopolitical and cultural centralization. Grammar, poetics, and unitary language theory are modes whereby the prestige language simultaneously canonizes itself, regularizes and endorses its system and boundaries, makes itself teachable and assimilable in educational practice and above all 'naturalizes' itself over against all competing sociolects, dialects, registers. (140–143)

This is precisely the case with grammar study. So Volosinov's answer to the question I raised in my title is "no." Formal study of language is a fiction, though a useful fiction for those in power, for those who rule. It is, as Volosinov puts it, an ideology of an ideology, since language is a concrete dynamic set of linguistic forces and the linguistic approach to study makes language into a static, regularized, normed thing. Volosinov is reminding us that any grammar of a language is in that language, after all. It is no less politicized than oratory in the Senate or debates on abortion. Grammar is a "high language," as Allon White calls it. It presents a purity, a rule-governed system, that finds its best examples in the ruling languages of those in power or in the systematicity of the alien world which is no longer used in the daily life of the people. The more distant from everyday life, as a matter of fact, the more "unified" the language and the grammar, which goes far to explain why traditional English grammar uses categories closer to Latin than to English in its analysis of parts of speech and parts of sentence. Obviously Volosinov is not saying we should never study language under any conditions. He is arguing, rather, that we need to avoid the itch for security that grammars and formal studies of language represent. And we have to realize that that itch for security has clear ties to who has power and who does not.

In fact, Volosinov is arguing for a more lively and more rigorous kind of language study, which approaches a kind of applied populist ethnography. To begin to move toward such a people's study of language, Volosinov argues in the last third of his book for the study of reported speech. Reported speech is both speech within speech and speech about speech. Volosinov finds reported speech, probably the most common form of language, to be a useful speech genre to study for the very reason that it is so common, it is dialogic in its essence, and the relations of power between speaker and the other are so transparently reflected in the boundaries between the reported speech and the reporting context. Volosinov finds there is an interesting parallel between our theories of language, the prevailing social forces of an historical period, and the boundaries we create in our reported speech. Abstract grammars, times of political repression, and hard and fast boundaries between the reported word and the reporting context go together; generative theories of language, revolutionary periods in history, and soft, infiltrated boundaries between the authoritative word and the people's word go together.

A Call for Teacher Research

In conclusion, let me say that in all of this controversy, I find the classroom teacher curiously absent. Researchers from both sides bombard each other with arguments and counterarguments, year after year, the same voices. But what the teacher in the trenches thinks of all of this has been completely ignored. Who speaks for the teacher? Where is the study that recreates the teacher's world and examines the teacher's motives? This is a very strange omission, considering that research on grammar instruction supposedly has been going on for over eighty years.

It gets even stranger. Evidently the only thing that has failed more miserably than traditional grammar instruction has been the researchers' injunction to teachers not to teach traditional grammar. I do not dispute what the researchers have to say about grammar. But I strongly contest the apparent right of researchers to lord it over classroom teachers, to determine what is a worthy subject of research, to determine what the appropriate methods of inquiry are, to say what truth is and to speak for and at the teacher. I also want to raise questions about the language in which researchers have formulated the anti-grammar dicta, for that language itself has too often been the "high language" of quantitative research. I have more respect for the classroom teacher who may teach grammar but is questioning, is trying to understand the issue, not just as it appears abstractly in the journals, but as it is embodied in the life of the actual classroom and community.

I suspect the reason we have no studies of the teacher's view of all of this and of how it fits into the classroom and community is that such a study would be too politically explosive. First, such a study would put the authority of the researcher into question. Difficult questions would arise, like how many composition courses does the researcher teach? Or when was the last time the researcher taught freshman composition? Or what kind of students were in the course and at what kind of school? Such a study would inevitably seem to raise the issue of classloads. For if the typical classroom teacher had the time to reflect, to read widely on the issue, to try out some new approaches in the classroom without being penalized either for veering from the given department syllabus or for taking time and attention away from class preparation or paper grading, then I think that teacher could draw her or his own conclusions about the grammar controversy.

I believe a study of teachers and their workplace would show that it is because teachers don't have time to do any of these things— don't even have time to take a vacation, unless they can call it a conference—that they often resort to grammar. Robert Connors's remarks seem fitting here.[4] Although he was discussing the rise of mechanical correctness as the primary goal of composition courses in nineteenth-century America, he states:

> Faced with this gross overwork and with growing social and pro-
> fessional pressure to enforce the basics, teachers were forced to
> evolve strategies to protect themselves from insanity and to get on
> with the work . . . The new emphasis upon mechanical correctness
> grew out of the furor over 'illiteracy'. . . but also out of the under-
> standable need of teachers to somehow deal with their huge stacks
> of student themes. (67)

Lest we kid ourselves that we are all beyond that now, let me suggest that one of the reasons for the rise of the so-called process approach to composition in the last twenty years is that it too allows us to process more students, and shuffle more student papers, with less guilt. So, it is unlikely that many future studies of the grammar controversy will consider what teachers have to say and the condi- tions under which they labor. If teachers are going to raise their voices on this or any other literacy issue, they are going to have to do it on their own, in spite of those who supposedly have more knowledge, but actually only have more power. Patrick Hartwell is right to say that this issue comes down to the question of power. But not simply the power of the teacher over the learner. It is far more complicated than that. The grammar controversy involves the power of administrators over teacher and parents over schools and the capitalist economic system over the working middle and lower classes.

Volosinov, toward the end of his work, cites a scholar, Lorck, who says the right words but really has no understanding of what they mean. Volosinov takes those words out of the mouth of that scholar and makes them his own, implanting his own accents into them. (Volosinov does this in the very section of the book where he is talking about imported speech and the boundaries between the other's word and one's own word.) He says "There is only one possibility for its (the language's) rejuvenation: the proletariat must take command of the word from the bourgeoisie."

So too teachers must take command of the grammar controversy (and composition generally) from the so-called experts.

Notes

1. Patrick Hartwell. 1985. Grammar, grammars, and the teaching of grammar. *College English* 47(2):105–27.

2. See Katerina Clark and Michael Holquist, *Mikhail Bakhtin* (Cambridge, Massachusetts: Harvard University Press, 1984) for one view of the authorship of the "disputed" texts, and Gary Saul Morson and Caryl Emerson *Mikhail Bakhtin: Creator of a Prosaics* (Stanford, California: Stanford University Press, 1990) for a very different view. Only more tedious than whether English teachers need to teach traditional grammar in composition classes is whether Bakhtin was or was not the author of certain disputed books.

3. See Arthur N. Applebee, *Tradition and Reform in the Teaching of English: A History* (Urbana, IL: NCTE, 1974) and David Foster, *A Primer for Writing Teachers: Theories, Theorists, Issues, Problems.* 2nd ed. (Portsmouth, NH: Boynton/Cook, 1992).

4. Robert Connors. 1985. Mechanical correctness as a focus in composition instruction. *College Composition and Communication* 36(1):61–72.

Chapter Fifteen

The End(s) of Theory

It would be nice, it might seem, if we could just get our theory together, to think things through once and for all, and then act on the basis of that theory. But we are called upon to act and to be answerable, even though our theory is unfinished, in process, under construction. There can be no "after-composing theory." I cannot wait until I have a relatively complete theory of writing to teach. I have to teach now, working with what I have. I have to write even though I am not always sure where I stand and what I think. I have to go forward with an intellectual project even though the pieces don't always seem, to some, to fit together in an obvious, conventional way. I have to get up in the morning and face myself in the mirror even when I doubt who I am and what I believe.

The existentialists didn't think this situation a bad thing, but rather saw this as an inherent part of the human condition that made authentic living a possibility. In my doubt, I have the chance to see life differently, to break out of old conceptions, to glimpse, perhaps, freedom. But doubt, though it has a long and illustrious history in our tradition, is, despite what Peter Elbow says in his believing and doubting game distinction, rarely considered an appropriate trait of the academic discourse that I read and hear. There is, it is true, a lot of criticism, critique and even skepticism, of course, put forward more often in strong, assertive forms. Current academic discourse, more often than not, pretends that it doesn't doubt.

I feel more comfortable with a kind of doubleness, a nearly simultaneous belief and nonbelief, than I do with much of the directness and assertiveness that I read in our journals and our scholarly books. That doubleness can be seen in my use in this book of section headings that no doubt would drive a tranformational grammarian to distraction, suggesting an ambiguity that I do not feel the need to decide, an ambiguity that may well be undecideable. Is "Composing Theory" a verb or a noun? Is this essay about theory constructed in the field of Composition *about* writing or is it about the activity or process or event *of* creating theory? And so with the heading "Composing Context," "Composing Text," "Composing Self," "Composing Society." This doubleness can also be seen in the repetition of parts of text across essays, in the acceptance of theory but the rejection of Theory, in the order of texts, in the recursiveness of the book. Make up your mind some might say. Yes, that's it exactly.

So, for example, I approach the question of poststructuralist Theory and its place in Composition in doubt. Since 1982 I have read poststructuralist Theory sympathetically, discovering in it a similar critique of the communication model of language (and writing) that I found attractive in the Russian theory of Vygotsky, Bakhtin, and others. As James Comas pointed out to me, it is understandable that poststructuralist and Russian theory share some similar arguments and tropes, since Russian and Eastern European language theory of the 1920s can be seen as one of the origins of the poststructural Theory of the late 1960s and early 1970s. Roman Jakobson is the most apparent bridge between the intellectual traditions of Russia and the linguistic turn in Western European philosophy of the second half of the twentieth century. In France, Kristeva's reintroduction, and Todorov's further explication, of the work of Mikhail Bakhtin form another link between the sort of theory I have examined in this book and poststructuralist Theory frequently practiced in English departments in the U.S. I had hoped that alliances might be formed among the literary Theorists and composition theorists. This was one reason why I came to Syracuse University in 1987 to work with Louise Wetherbee Phelps and Steven Mailloux in constructing such bridges through the key concept of *rhetoric*. The following essay then needs to be read with this dialogue in mind. I am raising the question of what role, if any, that poststructuralist Theory should play in the field of composition studies. I am also questioning how this Theory already tends to function in professional conversations between literary studies specialists and composition studies specialists. I am not arguing against the sort of theory that this book enacts, but rather I am questioning the position of theory in English departments where Theory is becoming the hegemonic discourse. I have doubts about poststructural Theory that I have so far encountered. I do *do theory;* but I don't at this time see much reason to *do Theory.* What follows are some of my reasons.

In the summer before I entered the sixth grade, my father decided to take his mother back for one last trip to the tiny town deep
in the middle of Pennsylvania from which she came. My grandmother, white haired and proper—not at all the old world ba-
bushka—came from Rossiter, Pennsylvania, a miniscule coal-mining
company town populated largely by Polish Americans who stopped
there almost right off the boat to work the mines. The trip was a
great adventure for an eleven-year-old, so much so that when, in the
fall, Mrs. Weaver, my sixth-grade English teacher, asked us to make
our first speech in front of class about some topic we knew, I spoke
about this weekend venture from the homey warmth of Northeast
Ohio with its monster steel mills and its smelly, smokey skies to
what seemed the wilds of Pennsylvania's inner, endless, unchartable
guts. It took us all day to drive there; this was before interstates. I
can vividly remember that my grandmother pointed out huge hills,
strange hills on which nothing but grass grew and it was puny grass
at that. My grandmother sat shotgun in my father's old white Dodge
with its enormous fins and push-button gearshift, me in the backseat
getting car sick on and off as befits the two-lane highways that wove
around the hills of Pennsylvania. She told me that those hills had
been strip-mined years ago and while there wasn't any evidence of
strip-mining visible to the eye in 1963, my grandmother said that
something important had been taken out of these strip-mined hills
and that nothing but puny grass would grow there ever after. A
peculiar creation of human beings and nature, these huge barren
piles. The same jobs that made making a living in Rossiter possible,
ripped the topsoil and minerals off these hills and made life impossible.

But Rossiter wasn't what I expected. It was a pleasant, clean,
small town. A big Catholic church up against one of the hills, the
streets inclining upward. Plain, but neatly kept clapboard houses
with big front porches. Not much to it. But the mines were still
working then, so for the few who remained there was still something
that passed for prosperity. In fact, we went out to the mine and my
Dad, a factory worker and union man back in Warren, talked with
one of the miners at the mineshaft entrance. The mine wasn't a huge
operation, but it was big enough and the mine was deep enough to
scare me. When the miner invited my Dad and me to go down into
the shaft I said no, more because I had to go to the bathroom—it had
been a long trip for an eleven year old—than because I was afraid,
but I was afraid too. We went over to the house of my grandmother's
people and they seemed happy to see us, and we stayed a while
visiting with them in the parlor. Then as late afternoon turned into
early evening, we left Rossiter for the last time. My grandmother and

father, both dead now, never returned. Neither did I. We drove on to find motel rooms in what seemed, in comparison to Rossiter, to be the big, progressive, and much more modern town—Indiana, Pennsylvania, home of the Jeep.

My grandmother spoke English without an accent, though unlike my father, she knew and would speak Polish in front of the children and grandchildren. My father, in contrast, never spoke anything but English, though I discovered twenty years later, by chance, that he knew Polish, Slovak, and Russian. From these experiences, it always seemed strange that people who came to America—and there were stories in my family about these very people, stories, for example, about those who after immigrating to the U.S. decided they had had it better in Poland and left the U.S. to return to Poland, stories about my grandmother's people working in the old country as maids in the house of my better-off grandfather's people—it seemed strange that there were such people in the family who were *not* like my grandmother and my father, people who still spoke Polish as their first language, people who seemed to prefer Polish to English after being in the country for decades. What was going on here? Why didn't my father's old aunts and great aunts learn and use the ruling English language? Why didn't they keep a little Polish on the side, bringing it out for special occasions like we brought out the kalache, kapusta, and kielbasa, at Christmas? Why in the world did these old ones, these old timers who my father told me still talked of the the religious pilgrimages in the old country to the Shrine of the Black Madonna at Czestochowa, sometimes refuse to yield to English? Why did they still speak what English they used with an accent, a sort of "broken English" after some had been in this country for decades, sometimes even for their whole lives? That seemed to me, at the time and for a long while after, a mystery as profound and inexplicable as Czestochowa.

Why, for example, did the old ladies of the Rosary Society at Cyril and Methodius Church where we were members insist on chanting the Rosary in Slovak before the ten o'clock high mass? Why did Monsignor Krispinsky continue to do the sermon first in Slovak, then English? Why were these people so different from my people who still made occasional forays to Rossiter and in Polish, but who seemed to be at home in the mill country of the Mahoning and Shenango Valleys and with the English language?

The trip to Rossiter did throw a bit of light on this. In a town like Rossiter it might well be easier to retain and preserve traditional language and customs in the new setting. Much of the life of that first generation of immigrants had to have been preserved as much as transformed. A high price had already been paid in coming to the

New World. Keeping the language and ways of the old country would have been easy in a community the size of Rossiter, no doubt populated mostly by people in identical circumstances, even at times from related families. To come half way around the world may have seemed a steep enough price to pay. If you knew the people that went with you on the journey and that had gone before you, it would be easy to stay with your native language. At least for a while. The Polish language would have been a great comfort in lives that had little other comfort. Maybe it was because my grandmother had made her own journey out of Rossiter, to Sharon, Pennsylvania, just as her people had left Poland, that I hadn't a clue about any word in Polish.

But keeping the language of the old country wasn't simply an easy and comfortable move. The operative phrase is *for a while.* For a while, perhaps speaking Polish gave comfort and support but after a not very long time, it would begin to cause its own set of problems. Even in a place like Rossiter it took an act of will, an ongoing commitment to keep Polish alive especially when you would inevitably encounter a harsh negative judgment, stated outright or suggested by tone and look, from the native speakers of English whom you'd inevitably meet. Retaining Polish in the homogenizing-Wonder-Bread-White-Bread atmosphere of the United States was (and is) an act of resistance.

This resistance, as much a political act and a message of rebellion as picketing or voting, a kind of erecting of barricades not in the streets but around the subject, has only become sensible to me with age. At twenty, I wouldn't be caught dead talking about this with anyone. Any of these sorts of gory details, of itchy, persistent questions about my identity and background that might set me apart, that might prevent me from fitting in, from being like everybody else would have been (were) completely, totally suppressed. That, after all, is the reason I refused to work in the factories when in 1970 summer jobs in the factories were easy to come by and paid handsomely. Jim Baughman, my friend and the son of the town's banker, worked at Republic Steel between college years at Harvard. But not me. In the deeper recesses of my twenty-year-old mind—if there can even be said to be such a place—I had an accurate intuition. I knew even then that if I wanted to be a "professional," a price would be paid. That price required that, like my grandmother and then my father, I leave my hometown, maybe even my home state. And more, that I frequent the places—regardless of the pay—where it was likely I'd pick up the ruling language and the ways of knowing that accompany that language. That was not the factory, where it was hot, dirty, smelly—I can still remember the ozone electric transformer odor that came off my father's clothes when he returned from work at Packard Electric. It was not the factory where talk would be about unions and management, take home and taxes, Minotti's Tavern and overtime and Friday nights at the Moose Lodge. (A way of talking makes possible a way of knowing and even things to know about.) No, just as my grandmother had left Rossiter, and then my father had left the steel mills for the more prestigious job at an electrical machine factory, so I left to work—in of all places—the public library. If you want to learn the language of the intellectual, you go where the intellectuals go. And you do this at the earliest possible age. You go to the books as a youth so you can absorb the rhythms and nuances of tone of the ways of thinking, of the lines of argument—you get the feel of the language early on from the inside, even if that means, as it no doubt will, that you sever yourself from the old world—whether Poland, or Rossiter, or Packard Electric in Warren, Ohio. Unlike Lot's wife, you never turn back or even suggest you'd like to turn back.

Not, at least, until you are far down the road, after you have established your new life, mastered the new language, made the commitments that in youth seemed absolutely necessary and with age seem at best zealotry, at worst delusions. After you have paid the heavy price required of giving up a language, and a self, then you can turn back.

It is especially easy to turn back if you are not a great success in your new world. That leaves more openings to the past. Richard Rodriguez has it far harder than I, since I make these memories the substance of my work as a composition teacher—I can write of them and to the extent they are written make the issues they raise the material out of which my teaching is made. Then too because I haven't risen to Richard Rodriguez's heights—don't expect that sort of book from me—I can also go home. My younger brother works in the mill. We can talk. We share a lot. We vote for the same unsuccessful presidential candidates. We like the same rock & roll. We feel similarly about the institutions in which we work. I feel none of the angst Rodriguez does about the loss of home.

Rather, my loss—if any—is here in the university. In academe, who can I talk with about these experiences, these languages? As I linger in my late thirties I say almost daily—*no more deals.* No more little bargains with the devil where I gladly exchange my language, my self, for some promise of better things. First, the devil is a notoriously untrustworthy bargainer. I give up my language, my self, and he or she never comes through on the other end. I can give up my languages and take on a host of fashionable ones and get nothing, in fact lose a lot. Second, even if the bargain goes down as planned and the devil comes through with a shining bright bauble, the price is still too high. The price requires even further disruption of the few remaining ties to the old country, to the old language. To give up what there is left of my home language and the experiences and ways of knowing embodied, transmitted and preserved in it is a sacrifice I at this point of my life am unwilling to make.

I resist.

I will not take up a new language that promises all, but that has little place in it for me. As Zora Neale Hurston says, "I won't deny myself."

In our daily life we are often being presented with these little, seemingly innocuous bargains. The question of poststructuralist Theory and whether Composition should now consider accepting it, revising itself in poststructuralist terms, is preeminently the question of language. And the question of language is always the question of power—who is empowered to speak, who is silenced. Whether Theory is right or beautiful or moral or even useful is less the issue than what Theory *as a language* demands of and returns to me. How does Theory *function* in the new English department? What are the *ends* of Theory? Does it *work* to reproduce inequity? Does it add one more required elite language to the burden of already overworked writing teachers? What is then the *rhetoric* of Theory?

Theory is a set of discourses and discursive practices that allow certain sorts of knowledge but disallow other sorts. It is a language, like any local language, that the young pick up and speak easily, fluently, beautifully. I have no argument with that. For those who think they want to speak the language of Theory, I say good for you. But as for myself, at this point I could only learn to speak Theory with an evident and, for the native speaker, a grating accent. After eight years of seriously reading Theory hoping against hope to make it my first language, I now see that I could only speak a sort of "broken Theory," just like my distant Polish forebears spoke a sort of "broken English." If I were at the top of the social hierarchy, such an accent might well be seen to be charming. Witness Henry Kissinger or Zbigniew Brzezinski. As it is, I am not at the top of the social structure. For me to do Theory would mark me. I would never speak Theory like the native speaker. And to speak Theory with an accent might well be used against me. "Insufficiently theorized" is one of the phrases floating around, used against broken Theory speakers.

And ultimately, the pragmatic question is, would speaking Theory allow me to write and study the sorts of issues I raise in this essay and in my class in a more helpful way? I have not been persuaded that it would. If anything, since I've never encountered anything quite like this essay in the Theory I have read, I suspect Theory might well silence these experiences and issues and close off the very kind of things this essay, my book, and my work is about. The bargain offered though is tempting. Theory sounds to me a lot like the voice of Daisy in *The Great Gatsby:*

> I looked back at my cousin, who began to ask me questions in her low, thrilling voice. It was the kind of voice that the ear follows up and down, as if each speech is an arrangement of notes that will never be played again. Her face was sad and lonely with bright things in it, bright eyes and a bright passionate mouth, but there was an excitement in her voice that men who had cared for her found difficult to forget: a singing compulsion, a whispered "Listen," a promise that she had done gay, exciting things just a while since and that there were gay, exciting things hovering in the next hour.

For me, that's the sound of Theory. So even though the bargain sounds tempting, I think I'll pass for now. I will not deny anyone else's right to do Theory. But I don't do Theory. And now I have a better sense of why the old timers sat on their front stoops speaking in Polish of the Black Madonna of Czestochowa.